ZAMBIA

THE POLITICS OF INDEPENDENCE

1957–1964

Oxford University Press, Ely House, London W. 1

GLASGOW   NEW YORK   TORONTO   MELBOURNE   WELLINGTON
CAPE TOWN   SALISBURY   IBADAN   NAIROBI   LUSAKA   ADDIS ABABA
BOMBAY   CALCUTTA   MADRAS   KARACHI   LAHORE   DACCA
KUALA LUMPUR   HONG KONG   TOKYO

ZAMBIA
THE POLITICS OF INDEPENDENCE
1957-1964

BY

DAVID C. MULFORD

OXFORD UNIVERSITY PRESS
1967

To My Mother and the
Memory of My Father

PREFACE

This book is a study of constitutional change and the development of African nationalist political parties in Northern Rhodesia during the years 1957–64. These years saw dramatic political changes in Northern Rhodesia. In the short space of six years the Territory held three general elections, each under a different constitution. In 1958 Northern Rhodesia was governed exclusively by white men with African voters numbering less than a dozen in the Territory's electorate. In 1962, while still part of the Federation of Rhodesia and Nyasaland, Northern Rhodesia elected its first African Government under one of the most complex and controversial constitutions ever devised by a British Government. Two years later, after another constitution and general election, Zambia joined the ranks of Africa's independent states.

Research for this study was started at St. Antony's College, Oxford in April 1962. Under a grant that same year from the Department of Technical Co-operation (now the Ministry of Overseas Development) in London, I conducted a study of Northern Rhodesia's 1962 Constitution and the general election, held in October that year, which brought Africans to power for the first time. The results of that work were limited principally to the election and were published early in 1964 by the Oxford University Press.

The first field trip to Northern Rhodesia highlighted one of the major problems confronting students of contemporary African politics, namely, the lack of adequate materials for analysing political parties in depth. This was as true of Northern Rhodesia as it was of other African territories during the period leading up to independence. Political activity in Northern Rhodesia during the late 1950s and early 1960s appeared to revolve around either the various negotiations for constitutional changes or the contesting and/or boycotting of general elections. Research materials tended to be more plentiful for these periods as well, so that initially the most fruitful approach to a study of Northern Rhodesia politics appeared to lie within

PREFACEviii

the rather narrow frame work of constitutional development. As work progressed, however, it became clear that political parties would have to be researched in greater depth than I had yet achieved.

The present book was undertaken after a second field trip to Northern Rhodesia in 1963–4. At that time I was granted access by the Northern Rhodesia Government to a wide range of official material dealing primarily with political parties, security affairs, trade union activities, provincial administration, native authorities, political leaders, constitutional negotiations and elections. In addition, I was able to see other materials which included United National Independence Party (U.N.I.P.) and African National Congress (A.N.C.) documents, as well as correspondence between a number of the Territory's leading nationalist politicians. As a result, by 1965 I was prepared to produce a detailed study of African political parties, particularly for the period after 1957, when the first split occurred in A.N.C. and Kenneth Kaunda formed the Zambia African National Congress (Z.A.N.C.) and later the U.N.I.P.

In Northern Rhodesia during this period party organization and development was clearly and consistently related to constitutional development and elections. Therefore, the book has been organized as originally planned around these two broad themes. Assisted by the materials mentioned above, however, it has been possible to concentrate in depth throughout the book on the political parties themselves, particularly their growth, organization and leadership over the years. Detailed attention has also been given to the relationship between British administration in Northern Rhodesia and nationalist party development.

Research for this study was financed from three sources. The Woodrow Wilson Foundation, which awards fellowships for post-graduate study in the United States, kindly permitted me to use the second half of my fellowship to begin work at St. Antony's College in 1962. I should also like to acknowledge the support provided by the Ministry of Overseas Development in London for my first research trip to Zambia in 1962. Finally, I am particularly indebted to the Foreign Area Fellowship Program of the Ford Foundation in New York, which awarded me a two-year fellowship to return to Zambia in 1964 and to complete the writing of the manuscript during 1965. The Foreign Area Fellowship Program also very kindly agreed in 1966 to reactivate my fellowship for one month so that I could return to Zambia to clear my manuscript for publication in accordance with agreements entered into with the Northern Rhodesia Government at the time I was granted access to official materials in 1964. In this regard I should especially like to thank His Excellency, President Kaunda, who personally cleared the manuscript, and Mr. Vernon Atwood, Vice-President of the Ford Foundation, who assisted in reactivating my fellowship in 1966.

As with any endeavour of this kind, a number of people, too numerous to mention individually in this brief preface, have offered valuable support and assistance. Mr. George Bennett of Linacre College and Queen Elizabeth House, Oxford, supervised my doctoral work at Oxford for three years, always providing a blend of constructive criticism and sympathetic guidance. I should also like to thank Mr. Trevor Coombe both for his valuable efforts to improve the manuscript and for his sound judgement on many points of presentation; Miss Elena Plotnikoff and Mr. Albert Ammerman for their help at several points; Mr. Howard Nemerovski for his assistance at the publication stage; Mrs. Rose Cicala for her expert typing of the manuscript; and my colleagues in the White House Fellowship Program for their encouragement and kindness. Needless to say, responsibility for the manuscript is entirely mine. Finally, I should like to thank my wife, Astrida, and my two sons, Ian and Edward, for their faithful support and understanding during a long and difficult task.

DAVID C. MULFORD

July 1967
Brooklyn Heights
New York

Note on Unpublished Materials and Footnotes

Unpublished materials for the thesis were drawn from a number of different sources which are shown under separate headings in the bibliography. In the abbreviated form used in footnotes to the text the practice is as follows: references to materials drawn from 'Public Archives' include the file number and the notation, 'Lusaka Archives'; references to materials drawn from the 'Collection of Official Government Documents and Party Materials not in Public Archives' are indicated by the use of the file number alone; references to materials drawn from private collections or from the author's collection are noted by name (e.g., A.N.L.W. papers—the collection of Arthur Wina). Please see the 'Unpublished Materials' section of the bibliography for guidance to file titles and their location.

The list of abbreviations on p. xii provides a guide to footnotes.

CONTENTS

Abbreviations

Ad. Sec.	Administrative Secretary
A.M.W.U.	African Mineworkers Union
A.N.C.	African National Congress
A.S.	Assistant Secretary
A.S.(C.S.)	Assistant Secretary to the Chief Secretary
A.T.U.C.	African Trade Union Congress
B.N.G.	Barotse National Government
B.N.P.	Barotse National Party
C.E.O.	Chief Electoral Officer
C.S.	Chief Secretary
D.C.	District Commissioner
D.P.	Dominion Party
G.H.	Government House
M.I.R.	Monthly Intelligence Report
M.L.C.	Member of Legislative Council
M.N.A.	Minister of Native Affairs
M.P.	Member of Parliament
N.R.G.	Northern Rhodesia Government
P.C.	Provincial Commissioner
P.C.(N.P.)	Provincial Commissioner, Northern Province
P.S.	Permanent Secretary
R.C.	Resident Commissioner of Barotseland
R.R.P.	Rhodesia Republic Party
R.T.U.C.	Reformed Trade Union Congress
S.B.	Special Branch
S.O.	Special Officer
S.P.C.	Senior Provincial Commissioner
U.F.P.	United Federal Party
U.N.I.P.	United National Independence Party
U.N.F.P.	United National Freedom Party
U.S.	Under Secretary
U.T.U.C.	United Trade Union Congress
Z.A.N.C.	Zambia African National Congress

I

BACKGROUND

Introduction

ZAMBIA was born on 24 October 1964, Africa's thirty-fifth independent state. Like most of its sister nations in Africa, Zambia's transition to independence had been rapid and dramatic. For the ten years preceding independence Northern Rhodesia, as it then was, had been part of the Federation of Rhodesia and Nyasaland, a federation created and governed by white men, but resisted and ultimately destroyed by black men. As late as 1958 only eleven Africans were registered as voters in Northern Rhodesia; within five years that number exceeded a million. Three times between 1958 and 1964 Northern Rhodesia went to the polls, twice under Colonial Office constitutions imposed against the active and sometimes violent opposition of Africans. These were the years of militant resistance, the years during which Northern Rhodesia's African leaders organized the nationalist party which was destined to govern the new Zambia.

But there were important differences in Zambia, too. Seventy thousand whites, who over the years had settled among the Territory's approximately three million Africans, dominated Northern Rhodesia's economy, owned and operated its businesses, its copper-mines and most of its farms. In the early days of white settlement in Central Africa the Zambezi River had marked the beginning of black Africa. But Cecil Rhodes, who had secured a royal charter for the British South Africa Company, was out to alter this. Generously assisted by the British Government, Rhodes had already organized the first white settlement in Southern Rhodesia in 1890. At the same time white men, roused by reports of extensive copper deposits in the north, probed the vast area between the Zambezi and the Congo. White settlement remained slight in Northern Rhodesia at the turn of the century, limited primarily to a few Company

officials, small missionary groups, traders, and groups of pros-
pectors. In the next ten years, however, the railway opened the
Territory as far north as the Copperbelt. Additional copper
deposits were found; discoveries of zinc were made around
Broken Hill; and white settlement began to follow the 'line of
rail' from Livingstone in the south to the Copperbelt area along
the Katanga border.[1]

The Territory to which the British South Africa Company
had laid claim was a vast plateau area of relatively featureless
bush country, lying at an altitude ranging between 3,000 and
5,500 feet. It was not a land of great natural beauty, apart from
two magnificent exceptions, the mighty Victoria Falls in the
south and the 700-foot Kalambo Falls nearly 1,000 miles to the
north. Perhaps Northern Rhodesia's most striking physical characteristic was sheer space, 290,000 square miles, an area three
times the size of Britain, though with less than three million
people. Northern Rhodesia's Africans formed a diverse composite of tribal groups. More than eighty distinct tribes speaking
over forty linguistic dialects confronted the Company administration. For the most part these tribes had not shared a common
background; indeed, they had experienced little or no contact
between themselves before the intrusion of the white man.
Several major linguistic groups predominated. The largest, the
Ila-Tonga, spread its numbers across what later became
Southern Province and the western half of Central Province.
In the extreme west, dotted across the great Zambezi flood
plain, were the Lozi, the ruling group of the well-established,
highly centralized kingdom of Barotseland. These were the
people Livingstone first met in Northern Rhodesia, and it was
through Barotseland's King, Lewanika, that the British South
Africa Company first gained a foothold in what later became
Northern Rhodesia. In the Territory's north-western corner two
major groups, the Lunda- and the Lovale-speaking peoples,
were interspersed, the former spilling over into Katanga and
settled as far east as the western Luapula in Northern Rhodesia.

[1] For a detailed account of Northern Rhodesia history, both before and after
European penetration see: Gann, L. H., *A History of Northern Rhodesia*, London,
1964; Gray, Richard, *The Two Nations: Aspects of the Development of Race Relations
in the Rhodesias and Nyasaland*, London, 1960; Hall, R. S., *Zambia*, New York, 1965;
Rotberg, Robert I., *The Rise of Nationalism in Central Africa: The Making of Malawi
and Zambia 1873–1964*, Cambridge, 1965.

In the north the most militant of Northern Rhodesia's tribes, the Bemba, exercised domain over dozens of weaker tribes which for the most part spoke dialects of the Bemba mother tongue. To the east in what later became Eastern Province, were the Ngoni-speaking tribes, another proud and militant group which spread over into Nyasaland and which in the past had shared the great warrior traditions of the Zulu.[1]

As the Territory developed and Company rule gave way to direct British administration, few white men, apart from government officials and missionaries, ventured away from the Copperbelt and the narrow railway strip. More and more a landlocked Northern Rhodesia, virtually without access to its neighbouring territories to the north and west, looked to the south. Attachments with Southern Rhodesia developed rapidly as the white communities in both territories became increasingly aware of their common political and economic interests. During the Second World War Northern Rhodesia's copper industry boomed, and in the years immediately afterwards white immigration, especially in Southern Rhodesia, increased dramatically. White politicians, anxious to secure the economic and political advantages of formal union, sought to amalgamate the two territories, both of which were thought to be on the verge of great economic progress.

Northern Rhodesia's Africans shared no such interest in the white south. On the contrary, in both Nyasaland and Northern Rhodesia there were early signs of resistance to white rule.[2] Later, in the 1930's and 1940's, Africans in the north came to fear and despise the white south. For Africans the war and the far-reaching economic changes in Northern Rhodesia itself had been an awakening experience as well. As settlers in Northern and Southern Rhodesia sought to establish a closer bond between the two territories, northern Africans, now more united and increasingly hostile to the threat of white domination, began resisting white rule generally, whether directed by local settlers or by the British Government.

Half a century of white rule and all which that implied—

[1] For a detailed account of Northern Rhodesia's tribes, their origins, distribution through the country and linguistic diversity, see Brelsford, V. W., *The Native Tribes of Northern Rhodesia*, Lusaka, 1954.
[2] Rotberg, R. I., *The Rise of Nationalism in Central Africa*, pp. 55–91.

contact with Christian education, the undermining of traditional authority and values, new opportunities for travel and
exchange of ideas, racial discrimination, and exposure to the
harsh realities of government administration and the workings
of a cash economy—had given Northern Rhodesia's Africans a
measure of unity hitherto unknown. Reinforced by the colour
bar, by dissatisfaction among Africans with their new position
and above all by the threat of permanent white domination,
this unity took root, producing among those diverse groups the
beginnings of a common identity. In the beginning Northern
Rhodesia had been subjugated not by war but by treaties concluded between white men and the Territory's unsophisticated
chiefs. In 1924 Northern Rhodesia became a protectorate
instead of a self-governing colony like Southern Rhodesia. As
the term implies, the British Government maintained over the
years a special responsibility, variously defined, towards the
Territory's African population. Despite all this, the realities of
white political development were such that the Territory's
political future was highly uncertain. Was Northern Rhodesia
to be a white man's or a black man's country? This remained
an open question during much of the 1950's, particularly when,
after 1955, it became clear that the Federal Government was
attempting to extend its authority and to secure from London a
greater degree of independence.

Northern Rhodesia's future was ultimately decided in the
political upheaval which swept Africa in the late 1950's and
early 1960's. The rapid evolution to independence of British
and French territories in West Africa raised relatively fewer and
less complex problems than those which later confronted the
colonial powers in territories with large settled white populations. Experience in Algeria and Kenya, though quite different,
provided ample evidence of the cost to colonial governments of
attempting to protect the interests of white settlers by resisting
the rising forces of nationalism. The Congo, on the other hand,
graphically underlined the political and military dangers of
withdrawing too quickly from a colonial territory in which in-
adequate preparations had been made. Meanwhile, in East and
Central Africa white resistance to African political aspirations
stiffened. Before the late 1950's African government had never
been regarded as a serious possibility by white settlers in these

areas, certainly not before several generations, but by the end of the decade white attitudes had changed. Britain's capacity to withstand the mounting pressure for majority rule was now doubted by white settlers and civil servants alike. Two events were of particular significance in the undermining of white confidence; one was Britain's humiliation at Suez in 1956, the other was the granting of independence to Ghana and Britain's failure to condemn the path subsequently followed by Nkrumah. By 1960 a number of other African states were on the threshold of independence, and in January that year Prime Minister Macmillan completed a tour of the continent by speaking in the very heart of 'white' Africa about the inexorable 'winds of change' sweeping down Africa from the north.

In a sense the Federation of Rhodesia and Nyasaland was a microcosm of all these various conflicting forces. Constitutionally, the Federation combined the white-ruled, self-governing colony of Southern Rhodesia with two colonial protectorates, Northern Rhodesia and Nyasaland. Nyasaland was almost wholly black, while Northern Rhodesia's white population was approximately the size of Kenya's. Superimposed over the three territories was the Federal Government, itself neither fully independent, nor in a position to control the constitutional development of its respective territories. The Federation had been formed by a British Government as yet unaware of the magnitude of the changes which would later appear in Africa. Once African political consciousness emerged and Africans began organizing, white solidarity and defensiveness increased. Race came to dominate not only politics but almost all relations between Africans and Europeans. What one group gained the other felt it had lost, and by the end of the decade multi-racial political groups had all but disappeared.

Federation had never gained acceptance among the vast majority of Africans, so that from the beginning its survival depended upon the maintenance of white control in at least two of the three Federal territories. Thus, all attempts by the British Government to include 'responsible' African elements in the Federal and territorial governments were always limited to minority representation based on qualified franchise arrangements, provisions for indirect election or appointment by the Governors of one of the territories. The Federal franchise provided for a small

African electorate and six African seats in the Federal legislature. In Northern Rhodesia approximately 7,000 Africans were enfranchised under the 1959 Constitution, which provided for eight African seats in a Legislative Council of twenty-six members. In Southern Rhodesia the 1961 Constitution created the Territory's first African seats filled by direct election. There were fifteen such seats in a Legislative Assembly of sixty-five members. Not surprisingly, these attempts to create a semblance of 'multi-racial' government in territories where it appeared that white domination would continue indefinitely were rejected by Africans, who opposed the maintenance of Federation in any form.

As the Federal Government sought after the first few years to enhance its power, African political consciousness grew and African organizations spread their influence through both the northern territories. Of the two protectorates, Nyasaland could not compare in importance to the Federation with Northern Rhodesia. Despite Nyasaland's role in the African campaign against Federation, the small protectorate had never been wanted by the Federation's white politicians in the first place. Economically, Nyasaland was dependent on the two Rhodesias, and politically its secession, though of symbolic importance to Africans, could have been survived easily by Salisbury. It was Northern Rhodesia with its relatively large white population, its great mineral wealth and its importance as a market for Southern Rhodesia that was the coveted prize. For Africans the control of Northern Rhodesia was the key to breaking Federation. Sir Roy Welensky knew this well and sought with great ingenuity to prevent all constitutional changes in Northern Rhodesia which would effectively increase the power of Africans. In the end Welensky failed, and with him the Federation. In both protectorates power passed from European to African hands, and once again the Zambezi became the frontier it had been in the past between black and white Africa.

Constitutional Development

Europeans dominated Northern Rhodesian politics until the late 1940's. Their first demands for a share in the Territory's government, raised initially as early as 1910, met with limited success in the form of an Advisory Council granted to the settlers by the British South Africa Company in 1918.[1] Company rule ended in Northern Rhodesia in 1924, when the Territory was placed under the direct administration of the British Government. An order in council that year established Northern Rhodesia's first Legislative Council, which comprised nine officials and five unofficial elected members. The order also called for an Executive Council composed entirely of officials.[2]

Despite officials controlling both councils, it was generally assumed by settlers and officials alike that Northern Rhodesia would soon receive a greater measure of responsible government and that in due course the protectorate would achieve self-government under a constitution similar to that granted Southern Rhodesia in 1924. An increase in the Legislative Council's unofficial membership in 1929 appeared to confirm these hopes, but the following year the settlers received a sharp rebuff which was to influence their political ambitions for more than two decades. Lord Passfield, then Secretary of State for the Colonies, issued a White Paper in which he extended the so-called doctrine of paramountcy to Northern Rhodesia. Though the doctrine had appeared originally in a 1923 White Paper dealing with the position of the Indian community in Kenya, as re-stated by Lord Passfield in 1930 it held 'that the interests of the African natives must be paramount, and that if . . . those interests and the interests of the immigrant races should conflict, the former should prevail. . . . His Majesty's Government regard themselves as exercising a trust on behalf of the African population, and they are unable to delegate or share this trust, the objective of which may be defined as the protection and advancement of the native races.'[3]

The Passfield Memorandum provoked an angry wave of protests among Northern Rhodesia's white settlers, who interpreted the pronouncement as a blunt rejection of their most

[1] Davidson, J. W., The Northern Rhodesia Legislative Council, London, 1948, p. 18.

[2] The basic documents of Northern Rhodesia's original constitution were the Northern Rhodesia Order in Council, 1924; the Northern Rhodesia (Legislative Council) Order in Council, 1924; and the Instructions passed under the Royal Sign Manual and Signet to the Governor and Commander-in-Chief of Northern Rhodesia. These are printed, with amendments up to 1930, in the Laws of Northern Rhodesia, Vol. IV, pp. 1206–17, 1267–71, 1287–94.

[3] Statement of the Conclusions of His Majesty's Government in the United Kingdom as Regards Closer Union in East Africa, Cmd. 3574, 1930.

basic political objectives. Efforts by local officials, including both
the Governor and the Chief Secretary, to assure the settlers that
no policy change had taken place were of no avail.[1] In both
East and Central Africa white politicians, supported by their
friends in Britain, continued to protest, until late in 1931 a Joint
Select Committee of Parliament issued a report which significantly altered the emphasis of the paramountcy doctrine.
According to the Committee's report, paramountcy now meant
'no more than that the interests of the overwhelming majority
of the indigenous population should not be subordinated to
those of a minority belonging to another race, however important
in itself'.[2] This only partially restored the confidence of the
settlers, who continued to distrust the intentions of the British
Government. Three years later, in 1934, paramountcy was
finally diluted beyond recognition. Arriving in Northern
Rhodesia to take up his appointment as Governor, Sir Hubert
Young stated that paramountcy meant no more than what the
Select Committee had already stipulated and 'no less than that
the interests of the non-native minority must not be subordinated to those of the native majority'.[3]

The threat implied to white political objectives by the Passfield Memorandum had been successfully countered, but the
effect on European and African politics in Northern Rhodesia
was a lasting one. For the white settlers amalgamation with
Southern Rhodesia suddenly assumed overriding importance,
and though the urgency with which it was pursued varied
during the ensuing years, amalgamation remained a major
goal for European politicians in Northern Rhodesia until the
formation of the Federation in 1953. Neither was the lesson of
the paramountcy struggle lost on thoughtful Africans, particularly as they looked back in the late 1930's and 1940's. The
settlers' drive for political domination was now unmistakably
clear. Less apparent, however, was the position of the Colonial
Office; whereas in the past Africans had depended upon the
Colonial Office to protect their basic interests, the future now
seemed uncertain.

The settlers pursued their new tack with characteristic

[1] Gann, L. H., *A History of Northern Rhodesia*, p. 394.
[2] *Report of the Joint Select Committee on East Africa*, December 1931.
[3] *Northern Rhodesia Legislative Council (Leg. Co.) Debates*, 1 December 1934, col. 12.

vigour. In 1936 Northern Rhodesia's elected Legislative Council members conferred at Victoria Falls with representatives of Southern Rhodesia's various political parties. The conference, the first of several such meetings over the next two decades, strongly endorsed the view that Northern and Southern Rhodesia should be amalgamated and granted self-government.[1] Within two years the British Government had appointed a royal commission, the Bledisloe Commission, to study the problem, though its terms of reference—to explore the feasibility of closer association between the two Rhodesias and Nyasaland—were a good deal broader than the settlers might have liked.[2]

The Commission's subsequent report, published in 1939, accepted in principle that closer association was desirable, but did not recommend immediate steps to achieve it. The Commission considered that all three territories would tend naturally to become increasingly interdependent, but for the time being it ruled against a formal link between them. In reaching this decision the Commission had been impressed by two findings in particular: one was the important differences which it believed existed between the native policies followed north and south of the Zambezi; the other was the widely expressed fear amongst northern Africans that any association with Southern Rhodesia would adversely affect their status as British protected persons. For the settlers, the Commission's report was a grave disappointment. Its only positive recommendation was that the three territorial governments should attempt to find ways of co-operating more closely on matters of mutual interest.[3]

Shortly afterwards the war intervened and nothing concrete came of the Commission's proposals until 1944. At that time the British Government proposed that an interterritorial council be established to facilitate co-operation between the respective governments without compromising the British Government's own special responsibilities in the two northern protectorates. The Central African Council, as it was named, first met in Salisbury in 1945. Despite a brief period of optimism at the

---

[1] Rotberg, R. I., *The Rise of Nationalism in Central Africa*, p. 108.
[2] *The Rhodesia-Nyasaland Royal Commission Report*, Cmd. 5949, 1939, p. 4.
[3] Ibid., *passim*.

beginning, however, the Council failed to satisfy the white politicians, who never regarded it as anything more than an intermediate step towards amalgamation.

Meanwhile, the settlers in Northern Rhodesia resumed their drive towards self-government. In 1938 the number of officials and unofficials in the Legislative Council was brought into balance by reducing the number of officials from four to three and adding a nominated unofficial to represent African interests.[1] The formation of a national Government the following year, ostensibly a temporary measure for the duration of the war, introduced elected unofficials into the Executive Council for the first time.[2] In 1941 they were granted an additional seat in the Legislative Council, but to maintain balance between the two sides the Government raised the number of officials to four once again.[3]

In 1945 constitutional changes were introduced in Northern Rhodesia which radically altered the existing balance between the settlers and the officials. The number of officials and unofficial elected members remained unchanged, but the hitherto single nominated unofficial member was joined by four other nominated Europeans, three of whom were also charged with representing African interests.[4] Thus unofficial European members, eight of whom were elected, held a majority of thirteen to nine over the officials. The traditional characteristic of crown colony government, the official majority, had been dropped, though, theoretically at least, officials retained control in matters which affected African interests. The conventional powers of the Governor remained intact, but in practical terms it was now extremely difficult for him to force legislation through the Legislative Council against the combined opposition of the unofficial members. In the Executive Council officials retained a majority of five to three over their unofficial colleagues, none of whom were granted portfolios.

The war had been extremely valuable politically to the European politicians. By the time it was over elected unofficials,

[1] The Northern Rhodesia (Legislative Council) Amendment Order in Council, 1938.

[2] Davidson, J. W., *The Northern Rhodesia Legislative Council*, p. 58.

[3] The Northern Rhodesia (Legislative Council) Amendment Order in Council, 1941.

[4] The Northern Rhodesia (Legislative Council) Order in Council, 1945.

in particular Roy Welensky (later Sir Roy), had gained six years' administrative experience and considerable political leverage in the Territory's Government. Led by Colonel Stewart Gore-Browne (later Sir Stewart) and Welensky, the settlers had tempered their demands for constitutional advance during the war years, and in part the 1945 Constitution, like the Central African Council at the interterritorial level, represented something of a reward for the settlers as well as recognition of Central Africa's growing economic and political importance to Britain. With the war over, however, white demands for constitutional reform in Northern Rhodesia and amalgamation with Southern Rhodesia were raised with renewed intensity. Their position secured by the 1945 Constitution, Northern Rhodesia's settlers seemed poised for their final assault on Colonial Office rule.

Progress was slow in the immediate postwar years. Labour's victory at the polls in Britain brought men to power who were less sympathetic to the settlers' objectives. In Northern Rhodesia relations between officials and unofficials deteriorated under a constitution which set the executive directly against the legislature.[1] On the question of amalgamation the Government stood firm. A motion on the issue introduced into the Legislative Council by Welensky in August 1945 was defeated by thirteen votes to nine. The three elected unofficials representing African interests and one nominated unofficial had voted with the Government.[2] For the time being the settlers' united front had been divided. In Southern Rhodesia the general election result of 1946 produced near disaster for the Prime Minister, Sir Godfrey Huggins (later Lord Malvern), whose majority was so severely cut that he found an all-out campaign for amalgamation with the north impossible to mount.

The year 1948 marked a turning-point both in Northern Rhodesia and in Central Africa as a whole. In Northern Rhodesia the unofficials, led now by Welensky instead of Gore-Browne,[3] won several important concessions in a new constitution. The Legislative Council's life was extended from three to

[1] Gann, L. H., *A History of Northern Rhodesia*, p. 389. Welensky, in fact, resigned from the Executive Council in 1947; Davidson, J. W., *The Northern Rhodesia Legislative Council*, p. 58.
[2] Leg. Co. *Debates*, January 1945.
[3] Gann, L. H., *A History of Northern Rhodesia*, p. 58.

five years, and the Governor was replaced as President of the Council by an elected Speaker. Elected unofficials and officials were given ten seats apiece. The number of nominated unofficials was reduced from five to four, all representing African interests, and for the first time two of the unofficials were Africans, selected by the Territory's African Representative Council and appointed by the Governor.[1]

Officials maintained control over the Executive Council, which was now expanded to a total of eleven members. Four seats went to unofficials, one of whom had to represent African interests. At the same time, official recognition was given to a constitutional convention which lent considerable strength to the position of the unofficial members. The convention stipulated that, 'if all the unofficial members . . . advised the Governor unanimously in one sense, he was bound to regard that advice as the advice of the Executive Council, even though all the officials . . . advised otherwise. The Governor had then either to accept the advice or to exercise his right to reject the advice of Council and to refer his decision to the Secretary of State in accordance with the Royal Instructions.'[2] In a further change the following year two elected unofficials were given portfolios.[3] Apart from the several instances during the war, this was the first occasion on which elected members assumed direct responsibility for government business.

By early 1948 the campaign for closer association had been resumed, this time under the banner of federation, which Welensky had accepted as the only possibility with any hope of securing Colonial Office backing. Huggins, meanwhile, had more than regained his former ascendancy in Southern Rhodesia with a crushing victory in the 1948 general election. In the Colonial Office itself the idea of a larger state of some kind in Central Africa appeared to be gaining ground. Federation seemed to offer the best basis on which to proceed, and late in 1948 the Secretary of State encouraged Welensky and his colleagues to take the initiative in producing a solution.[4] The

[1] The Northern Rhodesia (Legislative Council) Order in Council, 1948.
[2] *Advisory Commission on the Review of the Constitution of the Federation of Rhodesia and Nyasaland*, Appendix VI, 'Survey of Developments Since 1953', October 1960, p. 40.
[3] The Northern Rhodesia Order in Council, 1949.
[4] Gann, L. H., *A History of Northern Rhodesia*, p. 404.

result was an unofficial conference at Victoria Falls early in
1949 to explore the feasibility of federation in Central Africa.
African representatives were not invited to the conference, and
Huggins, in his opening address, made it clear that Africans
in the three territories could not expect to participate for many
years in the political life of any proposed federal state. The conference closed with unanimous endorsement of the federal
solution; the stage was set for a bitter political battle which in
the next four years would radically alter the face of Central
Africa. /

The Beginnings of African Politics

African national consciousness appeared in Northern Rhodesia
after the Second World War as a direct counter response to the
settlers' drive for political power. The seeds of African reaction
were sown decades earlier as the Territory developed and the
two racial communities, distinctly separate and often antagon-
istic, became increasingly interdependent. African reaction to
white rule, especially to the white man's taxes, appeared as
early as the first decade of the Company's administration.[1]
In 1915 the Chilembwe rising in Nyasaland provided the first
serious warning of African discontent. Northern Rhodesia's
first protest movements were for the most part local religious
sects or native welfare societies, both of which emerged in some
strength during the 1920's. This pattern continued into the
next decade, but before long African discontent began to
appear more openly, particularly in the railway towns and on
the Copperbelt.[2] In 1935 African miners rioted on the Copperbelt and minor disturbances occurred in several rural areas of
Northern and Southern Provinces. Five years later a second
more serious outburst shook the Copperbelt.[3]

Meanwhile in 1938 the Government took steps to liberalize
the Native Authorities and to encourage co-operation between
the chiefs and the more progressive young men of their respective communities. As a first step, the Government established a
system of African councils at the Native Authority level in rural

[1] Rotberg, R. I., *The Rise of Nationalism in Central Africa*, p. 73.
[2] Ibid., pp. 124–34; Hall, R. S., *Zambia*, pp. 111–26; Gann, L. H., *A History of Northern Rhodesia*, pp. 303–7.
[3] Rotberg, R. I., *The Rise of Nationalism in Central Africa*, pp. 161–77.

areas.[1] Later, Urban Advisory Councils were formed, and in 1943 the first African Provincial Councils, their members drawn from the existing lower councils, came into operation.[2] In developing the council system the Government's guiding principles were to combine popular with traditional elements and to introduce the elective principle on a limited scale to 'responsible' and 'advanced' Africans.

Despite these early signs of growing political awareness, Africans in Northern Rhodesia had yet to create a national organization of any kind. African leadership up to 1945 remained largely in the hands of the chiefs, religious ministers and school-teachers, most of whom were scattered about the rural areas. In 1946 two bodies purporting to represent the Africans of Northern Rhodesia were formed. Both were to have a significant influence on the African political scene. One was the African Representative Council, which brought together twenty-five Africans elected by their colleagues on the various Provincial Councils and four appointees of the Paramount Chief of Barotseland.[3] The other body was the Federation of African Societies, which sought to bring the various African traders' groups, shop assistants' associations, farmers' organizations, and welfare societies into one association. The Federation of African Societies, which initially included the welfare societies of only six towns, was formed on 18 May 1946 by Dauti

[1] Davidson, J. W., *The Northern Rhodesia Legislative Council*, pp. 28–29.
[2] Ibid., pp. 79–80.
[3] Unpublished manuscript of A. N. L. Wina, 1960, p. 13, A.N.L.W. papers. Wina makes several other interesting suggestions. The major tribes of Northern Rhodesia were removed from the European centres, which traditionally were areas inhabited by less well-organized 'tribelets' which were not as capable of resisting the whites (Lamba, Saka, Lenji, and Soli). In the early years of African nationalism none of these tribes produced a leader of national standing.

Wina also claims that the real clash between Africans and Europeans did not come until after Africans who secured their education at rural missions began to seek better opportunities in urban areas. He notes that many of the early leaders were closely connected with chiefs. Harry Nkumbula, often referred to as the father of African nationalism in Northern Rhodesia, was teaching in the rural areas during the war and was the son of a subchief in Chief Mugaila's area in Southern Province. Godwin Lewanika, the first President of the African National Congress, was the private secretary of the Paramount Chief of Barotseland and a member of the royal family. Dauti Yamba, a major figure in the formation of the Federation of Welfare Societies, was from Chief Kazembe's capital in Northern Province. Lawrence Katilungu, the first President of the African Mineworker's Union, was a cousin of Chief Chitimukulu in the Northern Province.

Yamba, a schoolmaster, and George Kaluwa, a trader and
farmer in Mazabuka.¹ The Society set itself the goal of collecting £1,000 from its own constituents and from the European
public. In late October the Society held its first general meeting
in Lusaka, after which a deputation met with the Assistant
Chief Secretary (Native Affairs) and requested official recognition by the Government and five seats on the newly formed
African Representative Council.² The Government's position
was stiff and uncompromising. The Society did not represent
Africans generally; its leaders had not been chosen by the
people, nor had it been authorized by law or appointed by the
Governor. Rather surprisingly, however, the deputation's
requests were thought to warrant consideration in the Executive
Council, where it was decided that a special effort should be
made not to antagonize the Society's leaders.³ In the end,
Yamba's and Kaluwa's demands were rejected, but only after
the Government's position had been explained personally by
the Secretary of Native Affairs.⁴

The Society was soon preoccupied with two explosive issues:
the settlers' agitation for self-government and for closer association with Southern Rhodesia. The effect on Africans was a
shift towards more radical views, which received sudden and
lasting impetus from the resurgence of white political activity
in 1948. To the surprise of both government officials and
Africans, the new drive was launched by Gore-Browne, one of
the unofficials charged with representing African interests and
a long-standing opponent of amalgamation. Speaking in the
Legislative Council in January 1948, Gore-Browne demanded
responsible government for Northern Rhodesia and suggested
that the unofficials might be forced to use their existing power
to paralyse the Government unless their demands were met.⁵
In March that same year Gore-Browne came out in favour of
federation between the two Rhodesias and Nyasaland as the
only possible arrangement which would satisfy Central Africa's

¹ The towns included Kitwe, Lusaka, Luanshya, Broken Hill, Monze, and
Mazabuka, Sec/Nat/353. See also Gann, L. H., *A History of Northern Rhodesia*, p. 386.
² The deputation consisted of Yamba, Kaluwa, N. S. Liyanda, Godwin
Lewanika, Sykes Ndilila, and N. Nalumango, Sec/Nat/353.
³ Executive Council (Exec. Co.), 4 November 1946, ibid.
⁴ Ibid.
⁵ Leg. Co. *Debates*, 12 January 1948, col. 829.

whites, protect the rights of Africans and realize the economic advantages of mutual co-operation.[1]

Gore-Browne's hope for a united European-African front against the Colonial Office misfired disastrously. The African Representative Council shed its formerly deferential behaviour and passed a strong resolution pointing out that Northern Rhodesia was a black man's country and condemning any move which might give the Territory responsible government before Africans were suitably prepared to assume responsibility.[2] The Society sent a delegation to the Secretary of Native Affairs, which stated its opposition to Gore-Browne representing African interests at the forthcoming constitutional talks in London and requested that one of its members rather than one of the African Representative Council's members be added to Northern Rhodesia's delegation.[3] What was needed in London was 'an experienced opposition', claimed the Society's spokesmen, and the Federation of African Societies was accustomed to this role by virtue of its long opposition to the African Representative Council. The Secretary was not impressed and rejected the Society's pleadings out of hand.[4]

In July 1948 the Society held its second and last general conference. Despite the air of crisis which surrounded the meeting, both Welensky and Gore-Browne had been invited to address the meeting. Both had declined. The meeting passed several strong resolutions, one reiterating the Society's demand for its own delegate to the London talks, another opposing the return of Gore-Browne to the Legislative Council as a member representing African interests, and a third restating African opposition to any form of closer association with Southern Rhodesia, whether amalgamation or federation. But the meeting's most important decision concerned the Society itself. By a unanimous vote it was agreed that the Federation of African Societies should become the Northern Rhodesia African Congress.[5]

---

[1] Leg. Co. *Debates*, 24 March 1948, cols. 439–41.

[2] *Proceedings of the African Representative Council* (a.r.c.), July 1948, cols. 8–51.

[3] Report of meeting between the s.n.a. and representatives of the Society, 29 June 1948, Sec/Nat/353, Lusaka Archives.

[4] General Secretary of the Society to s.n.a., 10 July 1948, Sec/Nat/353, Lusaka Archives.

[5] Record of the annual general meetings of the Federation of African Societies

Congress represented itself as the voice of the people. In addition to the specific objectives contained in its first resolutions, Congress set itself the task of promoting the educational, political, economic, and social advancement of all Africans, irrespective of sex, social standing, or tribe. The Society's practice, in part the result of the Government's policy, of working outside the African council system appeared to have been reversed, the new approach being one of 'full co-operation with Government, Native Authorities, Missionary Societies, the African Representative Council and other such organizations which have the welfare of the Africans at heart'.[1]

The Government's negative attitude to the Society carried over without change to Congress. The Secretary of Native Affairs observed that welfare societies had existed for some years and had 'always interested themselves more in politics than in welfare'. It was hoped, he recalled, that the establishment of African councils would lead to the decline of the welfare societies, and until recently the policy had been reasonably effective, certainly more so than the approach in Southern Rhodesia and Nyasaland. But the Secretary also warned against needlessly offending Congress officials: 'We must avoid snubbing the members', he wrote, 'but at the same time do nothing to give the Congress official recognition as a representative body, which it is not. Many of its members are well meaning . . . intelligentsia and many . . . are politically ambitious Africans who have rather wild ideas. Unless carefully handled it will be a focus for political agitation and it might become an embarrassment.'[2] The next few years were to justify the Secretary's worst fears.

Meanwhile the Government remained friendly. Congress invited the retiring Secretary of Native Affairs to address its first annual conference at Munali Secondary School in December 1948. Without compromising the Government's non-recognition policy, the Secretary did, in fact, give a short

---

of N.R., 9–13 July 1948, Sec/Nat/353, Lusaka Archives. The first office-bearers of Congress were Godwin M. Lewanika (President); R. N. Nabulyato (General Secretary); M. Kakumbi (Treasurer); L. M. Lipalile (Vice-President); J. Richmond (Assistant Secretary); George Kaluwa (Assistant Treasurer).

[1] N.R. African Congress Constitution, ibid.
[2] S.N.A. to Governor, 25 September 1948, ibid.

speech, the first and last time a senior government official
addressed a political party conference, and was given a small
gift for his service to the country.[1] A similar invitation to the
Governor was politely declined.[2]

Once Northern Rhodesia's new Constitution had been
introduced in 1948, white political agitation shifted to the
campaign for Federation. Despite the British Government's
refusal to extend official recognition to the Victoria Falls
Conference of 1949, African suspicions continued to grow. That
opposition to a link of any kind with Southern Rhodesia was
widespread in Northern Rhodesia could hardly have been more
obvious. The Bledisloe Commission had recognized and recorded this as early as 1939. Gore-Browne in 1947, after a tour
of the Northern Province, wrote that 'Northern Rhodesia
politicians would be surprised at the strength of feeling [against
amalgamation] in all the rural areas. It is not a subject I raise
deliberately but it invariably crops up.'[3] Even in Barotseland,
long considered remote and politically contented, Gore-
Browne encountered 'a great deal of talk, as at all my meetings
lately, about amalgamation. The meeting [in Mongu] [was]
unanimous against the idea and kept coming back to the
subject. There is no doubt that people in rural areas are exercised on this matter just as much as those in towns.'[4] In 1948
the Kitwe African Society passed a resolution condemning
both responsible government for Northern Rhodesia and
amalgamation with Southern Rhodesia,[5] views which the
Society reiterated in 1950.[6] A meeting in Chingola in May
1949 between Gore-Browne and representatives of eight local
bodies passed a similar resolution against federation, which they
viewed as merely another means of achieving amalgamation.[7]

[1] Record of the first annual conference of the N.R. African Congress, 24–27
December 1948, Sec/Nat/353, Lusaka Archives.
[2] S.N.A. to Governor, 22 October 1948, ibid.
[3] Gore-Browne to P.C.(N.P.), 20 January 1947, Sec/Nat/117, Lusaka Archives.
[4] Gore-Browne to S.N.A., 23 February 1947, ibid.
[5] Resolution of Kitwe African Society, 5 February 1948, ibid.
[6] Meetings held by Nominated Members of Legislative Council with Kitwe
African Society, 13 February 1950, N/0073, Box 203.
[7] The meeting was in May 1949, between Gore-Browne and the following
bodies: Chingola Urban Advisory Council; African Mineworkers Union; African
Lorry Driver's Association; African Shop Assistants; African Contractors' Employees Union; Chingola African Welfare Society; Kasempe African Township
Management Board; African Civil Servants' Association; N/0073, Box 203.

Yet plans for closer association proceeded, despite the opposition of Africans. An exploratory conference of officials met in London early in 1951 and produced a report which unanimously and urgently called for some form of closer association in Central Africa.[1] A second Victoria Falls Conference, convened in September 1951 by the British Government and the three territorial governments, reached agreement, with the exception of Northern Rhodesia and Nyasaland's African representatives, on the principle of federation.[2] Britain's general election that autumn altered the situation dramatically. In a matter of weeks the new Conservative Government decided to press ahead with the formation of a federation, and the conclusions of both the London Conference of officials and the recent Victoria Falls Conference were accepted as the basis for drafting a detailed federal scheme.[3]

In March 1953 the proposals for Federation were approved by the House of Commons, and the following month motions approving the scheme were passed in the Legislative Councils of Northern Rhodesia and Nyasaland. In Southern Rhodesia the proposals were accepted by referendum amongst the Colony's white electorate, and in October 1953 the Federal Constitution came into operation.

The years 1950 to 1953 and the bitter battle over Federation were crucially important for the whole of Central Africa, both at the time and during the decade to come. In particular, the impact on African politics in Northern Rhodesia was decisive. African nationalism, still only in its infancy, was suddenly thrust into a period of painful adolescence. These were the first years of national protest, during which African leaders attempted simultaneously to prevent the Federation and to build a national political party. In the rush of events, however, the struggle against Federation took precedence over laying the foundations of a sound political organization. African leaders constantly found themselves on the defensive in a

[1] *Central African Territories: Report of Conference on Closer Association*, Cmd. 8233, London, March 1953.
[2] *Conference on the Closer Association of the Central African Territories: Proceedings of a Conference held at the Victoria Falls Hotel, Southern Rhodesia on September 18 to 21, 1951*, p. 3.
[3] *Closer Association in Central Africa: Statement by His Majesty's Government in the United Kingdom*, Cmd. 8411, 21 November 1951.

campaign which became more futile with each day that passed. The imposition of Federation was a stinging defeat for Congress, one from which it required several years to recover. But the struggle had had its positive effects as well. Africans in Northern Rhodesia had joined in a common cause for the first time; important political alignments had occurred; new men had moved into positions of leadership; and political attitudes of quite a new stamp had been formed in the heat of self-righteous opposition.

The African National Congress

We must tell the white settlers in our Protectorate and the British Government that we cannot trust them any more. We have been much humiliated. We have suffered from the hands of our supposed partners. Perhaps this has been a blessing in disguise. There is now a rising tide of nationalism among our people. Our national spirit, now ripe, is an upthrust from our long suffering. There is no going back. We are a nation and like any other nation on earth we love to rule ourselves.[1]

Congress became the African National Congress (A.N.C.) on the day that Harry Nkumbula took over its presidency in August 1951.[2] Nkumbula, who had long opposed any form of closer association with Southern Rhodesia,[3] was widely known amongst his countrymen as a fearless advocate of African rights.[4] He was born in 1914 at Namwala in Southern Province, a member of the Tonga-speaking Ila tribe. Nkumbula passed his standard VI at the Kafue Training Institute, a Methodist mission near Lusaka, about 1934 and stayed on a further four years to teach at the mission. In 1938 he joined the government service as a teacher and became headmaster of the Wusukili

[1] Excerpt from an address by Nkumbula to a Congress working committee meeting at Kitwe, 25 December 1951, Emanuel collection.
[2] Historical Extract of the African National Congress, Its Activities and Growth, 1951–1960, J. E. Michello, 1960, author's collection.
[3] Nkumbula gave a strong speech against closer association as early as 1943, when he was a representative of the Kitwe Urban Advisory Council to the African Provincial Council of Western Province; Regional Council, Western Province, Chairman's Report of First Meeting, 20 December 1943.
[4] Kenneth Kaunda, Zambia's first President, who had split with Nkumbula in 1958, recalled being deeply impressed by Nkumbula on their first meeting in 1944. Nkumbula had dared to speak to a passenger-lorry driver in strong terms on behalf of an ill fellow passenger at a time when lorry drivers 'were virtually kings unto themselves'; Kaunda, K. D., Zambia Shall Be Free, London, 1962, p. 45.

African School in 1944. Two years later Nkumbula resumed his
own education, first at Makerere University College in Uganda,
and then in London on a British Council scholarship to the
Institute of Education. There Nkumbula won a four-year
scholarship to the London School of Economics, where he was
caught up before long in the campaign against Federation. He
became friendly with Dr. Hastings Banda of Nyasaland, dedicated more and more time to politics, and in 1949 helped Banda
prepare a lengthy memorandum setting out the case of Northern
Rhodesia and Nyasaland Africans against Federation. Meanwhile that same year Nkumbula failed all five subjects of the
special intermediate B.Sc. (Economics), his bursary was cancelled, and he returned, bitter and dejected, to Northern
Rhodesia in January 1950.[1]

After a brief business venture Nkumbula turned to politics.
He immediately established himself as an aggressive opponent
of both the Federation and the Northern Rhodesia Government, so that the following year, when he challenged Lewanika
for the Congress presidency, Nkumbula won a sweeping victory.[2]
There was no time to lose. Nkumbula quickly set about preparing Congress (now A.N.C.) for the campaign against Federation. A national headquarters was set up in Chilenje township at
Lusaka with a full-time clerk-bookkeeper to handle administrative matters; field officers were appointed in a number of provinces and new branches formed in many towns and rural
areas, with several as far afield as Southern Rhodesia and South
Africa.[3] By February 1952 the field officers had been replaced
by provincial executives, supported in some areas by district
organizations to maintain closer contact with the growing
number of branches. That A.N.C. was clearly gaining ground
amongst 'responsible' Africans was demonstrated by its increased influence during 1951 in the African Representative
Council, the body responsible for selecting the two African
members for the Legislative Council. Reverend Kasokolo and
Nelson Nalumango were both replaced that year on the

[1] Extracts from the Biography of Nkumbula, 27 November 1962, S/S201/015;
also biographical notes on Africans, N/0118, Box 205, Lusaka Archives.
[2] Nkumbula defeated G. M. Mbikushita (who later added Lewanika to his
name) by nineteen votes to five; Historical Extract of A.N.C., 1951–1960, J. E.
Michello, 1960, author's collection.
[3] Ibid.; Gann, L. H., *A History of Northern Rhodesia*, p. 424.

Legislative Council by active Congressmen, Dauti Yamba and Paskale Sokota.[1]

At A.N.C.'s annual conference in August 1952 further changes were introduced. A supreme action council was formed to direct the campaign against Federation, plans were made for the creation of a radical youth wing and the constitution was amended to allow office-bearers and conference delegates to be elected every three years.[2] The Federation issue also brought an unprecedented response from the chiefs. Over 100 attended the conference from all parts of the Territory except Barotseland. During the course of the conference, which lasted a week instead of the usual three days, a delegation of chiefs met with Clement Attlee, M.P., the Leader of the Labour Party, to represent their views on Federation. A few days later the Secretary of Native Affairs requested the chiefs to attend a meeting with government officials at which the chiefs were told not to support or subscribe money to A.N.C. Their reply indicated that the chiefs' interest in A.N.C. was the direct result of A.N.C.'s campaign against Federation: 'The only chief who is not interested in Congress efforts . . . is the one whose country is not included in the Federal Scheme.'[3] Before the conference ended the chiefs agreed to help A.N.C. raise funds for a joint delegation to London to represent the African case against Federation.[4]

A.N.C.'s conference gave new impetus to the anti-Federation campaign. Provincial and branch officials returned to their respective areas with renewed initiative, and Nkumbula himself travelled tirelessly in the rural areas, spreading A.N.C.'s influence and gathering support against the proposed Federa-

[1] Yamba, a Bemba and one of the founders of the Federation of African Societies, was headmaster of the Luanshya African School from 1941 to 1947, before being appointed Education Councillor to the Lunda Native Authority. In 1953 Yamba became a Federal M.P., a move which fatally damaged his political career. Sokota, also a Bemba, was headmaster of the Kitwe African School from 1941 to 1951. In 1949 he became a member of the Western Province African Provincial Council and the African Representative Council. After his 1951 term in the Legislative Council, he was re-elected in 1954 for a second term. Biographical notes on Africans, N/0118, Box 205, Lusaka Archives.

[2] The supreme action council had nine members, five of whom were to represent the African Trade Union Congress, but Kaunda later expressed disappointment with the council's effectiveness; Kaunda, *Zambia Shall Be Free*, p. 49.

[3] A.N.C. Official News Bulletin, Vol. 2, No. 1, Chiefs and Delegates Conference, Lusaka, August 18–25, 1952, author's collection.

[4] Ibid.

tion. Despite widespread activity, however, Congress's growth during these early years was not uniform throughout the Territory, nor, judged by later standards, was it particularly impressive. Branch formation was most rapid in Northern and Southern Provinces with Central and Western (the Copperbelt) Province close behind. Branch activity in Eastern Province was minimal, while in Barotseland and North-western Province a.n.c. had formed no branches at all.[1] Nevertheless, the movement's influence on rural African opinion was quite dramatic; the African Affairs Department conceded the point in its annual report for 1951. 'There is no doubt that local leaders of African opinion are being briefed as to what they should say [against Federation] from Congress headquarters.'[2] But Congress's success in building a political organization capable of sustaining itself in the future and maintaining a more or less permanent following was quite another question. At this time the party offered little beyond resistance to Federation. Had Congress decisively shaped the political attitudes of Africans in Northern Rhodesia, or had it simply ridden the crest of African discontent and fear of amalgamation? After all, African opposition to amalgamation with Southern Rhodesia was widespread well before the formation of Congress; and though Africans of diverse tribal and linguistic backgrounds might prove relatively easy to unite against Federation, it did not necessarily follow that cohesion would survive on issues closer to home.

African opposition to the Federation was more emotional than reasoned. With deeply held suspicions born of long experience with the white man and limited knowledge of his institutions, great numbers of Africans, most of them with no detailed knowledge of federalism, opposed the Federation with a fervour which shocked and confused government officials. The safeguards offered in the Federal Scheme by the British Government were meaningless when set against this kind of opposition. Years of looking to the south had made even the unsophisticated

---

[1] Actual figures for branches in 1952 by Province were: Northern, 24; Southern, 13; Western, 11; Central, 9; Eastern, 4; Southern Rhodesia, 13; South Africa (Johannesburg), 1. These figures, attributed to government sources and probably inaccurate on the conservative side, are cited by Gann, L. H., *A History of Northern Rhodesia*, p. 424.

[2] *Annual Report of the Department of African Affairs*, 1951, p. 23.

African too wise to accept his protector's assurances at face value.

A.N.C. encouraged and articulated these suspicions. Among 'ordinary' Africans the most widespread fear was that their land would be taken, as it had in Southern Rhodesia. It was also widely assumed that African educational and occupational opportunities would be restricted by new forms of racial discrimination from the south. The most prominent fear of politically conscious Africans was their belief that Federation posed a grave threat to African political advance in the northern territories. 'The Europeans of Central Africa want Federation, hence Dominion status, in order to gain absolute power over Native policy . . . to remove British influence altogether from African affairs . . .'.[1] The Government's rejoinder that the African policies of the three territories were similar, differing only in methods of approach and timing (a claim supported by the Colonial Office but rejected by Northern Rhodesia's Governor)[2] was dismissed with the authority of personal experience. 'Their law [Southern Rhodesia's] may say that Africans are partners of Europeans. This may work theoretically, but in practice it does not, and we the people on the spot can bear witness to that!'[3]

The main safeguards for Africans contained in the federal scheme—the maintenance of protectorate status in Northern Rhodesia and Nyasaland, territorial responsibility for matters directly affecting African affairs, and the proposed African Affairs Board, a body with certain powers to refer discriminatory legislation to the Secretary of State—were also discredited by

---

[1] *Resolutions passed by the Northern Rhodesia African Congress at its Central Meeting . . .*, Lusaka, 21 July 1951.

[2] Speaking about the statement in paragraph 18 of the Report of the London Conference of 1951, which claimed that the native policies of the three territories were similar, the Governor wrote: 'I felt that this [paragraph 18] had aroused a certain amount of justifiable criticism, since in fact the divergences were numerous and in some respects important. I pointed out that we had invariably taken the line with Africans that Native policy would remain a territorial subject and that there was no need for those who objected to the Southern Rhodesia policy to have any fears, as what was done in Southern Rhodesia could in no way affect this Territory'. Minute from the Governor to the Chief Secretary, 25 October 1951, C/1016, Vol. I, Box 4349, Lusaka Archives.

[3] Memorandum by the Livingstone Africans on the Proposed Federation of Rhodesias and Nyasaland, p. 4, n.d. 1951, author's collection. See also A.N.C.'s 'A Case Against Federation', 4 August 1951, author's collection.

African leaders. 'When Southern Rhodesia received autonomous status in 1923', A.N.C. argued, 'reserved powers were vested in the Commonwealth Race Relations office to veto any legislation . . . detrimental to the interests of Africans. Despite class legislation, racial segregation, economic discrimination which adversely affect the interests of the Africans, those reserved powers have never been used.'[1] A.N.C. undoubtedly represented Africans in Northern Rhodesia between 1950 and 1953, but articulating African opposition to the Federation was vastly different from giving force to that opinion through effective action. It was here that A.N.C. fell short, not because it was unable to prevent Federation, but because it failed to mount a single action which involved more than a handful of officials and sympathetic supporters. Part of the reason lay in its organization. Provincial, district, and branch executives were poorly co-ordinated, each enjoying more autonomy than its inexperienced officials could wisely utilize. Provincial officials were not appointed by A.N.C. headquarters, but elected by subordinates at lower levels, a system which further weakened central control. Nor was the party well organized at its headquarters. Nkumbula's prolonged tours were usually accompanied by a somewhat chaotic situation at Chilenje. A.N.C. also lacked the steady income required to finance its operations. Most of its money was raised locally, but the absence of effective financial arrangements encouraged misappropriation of funds by officials at all levels. It has been estimated that A.N.C. managed during 1952 to collect approximately £7,000,[2] a figure which clearly represented a high point and a considerable portion of which went to support Nkumbula's London delegation. At the end of 1952, with no other accomplishments to its credit, A.N.C.'s accounts were overdrawn.[3]

Perhaps Congress's most serious tactical failure was its inability to establish an effective working relationship with the African trade-union movement. Industrial unrest in Northern Rhodesia would have been a potent weapon. The Supreme

[1] Resolutions passed by the Northern Rhodesia African Congress at its central meeting, Lusaka, 21 July 1951, author's collection.
[2] Gann, L. H., *A History of Northern Rhodesia*, p. 424.
[3] Ibid., p. 425.

Action Council which Congress established in 1952 represented an effort to secure closer party-trade union co-operation, but the Council barely functioned. Part of the difficulty was financial; Congress funds were insufficient to support a lengthy strike by African miners. More immediately relevant, however, were the attitude of Northern Rhodesia's leading trade unionist, Lawrence Katilungu, and the trade-union policy of the Government. African trade unions were not permitted in Northern Rhodesia until after the Second World War, and their position was by no means independent and secure. Though at this time no official barriers prevented trade unionists from maintaining personal political affiliations, they were strongly discouraged from holding party offices and introducing politics into trade-union affairs. Katilungu, who headed both the African Mineworkers Union (A.M.W.U.) and the African Trades Union Congress (A.T.U.C.), was himself against Federation and joined Congress's 1952 London delegation. However, for many years Katilungu was also a faithful supporter of the Government's trade-union policy, a position which became increasingly difficult to maintain after 1954, when he was driven more and more to depend on government assistance.

The conflict came to a head in April 1953 when Nkumbula, as a climax to Congress's campaign against Federation, organized two days of national prayer which were to be supported by a general strike among African workers. Katilungu expressed personal agreement with the plan, but refused to call out African workers in support of it.[1] To Africans the future was all too clear: Federation was inevitable and there was little sense in still another futile demonstration. Government officials and white politicians congratulated themselves on being right all along about 'whipped-up' African opposition, while Congress, defeated and demoralized, entered a period of disenchantment and decline.

Government Policy and African Opposition to Federation

The official policy towards Congress during the period 1950–3 remained one of non-recognition, though as the campaign against Federation gathered momentum the Government's sympathetic attitude of the late 1940's disappeared. In part this

[1] Hall, R., *Zambia*, pp. 157–8.

was attributable to the new Secretary for Native Affairs, Ronald Bush, who was much less sympathetic than his predecessor, Rowland Hudson, towards the more progressive Africans who had organized Congress.[1] But Congress itself had changed. The new militancy which Nkumbula brought to the movement had markedly influenced African opinion in the Territory. In the Government's eyes the effect on chiefs was particularly serious. Congress now posed a double-edged threat to the Government; Congress would reap the credit if Federation failed and welcome disgruntled Africans if it were imposed.

The Northern Rhodesia Government was committed at an early stage to some form of closer association. After the report of the conference of officials in London had been issued in March 1951, the three territorial governments agreed that in explaining the report to Africans 'a positive line should be taken by officials', who should point out that 'the report had been signed by senior officials of the territories and . . . United Kingdom Government, who had the welfare of Africans at heart and who firmly believed . . . they [the proposals] would be for the lasting benefit of all inhabitants of the three territories'.[2]

As a first step the Government convened a July meeting of the African Representative Council, where, in committee, the Chief Secretary and the Governor commended the report of the London Conference to the Council's members.[3] In the hope of achieving a favourable reaction, which might then be passed on to their respective communities, the proposals were explained in great detail. In the face of such an effort, the Governor's assurance that he was in no way committed to the plan did little to offset the suspicions roused amongst the Council's members. Six weeks later, after the members had consulted their people, the Council unanimously disapproved of the report on the ground that its implementation would be detrimental to the interests of the African people.[4]

[1] Bush succeeded Hudson in 1949.
[2] Extract from the minutes of a meeting of the S.N.A. at Salisbury on 10 May 1951, included in a note from the C.S. to the Governor on the policy to be adopted in explanation of the Closer Association proposals, 9 November 1951; C/1016, Vol. I, Box 4349, Lusaka Archives.
[3] Records of statements by the C.S. and the Governor to A.R.C. in committee on 20 July and 27 July 1951 respectively, ibid.
[4] A.R.C., Proceedings, 12 September 1951, col. 6.

By the time of the second Victoria Falls Conference, which agreed on the principle of Federation, the Government could no longer ignore the obvious strength of African opposition to any form of closer association with Southern Rhodesia. An effort had to be made to counter the claims of widespread African opposition to Federation which were constantly being made by Congress. Ironically, it was Northern Rhodesia's two African representatives to the conference, Yamba and Sokota, both active Congressmen, who provided the Government with the opportunity it needed. Yamba and Sokota had agreed to attend the conference only after an assurance was given that any decision reached would not be binding on the participating governments.[1] Throughout the proceedings the two Africans faithfully recorded their opposition to Federation, but at one point, apparently to avoid a complete breakdown of the conference, they agreed to what seemed a minor concession. Speaking on their behalf, John Moffat (later Sir John), one of the European Legislative Council members charged with representing African interests, stated the position.

Minor alterations in the proposals would not change their [Africans'] views but they would be prepared to consider the Report [Cmd. 8233] again if an effective policy of partnership were prepared and implemented . . . They accordingly requested that after the Conference further consideration of the proposals should be left over until the principles of partnership had been defined and put into effect and adequate safeguards of the legitimate interests of all races [had been] provided, after which a more dispassionate examination of the Report could be made.[2]

Yamba had made it clear, however, that Africans meant to wait to consider the report until 'they were taking a full part in the government of the country',[3] a crucial point which was conveniently ignored both in the final press communiqué and later by all the governments.[4]

[1] *Conference on the Closer Association of the Central African Territories*, 18–21 September 1951, pp. 11–15.
[2] Ibid., p. 14.
[3] Ibid., p. 14.
[4] In the final communiqué of the conference, the condition allegedly agreed to by the African representatives from N.R. was subtly different in its wording from Moffat's statement. The communiqué said: 'The representatives of African interests in N.R. explained that Africans would be willing to consider the question of

Essentially, the Government's plan was to persuade African members of the various councils in Northern Rhodesia to participate in framing a definition of Partnership which was acceptable to the African people. Since Partnership had been the official policy in Northern Rhodesia since 1958, the Government believed that it could represent its intentions to secure the definition as purely a territorial matter, quite separate from the question of Federation. Once secured, however, the Government would be in a position to argue that the definition also met the conditions laid down by Northern Rhodesia's representatives at Victoria Falls, and therefore that African objections to Federation had been satisfactorily resolved.

The Government set its plan in motion almost at once. At an Executive Council meeting in early October, Moffat reported on African reaction to the Victoria Falls Conference. In view of the need for prompt action before detailed discussions on a draft Federal scheme were begun in London (April 1952), 'the Council advised that immediate steps should be taken to proceed with the preparation of a definition of the policy of Partnership'.[1] Moffat and W. F. Stubbs, Acting Secretary for Native Affairs, were instructed to tour Lusaka, Broken Hill, and the Copperbelt to explain the Victoria Falls statement to Africans. In addition a 'brief' was to be prepared and issued to Provincial Education Officers in order 'that the statement might be explained during civic lessons in schools'.[2]

Moffat prepared a preliminary statement of the principles of Partnership,[3] but Africans on the Copperbelt had already rejected their representatives' concession at the Victoria Falls Conference. Partnership, it was held by a joint meeting of Urban Advisory Councillors, trade unionists, and Congress officials, was incompatible with Northern Rhodesia's status as a protectorate, a sop to obtain African agreement to Federation, which, if implemented, would prevent Africans from achieving

federation on the basis of the Report of the London Conference of officials after the policy of partnership in N.R. had been defined, and so defined, put into progressive operation.' Final Communiqué, 21 September 1951.

[1] Executive Council, 2 October 1951, C/1016, Lusaka Archives.
[2] Ibid.
[3] Moffat to Governor, 30 October 1951, ibid.

majority rule and independence within the Commonwealth.[1] Faced with the need to maintain its position, the Government quickly convened the African Representative Council, first to seek its co-operation in defining Partnership and, second, to secure confirmation of the statement made on its behalf by the African representatives at the Victoria Falls Conference.[2] It was essential, the Governor wrote, that Partnership be defined before the 'full campaign about federation'.[3]

At the Council's opening session on 3 December 1951 the Governor gave a lengthy speech,[4] which had been prepared in close consultation with the Chief Secretary, the Secretary for Native Affairs, the Colonial Office, Moffat and, rather surprisingly, Welensky, who at this time was not an Executive Council member.[5] In his speech the Governor took great pains

[1] The meeting took place on 28 October 1951; demi-official letter from the s.n.a. to all p.c.s and d.c.s, 15 November 1951, N/0052, Vol. II, Box 1682, Lusaka Archives. See also Gann, L. H., *A History of Northern Rhodesia*, p. 432.

[2] Executive Council, 13 November 1951, N/0052, Lusaka Archives.

[3] Governor to c.s., 12 November 1951, C/1016, Lusaka Archives.

[4] A.R.C., *Proceedings*, 3 December 1951, cols. 1–11.

[5] s.n.a. to Governor, 30 November 1951; telegram from c.o. to Governor, 16 November 1951; Welensky to s.n.a., 28 November 1951: N/0052, Lusaka Archives.

The draft produced originally took a very much stronger line than the final speech and shows up clearly the thinking of the Native Affairs Department at this time. The original draft sought more vigorously to establish the early roots of the policy of Partnership (see footnote 1, p. 31). More important, it contained a remarkable and scarcely veiled threat to Africans which, though dropped from the Governor's final version, probably reflected the line being followed on this question by Provincial Administration officials in the field. It said: 'A refusal [by Africans] to collaborate on the grounds that Africans are protected, would only mean that the other communities would be forced to pursue alone their own paths towards their political and economic goals. In view of such refusal the non-African communities would be forced to deal with the Government and the Secretary of State for the Colonies and would be under no obligation to consult or consider the views of Africans.'

The s.n.a.'s minute to the Governor, 30 November 1951, indicates that Welensky was brought in only at the final stages. Welensky had discovered that Moffat possessed a copy of the Governor's draft speech and was annoyed that he had been left out. The s.n.a. then showed Welensky his copy (without consulting the Governor) and Welensky's letter of 28 November was the result. Welensky's ideas were sympathetically treated by the s.n.a., the c.s., and Moffat, though not all his suggestions were included in the final speech. On 2 December the c.s., s.n.a., and Moffat met together and decided on the various points in the s.n.a.'s covering minute for the final draft of the speech.

One other point of considerable interest comes to light in the s.n.a.'s minute. Moffat informed the s.n.a., in strictest confidence, of his intention to attend a meeting between the European unofficial Legislative Council Members and God-

to demonstrate that the policy of Partnership, officially introduced in 1948, had, in fact, been established in practice for a
very long time.[1] In 1945 a motion embodying the essential
meaning of Partnership, though not employing the actual word,
had been passed in the Legislative Council; during the subsequent debate the word had been used twice, once by Gore-
Browne and again by the Chief Secretary.[2] In 1948 at the
Territory's constitutional conference in London, which two
representatives of the African Representative Council had
attended, a summary of Partnership had been prepared and
approved, which in July of that year the Secretary of Native
Affairs communicated to the Council.[3] Africans knew full well,
the Governor argued, that Partnership was not a new policy,
and that they had been assured repeatedly that its implementation would in no way affect the British Government's ultimate
responsibility towards Africans.[4]

The Council subsequently dissolved into committee to consider the Governor's proposals. Moffat spoke to the meeting,
despite considerable reluctance at first to accord him a hearing.[5]
When the Council reconvened on 5 December several motions
were debated. The Council refused to participate in the preliminary definitions of Partnership and instead moved that a
government definition be referred to Native Authority Councils,
Urban Advisory Councils, and African Provincial Councils
before finally being considered in the African Representative

frey Huggins on the night of 2 December. Though it is not known what took place
at the meeting, Moffat's behaviour in this whole business, and in the A.R.C.
meeting which followed, strongly suggests that he advised the unofficials on African
opposition to Federation, and perhaps on how African opposition might be over-
come. It seems clear that Moffat sympathized with federation at this stage.

[1] In the original draft of the Governor's speech, it was stated that the concept of
Partnership was twenty years old, dating back to the findings of the Joint Select
Committee of Parliament of 1931, 'although we did not make use of that useful and
descriptive word until 1948'; N/0052, Lusaka Archives.
[2] A.R.C., *Proceedings*, 3 December 1951, cols. 3–4. For the use of the word
'Partnership' in the 1945 debate, see Leg. Co., *Debates*, 4 July 1945, cols. 468 and
471.
[3] A.R.C., *Proceedings*, 3 December 1951, col. 7. For the S.N.A.'s statement, see
ibid., 10 July 1948, col. 311.
[4] This point was emphasized by the C.O. telegram to the Governor, 16 November
1951, N/0052, Lusaka Archives.
[5] Circular from the S.N.A. to all P.C.s and D.C.s, 16 December 1951, ibid.

Council.[1] Two attempts to amend the motion to include the
Council more directly in the Partnership discussions were de-
feated.[2] A second motion recorded the Council's concern over
the Secretary of State's statement on Federation in the Commons
on 21 November and indicated that the Council felt it was too
early for any such statement.[3] The third motion, 'that this
Council confirms the statement which was made by the African
Representative Council's representatives at the Victoria Falls
Conference', was narrowly defeated on the grounds that while
Partnership and Federation were discussed at the conference, it
was never intended by Africans that the two should be tied
together on condition that the former would help to bring about
the latter.[4]

The defeat of the third motion represented a severe setback
to the Government's plans. At an 'informal' committee meeting
that evening the Secretary for Native Affairs and his assistant,
Stubbs, set about persuading the Council to reverse its position.[5]
In the end it was agreed to expunge the third motion from the
record and to replace it with a compromise motion which indicated that Africans 'might' be willing (as opposed to the phrase
'would be willing' which appeared in paragraph 6 of the
Victoria Falls Conference statement) to consider Federation
after the policy of Partnership had been defined and implemented.[6] Though the Secretary of Native Affairs was displeased
with the compromise, because he believed it to be a repudiation
of the original Victoria Falls statement and a victory for the line
that Partnership and Federation were not tied together,[7] the
Government had salvaged enough from the Council's meeting
to carry on its policy.

In April 1952 a draft statement of Partnership was issued to
all Provincial and District Commissioners to guide their dis-

[1] A.R.C., *Proceedings*, 5 December 1951, col. 11.
[2] Ibid., cols. 11-49.
[3] Ibid., col. 52. The motion was passed by twenty-five votes to nil.
[4] Circular from the s.n.a. to all p.c.s and d.c.s, 16 December 1951, N/0052,
Lusaka Archives. The motion was defeated by seven votes to five. with fourteen
abstentions.
[5] Ibid.
[6] A.R.C., *Proceedings*, 6 December 1951, cols. 65-68. The motion was passed by
nineteen votes to three.
[7] Circular from the s.n.a. to all p.c.s and d.c.s, 16 December 1951, N/0052,
Lusaka Archives.

cussions with Native Authority Councils and African Urban Advisory Councils.[1] African opposition in the local councils was as strong as it had been in the African Representative Council, and the Government's sudden interest in defining Partnership only made matters worse. Africans wanted to know why, if Partnership had been the policy since 1948, it was not defined then? They had seen little change in European attitudes since 1948 and felt that defining Partnership would prove fruitless until Europeans demonstrated their sincerity by treating Africans as human beings.[2]

At the next African Representative Council meeting in December 1952, African hostility towards the Government and Europeans in general broke into the open. A motion put forward by Donald Siwale declared that since it was the policy of both the Northern Rhodesia and the British Governments that no race in Northern Rhodesia should dominate another, the time was 'ripe in fact overdue' for representation in both the Legislative and Executive Councils to be based on parity.[3] Supporting his motion, Siwale complained that Partnership was not being offered for today, but for some unspecified date in the future.

Does the Government of Northern Rhodesia think that Africans . . . do not understand what is taking place? I have already said that we are not blind . . . We have been co-operating with our European friends for many years and we wonder why they want partnership now at this present time. There is something behind partnership. The African is beginning to suspect . . . some danger . . . If they [the Government] want trouble in Northern Rhodesia, let them continue with the policy that they have got . . . It has already been said that no nation will dominate another. Now we see we are already dominated and the attitude of the Europeans is to dominate the Africans of Northern Rhodesia for ever. I am afraid that the Africans will not tolerate that.[4]

Later in the debate Titus Mukupo, who was active in Congress and in 1958-9 served as the party's General Secretary,

---

[1] S.N.A. to all P.C.s and D.C.s, April 1952, N/0047, Vol. I, Box 1682, Lusaka Archives.
[2] African reaction was reported by P.C.s and D.C.s during the months which followed the S.N.A.'s circular; ibid.
[3] A.R.C., *Proceedings*, 19 December 1952, cols. 73-74.
[4] Ibid., cols. 75-77.

succinctly summed up the confusion and frustration Africans
felt towards the Government's policy.

As regards partnership, the Government says the time is ready;
federation, the Government says the time is ready; but when we
bring up . . . representation, the Government says the time is not
ready . . . How is it that for the other things the time is ready, but
for representation the time is not ready? (Hon. Members: Hear,
hear!) We cannot understand our Government at the present
stage.[1]

In 1953 the Government made a final attempt to secure
African co-operation in defining the policy of Partnership. The
African Representative Council had reached the end of its prescribed term, and for some time the Native Affairs Department
debated whether the Council's term should be extended to fit
in with the proposed 1954 Legislative Council elections, or
whether African councils throughout the Territory should hold
elections.[2] The present councils had already rejected the idea of
Partnership, and new councils, it was felt, 'would be more
representative of up-to-date opinion'.[3] In the end it was decided
to extend the life of the present African Representative Council[4]
and to concentrate on influencing African political thought in
the lower councils.[5] If the lower councils could be persuaded to
define Partnership, as well as to accept a draft definition, their
delegates to the next meeting of the African Representative
Council would be compelled to follow suit.

The Native Affairs Department, assisted by Moffat, then
prepared a list of general motions on Partnership for discussion
in the African Provincial Councils.[6] Explaining the motions to
the Secretary of Native Affairs, their author wrote: 'I did not
want to go into too much detail, but I felt that if these motions
were approved (and they do seem harmless enough in all conscience) it could be claimed that the African councils had supported the fundamental principles of partnership.'[7] Provincial

---

[1] A.R.C., *Proceedings*, 19 December 1952, cols. 99–100.
[2] See correspondence among officials in the N.A. Department during February
and March 1953, N/0052, Lusaka Archives.
[3] Thomas to S.N.A., March 1953, ibid.
[4] S.N.A. to all P.C.s and D.C.s, 26 March 1953, ibid.
[5] Thomas to S.N.A., 1 April 1953, ibid.
[6] Ibid.
[7] Ibid.

Commissioners, it was decided, were to present the motions to the councils in committee, pointing out that the African Representative Council was awaiting the views of the African Provincial Councils as well as their authorization to discuss the draft statement of Partnership both with the Government and, if necessary, with the unofficial members of the Legislative Council.[1]

African reaction in the Provincial Councils was less hostile than the Government had anticipated. There appeared to be a growing element of moderate African opinion which favoured co-operating with the Government in working out the federal plan in order to ensure that the Government's assurances to Africans would, in fact, be carried out.[2] Preparations went ahead for the African Representative Council meeting scheduled for July 1953. Moffat planned meetings with Africans up and down the 'line of rail', and Provincial Commissioners were asked to prepare a list of Africans whom it would be 'useful' for Moffat to meet.[3]

At the African Representative Council meeting, however, the Africans stood firm in their opposition to Federation. A motion deploring the decision taken by the British Government to implement the Federation against the expressed opinion of Northern Rhodesia's overwhelming indigenous population and calling for an all-African conference on the subject was passed unanimously.[4] In the debate which followed nearly every speaker expressed loss of confidence in the Government and considerable antagonism towards Central Africa's Europeans.[5] They warned repeatedly of the serious consequences which would follow if the Government decided to disregard African opposition to the Federation, which many speakers already appeared to recognize as an established fact. Several lamented the political weakness of the Africans; they had wanted to

[1] Executive Council, 8 April 1953, ibid. One P.C., at Livingstone, protested against the proposed plan and was told that there were certain 'reasons why partnership has to be discussed'. Fortunately, the S.N.A. noted, it would not now have to be in open council. This suggests that N.R.G. was negotiating with the C.O. on this question; P.C. (Livingstone) to S.N.A., 7 April 1953, N/0052, Lusaka Archives.
[2] S.N.A. to all P.C.s, 28 May 1953, N/0052, Lusaka Archives.
[3] Thomas to all P.C.s, 18 June 1953, ibid.
[4] A.R.C., Proceedings, 22 July 1953, col. 93.
[5] Ibid., cols. 93–114, passim.

co-operate with the Government and with Europeans, but African feelings had been disregarded and their trust in the Government's alleged concern for them destroyed. But despite the air of disillusionment and rather pathetic resignation which ran through much of the debate, there were several manifestations of the more violent reaction and the bitter opposition to Federation which would become widespread in the coming years.

. . . in the past we have had the Secretary of State for the Colonies as our guardian in every sense of the word, but once we realize that we are not regarded as a protectorate any more everyone is likely to do his own will. Even fowls, if you have kept a crate of fowls, and they are not looked after will scatter. To those who are under-estimating us by saying 'What can they do, it does not matter', I can assure them that even to collect those fowls again it will cost time and money. Sir, I say that if four men have walked away from the law, the Government will have to send ten askaris (soldiers) to see what is happening . . .[1]

African National Congress, 1953–7

The immediate reaction of Africans to the formation of the Federation was one of disillusionment and resignation. Discredited to some extent by its failure to prevent Federation, A.N.C. quickly lost much of the attraction and unity of purpose which it possessed before 1953. The movement entered a period of disintegration and decline characterized by inconsistent policies, petty bickering amongst officials, poor relations with the African trade-union movement, and apathy among the African public.

A.N.C.'s difficulties began several months before Federation's formal implementation in October 1953. For some time there had been disagreement within the party over the methods to be adopted for the final stand against Federation. The failure of the day of national prayer which Nkumbula had called in April weakened A.N.C. further by widening the breach with the trade-union movement.[2] The elections at A.N.C.'s annual conference

[1] Chimkoko speaking. Ibid., col. 112.
[2] Epstein, A. L., *Politics in an Urban African Community*, Manchester, 1958, p. 162. Epstein's entire chapter, 'The National Congress and Local Politics', supports the view that A.N.C. disintegrated during this period, both nationally and at the local level on the Copperbelt; see especially pp. 164, 179–82.

in August 1953 provided an indication of the party's new mood. Nkumbula, who was returned with overwhelming support, was provided with a new and more militant group of office-bearers, which included Kaunda as Secretary-General.[1] The conference closed by adopting a policy of 'non-cooperation without violence towards any move considered detrimental to African interests'.[2]

Within two months, however, A.N.C. compromised its 'non-cooperation' policy by announcing that it would contest the first Federal elections.[3] Though Federation was still deeply opposed by Africans, A.N.C.'s leaders feared that boycotting the election would lead to the appointment of African 'stooges' by the territorial Governors. In fact, A.N.C.'s decision made little difference, since Northern Rhodesia's African members in the Federal Assembly would be elected by the African Representative Council from among its own membership. A.N.C. could only endorse the candidates it preferred. Initially, A.N.C. attempted to obtain representation for itself and the trade unions in the African Representative Council.[4] When this failed it demanded instead that membership in the Council be dropped as a requirement for candidates for the Federal Assembly.[5] Nkumbula and Kaunda alleged that the regulations for candidates were *ultra vires* the Federal Constitution on the ground that it contained no authority to restrict candidature specifically to members of the African Representative Council.[6] The Government rejected this demand as well and ignored the legal argument which it raised. In large part this was because the regulations, as drafted, successfully excluded 'professional politicians' from the field,[7] but the Government was also aware of its own rather shaky legal position.[8] When the Federal elections took place, neither

[1] Kaunda to Commander Fox-Pitt, 16 October 1953, Emanuel collection.
[2] Epstein, A. L., *Politics in an Urban African Community*, p. 162.
[3] Press communiqué, 13 October 1953, cited by Kaunda, *Zambia Shall Be Free*, pp. 56–57.
[4] Norman Price to C.S., 14 November 1953, MN/1/3, Vol. I, Box 1672, Lusaka Archives.
[5] Exec. Co., 24 November 1953, ibid.
[6] A.N.C.'s case was also put in a letter from Nkumbula and Kaunda to the Governor-General of the Federation, 30 November 1953, ibid.
[7] S.N.A. to V. Strangeways, Secretariat, Zomba, Nyasaland, 4 March 1954, ibid.
[8] Solicitor-General to Attorney-General, 30 September 1953, ibid. Unknown to Nkumbula and Kaunda, they had hit upon an extremely sensitive point which if

of A.N.C.'s candidates was successful,[1] despite threatening handbills distributed by A.N.C. to the African Representative
Council's members shortly before the vote. The Council was
offended, not only by the handbills, but also by A.N.C.'s allegations that the Council was not the proper body to elect African
representatives to the Federal Assembly; relations between the
party and the Council, formerly good, now began to deteriorate.[2]

The first three years of Federation did not confirm the earlier
fears of most Africans; indeed, living standards improved and
job opportunities were more numerous. A.N.C. sought to keep
African resentment alive by seizing on local issues and by
encouraging Africans to demand equal rights as a means of
testing the official policy of Partnership. In January 1954 A.N.C.
organized a boycott of Lusaka butcheries which aimed at ending the discriminatory practice of serving Africans pre-wrapped,
often spoiled, meat through a hatch in the wall of the shop.
Attempts to extend the boycott to the Copperbelt in February,
however, were largely unsuccessful.[3] With the exception of the
1956 boycott of European and African traders, the same was
true of most other A.N.C. boycotts during the period.

By late 1954 Kaunda, A.N.C.'s Secretary-General, realized
'that some constructive thinking would have to be done if
Congress were going to hold together'.[4] Africans had come to
believe that the Federation was so firmly entrenched that it was
useless to continue the fight to break it. The position in A.N.C.

---

pursued with ingenuity and followed up in court might have resulted in a major
A.N.C. triumph. In 1958, when the system of electing African members to the Federal
Assembly was altered, the opinion of the legal draftsman was that the original
provision on candidature in 1953 was *ultra vires*. 'It is just as well that the life of
the first Federal Assembly is over, as I have little doubt that any one of the other
two million Africans in this country who were not members of the A.R.C. could
have taken legal action to set aside the original election of the specially elected
African members'; Acting Legal Draftsman to S.N.A., 6 November 1958, ibid.

[1] A.N.C. endorsed Paskale Sokota, M.L.C., and D. R. Siwale, but the successful
candidates were M. Kakumbi and Dauti Yamba; *Central African Post*, 24 November
1953.
[2] Draft letter from S.N.A. to Marnham at the C.O., 14 December 1953, N/0052,
Vol. III, Box 1682, Lusaka Archives.
[3] Epstein, A. L., *Politics in an Urban African Community*, pp. 171–9.
[4] Kaunda, *Zambia Shall Be Free*, p. 60.

remained unchanged through most of 1955. Nkumbula and
Kaunda were arrested for possessing copies of a banned publication, *Africa and the Colonial World*, and sentenced to their first
term in prison, two months with hard labour. Branch morale
remained low; it was difficult to get people to organize and
several provincial officials were arrested and jailed for various
offences. Towards the end of the year Kaunda drew up a five-
year plan aimed at revitalizing the party.[1] Kaunda saw A.N.C.'s
next five years as crucial ones, particularly for the fight to prevent the Federation from attaining its intended goal of dominion
status. The fight, as Kaunda saw it then, was not to achieve
self-government in Northern Rhodesia but instead to remain a
protectorate under the direct control of the Colonial Office
until Africans were ready to participate fully in the Territory's
affairs.[2]

Before the year was out there were signs of a resurgence of
A.N.C. activity in some areas, notably the Northern Province
and the Copperbelt. In April 1955 A.N.C.'s district committee
in Chinsali decided to form six action groups whose function
was to precede government officers on tour, dissuading villagers
from showing respect to Native Authority and Boma representatives as well as refusing to supply them with food, water, and
firewood.[3] In June it was reported that Northern Province was
experiencing an unusual amount of 'A.N.C. infiltration just
lately'.[4] A touring officer in Mporokoso District found villagers
unco-operative and disrespectful, completely changed since his
last tour of the area in 1953, and he recommended that chiefs
and Native Authorities be encouraged to take stronger action
against dissident elements.[5]

'We are dealing with something more organized than a
seasonal outburst of political high spirits', wrote the District
Commissioner at Chinsali. In his opinion, the heart of the
problem was the failure of the Native Authority in recent years
'to assert itself against the hard core in the Lubwe-Chinsali

[1] Kaunda, *Zambia Shall Be Free*, p. 60.
[2] Ibid., p. 65.
[3] Ag.P.C.(N.P.) to S.N.A., 22 April 1955, N/0001/2/15/4, Box 188, Lusaka
Archives.
[4] D. C. R. Bailey to A.S. (Native Affairs), 17 June 1955, N/0003/2/15/3, Box 188,
Lusaka Archives.
[5] Tour Report No. 2 of 1955, ibid.

Boma areas'.[1] A.N.C.'s chief organizer in the province, Robert Makasa, adopted tactics which later became widespread among rural organizers, especially after the formation of the United National Independence Party (U.N.I.P.) in 1960. Makasa's approach was to attempt to split the Native Authorities from the Boma by impugning the chiefs as creatures of the Government. At the same time, Makasa issued circulars to all chiefs in the province urging them to give a lead to their people by ceasing to show respect to government officials and taking the initiative in forming small A.N.C. groups to tour their respective areas fomenting discontent on a wide range of local issues.[2] According to the Provincial Commissioner, Makasa also encouraged support for the Lumpa Church, a separatist religious sect headed by Alice Lenshina, which was extremely active and popular in the Chinsali area, and attempted to use the church's gatherings for political meetings.[3]

At this time field officers exercised a decisive influence on Government policy towards A.N.C. It was generally believed in the Provincial Administration that where Congress agitators caused disturbances resulting in criminal prosecutions subversive activity tended to decline sharply. On the other hand, where A.N.C. organizers succeeded in maintaining a constant nuisance value without laying themselves open to prosecution, as in Chinsali, it was felt that they managed to create the impression of 'apparent immunity', which deluded the ordinary villager and led to a deterioration in law and order.[4] Thus most field officers subscribed to the view—as indeed they did until 1963, though their influence on official policy declined after 1961—'that the key to coping with incipient subversion lies with the Chiefs'.[5] Until they were firmly committed there was 'little hope that the ordinary people will produce the evidence to convict the agitators . . .'.[6]

In Chinsali District the Provincial Administration took a strong line with the chiefs in an effort to force them to exert their authority against A.N.C. Arrangements were made for Chiti-

[1] Tour Report No. 2 of 1955, N/003/2/15/3, Box 188, Lusaka Archives.
[2] D.C. (Chinsali) to P.C.(N.P.), 22 April 1955, N/0001/2/15/4, Lusaka Archives.
[3] Ag.P.C.(N.P.) to S.N.A., 5 May 1955, ibid.
[4] See, for example, Ag.P.C.(N.P.) to S.N.A., 2 June 1955, ibid.
[5] Tour Report No. 4 of 1955 (N.P.) Annexure I, ibid.
[6] Ibid.

mikulu, the Paramount Chief of the Bemba, to visit Chinsali to bring his subchiefs there into line. The Provincial Commissioner's subsequent report was illustrative of the approach the Government took towards chiefs and Native Authorities in areas beset by nationalist agitation during these years.

He [Chitimikulu] was there and announced his intention of having local Congress organizers on the mat in regard to their connection with local disrespect to constituted authority. He undertook to consider some public acknowledgement of bad manners to atone for the repeated uprooting of the Coronation Tree [a tree planted near the Boma on the occasion of the Queen's Coronation]. He also said he was going to bring Chief Nkula to book for having fined several offenders for contempt of his court and then cancelling his sentences. I went over all these matters with him in the presence of the District Commissioner and gave him as big a head of steam as possible, but I would not as yet wager upon the results. He is, however, feeling somewhat ashamed of himself for a disgraceful exhibition in the Welfare Hall in Kasama about a week ago, when he allowed a formal interview at which he was supposed to preside, to degenerate into a Congress meeting at which he and Senior Chief Mwamba were the principal exhibits. He was not sober and ended up by standing on the table and leading a crowd of some fifteen hundred in cheers and tipsy self-congratulation in which everyone but Government was favoured. The District Commissioner reports that Chief Nkula has now been doing his shaky best to assert himself and I do not at present expect to have to recommend his suspension.[1]

Nor was A.N.C.'s suspected connexion with the Lumpa Church ignored by the Government. Officials in Lusaka realized that dealing with Lenshina might well prove difficult, though, at the same time, they assumed that the Acting Provincial Commissioner of Northern Province was seeking the co-operation of Chinsali mission groups, notably the White Fathers, to invoke sanctions which would deprive Lenshina of much of her support. 'After all,' it was argued, 'if any person attempts to start up what is in effect another religion, surely the missionary society will want to call out their commandos.'[2]

Towards the end of 1955 violence on the Copperbelt increased, especially the stoning of houses and cars, blame for

[1] Ag.P.C.(N.P.) to S.N.A., 15 May 1955, ibid.
[2] Bailey to A.S. (Native Affairs), 11 May 1955, ibid.

which was generally laid on A.N.C. Nkumbula denied the party's
involvement in the outbreaks and asked those responsible to
stop immediately.[1] He was supported by his old friend, Harry
Franklin, a European M.L.C. responsible for African interests, who, after making an exploratory trip to Chingola
and meeting with a number of leading Africans, assured the
public that the stonings were not politically inspired.[2] The fact
that both Europeans and Africans were victimized, apparently
indiscriminately, suggested to Franklin that the violence was
due entirely to the kind of hooliganism which resulted from
inferior housing, insufficient education facilities, and deteriorating family life among urban Africans. Whatever the reasons,
African discontent on the Copperbelt, often referred to as 'the
loafer problem', was clearly on the increase, and A.N.C.'s more
militant leaders lost no time in taking advantage of the rise in
tensions.

At the same time industrial disputes flared up on the Copperbelt, and A.N.C. began to extend significantly its influence over
the African trade-union movement. Katilungu's refusal in 1953
to throw the full support of the African unions behind A.N.C.'s
anti-Federation campaign had won him many enemies, some
of whom worked for the next seven years to break his power in
the dominant African Mineworker's Union (A.M.W.U.). As
Katilungu backed away from trade-union involvement in
nationalist party politics, his more extreme opponents, who
favoured a closer link with A.N.C., sought to strengthen their
position in the trade-union movement. The group was led by
Robinson Puta, at that time (1954) Vice-President of the
Northern Rhodesia African Trade Union Congress (A.T.U.C.),
Chairman of the Chingola branch of the A.M.W.U., and an
official in A.N.C.; Mathew Nkoloma, General Secretary of both
the A.T.U.C. and the A.M.W.U.; and Dixon Konkola, President of
the Northern Rhodesia Railway African Worker's Trade Union
(R.A.W.U.) and an active A.N.C. organizer during 1952–3 at
Broken Hill. They were joined by several other trade unionists
who favoured closer co-operation with A.N.C.: Jameson Chapaloko, Mathew Mwendepole, and Gordon Chindele, all A.M.W.U.
branch secretaries, and Justin Chimba, Organizing Secretary

[1] *African Eagle*, 11 October 1955.
[2] *Central African Post*, 21 October 1955.

of the Northern Rhodesia General Workers Trade Union
(G.W.T.U.), who had been an active and vociferous A.N.C. leader
in the anti-Federation campaign. During the fight against
Federation most of these men had been closely associated with
Simon Ber Zukas, an alleged Communist who was active in
A.N.C. during the early 1950's before being deported from
Northern Rhodesia in 1952. In the years ahead several were to
continue to maintain their contacts with Zukas in London.

In January 1955 the A.M.W.U. called a strike over the issue of
African advancement, which lasted nearly two months and resulted in something of a breakthrough for African miners.
During the course of the strike, which gave rise to ill feeling on
both sides, A.N.C. leaders played an active part in encouraging
the miners to remain out until the mining companies had met
their demands.[1] That the strike had a political aspect and represented something of a triumph for Puta and Nkoloma could
be seen in the remarkably high pay increase of 10s. 8d. per shift
which Katilungu allowed to go forward as the union's demand.
Had it been obtained, the increase would have brought African
miners within reach of qualifying for the vote under Northern
Rhodesia's existing franchise arrangements.[2]

Though the pay increases awarded to the A.M.W.U. fell far
short of the union's original demand, the movement to establish
a more militant trade union-A.N.C. link continued to develop.[3]
By mid-1955 Katilungu's opponents turned their attention to
the A.T.U.C. and in August gained control of its executive.
Konkolo replaced Katilungu as President; Puta and Nkoloma
retained their positions as Vice-President and General Secretary
respectively; and both Chimba and Chapaloko became Executive Committee members.[4] The A.T.U.C. then formed a subcommittee of nine, headed by Konkola and Nkoloma, to deal
with political matters.[5] Its membership was almost exclusively composed of the more militant trade unionists,[6] who

[1] Labour Commissioner for record from N. Hunt, 19 February 1955, N/2709/4,
Box 225, Lusaka Archives.
[2] 'Subversion in the Trade Unions of N.R.', 17 October 1961, S/S128/64/01,
p. 8.
[3] Ibid., p. 9.
[4] Ibid., p. 14.
[5] Northern News, 24 October 1955.
[6] Its members were Konkola, Nkoloma, Kaluchini, Mwendepole, Namitengo,
Mubanga, Chanda, Chapaloko, Chindele, Northern News, 24 October 1955.

maintained external connexions with the World Federation
of Trade Unions (w.f.t.u.) and favoured a united party-trade
union front to further African economic and political advance.
Despite these developments in the a.t.u.c., Katilungu's position in the a.m.w.u. remained relatively safe. The a.t.u.c., even
under Katilungu's leadership, had never achieved significant
unity or financial independence, primarily because of the de-
plorable state of its member unions and its consequent depen-
dence on the a.m.w.u., the only really powerful and wealthy
African trade union in Northern Rhodesia. Before the a.t.u.c.
group could consolidate its position in the a.m.w.u., however,
Katilungu seized the initiative by suddenly resigning from the
presidency in November 1955. After allowing himself to be persuaded to return to his post, Katilungu regained his position
with new strength at the a.m.w.u.'s annual conference early in
1956. Nkoloma retained his office as General Secretary, but
Puta was dismissed.[1] For the time being, the a.t.u.c. remained
relatively inactive, though only partly owing to Katilungu's
manoeuvres; for in early 1956 it appeared that the trade unions
and a.n.c. had begun to work together.

In April 1956, not long after Nkumbula had sent out a virulent circular to all a.n.c. branches which alleged that racial
discrimination and the social colour bar were worse in Northern
Rhodesia than in South Africa, there was an outbreak of boycotts organized by a.n.c. against European and Asian shops.
At first dissension appeared in a.n.c. ranks, and Nkumbula
called off the boycotts on 23 April.[2] In May and June, however,
they were resumed, this time more effectively and in a larger
number of centres.[3] In most cases, a.n.c.'s district secretary
wrote letters to the local European and Indian Chambers of
Commerce, setting out African grievances and requesting a
meeting.[4] When the reply had been received—usually that
a.n.c. should take the matter to the African Urban Advisory

[1] 'Subversion in the Trade Unions of N.R.', 17 October 1961, S/S128/64/01,
p. 9.
[2] Mason, P., Year of Decision, Oxford, 1960, pp. 114–15.
[3] In addition to most of the major urban centres, boycotts were organized in
Fort Jameson, Monze, and Kasama.
[4] See, for example, a.n.c. district secretary to the secretaries, Ndola Dist.
Chamber of Commerce, Indian Chamber of Commerce and Industry, African
Chamber of Commerce and Industry, 14 May 1956, MN/2154/2, Box 189,
Lusaka Archives.

Council with whom the local traders were prepared to meet—
the boycott began at once, often proving almost totally effective.
The District Commissioner at Broken Hill, reporting that A.N.C.
action groups were intimidating people in the townships, admitted that he had previously underestimated A.N.C.'s local
strength.[1] His immediate superior, the Provincial Commissioner,
disagreed, but even he conceded that many Africans had not
required intimidation to support the boycott.[2]

At about the same time the famous 'rolling strikes' began on
the Copperbelt.[3] The A.M.W.U. had been engaged for several
years in a bitter struggle against the Mines African Salaried
Staff Association, an organization of African clerks and foremen
which the copper companies had formed in 1953. In June 1956
Katilungu appeared to be moving closer to Nkumbula, who had
also opposed the division of Africans on the mines into two rival
groups. Katilungu began speaking of Nkumbula as Northern
Rhodesia's national leader,[4] and in late June the first of the
strikes began, ostensibly over the regulation which required
African, though not European, underground workers to wear
protective leg guards. While Katilungu was away in Northern
Province, A.N.C. and the A.M.W.U. held a public meeting together
on 23 June which gave further impetus to the leg-guard question and underlined the growing co-operation between the two
organizations.[5]

Europeans, alarmed by the sudden burst of African aggressiveness, demanded that the Government take action. The European Press remarked on the growing link between A.N.C. and
the A.M.W.U.,[6] and the Acting Deputy Labour Commissioner
reported that Copperbelt Europeans believed the strike action
to be an extension of A.N.C.'s boycott.[7] As with the boycott,
Europeans tended to regard strikes by Africans as 'racial and

[1] D.C. (Broken Hill) to P.C. (Central Province), 28 May 1956, MN/2154/2, Box 189, Lusaka Archives.
[2] P.C.(C.P.) to S.N.A., 11 June 1956, ibid.
[3] The term was used because no sooner had one strike ended than another began somewhere else; Mason, op. cit., p. 116.
[4] Ibid., p. 116.
[5] R. Philpott for record from Ag. Dep. Labour Commissioner, 24 June 1956, N/2709/4, Box 225, Lusaka Archives.
[6] *Central African Post*, 11 June 1956.
[7] R. Philpott for record from Ag. Dep. Lab. Comm., 22 June 1956, N/2709/4, Lusaka Archives.

nationalistic in origin, rather than due to industrial or economic causes'. From the Copperbelt itself, Labour Department officials reported that Europeans were wondering why the Government had failed thus far to act.[1]

Encouraged by such sentiments, the Government instituted a Crown prosecution in Mufulira against four A.N.C. officials, including the Provincial President and his deputy, for conspiracy to injure the business of European traders. A.N.C. engaged a senior member of the Southern Rhodesia Bar to fight the case.[2] When proceedings opened on 3 July the Government thought it significant that Nkumbula and Nkoloma attended together.[3] In the ensuing deliberations the judgement went against the Government; the four accused, amid the jubilation of A.N.C. supporters who had gathered outside the court, were acquitted. Mufulira's decision greatly enchanced A.N.C.'s reputation in the eyes of Africans throughout the country, and A.N.C. leaders, both at the time and years later, tended to regard the victory as one of the great milestones in their struggle.[4]

In July and August 1956 the industrial situation continued to deteriorate. The Mines African Salaried Staff Association (M.A.S.A.), which since its formation in 1953 had been vigorously opposed by A.M.W.U., withdrew from arbitrations on African advancement after a dispute with the A.M.W.U. A series of short stoppages in August, together with threats of a general strike and, finally, a strike by both the A.M.W.U. and the R.A.W.U. in early September provoked the Governor into declaring a state of emergency in the Western Province. Katilungu was in Southern Rhodesia at the time, attending a meeting of the Railway Arbitration Board in Bulawayo.[5] Forty-five union leaders were detained, many of them Katilungu's opponents.[6] When he returned to the Copperbelt shortly afterwards industrial peace was quickly restored and Katilungu's position considerably strengthened.

[1] R. Philpott, for record from Ag. Dep. Lab. Comm., 22 June 1956, N/2709/4, Lusaka Archives.

[2] Kaunda, *Zambia Shall Be Free*, p. 75.

[3] Ag. Dep. Lab. Comm. for record, 3 July 1956, N/2709/4, Lusaka Archives.

[4] Kaunda, *Zambia Shall Be Free*, p. 77.

[5] Trade Unions in N.R., S/S128/64/01, p. 9.

[6] Mwendepole, Puta, and Nkoloma were all detained, though Konkola, who was in England at the time, escaped; ibid. See the account given by Rotberg, R. I., *The Rise of Nationalism in Central Africa*, pp. 208-9.

By the end of 1956 constitutional issues, both territorial and Federal, began to loom large on the horizon. A.N.C., which had followed a less aggressive line since August, when Nkumbula had pledged the party to work for improved race relations,[1] began preparing for the conflict which lay ahead. This was reflected in the main resolutions which A.N.C.'s annual conference passed in October 1956 and forwarded to the Colonial Secretary. The party's first demand was that the state of emergency in Western Province be ended; the second that Northern Rhodesia should be granted the right to secede from the Federation at the time of the Federal Review; and the third that parity of representation be introduced in both the Legislative and Executive Councils with British protected persons given the right to vote.[2]

Looking back, the year 1956 marked the beginnings of an important change in A.N.C. Arthur Wina, later Zambia's Minister of Finance, writing in 1960, provided a concise assessment of A.N.C. development during the mid-1950's.

The anti-federation movement was really more of a protest manifestation against white settler domination than a nationalist programme. True the implication was always that settler domination should be withdrawn and African self-government achieved in its place, but once Africans were placed in a defensive position it was difficult for them to demand African self-government from the British Colonial Office when there was already a second obstacle to this end—white domination, which appeared the worst of the two evils . . . In this sense, then, the federation period marked the highest point of the 'protest' movement and at the same time the birth of a truly nationalistic movement under determined leadership. Like everything else, adolescence is a difficult period of life in which one makes many false steps . . . There was, however, no definite programme laid out to bring about this dismantlement [of Federation]. The African Representative Council . . . was unanimous in opposing federation but did not see the incongruity of sending two representatives from among its members to the institution they were opposing. The protest movement can be said to have come to an end with the African boycotts of commercial premises which discriminated against Africans purely on racial grounds.[3]

[1] Mason, P., *Year of Decision*, p. 117.
[2] Ibid., p. 118.
[3] Wina manuscript, 1960, pp. 26–27, A.N.L.W. papers.

Already in 1957 the Europeans had begun gathering their
forces for the final assault on Colonial Office rule. A.N.C. had
survived its period of decline and disillusionment; internal
changes had already begun in the party. Though at first barely
perceptible, the most important of these was a shift towards
greater militancy in nationalist thinking. A group of young
nationalists, whose single-minded purpose was to break the
Federation by first achieving self-government in Northern
Rhodesia, was soon to grasp the reins of leadership. Embracing
a new strategy, however, was one thing; building a modern
nationalist party was quite another.

The European Drive for Power, 1953–8

With the achievement of Federation, Northern Rhodesia's
Europeans expected a major constitutional advance at the
territorial level early in 1954. The Colonial Office, having demonstrated its confidence in Central Africa's whites by supporting Federation, was hardly in a position to refuse some measure
of constitutional progress for Welensky's elected unofficials in
the north. The composition of the Legislative Council had not
been altered since 1948, when officials and elected unofficials
were brought into balance with ten seats apiece. The remainder
of the Council included two Europeans nominated to represent
African interests and two Africans selected by the African
Representative Council and appointed by the Governor.
Nevertheless, the position of the settlers had been considerably
strengthened, first, by the convention agreed to in 1948 that the
Governor would not overrule the unanimous advice of elected
unofficials, and later (1949) by the provision of portfolios for two
elected unofficials in the Executive Council.

Welensky now demanded a majority of elected unofficials in
the Legislative Council. Negotiations in London with the
British Government in September 1953 proved abortive, however, and several days later Welensky withdrew from the
Northern Rhodesia scene to take up his appointment as Minister
of Transport and Development in the new Federal Government.
At the end of October the Colonial Secretary imposed his own
solution to Northern Rhodesia's constitutional impasse. The
new Legislative Council was to number twenty-six members,
and elected unofficials were given their majority over the

officials, twelve seats to eight. However, the whites' demands for a clear majority were again frustrated. Two Europeans were again nominated to represent African interests, and the number of Africans selected from the African Representative Council was increased from two to four. In the Executive Council the officials' majority was cut to one seat, though the four unofficial Council members included in their number one of the Europeans nominated to represent Africans.[1]

Despite failing to obtain self-government, Northern Rhodesia's whites were satisfied that they had at least made some progress, while Africans had been prevented from any significant advance at all. Most important in this respect was the franchise, which retained virtually the same requirements it had in 1924 and in practice excluded all but approximately a dozen Africans.[2] In December 1953 the settlers agreed to the constitutional changes in return for an assurance from the British Government that the new arrangements, including the franchise, would remain unchanged for the full five years of the Legislative Council's life.[3]

The initiative for European advance then shifted to the Federal Government. Before 1954 was half over, Huggins and Welensky started what later became their drive for dominion status for the Federation. Proposed Federal legislation that year aimed at removing certain functions from the Federal Constitution's concurrent list. When the proposals were referred to the Northern Rhodesia Government in May, the Governor, Sir Arthur Benson, who had enthusiastically supported Federation when he assumed his post in 1954, advised Huggins to take a more moderate course. Benson suggested that if Huggins concentrated his efforts on winning Africans over by implementing the agreed policy of Partnership, dominion status would eventually 'fall into his lap'.[4] Huggins disregarded Benson's advice and soon afterwards publicly espoused dominion status in the

[1] The Northern Rhodesia (Legislative Council) Order in Council, 1953.

[2] A person qualified for the vote if he was a British subject of 21 years or older, fulfilled certain residence requirements and was: (a) in occupation of a house or building in the Territory valued at £250; or (b) possessed a mining claim; or (c) received an annual income of £200. For details see *Report of the Advisory Commission on the Review of the Constitution of Rhodesia and Nyasaland*, Cmd. 1148 (The Monckton Commission Report), Appendix IV, October 1960, p. 39.

[3] Mason, P., *Year of Decision*, p. 101.

[4] Interview with Sir Arthur Benson, 27 November 1963.

Federation.[1] During the next year additional Federal legislation
was proposed which sought to strengthen the Federal Government's position, and public statements on dominion status by
white politicians, both in Northern and Southern Rhodesia,
continued to appear.[2] By 1956 Benson's initial faith in the
Federation and the sincerity of its leaders was badly shaken.[3]

Benson faced difficulties in Lusaka as well. Not only had
A.N.C.'s rather sudden resurgence in the Copperbelt and in
Northern Province alarmed the Government, but the Federal
Party, led by Welensky's successor in the Broken Hill constituency, John Roberts, took an increasingly aggressive line as
well. Roberts demanded stricter control over African trade
unions,[4] the recruiting of more local-born white Rhodesians
into the police,[5] and the introduction of riot damage legislation
which would give the Government powers of collective fining for
personal injury and destruction of property caused by African
riots.[6] In the constitutional sphere, Roberts demanded additional and more important portfolios for the elected unofficials.[7]
Early in 1956 the *Rhodesia Herald*, in a leader entitled 'Government in the North', commented on the settlers' growing
strength. 'The highest officials in Northern Rhodesia make no
secret of the fact that since the general election in February 1954
the Executive Council has operated virtually as a Federal Party
Government. If the three elected members stand firm on any
issue they are almost certain to carry the day.'[8]

Speaking in Broken Hill in May 1956, with Welensky present
and offering encouragement, Roberts demanded that he be
given the post of Chief Minister in a Government controlled by
the elected unofficials. Claiming that he was tired of defending

---

[1] In fact, both Huggins and Welensky claimed that dominion status was their
goal for the Federation at political meetings in Bulawayo in November 1953;
Franklin, H., *Unholy Wedlock: The Failure of the Central African Federation*, London,
1963, p. 97.

[2] In October 1955 Welensky voiced his confidence that the Federation would
achieve dominion status. 'If we continue to show we can govern with firmness,
tolerance and justice, there will be no difficulty in persuading H.M.G. to offer full
self-government to the Federation'; *Northern News*, 5 October 1955.

[3] Interview with Benson, 27 November 1963.

[4] *Northern News*, 18 October 1955.

[5] Ibid.

[6] Ibid., 29 September 1955.

[7] Ibid., 9 September 1955.

[8] *Rhodesia Herald*, 6 March 1956.

a Government over which he did not have full control, Rober\
insisted that the time was ripe for another round of constitu\
tional talks. Growing uncertainty in the Territory required that\
the constitutional issue be settled once and for all.[1]
But it was the Federal Government, led now by Welensky,
who became Federal Prime Minister in November 1956, which
secured the next constitutional advance. Preparations for the
move were begun behind the scenes as early as 1955, and received sympathetic support at the Commonwealth Relations
Office. Benson's reservations about the Federal Government's
drive for greater independence had become serious enough by
mid-1956 for him to write an outspoken memorandum on the
subject to the Colonial Secretary, Lennox-Boyd. The Colonial
Office was unreceptive; indeed, Benson soon discovered, much
to his chagrin, that this memorandum had been passed to Lord
Home at the Commonwealth Relations Office and thence to his
adversaries in Salisbury.[2] Over the crucial months of late 1956
and early 1957 the Colonial Office proved unwilling to take a
stand against its sister office for the Commonwealth, and
Welensky eventually won the day.

On 26 April 1957 the extent of agreement between Welensky
and the Commonwealth Relations Office became public. While
much remained to be settled in detail, agreement had been
reached on the following matters: (a) the Federal Government
would be given additional responsibilities for external affairs;
(b) the British Government agreed not to exercise its right, conferred by the Federal Constitution, to legislate for the Federation, except at the Federal Government's request; (c) Civil
Servants, whether Federal or territorial, would eventually be
locally based and look for their future to the Federal area;
(d) proposals for the enlargement of the Federal Assembly were
accepted in principle; (e) the three territories would not be
allowed to amalgamate or to secede from the Federation; (f)
the Federal Review Conference, which had been provided for
in Article 99 of the Constitution, would be convened at the
earliest possible time in 1960; (g) the purpose of the conference

[1] *Central African Post*, 30 March 1956.
[2] Hall, R. S., *Zambia*, p. 164. Benson confirmed this account in an interview
with the author on 27 November 1963, though Benson refused to reveal the name
of the person who was actually responsible for releasing his memorandum to the
C.R.O.

would be to agree on constitutional advance for the Federation and to consider a programme for the attainment of independence.[1]

Armed with these assurances, the Federal Government introduced two highly controversial Bills, the Constitution Amendment Bill[2] and the Federal Franchise Bill.[3] The first Bill provided for the enlargement of the Federal Assembly from thirty-five to fifty-nine members (excluding the Speaker), while the second introduced a complicated qualified franchise system with two separate classes of voters.

The combined effect of the two Bills was to devalue African representation in the Federal Assembly, notwithstanding the fact that the proportion of Africans and Europeans charged with representing African interests remained constant at one-quarter of the Assembly's total membership.[4] Under the old arrangements, nine members represented African interests, two Africans and a European from each of the three territories. In Southern Rhodesia all three were elected by the overwhelmingly European common roll. In the northern territories the four Africans were indirectly elected by African electoral colleges, while the Europeans were appointed by their respective territorial Governor. Under the new arrangements, the method of returning the nine members remained unchanged, but the six additional members representing African interests, two from each territory, were returned by electorates, which, because they combined both 'ordinary' (higher franchise) and 'special' (lower franchise) voters, were predominantly European. The effect was that although six new African members, whose electorates included a modest number of newly enfranchised Africans, had been introduced into the Federal Assembly in practice the new members were wholly dependent on European support.

The African Affairs Board, a standing committee of the Federal Assembly and the chief safeguard of African interests under the Federal Constitution, invoked for the first time its

[1] *The Times*, 27 April 1956.
[2] Introduced in May 1957.
[3] Introduced in September 1957, though the franchise proposals were first made public by Welensky in London in June 1957.
[4] See *Monckton Commission*, Appendix VI, pp. 5–11, for details. Also see Mason, P., *Year of Decision*, pp. 70–87, and Leys, C., and Pratt, R. C., *A New Deal in Central Africa*, London, 1960, pp. 109–18.

power to reserve 'discriminatory' legislation for the consideration of Her Majesty's Government by declaring both Bills
'differentiating measures', on the ground that together they
reduced the proportion of effective African representation in the
Federal Assembly. In view of the earlier assurances given to
Welensky, it was hardly surprising that the British Government
overruled the Board on both Bills. Unfortunately for the Board,
which had staked its reputation on this single issue, the decision
was fatal: Moffat, the Board's Chairman, angrily resigned, and
from then on the Board was regarded as a dead letter. The effect
on African opinion in the north was particularly serious, because
of the Board's prominence as the most important, albeit weak,
safeguard for African interests at the Federal level. What small
faith Africans had retained in the British Government after the
formation of the Federation was now utterly destroyed. African
leaders in the north now believed that unless drastic action were
forthcoming in the next months Central Africa's whites would
inevitably achieve their goal of dominion status in 1960. Though
African leaders might prescribe a different remedy to the problem, they were not alone in their concern over the Board's
demise. Northern Rhodesia government officials were also
troubled, and Benson himself even considered resigning at the
time.[1]

When Benson became Governor of Northern Rhodesia he
was charged with the responsibility of designing a constitution
which would see the Territory through its next stage of political
development. By 1957 Benson's position had become impossibly
difficult. The Federal Party, fresh from a string of successes at
the Federal level and keenly aware that time was growing short,
displayed a new militancy. At the same time, the obvious failure
of Partnership reinforced by the Federation's open drive towards dominion status gave rise to a more extreme form of
African nationalism.

Roberts continued to press his demands for additional unofficial portfolios, including the new post of Chief Minister for
himself, before the next round of constitutional changes were
negotiated. Certainly after thirty-one years, Roberts argued,
the unofficials had proved themselves. An imposed solution,
such as that of 1954, would be unacceptable, and, in any case,

[1] Interview with Benson, 27 November 1963.

Roberts could not imagine that the British Government would override the Federal Government's views on a proposed constitution for any one of its territories. As for extending the franchise to Africans, Roberts took the line that if British-protected persons were eligible to vote, a greater measure of responsible government was axiomatic. A situation in which a person who was eligible to vote still looked for protection to London, where in Roberts's words 'he imagined his grandmother . . . lived', was intolerable.[1] Indeed, Roberts even went so far as to claim that British protection, in effect the close control the Colonial Office and the Provincial Administration exercised over African affairs, had prevented European elected members from 'getting among the African population generally'.[2] The statement caused a furore in the secretariat and Benson firmly requested that Roberts either retract or correct his comments.[3]

Early in 1957 Benson initiated consultations on a new constitution, later known as the Benson Constitution, which in 1958–9 was to produce a crisis in Northern Rhodesia politics. The proposals submitted by the various political groups ranged over a broad spectrum. The right wing Dominion Party (D.P.), a minority white party with support among farmers in Southern Province and South African miners on the Copperbelt, proposed that the Territory be divided into separate spheres of influence for Europeans and Africans. The United Federal Party (U.F.P.),[4] the governing party in all three territories as well as at the Federal level, favoured a constitution which would set the form and pace of political development for the foreseeable future. Despite its support for 'non-racial' political development, the U.F.P. adhered strongly to the view that political advance be based solely on 'merit', i.e. on financial and educational qualifications. The African leaders demanded parity of representation between the races, though A.N.C.'s

[1] *Central African Post*, 6 May 1957.

[2] Ibid., 16 October 1957.

[3] Roberts claimed that he had been misquoted, but Benson did not believe him; Governor to c.s., 23 October 1957, GHS/S201/09. The matter was brought up at an Executive Council meeting and Roberts promised to see that a corrected version appeared; Ex. Co., 22 October 1957, ibid.

[4] The name U.F.P. resulted from the merger of the original Federal Party, formed in 1953, and Garfield Todd's United (Southern) Rhodesia Party in September 1957.

definition of parity—equal representation between elected
Africans and elected Europeans and officials combined—would,
if implemented, have resulted in an African majority amongst
the unofficials in both the Legislative and Executive Councils.[1]
The Governor continued his consultation with European
politicians and African members of the Legislative Council
throughout 1957 and early 1958.[2] Throughout this period no
attempt was made to consult nationalist leaders until March
1958, a mere three weeks before the proposals were presented
to the Legislative Council. The meeting, when it did take place,
was little more than a formality.[3] Nkumbula and Kaunda presented A.N.C.'s proposals only to have Benson reject them out of
hand. But the meeting ended on a prophetic note. Benson had
argued that if he accepted A.N.C.'s plans, the whites might well
paralyse the Government. Kaunda responded by asking if this
implied that African demands would be met only when they,
too, threatened to paralyse the Government. 'My question',
Kaunda recalled later, 'was never answered.'[4]

[1] *Northern News*, 8 March 1958.
[2] The Governor held discussions with 'individual members and with other
groups of members of the Legislative Council and with certain other political
organizations'; *Proposals for Constitutional Change in N.R.*, Part III, 28 March 1958,
p. 4.
[3] *Northern News*, 8 March 1958.
[4] Kaunda, *Zambia Shall Be Free*, p. 87.

II

THE BENSON CONSTITUTION
CRISIS

The 1959 Constitution

THE Benson Constitution was the first of Britain's complicated 'multi-racial' constitutions to be introduced into Central Africa. As a political instrument the constitution clearly reflected the ideas on racial partnership, 'fancy franchises', and controlled political change which were fashionable both in the Colonial Office and amongst liberal whites in the Federation during the late 1950's and early 1960's. The British Government's main objective was to devise a constitution which could govern the Territory's advance for the next decade in such a way as to encourage politics to develop on party as opposed to racial lines. For its guiding principles the Government had turned to the Moffat Resolutions of 1954.

(1) The objectives of policy in Northern Rhodesia must be to remove from each race the fear that the other might dominate for its own racial benefit and to move forward from the present system of racial representation in the territorial legislature towards a franchise with no separate representation for the races.

(2) Until the objectives can be fully achieved a period of transition will remain during which special arrangements in the Legislative and Executive Councils must continue to be made so as to ensure that no race can use either the preponderance of its numbers or its more advanced stage of development to dominate the other for its own racial benefit.

(3) During this period of transition, special legislation must be in force to protect, to the extent that this may be necessary, the interests of either race. Meanwhile this Council notes and agrees with the Secretary of State that it is the duty of Her Majesty's Government to ensure that on contentious issues the balance is fairly held.

(4) Every lawful inhabitant of Northern Rhodesia has the right to progress according to his character, ability and industry, without distinction of race, colour or creed.[1]

Though Northern Rhodesia's franchise had been based on a common roll since 1925, in practice representation in the Legislative Council was by racial divisions—Europeans being directly elected by their own electorate and Africans being selected by the African Representative Council and appointed by the Governor. Under the 1959 Constitution a start was made towards replacing racial representation with a system under which all M.L.C.s would be elected by 'common machinery providing for the direct representation of all qualified voters in a geographical constituency'.[2] Government was to be maintained in the hands of 'responsible men' who would look to the whole community and not merely to the sectional interests of their respective race.

The common roll and the qualified franchise were retained, but voters could now qualify at two separate levels; in addition to the fixed and permanent 'ordinary' qualifications, 'special' (lower) qualifications were introduced as an interim measure to ensure that Africans who had not yet reached 'European standards' were adequately represented over the next decade. All voters were required to (a) complete the registration claim form unassisted and in English; (b) be at least 21 years of age; (c) be either a citizen of the United Kingdom and Colonies, a Federal citizen or a British-protected person by virtue of connexion with Northern Rhodesia; (d) have resided in the Federation for two years and in the constituency of registration for at least three months.[3] Registrants were then entitled to qualify as 'ordinary' or 'special' voters, depending upon which set of detailed requirements they were able to fulfil.[4]

[1] Leg. Co. *Debates*, 29 July 1954.

[2] *Northern Rhodesia Proposals for Constitutional Change*, Cmd. 530, September 1958, p. 20.

[3] Ibid., p. 25.

[4] I. Ordinary Voters

    (a) Four years' secondary education and *either* an income of £300 p.a. or ownership of property worth £500; or

    (b) A primary education and *either* an income of £480 p.a. or ownership of property worth £1,000; or

    (c) *Either* an income of £720 p.a. or ownership of property worth £1,500.

While initially Europeans and only a few Africans would qualify as 'ordinary' voters, Africans who qualified as 'special' voters would gradually advance towards the higher qualifications and be transferred to the 'ordinary' section of the voters' roll. Over a ten-year period the 'special' qualifications were to be progressively raised until one set of qualifications applied to all new applicants. No voter was to be disenfranchised if he ceased to possess the prescribed qualifications and persons registered as 'special' voters at the end of the ten-year period would remain registered and continue to participate in future elections.[1]

The Legislative Council, which was enlarged from twenty-six to thirty members, was to have twenty-two elected members, six officials, excluding the speaker, and two unofficial nominated members. Elected members were to be returned as follows: twelve from 'ordinary' constituencies consisting of the mainly

---

The following persons were exempted from the above requirements and entitled to register as 'ordinary' voters, provided that they were able to satisfy the general requirements:

(1) Ministers of religion who had undergone certain stipulated courses of training and periods of service in the ministry and followed no other profession or gainful occupation;

(2) Members of certain religious bodies with two years' secondary education who had been in the services of their religious body for four years and followed no other profession or gainful occupation;

(3) Chiefs recognized by the Governor or those certified to be of equivalent status in Barotseland;

(4) The wife (but only the senior wife of any polygamous marriage) of any person who was qualified as an 'ordinary' voter.

II. Special Voters

(a) Two years' secondary education and an income of £120 p.a.; or

(b) *Either* an income of £150 p.a. or ownership of property worth £500.

The following persons were exempted from the above requirements and were entitled to register as 'special' voters, provided that they satisfied the general requirements:

(1) Pensioners in receipt of a monthly or annual pension earned after twenty years' service with one employer;

(2) Headmen or hereditary councillors of two years' standing who were recognized by their chiefs, provided that they were performing this office without pay. In order to qualify for this privilege the headman had to be in charge of a village which had an unbroken existence since 1924 or contained at least twenty-five taxpayers;

(3) The wife (but only the senior wife of any polygamous marriage) of any person who was qualified as a 'special' voter.

[1] *N.R. Proposals for Const. Change*, Cmd. 530, September 1958, p. 7.

urban European areas; six from 'special' constituencies covering the African-dominated rural areas east and west of the railway line; two Africans from reserve constituencies covering the same area as the 'ordinary' constituencies; and two Europeans from reserve constituencies covering the same area as the 'special' constituencies.

Despite the fact that the Constitution was to encourage the development of 'non-racial' politics and that all candidates in an election would face multi-racial electorates, the Government held to the view that any move towards a 'non-racial' society had to be a gentle one.[1] This explained the special arrangements (reserved seats for urban Africans and rural Europeans) to ensure that all African and European voters were represented by at least one member of their own race. In the 'ordinary' and 'special' constituencies the voting strength of each category of voters was carefully balanced so as to ensure that the former returned Europeans and the latter Africans. Thus the Legislative Council's racial composition was easily discernible without a general election. Racial representation would fall far short of parity: of the Council's twenty-two elected members, fourteen members (twelve 'ordinary' and two reserved) would be Europeans, while eight seats (six 'special' and two reserved) would be filled by Africans.

The arrangements for balancing the influence of 'ordinary' and 'special' votes in the various constituencies proved to be a highly contentious issue. In the initial proposals of March 1958 the weight accorded to 'special' votes in both the 'ordinary' and the two European reserved constituencies was limited to one-third of the votes cast by 'ordinary' voters. The same was true for 'ordinary' as opposed to 'special' votes in the 'special' and the African reserved constituencies.[2] In the final White Paper of September 1958, however, the proposed limit on the influence of 'ordinary' voters was dropped. The Secretary of State explained that while it was reasonable to limit the influence of voters who had qualified on the lower franchise, it was not right to reduce the influence of the 'ordinary' voter who had met the higher qualifications. Furthermore, he continued, the practical considerations did not warrant such

[1] *N.R. Proposals for Const. Change*, Cmd. 530, September 1958, p. 27.
[2] *Proposals for Const. Change in N.R.*, 28 March 1958, p. 9.

limitation, a contention which proved quite untrue when tested the following year. In devising the constitutional proposals the Government had assumed that 'special' voters would out-number 'ordinary' voters by six to one in 'special' constituencies, not to mention the two constituencies specifically reserved for Africans.[1] The estimate was to prove wildly optimistic.

The decision to drop the limitation on the voting strength of 'ordinary' voters represented a considerable victory for the u.f.p. Shortly before the publication of the first White Paper and during the period March through August 1958, Roberts demanded that the devaluation of 'ordinary' and 'special' votes be accompanied by a system of single transferable votes, which would offset the advantage he believed would accrue to candidates with minority support. Failing this, Roberts argued for reducing the one-third figure to one-quarter. Both Welensky and the u.f.p.'s territorial caucus supported this demand, despite a written undertaking which Roberts had previously given to Benson to recommend the White Paper's proposals as a balanced whole to the people of Northern Rhodesia. On the day the White Paper was laid before the Legislative Council, Roberts infuriated the Governor and his officials by publicly dissociating the u.f.p. from certain sections of the scheme, disregarding completely the well-established principle of collective responsibility.[2]

Roberts claimed to have misjudged European sentiment with the result that he believed his very political life to be threatened. In particular he felt he could not risk accepting the March White Paper's Executive Council proposals. The u.f.p.'s minimal demand for an Executive Council comprising four ministers elected from 'ordinary' constituencies, three officials and one African, was rejected by the Colonial Secretary in September 1958. The September White Paper substituted a Council composed of four officials and six unofficial members, four of whom had to be 'ordinarily' qualified elected members. The other two unofficials were to be Africans, both with full ministerial status.[3] For the first time, unofficials had gained a majority in the Executive Council; but the victory, such as it

[1] *N.R. Proposals for Const. Change*, Cmd. 530, p. 9.
[2] Leg. Co. *Debates*, 28 March 1958, col. 474.
[3] *N.R. Proposals for Const. Change*, Cmd. 530, p. 10.

was, rang hollow for the u.f.p. The crucial party majority for which it had struggled for many years had slipped through its fingers.

In addition to the White Paper's complicated voting arrangements and the proposed composition of the Legislative and Executive Councils, an attempt was made to encourage a closer link between the legislature and the Native Authorities system. Throughout Benson's term of office Native Authorities were encouraged to show more initiative and to use their influence against the rising tide of African nationalism. Thus under the 1959 Constitution 'special' candidates were required to obtain certificates indicating that two-thirds of the recognized chiefs in their respective constituencies did not object to the nomination.[1] Africans deeply resented this attempt to strengthen the authority of chiefs by establishing them as 'quasi-judges' of suitable African candidates. But as with the 1959 Constitution as a whole, Africans—for the last time in Northern Rhodesia's history—had remarkably little influence on the final settlement. And in the end the vast majority of Africans were to reject it.

Strains Within A.N.C.

In his annual report for 1954, Kaunda conceded that 'the masses thought a.n.c. had come to an end'. Most people evidently believed, he wrote, that a.n.c. had been formed only to fight Federation. The party's performance since mid-1953 hardly suggested any other conclusion. a.n.c.'s national executive and its working committee had met only once during the past year. Financial troubles, Kaunda claimed, had virtually immobilized the party and prevented even head office officials from touring in the rural areas. Part of the decline Kaunda blamed on Native Authority bans which had been imposed in Lundazi and Petauke District in Eastern Province, Mukushi District in Central Province, and in Gwembe, Kalomo and parts of Mazabuka District in Southern Province.[2] At a.n.c.'s annual conference in 1954, which drew only a handful of delegates and was the last conference to be held for two years, it was decided that senior officials should assess a.n.c.'s present

[1] *N.R. Proposals for Const. Change*, Cmd. 530, p. 11.
[2] Annual Report of a.n.c.'s Activities, September 1953–August 1954, Emanuel papers.

difficulties and prepare a five-year plan for the party.[1] 'The accent of our endeavour must always be on administration and organization', Kaunda observed, otherwise 'all our planning is moonshine'.[2]

In January 1955 Nkumbula and Kaunda served their first prison sentences, an experience which appeared to have a marked effect on both men. Kaunda resumed his organizing work more vigorously than ever after his release in March 1955. He published a series of monthly circulars which provided progress reports on branch formation and commentary on political developments in Northern Rhodesia and the Federation. In nearly every issue Kaunda stressed the need for dedicated leadership, personal sacrifice, improved party organization, and financial responsibility.[3] Nkumbula's prison experience appeared to weaken his resolve. His support for A.N.C.'s boycott actions was unenthusiastic on several occasions.[4] Nkumbula began seeing more of Harry Franklin, a white Liberal and member responsible for African interests in the Legislative Council, and even brought him along to meetings of the party's national executive council.[5] Nkumbula took little interest in party organization, gave few speeches and almost never toured in the rural areas away from the 'line of rail'. At the party's 1956 annual conference, held shortly after the 1956 emergency on the Copperbelt, Nkumbula's presidential address was notably moderate. He denied any connexion between A.N.C. and the trade-union movement, pleaded for improved race relations and defended a pledge which he had recently made to show a more co-operative spirit towards the Northern Rhodesia Government.[6] By comparison Kaunda's speech was far more militant. Reiterating his views on leadership and party organization, Kaunda warned of the years ahead and the

[1] A.N.C. circular to all Provincial Presidents, 13 September 1954, ibid.

[2] Annual Report of A.N.C.'s Activities, September 1953–August 1954, ibid.

[3] *Congress Circular*, selected issues published between April 1955 and December 1956, ibid.

[4] Sikalumbi, W. K. (ed. Harry W. Langworthy), 'The circumstances which gave rise to the banning of the Zambia African Congress of Northern Rhodesia' (unpublished manuscript, 1959–63), pp. 78, 80, 95–96, cited in Rotberg, R. I., *The Rise of Nationalism in Central Africa*, pp. 275–7.

[5] Kaunda to Fox-Pitt, 2 December 1958, author's collection.

[6] President's speech at seventh annual conference, 8 October 1956, Emanuel collection.

Federal Government's increasingly open campaign for dominion status by 1960.[1]

The shift in African nationalist thinking which emerged full-blown in 1957 had clearly begun in 1956. At first it was restricted to a mere handful of A.N.C. leaders. Gradually they built up branch organizations and began consolidating the party's more militant elements.[2] For the next eighteen months the build-up continued, slowly but steadily, until in October 1958 the split occurred which produced Kaunda's Zambia African National Congress (Z.A.N.C.)

One of the chief figures in the initial stages of this process was Munukayambwa Sipalo, who returned to Northern Rhodesia early in 1957 after completing his studies in India. Sipalo represented the first threat to Nkumbula's leadership since his rise to the presidency in 1951. Soon after his return Sipalo became a member of A.N.C.'s executive and immediately agitated for a more dynamic and aggressive party policy. He also set about rejuvenating A.N.C.'s ineffectual action groups and attempted to create a national youth movement, both of which he planned to use to force Nkumbula along a more extreme course. Not surprisingly, Sipalo soon ran afoul of Nkumbula and in September 1957, at Nkumbula's insistence, Sipalo was suspended from A.N.C.'s executive. Three months later at A.N.C.'s annual conference he was expelled from the party altogether.[3]

Meanwhile, aided by Nkumbula's and Kaunda's absence from June to September in London, Sipalo succeeded in raising the tempo of A.N.C. activity. In Southern Province the party was well enough organized early in 1957 to cause the Government concern over a rumour that A.N.C. would soon withdraw African labour from farms and missions in the area.[4] In Northern Province, the P.C. reported renewed interest in A.N.C.'s 'subversive activities', largely attributable, he believed, to the work of Makasa and Simon Kapwepwe as well as to the

[1] Secretary-General's speech at seventh annual conference, 8 October 1956, Emanuel collection.

[2] *Congress Circular*, selected issues published between April 1955 and December 1956, Emanuel collection. Volume II, No. 9, of August 1956, reported the number of A.N.C. branches registered with the Government to be 235 with a membership of approximately 100,000.

[3] Extracts from biography of Nkumbula, 27 November 1962, S/S 201/015.

[4] P.C.(S.P.) to S.N.A., 5 January 1957, S/S 123/7/01.

Government's failure to sustain a successful prosecution against important A.N.C. officials in the area.[1] In October Eastern Province's annual conference of District Commissioners considered the growing problem of A.N.C. action groups, which government officials blamed for the flare-up of boycotts and arson in the Territory.[2] By the time of Sipalo's dismissal from A.N.C.'s executive, the *Northern News*, commenting on A.N.C.'s beerhall boycotts in Luanshya, concluded that the 'most significant outcome is the disclosure of a rift in its (A.N.C.'s) leadership, with the junior officials challenging the authority of their seniors'.[3] In mid-September Nkumbula returned from Britain, while Kaunda remained behind to study political organization with the Labour Party. Nkumbula immediately condemned the methods employed in the boycotts[4] and a few days later overrode his executive's proposal to institute a beerhall boycott in Central Province.[5] In the field, junior party officials conducted operations as they saw fit,[6] a development that aroused European concern on the Copperbelt. 'The whole basis of the boycotts seems to be changed too. They have a look of nationalism, naked and unashamed.'[7] Nkumbula had created in A.N.C. a 'frankenstein' that was now beyond his control.[8]

With the help of a number of the trade unionists restricted in Lundazi District since the 1956 emergency, A.N.C. also mounted new attacks on Katilungu and the A.M.W.U. Katilungu maintained his position once again by threatening to resign,[9] but by mid-October he conceded that A.N.C. had successfully undermined the Territory's two largest trade unions, the A.M.W.U. and the R.A.W.U.[10] In his presidential address to the A.T.U.C. Katilungu declared 'war' on African politicians who attempted to undermine the power of both the trade unions and the chiefs

[1] Report from P.C.(N.P.), 16 January 1957, S/S 123/5/01.
[2] District Commissioners' Conference, 3–5 October 1957, DG 58/3/01.
[3] *Northern News*, 10 September 1957.
[4] Ibid., 19 September 1957.
[5] Ibid., 21 September 1957.
[6] Ibid., A.N.C.'s branch secretary at Fort Rosebery refused to call off a boycott of European shops, despite repeated orders to do so from his Provincial President; *Northern News*, 15 October 1957.
[7] Ibid., 21 September 1957.
[8] Ibid., 23 September 1957.
[9] Ibid., 13 September 1957.
[10] Ibid., 9 October 1957.

in rural areas. A.N.C., he declared, was seeking by violent means to destroy the Native Authorities system on which Northern Rhodesia's future pattern of self-government had to be based.[1] Even Chitimikulu, the Paramount Chief of the Bemba, had seen the danger and banned A.N.C. in three areas of Luwingu District.[2] In his anger, Katilungu turned to the moderate Europeans and helped launch the new multi-racial Constitution Party, founded by Dr. Alexander Scott, Federal M.P., Colonel David Stirling, Harry Franklin, M.L.C., and S. H. Chileshe, one of Northern Rhodesia's African M.L.C.S.[3]

With the approach of A.N.C.'s annual conference, set for mid-December, and with the Federal Government having introduced its franchise and constitution amendment Bills, nationalist agitation in Northern Rhodesia intensified. Speaking at Lusaka on 6 November, Nkumbula shocked the Territory by announcing that A.N.C. would reconsider its long-standing policy of non-violence at the forthcoming conference.[4] A.N.C. meetings on the Copperbelt were running at the rate of one per day, and press reports spoke of two schools in the area for training action-group members to commit acts of hooliganism. Europeans concluded that African moderates were quickly losing ground to their more extreme colleagues.[5] As if to confirm their fears, Katilungu suddenly resigned from the newly formed Constitution Party.[6] The *Northern News*, after weighing the arguments for and against the banning of A.N.C., came out in support of stricter legislation to control the party and to induce more sensible leadership.[7] African nationalism, the paper ruefully concluded, was a phenomenon of major importance, which would now be a permanent feature of political life in Northern Rhodesia.[8]

A.N.C.'s annual conference retained the party constitution's non-violence clause.[9] The return from Britain of Kaunda, who was emphatically opposed to a policy of violence, helped

[1] *Northern News*, 9 and 31 October 1957.
[2] Ibid., 31 October 1957.
[3] Ibid., 21 October 1957.
[4] Ibid., 7 November 1957.
[5] Ibid., 16 November 1957.
[6] Ibid., 3 December 1957.
[7] Ibid.
[8] Ibid., 31 December 1957.
[9] Ibid., 13 December 1957.

Nkumbula to bolster his position. Despite the defeat implied for A.N.C.'s militant elements, however, both by Nkumbula's apparent triumph and by Sipalo's dismissal, the party was far from unified. By this time, even men like Kaunda had serious doubts about Nkumbula's leadership.[1] African leaders viewed 1958 more and more as a year of great testing: only one opportunity remained for Northern Rhodesia Africans to obtain control over their Territory's Government before the Federal Review in 1960, and that appeared lost when Benson's constitutional proposals were concluded in September 1958.

During 1958 A.N.C. became increasingly unsettled. Government moves in late 1957 to tighten up territorial security arrangements, together with renewed pressure on chiefs and Native Authorities to take action against local nationalist leaders, further circumscribed A.N.C.'s area of legal operation and threw the party into frustrating confusion. The Emergency Powers (Amendment) Bill, the Societies Bill and the Northern Rhodesia Police (Amendment) Bill, all passed by the Legislative Council in November 1957, greatly strengthened the Government's hand.[2] The Emergency Powers (Amendment) Bill provided wide powers for government action to prevent the declaration of a full state of emergency.[3] The Societies Bill was aimed at controlling nationalist political organizations by requiring them to register their branches and to supply the Government with specific information about their activities and organization.[4] The Northern Rhodesia Police (Amendment) Bill provided the police with powers to control public meetings which took place outside Native Authorities' areas and off public roads and streets.[5] The Territory's Penal Code was also amended. To provide the Government with a more generally applicable weapon against politically inspired boycotts and strikes, section 29 of the Trade Union and Trade Disputes Ordinance, which dealt with offences such as the use of violence, intimidation and watching and besetting, was trans-

[1] Kaunda, *Zambia Shall Be Free*, pp. 92–94.
[2] Also Special Branch forces were to be greatly increased and operations generally tightened up; Governor to c.s., 17 January 1958, DG 58/4/01.
[3] Leg. Co. *Debates*, 20 November 1957, cols. 593–603.
[4] Leg. Co. *Debates*, 20 November 1957, cols. 603–12.
[5] Ibid., 8 November 1957, cols. 227–8.

ferred under the Code.[1] In addition the definition of 'seditious intention' was extended to include the bringing of any government of the Federation into hatred or contempt.[2]

Before A.N.C. had recovered from the Government's action, Benson introduced his proposals for constitutional change, which produced as much controversy within A.N.C. as they did between the Territory's various political groups. Faced with an increasingly hostile Government and almost total failure in its demands for constitutional advance, A.N.C.'s militants and moderates resumed their acrimonious debate over the party's immediate tactics.

By June 1958 militants controlled a number of important posts in the party hierarchy and were somewhat easier to identify as a group. Sipalo, who had taken a job with a Copperbelt commercial firm, continued to work against Nkumbula from outside the party. Three of his friends—Jeremiah Mulenga, Western Province President, Jonathan Chivunga, Provincial Secretary, and Hayden Dingiswayo Banda, Ndola District Chairman—were successfully guiding A.N.C.'s Copperbelt organization towards a somewhat confused militancy.[3] Perhaps the most outstanding example of this was the serious rioting which erupted on 8 and 9 April over an increase in house rents in Kabushi and Main townships at Ndola. Local A.N.C. officials attempted in March to institute a boycott of the African Area Housing Board elections. Nkumbula intervened and the boycott failed; but A.N.C. won only three of the Board's eighteen seats (Mulenga, Chivunga, and Banda). Local party officials then urged the people to boycott both the beerhalls and the Housing Board and to refuse to pay their house rents. Riots broke out the following day, leaving four wounded and one killed. Nkumbula's subsequent denial of A.N.C.'s responsibility was contradicted by African traders in the area, who claimed they had been intimidated by action-group members who were later seen leading the stonings of African shops.[4] Court proceedings the following month confirmed A.N.C.'s involvement in the riots; of the twenty-eight persons convicted, thirteen were

[1] Leg. Co. *Debates*, 20 November 1957, cols. 592–3.
[2] Ibid., 8 November 1957, cols. 223–4.
[3] Monthly Intelligence Reports (M.I.R.), April–June 1958, S/S 123/8/01.
[4] Ibid., April 1958, DG 58/8/01.

action-group members, six belonged to the women's league, and four, including two officials, were members of the main party.[1]
A.N.C. activity was increasing in Eastern Province as well, where two militant party professionals replaced local officials convicted and imprisoned for a variety of minor offences. One was Reuben Kamanga, formerly A.N.C.'s Deputy Treasurer, who became Acting Provincial President. The other was Frank Chitambala, recently released from prison, who assumed the post of Acting Provincial Secretary. In April Kaunda joined them for a month to reorganize A.N.C. in the Fort Jameson District. Efforts were made to seek closer co-operation between A.N.C., the Marketing Union, and local co-operative societies. Later, Kamanga and Chitambala were joined by Justin Chimba, formerly a close friend of Zukas's and one of the Territory's most ardent nationalists.[2]

A similar pattern of increased boldness and hostility in A.N.C.'s ranks also emerged in other provinces. In Southern Province A.N.C. opposed the Government's cattle-inoculation programme in the Choma and Mazabuka areas. On 18 March, twenty-three persons, all members of A.N.C., were charged before Chief Mpanza at Kachenje with failing to produce their cattle for inoculation under the Native Authority Order. Supported by A.N.C. members in court, they refused to acknowledge the authority of the chief and a small riot followed.[3] In Livingstone, A.N.C.'s district executive refused to accept a Nkumbula appointee as organizing secretary, because he was thought to be too moderate. Instead the executive sent a representative to Lusaka who took the matter up with Kaunda.[4]

In May Kaunda visited Northern and Luapula Provinces, where A.N.C.'s provincial organizations were far superior to those of most other areas. The Government reported 44 new A.N.C. branches in Kawambwa District alone,[5] while in Northern Province, Makasa, the Provincial President, claimed 165 A.N.C. branches, 97 of them in Kasama District.[6] Kaunda gave a series of impassioned speeches against the March constitutional proposals, and government officials reported that the White Paper was strongly opposed everywhere in the Province.

[1] M.I.R., May 1958, S/S 123/8/01.
[2] Ibid., April–June 1958.
[3] Ibid., March 1958, DG 58/7/01.
[4] Ibid., April 1958, S/S 123/7/01.
[5] Ibid., March 1958, S/S 123/4/01.
[6] Ibid., April 1958, S/S 123/5/01.

In June Kapwepwe visited the same area. Government officials were appalled; Kapwepwe surpassed even Kaunda in his preaching of 'racial hatred' and 'self-government by 1960'.[1]

By July 1958 control of A.N.C.'s policy was passing to the party's militant young leaders, who now saw Nkumbula as the main obstacle to radical party reform. Though Nkumbula continued to oppose the extreme policies advocated by his opponents in the national executive, he failed to prevent the council at its meeting in early July from adopting proposals for a more aggressive campaign, one feature of which was the encouragement of violent retaliation by the African public if provoked by the security forces. During the next three months Nkumbula made a determined effort to restore his position, announcing privately, as a first step, that he would not hesitate to order the 'annihilation' of any member who betrayed him.[2] However, his chief rival, Kaunda, was visiting India for six months at the time, having departed without Nkumbula's authorization from Dar es Salaam in May after attending a World Assembly of Youth Conference.[3]

Nkumbula had used autocratic methods in running his party before and he now reverted increasingly to them. In May he handed the C.I.D. at Ndola information against A.N.C. officials regarding party financial affairs; and although he claimed he had done so to rid the movement of its many dishonest officials, the C.I.D.'s subsequent investigations in July roused much bitterness amongst both officials and rank-and-file members of the Copperbelt organization.[4] Before Nkumbula left for England that month to attempt to secure alterations in Benson's first constitutional proposals, he dismissed or transferred numerous district and branch level officials in Western and Central Provinces.[5] At about the same time, the Federal Government's announcement of a decrease in the maize subsidy, which had the effect of raising the price of meal, sparked A.N.C. hostility and set off a new wave of threatened boycotts.[6]

When Nkumbula returned in August he launched a purge of

[1] M.I.R., May and June 1958.
[2] Nkumbula's biography, 27 November 1962, S/S 201/015.
[3] Nkumbula, H., 'How Right is Zambia', *Freedom*, January 1959, p. 4.
[4] M.I.R., May, June, July 1958, S/S 123/8/01.
[5] Ibid., July 1958, S/S 123/2/01 and S/S 123/8/01.
[6] *Northern News*, 23 July 1958.

A.N.C.'s senior provincial officials.[1] For the first time he publicly identified his enemies. Nkumbula claimed that the plotters were a group of party officials in Western Province who had been encouraged in their attack on his leadership by Kapwepwe, Chimba, and Chitambala.[2] Previously Chitambala had persuaded Eastern Province's executive to pass a motion of 'no confidence' in Nkumbula, which accused him of using delaying tactics to frustrate the Lusaka Conference decisions of July. The motion had also alleged that Nkumbula was afraid of going back to prison and concluded that, having outlived his usefulness to the movement, he was now simply an obstacle on the path to self-government.[3] On 27 August Nkumbula struck a blow at the Western Province executive. Appearing unannounced at a meeting of the executive in Ndola, he ruled the recent provincial election results null and void, placed his cousin, Moses Shankanga, in the post of Provincial Secretary and transferred Chivunga to Southern Province. Banda, the new Provincial President, who was still serving a prison sentence, was deposed and replaced by Wesley Nyirenda. Within a matter of days, however, Nyirenda resigned, professing disgust with Nkumbula's tactics. Mulenga was ignominiously transferred to the village of Serenje in Central Province,[4] whereupon Nkumbula concluded his visit by announcing that national executive elections would be held in late October.[5]

Not surprisingly, the new appointments were never implemented. Instead, Nkumbula's arbitrary actions provoked his opponents into attacking him publicly for the first time. Kapwepwe, Sipalo, Chivunga, Chitambala, and J. C. N'gandu all published attacks in the Press during the following weeks,[6] N'gandu referring to Nkumbula's leadership as 'a second-hand suit the nation does not intend to resew or patch'.[7]

Nkumbula then turned his attention to one of A.N.C.'s great strongholds, Luapula Province. The 'Luapulists' were easily the

[1] Nkumbula's biography, 27 November 1962, S/S 201/015.
[2] *Northern News*, 28 August 1958.
[3] M.I.R., August 1958, S/S 123/3/01.
[4] Ibid., August and September 1958, S/S 123/8/01; Nkumbula's biography, 27 November 1962, S/S 201/015.
[5] *Northern News*, 28 August 1958.
[6] Ibid., 6, 11, 17, 20 September 1958.
[7] Ibid., 23 September 1958.

most volatile, militant, and independent of A.N.C.'s cohorts. On 23 July approximately 200 officials and delegates of Kawambwa District branches met at Lukwesa village to hear Richard Bwalya, Mulundu branch chairman, report on A.N.C.'s national executive meeting some weeks earlier in Lusaka. Bwalya's speech contained the typical blend of provincial pride and fearless militancy. He boasted that 'Luapulists' had been first in committing violence in 1953, and that they would not wait, as the national executive wished, until 1959 to start again. Bwalya called for the holding of unauthorized meetings, attacks on government servants, the training of action and youth groups to disable government transport and to damage bridges and government buildings.[1] Feelings in Luapula were building up in a way they were not elsewhere. In September villagers reportedly welcomed news of an attack which seriously injured a European government official.[2] The Provincial Commissioner reported that since January over 120 cases of breaches of Native Authority Rules and Orders by A.N.C. members had occurred.[3]

Kapwepwe's appointment of several acting provincial executive officials in August at Kawambwa, as opposed to Fort Rosebery, the usual headquarters, represented a serious threat to Nkumbula, particularly as they began calling for national party elections to replace Nkumbula by 20 September.[4] Nkumbula arrived in Fort Rosebery on 18 September for a visit which must have been one of the least successful tours of his career. Initially he accused two leading Luapula officials, Sylvester Chisambele and Alex Sharpi, of embezzling party funds and later dismissed them. He also opposed the executive on the question of local boycotts.[5] In addition, the Provincial Commissioner, who had received two weeks' notice of Nkumbula's visit, worked to make his tour as profitless as possible.[6] Nkumbula experienced constant trouble in organizing public meetings. Though in part it was his own fault, because he seldom applied for the necessary permit forty-eight hours beforehand, as the law required, it was clear that chiefs and Native Authorities had been encouraged to follow an unco-operative policy towards A.N.C. applications.

[1] M.I.R., August 1958, S/S 123/4/01.   [2] Ibid., September 1958.
[3] P.C. (Luapula P.) to C.S., 5 September 1958, DG 58/4/01.
[4] S.B. to C.S., 9 September 1958, DG 58/4/01.
[5] M.I.R., October 1958, S/S 123/4/01.
[6] P.C. to C.S., 1 October 1958, DG 58/4/01.

It was the Provincial Commissioner's hope that Nkumbula would address an unauthorized meeting, as indeed his supporters encouraged him to do, because nothing in the Provincial Commissioner's opinion would lift the morale of the chiefs and Native Authorities higher than a successful prosecution against the President of A.N.C.[1] But, above all else, Nkumbula required his own freedom if he hoped to counter his opponents' efforts to oust him; so he followed a moderate line during his tour, taking great pains to keep within the law and refusing to address the large crowds which assembled as he moved around.[2] Ironically, Nkumbula's circumspect behaviour made him look dependent on government officers and chiefs, the sign of a moderate and one which hardly impressed Luapula's restless inhabitants.

While Nkumbula divided his time between the Luapula and the Copperbelt, party officials in Central and Southern Provinces continued to force A.N.C. along a more extreme course. The most serious incident occurred on 10 September in the Gwembe valley, where the Government was implementing a large-scale resettlement scheme to remove Tonga villagers from the low-lying areas in the path of the rising Lake Kariba.[3] A.N.C. had been active in the area for months, encouraging non-compliance with the Government's scheme.[4] Indeed, as early as June 1958 the Government encountered resistance from one of Chief Chipepo's villages.[5] In September villagers attacked the security forces sent to move them, and nine villagers were shot dead in the riot which followed.[6] This was followed in Lusaka and Broken Hill by a spate of arson attempts, a train derailment and boycotts—the boycotts being initiated for the most part by Chimba.[7]

With the approaching meetings of A.N.C.'s national executive and general conference, scheduled for 21 and 23 October, respectively, Nkumbula further identified himself with the forces of moderation by 'patching up' his quarrel with Katilungu. Katilungu was invited to a conference of provincial party

[1] P.C. to C.S., 5 September 1958, DG 58/4/01; P.C. to C.S., 1 October 1958, DG 58/4/01.   [2] M.I.R., October 1958, S/S 123/4/01.
[3] Governor's draft report on the Gwembe incident, September 1958, DG 58/7/01.
[4] M.I.R., July 1958, S/S 123/7/01.   [5] African Eagle, 17 June 1958.
[6] P.C. (S.P.) to S.N.A., 13 September 1958, DG 58/7/01.
[7] M.I.R., September and October 1958, DG 58/2/01.

delegates at Kitwe on 5 October, where Nkumbula once again appointed a new provincial executive. Both Katilungu and Nkumbula, stressing their high regard for one another, blamed Chivunga for the deterioration in A.N.C.-trade union relations. Nkumbula also chided junior officials present for their flirtations with violence and dismissed as nonsense the goal of achieving independence by 1960. Another decade would be required before Northern Rhodesians in sufficient numbers were suitably prepared for independence.[1] Nkumbula then set off for Northern Province to continue his preparations for the general conference.

When Kaunda returned from India on 12 October, only nine days before the national executive meeting, he discreetly refused to comment on the open rift in A.N.C.[2] He was painfully aware, as were many of his colleagues, that Nkumbula's recent behaviour and his comments at Kitwe posed a serious threat to party morale. The Federation was preparing for a general election in which Welensky claimed that the basic issue at stake was which party could secure increased Federal independence at the 1960 review.[3] In late September the Colonial Secretary had announced Northern Rhodesia's final constitutional proposals, which to Kaunda and his colleagues were less acceptable than those of March. Yet Nkumbula had neither accepted nor rejected the proposals. Attention focused on the forthcoming meeting of the national executive; the stage was set for an intraparty conflict of unprecedented proportions.

The A.N.C.-Z.A.N.C. Split

Few details are known about the A.N.C. split of 24 October 1958. The national executive met on the 21st at the party's Chilenje headquarters and quarrelled bitterly until the afternoon of the 24th, when Kaunda led a small group of his colleagues from the meeting.[4] At the party's general conference, which convened later that afternoon, Nkumbula announced his resignation to the 300 delegates present. He claimed that for the past three years there had been trouble in A.N.C., and that several times

[1] M.I.R., October 1958, S/S 123/8/01.
[2] *Northern News*, 15 October 1958.
[3] Ibid., 20 September 1958.
[4] M.I.R., October and November 1958, S/S 201/05; *Northern News*, 25 October 1958.

he had tried to resign. In August 1958 when he returned from Britain, he said that he had received letters accusing him of being a 'slow coach' and threatening him with death if he failed to achieve independence by 1960.[1] During the course of his speech all members of the Luapula and Northern Province delegations walked out.[2] On Sunday, 26 October, Nkumbula was re-elected unopposed amid scenes of 'wild enthusiasm and thunderous applause'; a choir and preacher sang his praises, women danced around him and telegrams came in from as far afield as Bulawayo and Cape Town. Letters of resignation from Kaunda and Kapwepwe were received the same day, announcing their intention of forming the rival Zambia African National Congress.[3]

The reasons for the A.N.C.-Z.A.N.C. split were more complex than the struggle over tactics during 1958 might suggest. Nkumbula was challenged, not simply because he had turned moderate and was prepared to consider giving the Benson Constitution a fair trial—though both charges could be made with justification later on—but because in the eyes of his colleagues the requirements of nationalist leadership itself had changed. Z.A.N.C.'s three most prominent leaders, Kaunda, Kapwepwe, and Sipalo, had all been deeply influenced by their respective visits to India. In their view if Africans hoped to achieve self-government in Northern Rhodesia and break the hated Federation, they would require, above all else, a well-organized and highly disciplined nationalist movement, led by men imbued not only with a spirit of self-sacrifice and complete commitment to the 'struggle', but also with ascetic qualities.[4] In no sense did Nkumbula fulfil this image. He indulged more and more in the pleasures of life; party organization and discipline did not genuinely interest him; and he was lax in his handling of party affairs, often, for example, arriving late at public meetings or failing to make an appearance at all.[5] Worse

---

[1] *Northern News*, 25 October 1958.

[2] M.I.R., October and November 1958, S/S 201/05.

[3] *Northern News*, 27 October 1958.

[4] Kaunda to Nkrumah, December 1958, p. 13, A.N.L.W. papers.

[5] He did this in June on the Copperbelt, M.I.R., June 1958, S/S 123/8/01; and in Luapula Province in September, ibid., September 1958, S/S 123/4/01. Kaunda claims that Nkumbula refused at the last moment to attend a meeting scheduled with the Colonial Secretary in 1957; Kaunda, *Zambia Shall Be Free*, pp. 93–94.

still, his refusal to delegate authority prevented others in the party from improving the situation. Those who tried, admittedly not always for the good of the party, felt the sting of his hostility and were alienated by his arbitrary decisions and increasingly autocratic methods.[1]

Those who disagreed with Nkumbula, for whatever reasons, he regarded as traitors who posed a threat to his leadership. That he invariably accused them of extremism and of favouring a policy of violence helps to explain why the militant-moderate conflict in A.N.C. both exaggerated and oversimplified the true position. Sipalo favoured an aggressive policy, but he also wanted a more efficient party with well-organized action and youth groups. Kamanga's decision to follow Kaunda surprised both government and A.N.C. officials in Eastern Province, who believed at the time that he was a moderate and loyal to Nkumbula.[2] Kapwepwe attacked the mishandling of party funds and advocated reform of A.N.C.'s financial arrangements: 'We are going to fly . . . motor . . . and boat; just in search of freedom. All this requires money. We are going to be prosecuted and fined and this also requires money. Where shall we get this money? Of course, from you people. No freedom can be got without co-operation, devotion, determination, and above all self-sacrifice.'[3] Indeed, some of A.N.C.'s so-called moderates were financially unreliable, and Nkumbula himself had never instituted an effective control system over the party's finances. The methods he employed against the men he accused of being militant extremists were not always characterized by moderation; on one occasion in May 1958 Nkumbula handed the party's Western Province accounts to the police for investigation.[4]

Nevertheless, Nkumbula, for all his faults, commanded mass support in Northern Rhodesia and had built up, albeit inadequately, the Territory's first and only nationalist movement. His acknowledged position as the 'father' of African nationalism made open attack on him a risky enterprise. When Sipalo published his anti-Nkumbula letter in the *Northern News* in July he was severely beaten at Chifubu beerhall a few days later.[5]

[1] *Northern News*, 9 July, 6, 11, 17 September 1958.
[2] M.I.R., October and November 1958, S/S 123/3/01.
[3] Report of the Treasurer-General of A.N.C. to the Ninth Annual Conference 5 July 1958, author's collection.
[4] M.I.R., June 1958, S/S 123/8/01.   [5] M.I.R., July 1958, TS/S 123/01, Vol. I.

Moreover, during the difficult months preceding the split, Nkumbula's opponents never threatened to create a rival organization. Their campaign aimed solely at removing Nkumbula and revitalizing A.N.C. When they had failed and formed Z.A.N.C., Kaunda realized that their most urgent task would be to convince the people that the split with Nkumbula was political and not personal.[1] This explains why all Z.A.N.C.'s early propaganda insisted that the split was purely over the question of accepting or rejecting the Benson Constitution.

Z.A.N.C. held its first general conference in Broken Hill on 8 November 1958. Sixty hastily summoned delegates elected Kaunda President, Sipalo General Secretary, and Kapwepwe Treasurer.[2] The Deputy President, Paul Kalichini, an A.T.U.C. official, was elected after Konkola, President of the R.A.W.U., refused to accept the post, because he had not been chosen as Z.A.N.C.'s President.[3] W. K. Sikalumbi and Kamanga filled the deputy positions under Sipalo and Kapwepwe. On 2 December, after some prodding from the Registrar,[4] Z.A.N.C. applied for registration as a political party under the Societies Ordinance.[5]

Politics after the Split, November 1958–March 1959

The A.N.C.-Z.A.N.C. split ushered in a particularly confusing period in Northern Rhodesia politics, culminating in the Government's banning of Z.A.N.C. during the general election campaign of March 1959. The split itself was not effectively completed until December 1958, when A.N.C. finally decided to accept the Benson Constitution and to participate in the forth-coming election.[6] Z.A.N.C.'s immediate objectives were clear: to boycott the election and to supplant A.N.C. as the Territory's major nationalist party.[7] But Z.A.N.C. lacked both the time and

[1] Interview with Kaunda, 9 July 1964.
[2] Memorandum to the Ridley Commission of Inquiry on Z.A.N.C. ban and the restriction of its leaders, 12 April 1959, S.M.K. papers; also Kaunda to Commander Fox-Pitt, 2 December 1958, author's collection.
[3] Kaunda, *Zambia Shall Be Free*, pp. 98–99.
[4] Registrar to Kapwepwe, 28 October 1958, S/S 82/81/01.
[5] Memo to Ridley Commission, 12 April 1959, author's collection.
[6] Circular to A.N.C. members, 21 December 1958, MS/2615/16, Box 4252; *Northern News*, 22 December 1958; M.I.R., December 1958, S/S 123/8/01.
[7] Z.A.N.C. Political Circular No. 1, December 1958, MS. 2615/16, Box 4352; also. Report on Registration of Voters to S.N.A., 17 December 1958, MN/1/4, Box 1672, 'African Administration, Territorial Election Procedure (Franchise)', Lusaka Archives.

resources to organize extensively throughout the Territory. The Government, too, was suddenly faced with a crisis. Two hostile nationalist parties, one intent on boycotting the election, inevitably complicated the security situation and posed a serious threat to the new Constitution. If the boycott succeeded, the influence of 'ordinary' voters in 'special' constituencies would be so great that African 'special' members would in effect be 'stooges' elected by Europeans. To prevent this the Government launched a massive campaign to register African voters in November.[1] In addition, increased attention was given to the Societies Ordinance as a means of controlling the two nationalist parties and preparing for possible security measures in the future.[2]

Although the split initially threw officials of both parties into disarray, rank-and-file members—apart from the 'Luapulists'—appeared to take little interest. Apart from the national leaders who followed Kaunda, z.a.n.c.'s initial support amongst lower-level officials in the provinces was small. November was largely given over to planning amongst z.a.n.c.'s leaders, while Nkumbula, apparently unperturbed by the split, ignored the Copperbelt and northern areas altogether.[3] Indeed, the split itself seemed uncertain. a.n.c. took no immediate decision on the question of participating in the election; and as late as 26 November, Chimba, one of z.a.n.c.'s most ardent leaders, was still able to propose a meeting of both parties' provincial officials to restore unity, on the condition that Kaunda should replace Nkumbula as President.[4]

In December the pattern of the split began to emerge. Shortly after z.a.n.c.'s formation, a.n.c.'s branch strength was given as 431 for the entire Territory.[5] With z.a.n.c. now in the field, the accuracy of this accounting was clearly open to question, especially the figure of 234 new branches which the Government suddenly registered (without the required copies of the party constitution) in mid-November.[6] The bulk of

[1] Circular from Ag. c.s. to all Heads of Depts. and p.c.s, 7 November 1958, 3/29/1, Box 3309, Lusaka Archives.
[2] Ex. Co., 21 August 1958, S/S 82/81/01; also, circular from c.s. to all p.c.s and d.c.s, 25 November 1958, ibid.
[3] m.i.r., November 1958, S/S 123/2/01, /3/01, /4/01, /8/01.
[4] Central African Post, 26 November 1958.
[5] Northern News, 18 November 1958.
[6] Ibid.; it was decided at an Ex. Co. meeting on 21 August to waive the requirement and to extend the registration period deadline to 2 December 1958, S/S 82/81/01.

A.N.C.'s registered branches were in Southern Province (106), with Northern (75), Eastern (72) and Luapula (68) close behind. Lusaka led in town branches, which normally were much larger than rural branches, with 36; Broken Hill came second with 13, while none of the Copperbelt towns could claim more than 10.[1]

Z.A.N.C. made its most rapid progress in the Luapula, Northern Province, Broken Hill, and Ndola. In Southern Province there was still no sign of the split in February 1959,[2] whereas in Luapula it was clear by December 1958 'that Z.A.N.C. had won the day'.[3] The situation in Northern Province was more obscure: Chinsali, Kasama, Mporokoso, and Mpika Districts followed Z.A.N.C.; while Isoka, Abercorn, and Luwingu remained loyal for the time being to A.N.C. A.N.C.'s provincial executive, led by Makasa, resigned and reapplied for registration under Z.A.N.C.'s name. By this time A.N.C. had dispatched two new officials to the area, and though both parties remained disorganized, by January the people were reportedly moving steadily towards Z.A.N.C.[4] On the Copperbelt, Kaunda and Kapwepwe addressed public meetings at Luanshya, Chingola, and Ndola, where for the first time they appeared in togas of the West African variety. Z.A.N.C.'s success, however, was almost entirely restricted to Ndola, where it had captured A.N.C.'s former provincial executive. Meanwhile, A.N.C. established its new provincial executive at Mufulira, where its first decision, on 20 December, was to accept the Constitution and to participate in the forthcoming election.[5]

In Central Province Z.A.N.C. appeared more successful in Broken Hill than in Lusaka, where A.N.C. adopted a strong anti-Z.A.N.C. line and continued its public meetings, despite somewhat reduced attendance. A.N.C. attempted to re-establish its Broken Hill's district executive, which Chimba had led over to Z.A.N.C. the previous month.[6] That same month, however, Chimba turned up with Kamanga in Eastern Province, where Z.A.N.C. reportedly had the better leaders, but A.N.C. the mass

[1] *Northern News*, 18 November 1958.
[2] M.I.R., November and December 1958, S/S 123/7/01.
[3] Ibid., S/S 123/4/01.
[4] Ibid., S/S 123/5/01.
[5] Ibid., S/S 123/8/01.
[6] Ibid., S/S 123/2/01.

of the people. Z.A.N.C.'s first meeting at Fort Jameson was effectively boycotted, but A.N.C.'s leaders, whose relations with local chiefs during the past few years had been unusually good, could not agree on whether or not to advise their supporters to register as voters. As a result, those chiefs who supported A.N.C. were undecided as well; Chief Kawaza, who had already registered, requested the return of his form and ordered his people not to register on pain of tribal sanctions. For this the Provincial Commissioner severely reprimanded Kawaza and cut his subsidy. Nevertheless, Kawaza and a number of other chiefs who had supported A.N.C. opposed the new Z.A.N.C., partly because its local leaders, unlike Nkumbula, believed that chiefs were not sophisticated enough to participate in territorial constitutional negotiations.[1]

Nkumbula took no tours after the split at all, except to Southern Province, where in November at a private meeting in Monze he appointed his top provincial officials for Southern and Eastern Province. Job Mayanda and Job Michello were named President and General Secretary respectively for Southern Province, while Amos Mweeba was appointed Provincial President for Eastern.[2] In the other provinces where nationalist activity had always been minimal or non-existent, Barotseland and North Western, the split went almost unnoticed.[3]

With the split less than two months old, both Kaunda and Nkumbula departed for Ghana to attend the All-African Peoples Conference. Nkumbula travelled via London, where during still another round of discussion on the Benson Constitution he went out of his way to create the impression that he had now become a man of moderate views.[4] Once at the Accra Conference, Nkumbula came into conflict with Kaunda and Dr. Hastings Banda of Nyasaland, ostensibly over a conference resolution which supported the right of freedom fighters to retaliate against violence in the struggle for national independence. Nkumbula found himself excluded much of the time, though not, however, from an agreement reached between all

[1] M.I.R., S/S 123/3/01.
[2] Ibid., S/S 123/7/01.
[3] Ibid., S/S 123/6/01; DG 58/1/01.
[4] S.B. to C.S., 29 December 1958, S/S 201/05.

the Congress parties of Central Africa to form a united front against Federation.[1]

Though the Government placed great importance on z.a.n.c.'s support for the Accra Conference resolutions and on the proposed united front against Federation,[2] the real significance of the conference for Northern Rhodesia politics lay elsewhere. The Government believed that Nkumbula and Kaunda had been informed before the conference opened that Nkrumah was unhappy about the split in Northern Rhodesia's nationalist movement and favoured a *rapprochement* between z.a.n.c. and a.n.c.[3] A meeting between Nkrumah and the various Central African delegations, in fact, took place on 14 December in Accra,[4] though both Kaunda and Nkumbula later denied that z.a.n.c. and a.n.c. had reunited.[5] It was significant, however, that Nkumbula returned to Northern Rhodesia shortly afterwards, while Kaunda remained in Ghana for another month. As a result of the meeting with Nkrumah, Kaunda attempted to convince the Ghanaian leader that z.a.n.c. was the party of the future in Northern Rhodesia. In a fifteen-page memorandum Kaunda set out the African case against both the Federation and the Benson Constitution. In the memorandum's concluding section, Kaunda acknowledged Nkrumah's great inspiration to Africa, emphasized z.a.n.c's intention to follow Ghana's example and intensify the 'struggle' in Northern Rhodesia, and appealed to Nkrumah for financial aid to enable z.a.n.c. 'to defeat the imperialists'.

. . . you [Nkrumah] have set for us in Africa a goal which we must work for; you have set for me a standard of behaviour or personal discipline exemplified in your famous three 'S's: Service, Sacrifice and Suffering—with which we must equip ourselves before we can even hope to start on the great task before us. With this you inspired your followers then as you do inspire us today . . .

You have proved to the world that black men can do everything else that a white man, brown or yellow man can do. The people of

[1] *Report of an Inquiry Into All the Circumstances Which Gave Rise to the Making of the Safeguard of Elections and Public Safety Regulations*, 1959, p. 9.
[2] Ibid., pp. 9, 14, 30.   [3] m.i.r., December 1958, S/S 123/2/01.
[4] Kaunda to Nkrumah, December 1958, p. 1, a.n.l.w. papers.
[5] Record of meeting between Nkumbula and c.s., 24 December 1958, S/S 201/05; Kaunda denied it when he returned from Ghana in January, *Northern News*, 18 January 1959.

Northern Rhodesia wish you to know, Sir, that they would like you to preserve this sovereign state of Ghana for upon it hangs FREEDOM, PEACE and JUSTICE for the rest of Africa. In other words, my people believe if you succeed here, as you are doing, we all are bound to do so in shorter periods than this world has ever dreamt of.

Kaunda outlined the party's five-year development plan and stressed the need for jeeps, loudspeakers, typewriters, duplicating equipment, and scholarships: '. . . Imperialists are now employing all methods against us which they used against you and they have naturally improved upon them. But against their improved methods we can, I am certain, depend upon you as our . . . brother and comrade.'[1]

When Kaunda returned from Ghana he claimed that Z.A.N.C. had been promised financial and other support by the Ghana Government. He denied any agreement between Z.A.N.C. and A.N.C. to reunite; indeed, Nkumbula, he revealed, had attacked and alienated both Banda and Nkrumah at the Conference.[2] In all probability Z.A.N.C. received little, if any, Ghanaian aid during the month preceding the Government's ban, but it seems clear beyond all doubt that Kaunda succeeded personally in winning Nkrumah's esteem. After Kaunda assumed the presidency of Z.A.N.C.'s successor, the United National Independence Party (U.N.I.P.), in January 1960, financial assistance from a variety of sources, including Ghana, was immediately forthcoming.[3] While undoubtedly Kaunda's reputation was enhanced in Pan-Africanist circles by his term in prison in 1959, the rapidity with which U.N.I.P. secured moral and financial support in 1960 depended to a large extent on Kaunda's success in Ghana at the time of the Accra Conference.

Meanwhile, the Government's registration campaign encountered serious difficulties. The number of Africans who applied under the 'special' franchise during the first three weeks was a mere trickle (2,134),[4] and there was grave concern, both in London and Lusaka, that the target figure of 25,000 African voters would not even be approached by the 31 December

---

[1] Kaunda to Nkrumah, December 1958, pp. 13–15, A.N.L.W. papers.
[2] M.I.R., January 1959, TS/S 123/01, Vol. I.
[3] S.B. to Ad. Sec., The Finance of the U.N.I.P., 9 July 1960, S/S 108/02.
[4] Circular from C.S. to all P.C.s and D.C.s, 15 December 1958, 329/1, Box 3302, Lusaka Archives.

deadline.[1] In late November the District Commissioner at Solwezi (North-Western Province) wrote a detailed report on registration in his district, which contained a series of extraordinary suggestions. He claimed that there was little party opposition in Solwezi District, and that Africans were not registering because they misunderstood both the constitutional proposals and the franchise. In addition, the presence on the application form of a small red tag, which enabled the applicant to register also as a Federal voter, discouraged many Africans, who believed that completing the Territorial form implied support for the Federation. The District Commissioner proposed to send officers out into the surrounding areas to explain the significance of the franchise proposals and the need for and mechanics of registration. The same procedure was suggested for the Boma's African staff, many of whom were able to fulfil the franchise qualifications. The District Commissioner believed that it should be made clear to Africans that abstentions would only result in the election of the wrong candidates. This, however, was not all.

The elementary exercise is, of course, to engage the confidence of the Chief or senior Native Authority representative. My officers have been instructed to stand ostensibly aloof from 'party' politics as such, but to make no bones about the fact that African National Congress is not regarded as a political 'party'. They are in fact regarded as a parcel of troublemakers whose apparent policies and intentions are little short of subversive. (One has to be careful these days!)

An alarming prospect is in fact that clearly the largest body of eligible voters—teachers and the like—are almost certainly Congress supporters and it is more than probable that Congress candidates will be returned. For this reason I consider that District Officers should go to considerable lengths (as we have done in this District) to obtain the registration of other eligible voters such as headmen and Government employees. This would have a leavening effect. The hard fact is that only about one in 50 headmen is literate in English and their knowledge of English is so sketchy that they are unwilling to come forward. When they do, they are immediately floored by words such as 'surname', 'sex', 'constituency', 'occupation' and the like. I consider that these people should be given considerable help (even practice) with the form provided so that, ultimately, they can

[1] D.C. (Solwezi) to Chief Electoral Office (C.E.O.), 24 November 1958, 329/1, Box 3302, Lusaka Archives.

sit down in front of the registering officer and fill in the necessary details unaided. One of the biggest obstacles to a man of 'simple' literacy is nervousness and it is often necessary to let him have a few practice goes with a clerk.[1]

In Lusaka the District Commissioner's letter received nothing but praise. Not only was the District Commissioner thanked 'for the keen and careful way in which he has done his best to make the registration campaign a success',[2] but the Chief Secretary took the matter up with the Secretary of Native Affairs, with the result that the District Commissioner's letter was duplicated and dispatched as a circular to all Provincial and District Commissioners, together with a covering letter instructing them to carry out their respective campaigns with the 'greatest vigour'.[3]

Additional encouragement was given to the Provincial Administration throughout December. The registration period was extended to mid-January, though this was not announced until late December, so that the campaign's sense of urgency might be maintained.[4] Copperbelt District Commissioners were instructed to request the mining companies to open registering offices on their premises and to enclose slips in African miners' pay packets advising those who were qualified to register.[5] On 16 December the Governor expressed disappointment at the small number of Africans who had registered:

It may be true that there is some apathy—in fact I am sure it is true —and we have always argued with Roberts and his boys that we shall be lucky if we get half those qualified to register. On the other hand a great deal of it may be due to procrastination and I would like to feel that we have taken every step possible to bring home to all qualified voters in the territory the fact that they must register at the very latest by the 10th January.

He then requested the Chief Secretary to consider sending telegrams to all District Commissioners, stressing the 10 January deadline, as well as a 'special circular to all heads of departments (for distribution) telling them that the responsibility lies fairly

[1] D.C. (Solwezi) to C.E.D., 24 November 1958, 329/1, Box 3302, Lusaka Archives.
[2] A.S.(C.S.)3 to C.E.O., 11 December 1958, ibid.
[3] Ibid. Covering circular: C.S. to all P.C.s and D.C.s, 9 December 1958, ibid.
[4] Ibid.
[5] Circular Ag. C.S. to Copperbelt D.C.s, 26 November 1958, ibid.

and squarely on their shoulders to ensure that their civil servants, qualified to become voters, do in fact take the opportunity to register (which should be specially provided for them)'.[1]

Though the Government's zealous efforts brought a rapid increase in 'special' voters, the figures at the close of registration were still far below the Government's targets. A total of 6,821 Africans registered as 'special' voters, while only 796 Africans qualified as 'ordinary' voters.[2] The increase in 'special' voters was chiefly confined to the rural areas which made up the 'special' constituencies, where the Government's influence over chiefs and Native Authorities could not be effectively challenged by the nationalist parties. In these areas the Government managed to secure the registration of slightly over half the number of estimated African voters. In the urban areas, which were covered by the 'ordinary' and reserved African constituencies, the picture was dramatically different: approximately only one-fifth of the estimated eligible Africans had registered.[3]

The Benson Constitution had received a setback from which it never recovered. Whereas in 'special' constituencies African voters would be in the majority and therefore would exercise a major, though not always perhaps a decisive, influence on results, Africans in the 'ordinary' and reserved African constituencies would not have anything like the influence on the election results which the Constitution intended. The Chief Secretary attributed the lack of success in registering Africans to the apathy of Africans generally (which was more true in rural than urban areas) and to A.N.C.'s indecisive attitude. But the pattern of 'special' registrations was too obvious for him to avoid admitting that Z.A.N.C.'s boycott 'may have deterred a number of voters until it was too late'.[4]

Despite the Chief Secretary's attempts to play down the importance of Z.A.N.C.'s boycott, by late January it was obvious to the Government that Z.A.N.C. was taking hold in several important areas. With the election set for 20 March and Z.A.N.C. threatening to continue its boycott at the polls, the problems of

[1] Governor to C.S., 16 December 1958, MS/2615/16, Box 4352, Lusaka Archives.
[2] N.R. General Election (March 20th) Distribution of Electorate, ibid.
[3] C.S. to all P.C.s and D.C.s, 30 January 1959, 329/1, Box 3309, Lusaka Archives.
[4] Ibid.

dealing with the new party became urgent. The poor response during registration had already seriously impaired the potential influence of African voters, and a low poll among Africans on election day would accentuate the deficiency with disastrous consequences for the Constitution. However, the Government's immediate ability to control z.a.n.c. was limited. The registration of z.a.n.c.'s branches under the Societies Ordinance, the Government's main tool for controlling nationalist parties, had not kept pace with branch formation, because of the confused struggle for power which followed the nationalist split. As a result, the Government did not possess an accurate record of z.a.n.c.'s strength and organization. Not only were the number and location of z.a.n.c.'s branches in doubt, and therefore the names and addresses of many of its office-bearers, but the Government was unable to determine which a.n.c. branches, in fact, had gone over to z.a.n.c. without re-registering under the new name. Officials of some former a.n.c. branches applied for re-registration under the name of z.a.n.c. soon after the split. This was the case with eighteen branches and z.a.n.c.'s provincial and district headquarters in Luapula Province. Initially the Registrar refused to register z.a.n.c.'s new branches, unless the branch office-bearers themselves notified him of the change, because he believed that ambitious provincial-level officials were transferring their branches to z.a.n.c. without consulting their supporters. In some cases both a.n.c. and z.a.n.c. claimed the same branches with identical office-bearers.[1]

By February, however, the Registrar had been instructed to register all z.a.n.c. branches, despite double registrations, so urgent was the need to build up information on the new party.[2] Between 9 February and 11 March the Government registered eighty-five z.a.n.c. branches: seventeen in Northern Province; thirty-eight in Kawambwa District and twenty-five in Fort Rosebery District of Luapula Province; one at Chingola and three at Ndola in Western Province; and one in Fort Jameson in the Eastern Province.[3] z.a.n.c.'s headquarters was registered

[1] Registrar to General Secretary of z.a.n.c., 7 January 1959, S/S 82/81/01.
[2] c.s. to Registrar, 5 February 1959, ibid.
[3] *Report of an Inquiry Into All the Circumstances Which Gave Rise to the Making of the Safeguard of Elections and Public Safety Regulations*, 1959 (The Ridley Report), p. 8.

in Lusaka.[1] Other z.a.n.c. branches existed, however, which retained their a.n.c. registration; thirteen such branches were listed by the Government in Kasama District alone.[2]

a.n.c.'s position, on the other hand, had altered dramatically. Apart from minimal activity in Central, Eastern, and Southern Provinces, the party hardly appeared to function.[3] At the end of February, Nkumbula had still not visited the Copperbelt since the split.[4] On 20 February the Chief Secretary instructed the Provincial Administration not to prosecute a.n.c. branches which had existed in mid-1958, but which had failed subsequently to register under the Societies Ordinance. In recent months, he wrote, 'many had become so defunct or so inactive as to be regarded as defunct' that to prosecute them 'would serve no purpose and just stir up interest in a nearly dead organization'.[5]

That a.n.c. should have become less active at a time when it was planning to contest a general election is only partly explained by Nkumbula's apparent lack of interest in the party and his shift to a more moderate position. Of more significance perhaps were his increased contacts with the Government following his return from the Accra Conference. On 24 December 1958, Nkumbula met the Chief Secretary to discuss the registration of voters. In the course of the interview, Nkumbula complained that during his Ghana visit Banda informed Nkrumah that Nkumbula had secretly accepted Federation. Nkumbula said that at the time he had challenged Banda, who, though he refused to name his informer, claimed that he was reliable and close to the Governor. Nkumbula told the Chief Secretary that he intended replying publicly to Banda, but that before doing so, he wished to take the matter up with the Governor.[6]

Later the Chief Secretary raised the matter with the Governor, and the subsequent exchange between them was revealing.

[1] Registrar to c.s., 2 March 1959, S/S 82/81/01.
[2] c.s. to d.c. (Kasama), 12 March 1959, ibid.
[3] m.i.r., January and February 1959, S/S 123/2/01 to S/S 123/8/01.
[4] Ibid., February 1959, S/S 123/8/01.
[5] c.s. to all p.c.s and d.c.s, 20 February 1959, S/S 82/81/01.
[6] Record of meeting between the c.s. and Nkumbula, 24 December 1958, S/S 201/05.

I expect that in the circumstances Your Excellency will not think it necessary to grant a personal interview to Mr. Nkumbula, but perhaps it would be as well if the Secretary of Native Affairs—who is the normal contact—were to see Mr. Nkumbula and to tell him that Your Excellency has no knowledge whatever of what Dr. Banda meant when he said that a source close to Your Excellency had accused Mr. Nkumbula of having acquiesced in the fact of Federation. The Secretary of Native Affairs could add that Your Excellency has frequently said that generally speaking the Africans in Northern Rhodesia are not so hostile to the concept of Federation but object rather to the policies and acts of the Federal Government [and wish to secede from the Federation, not because they dislike being a part of the Federation, but because they fear that if they remain a part of it they will be removed from the protection of Her Majesty's Government in the United Kingdom before long]; but rather that Your Excellency has never included Mr. Nkumbula in this category since his personal attitude on the matter is so well known.[1]

Nkumbula's interview with the Secretary of Native Affairs was arranged for 10 January 1959. The meeting was both lengthy and important. The Secretary refuted Banda's accusations and outlined the Government's view on the question of African opposition to the Federation, which Nkumbula accepted 'as a fair statement of the facts'. Nkumbula was then asked to agree to an insertion being made by the Chief Secretary to a proposed press statement which Nkumbula had submitted previously to the Chief Secretary. Nkumbula agreed to this as well. Finally, it was noted that Nkumbula had released to the Press a recent letter from the Secretary of Native Affairs concerning the Government's resettlement scheme in the Kariba area. In this particular case, the Secretary had no objection, but he felt that for the future he and Nkumbula should conclude a 'gentleman's agreement' on such matters. The Secretary proposed:

. . . that one would not release to the press letters or reports of meetings without first informing the other party. The Secretary of Native Affairs pointed out that in some cases he would not wish information he gave to Mr. Nkumbula to be released to the press and that unless they could come to a gentleman's agreement it

[1] C.S. to Governor, 30 December 1958, S/S 201/05. The section in brackets was added by the Governor.

would be difficult for him or any other member of the Government to write to Mr. Nkumbula or to grant him interviews.

Nkumbula indicated that he understood and accepted the agreement.[1]

In late February, at the time of nominations for the election, Nkumbula received secret assistance from the Government of quite another kind, which placed both Nkumbula and the Government in a suspicious light. Not only was the Government anxious about the difficulties being encountered by African 'special' candidates in the securing of the required chiefs' certificates,[2] more significantly, the Government took active steps to insure that Nkumbula should not fail to qualify for candidacy in the South-Western 'special' constituency, which he subsequently won in the election.[3] Nearly a month after nomination day Roberts publicly accused the Government of an 'abominable and shocking piece of administration' with regard to the nomination of African candidates.[4] On 30 March, G. B. Beckett, the u.f.p.'s unsuccessful candidate in the Southern 'ordinary' constituency, alleged that the Government had brought its influence to bear in favour of Nkumbula in South-Western.[5] As a result of these allegations, which the Government probably learned of before they became public, the Chief Secretary requested a Secretariat official to place on record any steps which had been taken to assist Nkumbula in lodging his nomination papers. The record, which (it must be emphasized) was compiled as a result of u.f.p. pressure, nearly a month after nomination day, is somewhat complicated and, in fairness to the parties concerned, worth quoting at some length.

The day before nomination day information was received in this office that Nkumbula was experiencing difficulty in obtaining the requisite number of Chiefs Certificates in support of nomination.

I was asked to verify the position using the utmost tact. I asked Mr. Woods, d.o. Lusaka, for his assistance in making enquiries in Chilenje at the a.n.c. headquarters as to how their campaigning was

[1] Record of meeting between the s.n.a. and Nkumbula, 10 January 1959, S/S 201/05.

[2] c.s. to all p.c.s. and d.c.s., 22 February 1959, MN 1/4, Vol. I, Box 1672, Lusaka Archives.

[3] Minute for record, 20 March 1959, ibid.

[4] *Northern News*, 20 March 1959.

[5] *Central African Post*, 30 March 1959.

going. He is well known in Chilenje and by the A.N.C. adherents, and his visit would therefore, in my opinion, have been less likely to arouse interest and comment than a visit from myself.

Woods spoke to Mukupo who volunteered the information that Nkumbula had left for Choma with his deposit and the requisite number of Chiefs Certificates in his pocket. He informed Woods that there had been a little doubt at one time as to whether Nkumbula would obtain the correct number of Chiefs Certificates, but everything had worked out in the end and Nkumbula was quite happy.

I then rang the D.C. Choma's office and spoke to Mr. Loggie, the D.O., in the absence of Mr. Aldous, to ask if Nkumbula had reached Choma. He had not at that time, i.e. the afternoon before nomination day, been seen in Choma. I told Loggie that Nkumbula intended to lodge a nomination paper and that we were anxious that, whilst there could be no question of there being any act of assistance contrary to the law afforded to Nkumbula in completing the nomination formalities, he should not have any obstacles placed in his way that would lead to a rejection of his nomination on some small technical point which he could have been made aware of before making his submission. Mr. Loggie was informed that this matter should be treated as absolutely confidential and that the utmost tact must be used.

I rang Mr. Aldous, D.C. Choma, on the morning of nomination day and asked if Nkumbula had lodged his nomination paper. I was informed that nothing had yet been seen of Nkumbula but Aldous understood the position and would put out tactful feelers to ensure that early news of Nkumbula's arrival reached him and that Nkumbula was aware that nominations had to be with the Returning Officer by 1 p.m. on that day.

Mr. Aldous rang the Secretary of Native Affairs very soon afterwards to say that Nkumbula had lodged his nomination papers, which were perfectly in order and had been accepted.

No action was taken with regard to assisting Nkumbula securing Chiefs Certificates. By the time we got wind of the information that he was experiencing some difficulty in this respect it was too late for anything to have been done about it, even supposing we had wished to do so.

All candidates, including those who had failed, for one reason or another, to lodge nomination papers in Choma, told the D.C. Choma that they were quite satisfied that they had received every possible assistance from D.C.s and there is no reason to suppose that Nkumbula received any more favourable treatment than any other candidate in the field.

In point of fact the U.F.P. candidate, Isaiah Mulondo, was probably helped more than any other candidate in that the D.C. personally pointed out to him that he was short of the required number of Chiefs Certificates and advised him that Chief Mapanza was in the vicinity should Mulondo wish to contact him. Mulondo did not bother to make any effort in this direction, and furthermore did not in fact submit a nomination paper to the Returning Officer. He told Mr. Aldous that his nomination by the U.F.P. had been confirmed too late, i.e. two weeks before nomination day, and he had told Roberts he could not hope to secure the necessary Chiefs Certificates in this time, but Roberts had said he 'would see that he was all right'.[1]

On the evidence available it is extremely difficult to reach a conclusive judgement on Nkumbula's contacts with the Government between December 1958 and March 1959. Did the Government assist Nkumbula with his nomination? The answer is unclear.[2] Apparently, Nkumbula had not required assistance (though even this is by no means certain); if he had, the general tone of the record suggests that assistance might well have been forthcoming. Prior to 1958 the Government had never concerned itself with Nkumbula's political fortunes; indeed, quite the contrary. Now, in February 1959, the Government was deeply concerned, and its actions went considerably beyond what was customary in the nomination of candidates.

Undoubtedly, Nkumbula had adopted a more moderate position than at any time in the past. A.N.C.'s marked swing towards moderation, Nkumbula's decision to accept the Constitution, his behaviour in London and in Northern Rhodesia after his return from Ghana in December 1958 confirmed this. But had Nkumbula passed the point of moderation and in effect become a tool of the Government? Again the evidence is insufficient to sustain a judgement.

[1] Minute for record, 20 March 1959, MN 1/4, Vol. I, Box 1672, Lusaka Archives.

[2] Welensky quotes Nkumbula on nomination day: 'I have travelled on foot or by bicycle over 600 miles in the past three weeks to get the chiefs' signatures. I still need two more, and one of the chiefs I must try to find today lives about 150 miles from the nearest road. I will have to cycle all the way'; Welensky, Sir Roy, *Welensky's 4,000 Days*, London, 1964, p. 135. With nominations closing at midday it would clearly have been impossible for Nkumbula to make his proposed bicycle trip.

Nkumbula's friendship with Harry Franklin, a former official government minister who was not favourably disposed to African majority rule, had angered Nkumbula's colleagues before the split and cast suspicion on his leadership.[1] As early as September 1958 Nkumbula, expressing confidence in his future, claimed that any 'rebel' group which broke away from A.N.C. would be banned within six months and its leaders removed from the political scene.[2] When the Government made the Safeguard of Elections and Public Safety Regulations, 1959, on 11 March, nine days before polling, the ban on political activity only applied to Z.A.N.C. The Government clearly hoped that Z.A.N.C.'s boycott threat would die with the party and that African voters would flock to the polls.[3] With Nkumbula in the Legislative Council, government officials hoped that A.N.C. might continue to pursue a moderate line,[4] but in April 1959 a report from Broken Hill noted that A.N.C. had so far failed to take advantage of Z.A.N.C.'s setback.[5] Yet the question remains: Was Nkumbula, in part at least, a party to the Government's plans; or was his shift towards moderation and a closer relationship with the Government simply a shrewd attempt to use the Government against his Z.A.N.C. opponents, thereby re-establishing himself as the indisputable leader of African nationalism in Northern Rhodesia? The absence of more substantial evidence, as well as Nkumbula's subsequent behaviour, suggests the latter as the more plausible explanation.

The 1959 Election

The 1959 election, like its many predecessors over the past thirty-five years, was essentially a contest among Europeans. The outcome was never seriously in doubt. European majorities in both the Legislative and Executive Councils were assured by the Constitution; nor could the U.F.P.'s continued dominance be seriously challenged by either the multi-racial Central African Party (C.A.P.) or the right-wing Dominion Party (D.P.). Nevertheless, the election introduced important new

---

[1] Kaunda, *Zambia Shall Be Free*, pp. 94–95.

[2] M.I.R., September 1958, S/S 201/05.

[3] Governor to C.S., 14 March 1959, MS/2615/16, Box 4352, Lusaka Archives.

[4] Secretary to Minister of Native Affairs (M.N.A.) to the M.N.W., 22 April 1959, S/S 82/81/01.

[5] M.I.R., April 1959, S/S 123/2/01.

developments. For the first time an election was fought largely on party lines by a number of political parties. A relatively large number of Africans, admittedly a highly selective group, voted for the first time. The election also brought the two African nationalist parties into direct and bitter conflict, A.N.C. accepting the Constitution and contesting the election, Z.A.N.C. boycotting the election and dedicating itself to the total destruction of the Constitution. Finally, and of paramount importance for future politics in Northern Rhodesia, the election set a severe test for the Constitution itself, particularly for its prescribed objective of encouraging the evolution of politics along 'non-racial' lines over the next decade.

In the 'ordinary' constituencies, the U.F.P. nominated a full team of twelve candidates, though in two electoral areas, Livingstone and Chingola, the U.F.P. was unopposed. The D.P. nominated nine candidates, preferring not to oppose Roberts in his home constituency of Broken Hill, while Moffat's C.A.P., the Territorial successor of the Constitution Party, contested only two 'ordinary' seats, Ndola and Lusaka West. Independents played only a minor role, except in Lusaka, where two independents stood in each of the three constituencies.

The U.F.P. also contested the four reserved seats, nominating African candidates for the first time in the two African reserved constituencies. In the seats reserved for Europeans the U.F.P. faced only C.A.P. candidates—Moffat, the party's leader in Eastern Rural, and Franklin in Western Rural. In the African seats the U.F.P.'s candidates, G. Musumbulwa in Copperbelt and W. Kazokah in South Central, each faced three opponents. Musumbulwa opposed three popular African independents— Katilungu, Puta and Sokota; while in South Central Kazokah faced equally impressive opposition in H. Habanyama (C.A.P.) and Chileshe (Ind.).

The 'special' constituencies presented quite a different picture. Only four of the six—Barotseland, North-Western, South-Western, and Eastern—were contested. The U.F.P. nominated two 'special' candidates, one in Barotseland and one in Eastern, while A.N.C. contested only South-Western and Eastern. Apart from A. H. Gondwe, the C.A.P.'s nominee in Eastern, the other eight 'special' candidates were independents.[1]

[1] For a full list of the candidates, see the *Northern News*, 28 February 1959.

Luapula and Northern, the two 'special' constituencies in which no nominations were forthcoming, served to underline one of the Constitution's most serious weaknesses. All eight prospective candidates in the north failed to lodge nomination papers, because they were unable to obtain the required certificates from two-thirds of the chiefs in their respective constituencies. The same pattern, though not as acute, persisted over the entire country. February marked the height of the rains, and most prospective African candidates found the task of collecting chiefs' certificates time-consuming, exhausting, and expensive.[1] In addition, and despite a Government circular advising chiefs to the contrary,[2] many chiefs proved unco-operative in signing the certificates, often refusing for purely personal reasons or because of local tribal and political considerations. In Barotseland, for example, the Paramount Chief rejected three candidates—two because he disliked them and another because he supported the hostile Barotse National Society and was a member of another branch of the royal family. In all, nineteen candidates were rejected for having insufficient chiefs' certificates, while only one failed for lack of the necessary financial deposit.[3]

Northern Rhodesia's election campaign proceeded almost unnoticed amid the events in the Federation in February and March 1959. Serious disturbances broke out in Nyasaland on 20 February and continued into March, when a full state of emergency was declared.[4] In Southern Rhodesia, Sir Edgar Whitehead's Government assumed emergency powers as a precautionary measure on 26 February and introduced legislation for the banning of the Southern Rhodesia African National Congress.[5] Despite the build-up of Z.A.N.C.'s 'positive action' campaign during February, Northern Rhodesia remained calm. Late in the month the Chief Secretary announced that he saw no need for the use of emergency powers in Northern Rhodesia; the Territory's Africans, he claimed, did not sympathize with events in Nyasaland.[6]

---

[1] M.N.A. to Governor, 10 April 1959, MN 1/4, Vol. I, Box 1672, Lusaka Archives.

[2] Circular from C.S. to all P.C.s and D.C.s, 22 December 1958, ibid.

[3] M.N.A. to Governor, 10 April 1959, ibid.

[4] *Report of the Nyasaland Commission of Inquiry*, Cmd. 814, 1959, pp. 54–73.

[5] *Rhodesia Herald*, 27 February 1959.

[6] *Northern News*, 27 February 1959.

Northern Rhodesia's Europeans took a different view. As a result of extreme speeches given by Kaunda and Sipalo, and frightened by events in Nyasaland, u.f.p. branches in Lusaka, Ndola and Kitwe cabled the Chief Secretary demanding Government action to prevent further inflammatory outbursts by z.a.n.c. leaders. The d.p., taking the same line, accused z.a.n.c.'s leaders of displaying 'criminal tendencies'.[1] On the other hand, the Government's monthly security reports for January and February indicated no significant increase in violence, despite rumours to the contrary in Central and Western Provinces.[2] Nevertheless, it was undoubtedly true that Kaunda's speeches had become more extreme, and z.a.n.c. experienced greater difficulty obtaining permission from the police to hold public meetings. In mid-February Kaunda asserted that z.a.n.c.'s policy for 1959 was to warn the Government three times on any contentious issue before taking positive action. If the Government banned z.a.n.c., the remnants of the party would go underground and its spirit would live on until the achievement of independence.[3] On 9 March z.a.n.c. officials, having been refused police permission, held an unauthorized public meeting in Lusaka. Kaunda announced the beginning of z.a.n.c.'s defiance campaign. The party was 'unalterably opposed' to the Constitution, he declared, and so long as other parties were allowed to hold public meetings z.a.n.c. would do so as well, with or without permission from the police.[4]

By late February the Government clearly feared the possible effects of z.a.n.c.'s boycott campaign. In an effort to discredit z.a.n.c.'s policies and leadership and to instil determination in African voters to go to the polls, the Government produced a special leaflet entitled, 'Don't Be Anybody's Stooge'. Though the leaflet was directed primarily at voters, it was issued both in English and in the major vernacular languages; District Commissioners were instructed to seek 'rather wider distribution'.[5]

Meanwhile, careful preparations began for the banning of

[1] *Northern News*, 20 February 1959.
[2] m.i.r., January, February and March, S/S 123/2/01 and /8/01.
[3] *Northern News*, 16 February 1959.
[4] Ibid., 10 March 1959.
[5] Circular from c.s. to all p.c.s and d.c.s, 21 February 1959, MS/2615/16, Box 4352, Lusaka Archives.

z.a.n.c. At an Executive Council meeting on 6 March the decision was taken to prepare orders for the ban on z.a.n.c. under section 21(2) of the Societies Ordinance.[1] A detailed report of a private z.a.n.c. meeting on 2 March at Kitwe provided evidence of z.a.n.c.'s immediate intentions. The report claimed that various provincial-level officials believed that the Government had been deceived by z.a.n.c.'s constitutional policy of non-violence. These same officials believed that the positive-action campaign, which according to the reports was planned by z.a.n.c's leaders at Accra, would be impossible for the Government to control. African candidates and voters who participated in the elections would be assaulted or if necessary assassinated. A. J. Soko, z.a.n.c.'s secretary for Western Province, was quoted: 'We are the elephants of this country, prisons are our playing fields and death is our game.'[2] The Government also knew that Kaunda and Sipalo had visited Eastern Province in early March at the height of the Nyasaland disturbances to meet Banda and other Nyasaland nationalists, a plan which was frustrated by the Nyasaland emergency on 3 March.[3]

On 11 March the Governor, acting under the authority of section 2(1) of the Emergency Powers Ordinance, issued the Safeguard of Elections and Public Safety Regulations, 1959.[4] z.a.n.c.'s leaders were arrested in the early hours of 12 March and immediately rusticated to various remote areas. The Governor also declared z.a.n.c. and all its registered branches in the Territory illegal under section 21(2) of the Societies Ordinance.[5] Other z.a.n.c. branches were also treated as unlawful, since they had not applied for registration under the Ordinance.[6]

Benson, defending the Government's action in a radio broadcast, referred to a joint plan for violent revolution in Central Africa, which he alleged had been prepared by the Federation's nationalist leaders at the Accra Conference of 1958. However, Benson carefully distinguished between z.a.n.c. and a.n.c.,

[1] Exec. Co., 6 March 1959, S/S 82/81/01.
[2] s.b. to c.s., 9 March 1959, S/S 201/07.
[3] p.c.(e.p.) to c.s., 5 March 1959; and m.i.r., March 1959, DG 58/3/01.
[4] Government Notice No. 81, of 1959.
[5] *Northern News*, 13 March 1959.
[6] *Ridley Report*, 1959, p. 8.

claiming that Nkumbula had left Ghana early and refused to take part in the proposed plan. In fact, Benson went so far as to attribute the A.N.C.-Z.A.N.C. split to this disagreement between Kaunda and Nkumbula, ignoring the fact that the split had taken place nearly two months before the Accra Conference.[1]

According to the Governor, the nationalists' plan consisted of three distinct phases: the first was to be widespread civil disobedience; the second, the provocation and 'stretching' of the forces of law and order; the third, outright revolution, which aimed at violent attacks on persons in authority, as well as the killing of Africans, Asians, and Europeans who resisted the imposed order. The first stage had been reached in Northern Rhodesia, Benson claimed, and in Nyasaland the plan had already 'gone off at half cock'. Nyasaland's leaders, he reported, had already met Kaunda and Sipalo and encouraged them to follow Nyasaland's example; z.A.N.C., however, was not yet prepared, though its plans were expected to be completed by mid-March. Already, z.A.N.C. had spread uncertainty and fear in the country to prevent registered Africans from voting in the elections; but this, claimed Benson, was only what z.A.N.C. had done in public. In private, in the villages and towns at night, z.A.N.C. had instituted a virtual reign of terror, threatening women and children with death, 'invoking witchcraft and unmentionable cursings'. Benson then made his well-known comparison between z.A.N.C. and Chicago's 'organization of killers' of the 1930's, 'Murder Incorporated'.[2]

Thus z.A.N.C. was decapitated in one swift blow. Scattered incidents of violence and arson followed both in Lusaka and Broken Hill and in Northern and Luapula Provinces.[3] With z.A.N.C. 'safely out of harm's way', as Roberts put it,[4] the election campaign moved to its climax. Benson noted a 'surge' of African confidence after the Government's action, though he feared the new confidence might collapse before the 20th. Accordingly posters were issued encouraging people to vote and reminding them that the police reserve would be out in full strength on polling day to keep order.[5]

[1] *Northern News*, 13 March 1959.
[2] Ibid.
[3] *Ridley Report*, 1959, pp. 25–29.
[4] *Northern News*, 13 March 1959.
[5] Governor to c.s., 14 March 1959, MS/2615/16, Box 4352, Lusaka Archives.

In the event, the election was held without serious incident. Voting was heavy among Africans, who recorded an average poll among 'special' voters of 85.7 per cent. European apathy, which had marked the entire campaign, held the percentage poll among 'ordinary' voters down to 61.2 per cent. The u.f.p. won thirteen of the twenty-two elected seats, eleven 'ordinary' and both African reserved seats. The c.a.p. secured the two European reserved constituencies as well as one of the 'special' seats. Nkumbula won South-Western for a.n.c., and the d.p.'s candidate upset his u.f.p. opponent by a majority of five votes in Southern 'ordinary' constituency. The two remaining 'special' constituencies contested were both won by African independents.[1] The party and racial composition of the Legislative Council's elected membership immediately after the general election is shown below.[2]

Legislative Council, March 1959
Composition of Elected Members by Party and by Race

Party	Number of Members	Africans	Europeans
U.F.P.	13	2	11
C.A.P.	3	1	2
A.N.C.	1	1	
D.P.	1		1
Independents	2	2	
	—	—	—
Total	20*	6	14

* Two 'special' seats for which there were no nominations at the time of the general election are excluded here. In subsequent by-elections Africans won both seats.

In forming the new Government, the Governor was bound to consult and pay due regard to the advice of the majority party's leader before selecting the six unofficial ministers for the Executive Council.[3] The Constitution provided that two unofficial ministers be Africans, a requirement the u.f.p. could

[1] *Analysis of Polling on 20 March 1959*, Secretariat, Lusaka, 1959, author's collection.
[2] Mulford, David C., *The Northern Rhodesia General Election, 1962*, Oxford, 1964, p. 147.
[3] A point of clarification announced by the Colonial Secretary, *Northern News*, 19 December 1958.

fulfil because of its victories in both African reserved constituencies. Roberts naturally pressed for all six unofficial posts, a
demand which, if satisfied, would have given the U.F.P. its first
clear majority in the Executive Council. However, the U.F.P.
had failed to win an overall majority in the thirty-member
Legislative Council, and in forming his Government the
Governor appointed only five U.F.P. elected members and one
nominated African unofficial member.[1] Thus, the balance between officials and elected members was maintained.

The 1959 election produced two developments of fundamental importance for the future of Northern Rhodesia
politics. The first was the failure of the Benson Constitution,
despite the large turnout of African voters on polling day. The
second was the dramatic rise of Z.A.N.C. and the whole question
of the Government's repressive action against the party.

Voting analysis by constituencies revealed two noteworthy
patterns, both with serious implications for the 'non-racial' aims
of the Constitution. In 'ordinary' and European reserved constituencies, where Africans were forced to choose between
European candidates, the U.F.P. failed to attract African votes.
The U.F.P.'s share of the total 'special' vote amounted to only
6 per cent, lower than any other party or group, whereas the
U.F.P.'s right-wing rival, the D.P., secured 12 per cent. Indeed,
during the campaign Nkumbula had instructed Africans in
constituencies without A.N.C. candidates to vote for any candidate, irrespective of his party affiliation, who opposed the
U.F.P. In the two European reserved constituencies, where C.A.P.
candidates defeated both their U.F.P. opponents, the U.F.P.
secured only 120 of the 2,708 'special' votes cast. The U.F.P.'s
African candidates in 'special' constituencies fared no better;
in Eastern 'special', where four candidates shared 714 'special'
votes, the U.F.P.'s nominee came last with a mere 17 votes.[2]

The second pattern—the disproportionate influence of
'ordinary' votes in constituencies returning Africans—was far
more important than the first, because of the adverse effect on
African attitudes towards the Constitution. European 'ordinary'
voters exercised a decisive influence on the results in both
African reserved constituencies. In the Copperbelt seat,

[1] *Northern News*, 26 March 1959.
[2] *Analysis of Polling*, 26 March 1959, author's collection.

Katilungu led the field among Africans with 855 'special' votes; in addition, he received 1,819 'ordinary' votes, primarily from Asians and Africans, for a total poll of 2,674 votes. Yet the U.F.P.'s Musumbulwa, who polled only 67 'special' votes, won the seat easily on the strength of 4,384 'ordinary' votes from the U.F.P.'s white supporters. The other two African independents, Puta and Sokota, finished far behind, despite the fact that both heavily outscored Musumbulwa among Africans with 262 and 124 'special' votes respectively. In South Central, Chileshe suffered an even harsher fate. Though the U.F.P.'s Kazokah polled only 32 'special' votes, compared with Chileshe's 984, Kazokah won the seat by 3,404 votes to 2,102 for Chileshe.[1]

Against such blatant examples of white influence, it made little difference that the U.F.P.'s candidates in Barotseland and Eastern 'special' constituencies were both defeated. Indeed, here, too, white 'ordinary' voters were disproportionately influential, but 'special' voters predominated generally and were able to reverse the pattern. The best the U.F.P. could manage was second place among three candidates in Barotseland. In Eastern, however, A.N.C.'s C. J. Banda was defeated by the C.A.P.'s Gondwe, largely on the combined strength of 'ordinary' Asian, Coloured, and European votes.[2]

The only constituencies in which a significant number of 'special' votes had to be devalued, as provided for by the Constitution, were the European reserved constituencies, Eastern and Western Rural. In both cases the final result was not affected. Moffat and Franklin, the C.A.P.'s two leading figures, received overwhelming African support, Franklin outscoring even his U.F.P. opponent among 'ordinary' voters. Nevertheless, the devaluation was so large in both constituencies that it would have been impossible for an African party to contest the seats with European candidates.[3]

Africans were quick to grasp what had happened, and a wave of discontent swept the country. A.N.C. expressed bitter disappointment at the failure both of its own candidates and those it had supported, alleging that the election had been 'rigged' by an unfair Constitution.[4] Katilungu, too, was bitterly angry about his defeat in the Copperbelt seat and it was thought that

[1] *Analysis of Polling*, 26 March 1959, author's collection. [2] Ibid. [3] Ibid.
[4] M.I.R., April 1959, S/S 123/2/01, /7/01 and /8/01.

the A.M.W.U. might hereafter respond more readily to A.N.C. offers of co-operation. The Provincial Administration in Western Province regarded the adverse African reaction to the election results as a serious problem. The feeling that Africans had been tricked was not confined solely to A.N.C. members, and the Provincial Administration feared what it thought would be the repercussions on African attitudes towards the Constitution and the Government.

It was assumed by Africans that the object of the reserved seat was to ensure for Copperbelt Africans direct representation in the legislature, and Musumbulwa's easy victory, despite the almost 100% African poll from which only a handful of votes are believed to have gone to Musumbulwa, is said to demonstrate that even with the support of the anti-U.F.P. votes cast by members of other races the African vote is powerless against the European vote.[1]

At A.N.C.'s first National Assembly after the election, Nkumbula's leadership was challenged by Solomon Kalulu. Kalulu suggested that since Nkumbula's duties as a M.L.C. would limit the time he could devote to the party, he should be replaced and made honorary Life President. Nkumbula challenged and defeated Kalulu's proposals in the presence of the delegates, forcing Kalulu to resign as Treasurer-General and leave the party. The Assembly was in a militant mood. Nkumbula condemned the policy of moderation, which, he said, the British Government regarded as a sign of weakness. The campaign against the Constitution was to be intensified; proposals for a delegation to London were rejected as outworn and ineffective. Besides, it was argued, the African public would certainly resist calls to support still another London delegation. In the end, the Assembly drew up a petition to the Colonial Secretary which denounced the Constitution as a fraud. A mass procession was planned to deliver the protest to the Secretariat, but the police refused to grant the necessary permit on the ground that as long as Nkumbula was a M.L.C. he had ample opportunity to submit the protest himself.[2]

The hardening of African attitudes against the Constitution was only partly due to the failure of the Constitution itself. In retrospect, the Government's harsh action against Z.A.N.C. was

[1] M.I.R., April 1959, S/S 123/8/01.   [2] M.I.R., April 1959, S/S 123/2/01.

the election's most significant event, though its implications for
the Constitution were not immediately apparent. When Kaunda
left A.N.C. he had been forced to start almost from scratch.
Z.A.N.C.'s headway since October 1958, despite government
anxiety over the threatened boycott, had been limited, except
perhaps in Ndola, Broken Hill, and certain areas of the north.
However, none of these areas was contested by Africans in the
general elections. As for Z.A.N.C.'s propaganda and the speeches
of its leaders, they had undoubtedly been extreme. But the
Government knew in late February that Z.A.N.C.'s ability to
carry out its threats was severely limited.[1] Indeed, the Western
Province intelligence report for early March indicated that:
'Despite the many rumours circulating and the propaganda
put out by the Z.A.N.C. only minor incidents, conceivably per-
petrated by the Z.A.N.C. have occurred.'[2]

The Government's action against Z.A.N.C. on 12 March,
though effective at the time, produced long-term results which
weakened the Government's position. Z.A.N.C. had been be-
stowed suddenly with an element of martydom, which set its
leaders distinctly apart from and well above all other Northern
Rhodesia nationalists. In addition, the restriction of Z.A.N.C.'s
leaders to rural districts under conditions which allowed them
to move about freely in their respective areas provided new
opportunities for agitation, often in areas which had previously
been noted for their political quiescence.[3]

It is important to be clear about the Government's reasons
for banning Z.A.N.C. at the time the action was taken. This is
particularly necessary because in June 1959, three months after
the banning, the Government published a *Report of an Inquiry
Into All the Circumstances Which Gave Rise to the Making of the
Safeguard of Elections and Public Safety Regulations, 1959* (the
Ridley Report), which sought to establish the case against
Z.A.N.C. and to justify the Government's action. The Report
amassed considerable evidence, mainly from Special Branch
sources, most of it indicating that Z.A.N.C. was a highly militant
nationalist organization. The Report dealt with Z.A.N.C.'s

[1] M.I.R., February 1959, S/S 123/2/01.
[2] Ibid., March 1959, S/S 123/8/01.
[3] Report on Barotseland, S.B. to Ad. Sec., 22 December 1962, DG 58/1/01;
M.I.R., May 1959, DG 58/6/01.

formation and early activities and confirmed z.a.n.c.'s intention to boycott the general election. Heavy emphasis was placed on the activities of Kaunda and Sipalo, especially at the Accra Conference and afterwards, as well as on the alleged agreement between Central Africa's nationalist leaders to launch a coordinated 'civil disobedience campaign' throughout the Federation. The Report established, though not very effectively, that z.a.n.c. planned to use violent methods, including arson and attacks on Africans and Europeans, to achieve its aims.[1] Despite the mass of evidence, some totally irrelevant,[2] the Report never established that z.a.n.c. actually resorted to violence before being banned. The fact that z.a.n.c. supporters resorted to violence in several instances afterwards corroborated, so far as Ridley was concerned, earlier reports and evidence of z.a.n.c.'s violent intentions. The fact remains, however, that the Government had months to prepare its case against z.a.n.c. and it is not clear how much or precisely what material was known to the Government at the time it took action.

Though the Government subsequently destroyed the material from which the Report was compiled, enough evidence remains to provide quite a different account of the Government's action. z.a.n.c. undoubtedly posed a threat to the success of the election and therefore to the Constitution itself. Despite z.a.n.c.'s propaganda and the militant outbursts of its leaders, the Government knew that z.a.n.c. was not well enough organized to precipitate major violence.[3] Indeed, if limited violence had occurred, the Report conceded that 'individual actions could be and were dealt with under the ordinary law'.[4] Throughout

---

[1] The translation of a lengthy manuscript on the Action Group, which was recovered by the police on 16 March 1959 (Annexure III), provides an example. Though the manuscript's content is violent, it is not clear which nationalist party produced the document. There is no reference at all to z.a.n.c., which usually referred to itself as Zambia, though the word Congress, usually applicable to a.n.c., appears several times. The author of the manuscript is not named, nor is the date of its composition. Since neither the election nor the boycott is mentioned, it is perfectly possible that the manuscript was written by an a.n.c. man before the split in October 1958. *Ridley Report*, 1959, p. 46.

[2] Such as providing the figures for arson cases in Lusaka for the period 5 June to 3 October 1958, before z.a.n.c. was formed, in an attempt to support the argument that such incidents had a political motive. The motive is not specified. Ibid., p. 13.

[3] m.i.r., March 1959, S/S 123/2/01 and /8/01.

[4] *Ridley Report*, 1959, p. 33.

January and February 1959 the Press, apart from several reports of speeches given by Kaunda and Sipalo, recorded no important incidents which involved Z.A.N.C. Even the Government's own monthly intelligence at the time reported not only that Z.A.N.C. was too weak to carry out its violent aims but that the number of violent incidents was not unusually large and that in any case Z.A.N.C.'s responsibility for any such incidents was doubtful.[1]

On 26 February the Government announced that the political situation in Northern Rhodesia did not warrant the declaration of a state of emergency. From Eastern Province it was reported that as of 5 March the violence in Nyasaland had not spilled over into Northern Rhodesia; nor had Z.A.N.C.'s leaders succeeded in meeting the leaders of the Nyasaland African National Congress.[2] Undoubtedly, by early March the Government knew that violence was being discussed at private Z.A.N.C. meetings, though this in itself was nothing new in Northern Rhodesia politics. Against these reports stood Kaunda's public statement of 5 March reminding Z.A.N.C. members of the party's policy of non-violence and ordering them to refrain from interfering with voters or appearing near polling booths on election day.[3]

By early March events in Central Africa suggested that it was not only African organizations which had formed a united front. Welensky met the Governors of Northern Rhodesia and Nyasaland, the Southern Rhodesia Prime Minister and the Federal Governor-General on 20 February to plan concerted action against the build-up of nationalist activity in all three territories.[4] Emergencies were subsequently declared according to plan in both Southern Rhodesia and Nyasaland.[5] The Federal Government stood firmly behind the actions of both territorial Governments, which was perfectly understandable. The 1958 Federal election had been fought on the issue of greater independence for the Federation in 1960, and nothing posed a graver threat to the Federation's future than the rapid rise of militant nationalist parties in the northern territories.

[1] M.I.R., March 1959, S/S 123/8/01.
[2] P.C.(E.P.) to C.S., 5 March 1959, DG 58/3/01.
[3] *Ridley Report*, 1959, p. 18.
[4] Welensky, Sir R., *Welensky's 4,000 Days*, p. 116.
[5] Ibid., p. 118.

Thus one must ask whether the action of the three territorial Governments was part of a carefully planned attempt to decapitate major nationalist parties in Central Africa simultaneously in order to ensure the future survival of the Federation. The Northern Rhodesia evidence overwhelmingly supports this view. Furthermore, the main impetus appears to have come from the Colonial Office, backed by the Commonwealth Relations Office, rather than directly from Welensky and the Federal Government. An angry letter from Benson to the Colonial Office on 11 March, written after Welensky had given an aggressive speech on the Copperbelt about the Federation's determination to achieve independence in 1960, sets out the position clearly.

I enclose the front page of today's *Northern News*. You will see that Welensky, knowing fully all our plans, having talked to me for a quarter of an hour in the most cooperative way at Lusaka Airport yesterday on his way through to Kitwe, knowing that the one thing which everyone of our best Africans in this territory is scared about is independence in 1960, yet finds it necessary to talk about the Federal Government's determination on independence in 1960 on the very eve of our putting our plans into operation.

Nothing could be more calculated to wreck our plans. Nothing could be more calculated—and I say it is deliberately calculated, because whatever else he is he is not a moron—to persuade thousands of Africans to sympathize with the Zambia leaders. He knows that our plans have been based on the belief that if we declare Zambia to be an illegal society and put out of harm's way the fifty main leaders, the vast bulk of our Africans will be pleased and the few thousands on the fringe will at worst sit tight and gradually come over to our side. As a result of Welensky's talk at this particular moment about independence those few thousands will be very sharply pushed the other way and the vast bulk of our Africans will at best be miserably unhappy.

If we have bloodshed now as a result of going through with our plans the major share of the responsibility will rest fairly and squarely on Welensky's shoulders.

This speech, made in Southern Rhodesia, would have been enough. Made in Northern Rhodesia it is criminal. Made in Northern Rhodesia on the eve of our operation it is sadistic and evil. He is due to address a meeting in Broken Hill on Monday the 16th, and he could have made it then. The elections do not come off until the 20th March.

I shall be grateful if the Secretary of State could see this letter. Because of one of his telegrams to me I would like him to rest assured that neither on this subject, nor on the campaign which he mounted against me to declare a full scale emergency, has anything been said or will be said by me save to him and his advisers in the Colonial Office.[1]

Several points seem clear beyond all reasonable doubt. First, the theory, so clearly expressed in Benson's letter, that militant African nationalism could be stamped out in Northern Rhodesia (and presumably in the Federation as a whole) appears to have been widely accepted in the British Government as well as in Central Africa. Second, it was obvious that London, Salisbury, and Lusaka (and undoubtedly Zomba) all co-operated closely in the execution of a complicated and highly controversial action which embraced Central Africa as a whole. Third, the impetus for this kind of action clearly had not originated in Northern Rhodesia. Benson's aim—and this explains his intense anger over Welensky's speech—was to destroy a political party which, if not prevented from gaining mass African support, would pose a serious threat to the Federation itself. Benson's letter confirms that he successfully opposed the Colonial Office's demands for a full state of emergency of the Southern Rhodesia and Nyasaland variety in Northern Rhodesia. Finally, there was Welensky's role, which strongly suggests a powerful Salisbury–London axis, presumably with Lord Home and the Commonwealth Relations Office. This had been the pattern in the past, and Benson's letter had been passed on to Home immediately by the Colonial Secretary.[2] Within the Federation itself, Welensky took the initiative in co-ordinating the Government's actions, but it seems indisputably clear that in doing so he had not only the assent but the active support of the British Government.

The above explanation places the Ridley Report in quite a different light. While it remains useful as one interpretation of z.a.n.c. and its objectives in the period before the general election, the Report provides virtually no information of merit

[1] Author's collection.
[2] Welensky, Sir R., *Welensky's 4,000 Days*, p. 118.

about z.a.n.c.'s actual organization. z.a.n.c. was the most militant organization that Northern Rhodesia Africans had yet produced, and there is ample evidence for concluding that once z.a.n.c. had become well organized it would have been extremely difficult to control. But on this question the Report utterly failed to establish its case. The real reasons for the Government's action were concealed, and the question of why the Government had acted when it did was ignored. Any inquiry such as the Ridley Report invariably stands or falls on its essential credibility. Time would soon show that the Government, both in its ill-considered ban and its subsequent justification of that action, had seriously misunderstood the nature of African nationalism in Northern Rhodesia.

III

THE QUEST FOR AFRICAN UNITY

'ZAMBIA STILL EXISTS.'[1] The phrase was both a plea and a fact. Despite the ban and subsequent campaign against the remnants of Z.A.N.C., the Government was unable to crush the party completely. In Luapula Province, where vigorous action against party officials and members resulted in a large number of prosecutions—so many, in fact, that the jails were 'overflowing with convicted prisoners and detainees'—government officials conceded that Z.A.N.C.'s suppression could only be 'temporary'. Z.A.N.C.'s local officials refused to return to A.N.C., preferring instead to await the reappearance of Kaunda.[2] Even in September 1959 reports from Luapula indicated that Z.A.N.C.'s branch-level organization, though subdued, still remained intact, its activists quietly encouraging the popular belief that Z.A.N.C. would rise again.[3]

Part of the Government's problem was due to the fact that a number of Z.A.N.C. branches had never registered under the Societies Ordinance, while others, which had transferred their allegiance from A.N.C. to Z.A.N.C., continued to function under A.N.C. registration. Several Provincial Commissioners advocated banning A.N.C. branches that harboured Z.A.N.C. elements,[4] a proposal which found considerable support in Lusaka. Initially the Government's policy had been to act only against those A.N.C. branches which were obviously 'flying the Z.A.N.C. flag';[5] senior officials were reluctant to take action which might embitter A.N.C. and drive it from the moderate course it had

---

[1] Z.A.N.C. publication attached to letter from Registrar to C.S., 17 March 1959, S/S 82/81/01.

[2] M.I.R., April 1959, DG 58/4/01.

[3] S.B. to Ad. Sec., 22 September 1959, S/S 108/7/01.

[4] P.C.(N.W.P.) to C.S., 10 April 1959 and P.C.(E.P.) to C.S., 20 March 1959, S/S 82/81/01.

[5] A.S.(C.S.) 1 to C.S., 22 April 1959, ibid.

pursued since the split.[1] The Minister of Native Affairs advised his officials to adopt a wait-and-see attitude for the time being in the hope that branch officials might be prosecuted for specific local offences.[2]

The Government also encountered difficulties in attempting to prosecute known z.a.n.c. adherents individually under the Societies Ordinance. Under the terms of the Ordinance, it was necessary to prove: first, that the group to which the accused belonged was, in fact, a 'society' as defined in section 24(a) of the Ordinance (i.e. a group of ten or more persons which does exist or did exist at the time of the offence); second, that the accused was an office-bearer or manager, since it was not an offence simply to be a member, unless the accused acted as a member (e.g. paid a subscription, voted, canvassed support, carried or kept books).[3] Securing convictions proved exceedingly difficult, often because witnesses failed in court to abide by previous statements; hence a number of prosecutions failed, especially in Luapula Province. As usual, these failures produced complaints from the Provincial Administration that the position of Native Authorities was being undermined. In fact, field officers took the view that arresting z.a.n.c. supporters and failing to convict them was far more damaging than leaving them alone.[4]

Meanwhile, a.n.c. experienced something of a revival during April and May 1959. The party's National Assembly in early April condemned moderation and called both for better party organization and more militant action throughout the country. Nkumbula announced several new national and provincial appointments.[5] By late May government officials in all provinces except Barotseland reported an increase in a.n.c. activity as well as renewed militancy among lower level officials.[6] In Southern Province attempts were made to procure the appointment of a.n.c. men to Native Authority councils.[7] In Lusaka, on

[1] s.(m.n.a.) to m.n.a., 22 April 1959, ibid.
[2] m.n.a. to s.(m.n.a.), 24 April 1959, ibid.
[3] Judicial circular No. 16 of 1959, 29 June 1959, ibid.
[4] m.i.r., May 1959, DG 58/4/01.
[5] m.i.r., April 1959, S/S 123/2/01.
[6] m.i.r., April, May and June, S/S 123/2/01 through /8/01; and DG 58/2/01 through /8/01.
[7] m.i.r., May 1959, DG 58/7/01.

the Copperbelt and in Broken Hill, A.N.C. organized a campaign to test the colour bar in tea-rooms, hotels, swimming pools and churches in order to collect evidence of racial discrimination and the failure of Partnership for the 1960 Federal Review conference. A surge in A.N.C. activity was even reported in Kawambwa District of Luapula Province, where the old A.N.C. organization had followed Kaunda into Z.A.N.C. Mukupo, A.N.C.'s General Secretary and now a bitter opponent of the Benson Constitution, toured the Copperbelt in May, urging provincial leaders to improve their organization, to expand youth and action group activities and to prepare for trouble if the Constitution remained unchanged. Plans were also made for a delegation to London. Nkumbula issued a circular instructing branches to contribute £10 apiece, though for Luapula and Northern Provinces the required branch contribution was cut by half, a concession which frankly recognized A.N.C.'s weakness in the north.[1]

The pace of African politics was quickening in Northern Rhodesia. A.N.C.'s modest revival was based more on a general upsurge of African political awareness than it was on the efforts of the party itself. Indeed, as the pace quickened political alignments became more fluid: internal dissension reappeared in A.N.C.; new splinter groups emerged; Z.A.N.C. supporters continued to drift; restrictees established a broad network of contacts; and the African trade-union movement edged farther into the political arena. In short, an exhausting quest for African unity had begun, which in the coming months was to lead Northern Rhodesia's nationalist movement through bitter internecine strife. At the height of the struggle, September 1959, a future Zambian minister writing from restriction captured both the hope and the despair of a desperate situation.

But, and I don't know if I am pessimistic, one clear thing is that the nationalist movement has received a setback which will take years to correct. The only hope left in this gathering storm is the seeming awareness of the ordinary African to the danger of the Welensky-Settlerdom régime. . . . The post-mortem on the whole crisis seems to spotlight the fact that six years after the policy of Partnership was born some seventy-thousand settlers in the territory possess more power than its two million 700 thousand natives.

[1] M.I.R., S/S 123/2/01 and /8/01; also June 1959, DG 58/4/01.

If the objects of the Emergencies were to terrorise African sentiment into submission and break the hold the Congresses have upon African allegiance, it has failed ludicrously in both. Far from stilling African allegiance it has inflamed it; while by arresting moderates and radicals alike, it has offered its opponents the obduracy of extremes and linked them on the rack of Congress martyrdom. Above all, it has left the avenue of civil disobedience open to opposition, and stimulated the very violence against which it now pretends that it was obliged to protect itself.[1]

The Second A.N.C. Split: Preparations and Failure

The return of Katilungu from an International Confederation of Free Trade Unions Conference at Nairobi in May 1959 marked a new phase in relations between A.N.C. and the African trade-union movement in Northern Rhodesia. Katilungu, still bitter about his defeat in the March election, spoke out strongly against the colour bar. Labour Department officials whom he met soon afterwards attributed Katilungu's new militancy to his contacts with Tom Mboya in Kenya. During the course of these discussions, Katilungu claimed, reportedly in a state of great excitement, that it was time to suffer for human rights; that on such issues the trade unions would stand firm with political parties.[2] Katilungu also re-established friendly relations with Nkumbula. A series of meetings between the two leaders in May led to an agreement to intensify militant political activity on the basis of co-operation between political and trade-union organizations. The matter was taken a step further at a large private meeting on 5 June, where an A.N.C. delegation, led by Mukupo, and members of the A.T.U.C., headed by Katilungu, agreed to organize a full-scale conference of all African organizations in Northern Rhodesia.[3]

Meanwhile, Katilungu shared the platform with Nkumbula at numerous Copperbelt political meetings during June.[4] Katilungu's criticisms were not restricted solely to the copper companies and the Northern Rhodesia and Federal Governments. He urged A.N.C. to transfer its national headquarters to the

---

[1] Sikota Wina to Arthur Wina, 14 September 1959, A.N.L.W. papers.
[2] M.I.R., May 1959, S/S 123/8/01.
[3] Report on the 10th Annual Conference of N.R.A.N.C., 2 October 1959, TS/S 123/01.
[4] M.I.R., June and July 1959, S/S 123/8/01.

Copperbelt, because he believed that it was Copperbelt Africans who would lead the way to self-government.[1] A.N.C., he claimed, was a weak political party, and strike action was essential before Africans could hope to achieve independence and the break-up of the Federation.[2] Though Nkumbula did not accede to Katilungu's suggestions regarding A.N.C.'s national headquarters, he consistently emphasized the need for unity between A.N.C. and the A.M.W.U., predicting that strikes and boycotts would begin soon.[3]

Boycotts were also a popular topic of discussion among A.N.C. officials in Central Province. The party's Provincial Conference in Lusaka on 8 and 9 June produced a lengthy list of resolutions covering a wide range of national and local issues, including boycotts. In addition to the usual demands for self-government and Northern Rhodesia's secession from the Federation, several resolutions were directed against the local Indian community. One demanded that Indian bus inspectors employed by Central African Road Services (C.A.R.S.) be replaced by Africans, while another called for the removal of all Indians trading in rural areas. The conference also expressed alarm at the Governor's decision to appoint an Indian to the Legislative Council after the March elections. Lusaka's Chamber of Commerce was urged to seek price reductions in local shops, or alternately to put pressure on employers to raise African wages. Still another resolution called on the Municipal Council to allow Africans to run their own beerhalls on a rental basis. Finally, the conference announced that if its demands went unheeded boycotts would be organized against European and Indian shops, C.A.R.S., and the beerhalls. Simultaneously, Africans would be urged to refuse to pay taxes and to return their identity certificates (situpas) to the Government.[4]

In late May the first of several small splinter groups appeared, the African National Independence Party (A.N.I.P.).[5] A.N.I.P. was founded by Kalichini, Z.A.N.C.'s ex-Deputy President, and Frank Chitambala, one of Z.A.N.C.'s restrictees recently released

[1] S.B. to C.S., 25 June 1959, TS/S 123/01.
[2] Ibid., 17 June 1959.
[3] M.I.R., July 1959, S/S 123/8/01.
[4] M.I.R., June 1959, S/S 123/2/01; Northern News, 9 and 11 June 1959.
[5] M.I.R., May 1959, DG 58/8/01.

from Balovale District in North-Western Province, where a prosecution against him had failed.[1] A.N.I.P. was nothing more than
a fragment of Z.A.N.C. under a new name, but the Government
was quick to realize that other such groups might appear. On
18 June the Government issued a circular to the Provincial
Administration expressing concern that new political organizations of the A.N.I.P. type might attempt to take over assets
formerly belonging to Z.A.N.C. Under section 26 of the Societies
Ordinance the Governor-in-Council was empowered to order
that property of an unlawful society, both real and personal, be
invested in a duly appointed officer. Fourteen District Commissioners were appointed and instructed to confiscate, with as
little publicity as possible, Z.A.N.C. property, including cash in
banks or other deposit accounts, buildings, furniture, office
equipment, stationery, all records, and unused membership
cards. The officials were also instructed to discover if Z.A.N.C.
had outstanding debts, so that creditors might be paid out of
available assets at once.[2]

The outcome of this operation was almost completely fruitless. The reports which followed explained that Z.A.N.C.'s brief
existence had not enabled the party to establish 'the ordinary
machinery of office administration in many areas'. For the most
part, Z.A.N.C. had borrowed office equipment from its members,
most of which was destroyed in a fire at its Chilenje headquarters
on 23 March 1959. Fire had also destroyed Z.A.N.C.'s regional
office and a duplicating machine at Kasama in Northern Province. Pieces of corrugated iron found at the site, however, were
sold and several walls which remained standing were razed to
the ground. Z.A.N.C.'s monetary assets totalled only £5. 15s.,
and despite careful inquiries into private bank accounts, the
Government was unable to discover how Z.A.N.C. received and
held funds from overseas, which were used to pay expenses for
the trials of its restrictees.[3]

After Chitambala's release, he immediately attacked Nkumbula, claiming that he had 'gone soft' and was receiving a salary
from the Government.[4] Several other instances of dissatisfaction

[1] M.I.R., DG 58/6/01.
[2] C.S. to all P.C.s and D.C.s, 18 June 1959, S/S 82/81/03.
[3] Registrar to C.S., 19 October 1959, ibid.
[4] S.B. to C.S., 17 June 1959, TS/S 123/01.

QUEST FOR AFRICAN UNITY

with Nkumbula appeared about the same time. Nkumbula was criticized by A.N.C. officials in Livingstone for failing to make a promised visit to the town. The officials decided to send a delegation to Lusaka to inform Nkumbula that unless he paid a visit soon they would quit A.N.C. and join A.N.I.P.[1] In Eastern Province, shortly after Chitambala and Chapala Banda returned from restriction, a meeting of A.N.C.'s youth league called for Nkumbula's immediate resignation and attacked both the party's colour bar campaign and the proposed delegation to London.[2]

By July 1959 more serious dissension in A.N.C. emerged, largely over two issues: boycotts and the proposed unification conference of all African organizations tentatively scheduled for September. Meeting privately with Nkumbula on 26 June, Mukupo and Haswell Mwale, then A.N.C.'s General Treasurer, expressed their concern at Nkumbula's lack of interest in A.N.C. since becoming a M.L.C. and suggested that he step down from the presidency. Nkumbula threatened to resign and seek re-election by convening the National Assembly. But before Nkumbula could act, the boycott issue in Lusaka came to a head. As expected, C.A.R.S. refused to replace Indian bus inspectors with Africans, but what had not been anticipated was the sudden and incomprehensible change in Nkumbula's position. On 30 June, together with several independent African M.L.C.s, he issued a press statement condemning the proposed boycotts on the ground that there should be no job reservation on racial lines. Such action would only alienate C.A.R.S. and the Indian community; as an alternative, Nkumbula suggested that the matter should be pursued through the appropriate trade union. Then, as if his sudden reversal were not dramatic enough, Nkumbula denied all knowledge of the boycott plan, claiming that he had learned of it only recently from a journalist.[3]

Nkumbula's press statement angered his colleagues and provoked the first serious move against him since 1958. Central Province and national officials were bitter, since Nkumbula himself, they alleged, had put forward the original plan at the Provincial Conference in early June. Though some officials

[3] M.I.R., July 1959, S/S 123/2/01.
[2] M.I.R., June 1959, S/S 123/3/01.
[1] M.I.R., May 1959, S/S 123/7/01.

favoured implementing the full boycott plan in direct opposition
to Nkumbula, in the end a token boycott of Indian shops was
decided on to protest against the nomination of an Indian to the
Legislative Council. The boycott lasted only one week, but the
movement against Nkumbula was gathering momentum. An
action group meeting on 4 July in Lusaka, probably staged by
Mukupo, who now believed African unity under Nkumbula's
leadership to be impossible, called for Nkumbula's resignation.
Two days later Mukupo discussed with Kalichini the possibility
of uniting A.N.C. and A.N.I.P. Both leaders agreed on the necessity
of unifying all African groups. A.N.C., A.N.I.P., and the remnants
of Z.A.N.C. were joined by still another splinter group in late
May, the United National Freedom Party (U.N.F.P.), which was
formed by the R.A.W.U.'s President, Dixon Konkola. Kalichini
laid down specific conditions for any proposed merger, which
stipulated that M.L.C.s should not be allowed to hold office in a
united organization, that a non-violence clause should be excluded from the new constitution, and that restricted persons,
even those in prison (as Kaunda was after being convicted in
June for holding an unlawful meeting), should be eligible for
election.[1]

On 11 July Nkumbula retaliated, suspending eight national
and Central Province officials, including Mukupo, ostensibly
for their part in initiating the boycott of Indian shops without
the President's permission. Mukupo and his colleagues disregarded their suspension, and Nkumbula established an action
group guard around A.N.C.'s headquarters to prevent the suspended officials from returning to the office.[2] Mukupo now
admitted openly the existence of a united and determined
movement to depose Nkumbula and to absorb the various
splinter groups. 'The idea', he claimed, 'is not to break away
into another organization—only to get Nkumbula out. . . .
His incompetent leadership is responsible for the lack of united
nation-wide action.' To achieve this, Mukupo said he was
prepared to split A.N.C. in half initially and then to fight, with
the help of men such as Kaunda, Konkola, and Kalichini, to
reunite the entire movement.[3]

[1] M.I.R., July 1959, S/S 123/2/01.
[2] Ibid.
[3] *Central African Post*, 17 July 1959.

In the meantime, Nkumbula issued a lengthy circular announcing an All-African Parties and Trades Union Conference, beginning in Lusaka on 10 September and sponsored by A.N.C. and the A.T.U.C. The objects of the proposed conference were to be the creation of a common African front in Northern Rhodesia against Federation, exploration of ways and means of achieving immediate self-government, a new election for the presidency of A.N.C. and consideration of another delegation to London to protest against the present Constitution. The circular also proposed that an All-Party Committee be formed, which would convene on 3 August to prepare for the main conference and which would conduct, during the interim period, all African political affairs on a co-operative basis. Nkumbula was careful to ensure A.N.C.'s control over the interim committee by stipulating that its composition should consist of sixteen members from A.N.C. and only four from the various splinter groups.

Mukupo immediately attacked Nkumbula's proposals, particularly the composition of the proposed interim committee, which, Mukupo argued, would inevitably repel the splinter organizations and lead to certain failure. Instead, he proposed that Northern Rhodesia's top six African leaders, two each from A.N.C., A.N.I.P., and the U.N.F.P., should meet and agree on the composition of a representative sponsoring committee. This body could then act as the leaders' preparatory committee to organize the September conference on unification. Mukupo stressed the importance of achieving African unity quickly and urged Nkumbula to disregard his personal interests and to approach the unification question as a matter of national importance. Mukupo's letter was ignored.[1]

Nkumbula had apparently resumed the arbitrary behaviour which had periodically characterized his leadership in the past. In addition to the abrupt suspension of Mukupo and his colleagues, Nkumbula again began to disregard appointments, arriving hours late for public meetings or failing to attend altogether. On the Copperbelt he quickly lost sympathy.[2] Ndola's district executive expressed concern about the quarrel between Nkumbula and his officials in Lusaka, the majority placing the blame on Nkumbula and his autocratic methods. It was agreed

[1] Report on A.N.C.'s Annual Conference, 2 October 1959, TS/S 123/01.
[2] M.I.R., July 1959, DG 58/8/01.

that Ndola beerhalls should be boycotted without Nkumbula's
consent to test his reaction and thus to clarify the national
leadership question. Nkumbula's behaviour again alienated
Katilungu and several other trade unionists who shared his
desire for a strong and united nationalist movement.[1]

Katilungu set about repairing his relations with the Government. At a lengthy private meeting in Kitwe on 18 July with the
Senior Provincial Commissioner, Katilungu outlined his political views. The Provincial Commissioner reported that Katilungu was obsessed with the 1960 Federal review and believed
that African public opinion was completely unprepared for the
approaching showdown with Welensky. No single group or
party capable of representing Africans existed in Northern
Rhodesia, and Katilungu feared that the British Government
would accept 'stooges' or even U.F.P. Africans as the spokesmen
for African opinion. He condemned Z.A.N.C. for resorting to
violence and intimidation—'the maddest of actions' he maintained, if Africans wished to demonstrate their understanding of
constitutional procedures. A.N.C. was no better: the party was
in uproar, and most district and branch officials were irresponsible loafers both by trade and performance. Katilungu explained
that in recent months he had attempted to build up Nkumbula
as the only leader available with sufficient reputation to act as
the Africans' spokesman in 1960, but Nkumbula, he concluded,
was incapable of adequately filling the role. Further support for
him could only damage Katilungu's own position. The fact was
that Africans were further from having a spokesman for 1960
than ever before.[2]

The Government was quick to seize the opportunity; within
two weeks the Chief Secretary proposed that Katilungu be considered for appointment to the Advisory Commission to review
the Federal Constitution (the Monckton Commission). Apart
from the obvious advantage of having a man like Katilungu
represent Northern Rhodesia Africans in 1960, the Government
believed the appointment would remove Katilungu from active
politics.[3] Though government officials did not appreciate it at

---

[1] M.I.R., August 1959, S/S 123/8/01.
[2] Report of meeting between Senior P.C.(W.P.) and Katilungu, 18 July 1959,
DG 58/8/01.
[3] Ag. C.S. to Governor, 27 July 1959, ibid.

the time, the appointment would also take Katilungu away from trade-union affairs, a development they soon came to regret.

In response to the appearance of new splinter groups and the growing turbulence in nationalist politics, the Government during July also sought to improve its security arrangements. Particular attention was given to bringing the Societies Ordinance up to date.[1] For some weeks a stronger line had been taken against A.N.C. branches which the Government believed were controlled by Z.A.N.C. In North-Western Province the District Commissioner succeeded in getting an order passed by the Lundu Ndembu Native Authority banning A.N.C. in the Mwinilungu District, though in doing so he found it necessary to threaten Senior Chief Kanongesha with stoppage of his monthly subsidy and loss of title on the ground of age.[2] Subsequently it was decided not to apply a blanket ban in the district, but instead to ban selected branches under the Societies Ordinance on the ground that they had ceased to exist. The main branches in the district were then ordered, under section 17(1) of the Ordinance, to supply information regarding organization, membership, and finance. The Government's main objective, soon adopted as general policy, was to harass local party officials and to prosecute them if the information was not readily supplied in the hope of 'severing their relations with the law-abiding population'.[3] Where the Government was certain, however, as in Kasama District in early July, that A.N.C. branches had transferred their allegiance to Z.A.N.C., the branches were promptly banned.[4]

The Government hoped by its harassing tactics to build up information as well, primarily about branch-level organizations for use by the Special Branch. Little was known about the office-bearers of the various action group, youth brigade, and women's league formations because in the past such auxiliary groups had always been registered as integral parts of the branches.[5] The difficulties encountered in suppressing Z.A.N.C.,

[1] See correspondence between Registrar and Ag. c.s. during July 1959, S/S 82/81/01.
[2] D.C. (Mwinilungu) to P.C.(N.W.P.), 26 May 1959, ibid.
[3] Registrar to P.C.(N.W.P.), 4 July 1959, ibid.
[4] Ag. c.s. to Registrar, 2 July 1959, ibid.
[5] Registrar to Ag. c.s., 8 July 1959, ibid.

the emergence of new splinter groups, the threat to Nkumbula's leadership, as well as the large number of unregistered A.N.C. youth and action groups, caused concern among top government officials. An interesting attitude towards A.N.C. was revealed in a minute from the Registrar to the Acting Chief Secretary on 10 July. In questioning the effects of harassment on A.N.C., he acknowledged that: 'Now that Nkumbula seems likely to be deposed, it is possible that A.N.C. will become a much more formidable organization than . . . hitherto. But if it were to carry on as it has done in the past I feel . . . doubtful of the wisdom of using harassing tactics which might do nothing more than harden moderate Congress opinion against the Government.'[1]

Shortly afterwards a high-level meeting, which included various Secretariat officials and security officers, agreed on the policy to be adopted towards political parties, especially regarding application for registration under the Societies Ordinance. Applications had been received from A.N.I.P. and the U.N.F.P., both of which the Government regarded as open attempts to revive Z.A.N.C. Nevertheless, it was agreed that both parties should be registered at once, while most Z.A.N.C. leaders were still in restriction or in prison. The main arguments for registration were that new political parties should not be forced underground, or, equally undesirable, be encouraged to amalgamate or join other well-established political parties. A.N.I.P. and the U.N.F.P. reportedly opposed one another, and the Government was anxious not to discourage this enmity. The overriding factor in reaching agreement, however, was the advice of the Assistant Commissioner, Special Branch, who argued that if the Government wished to retain a measure of control over political parties, it was essential that as much information as possible be obtained under the Societies Ordinance. Similarly, on the question of the number of party branches which should be allowed to register in any one district, it was decided, as a general rule:

That on the assumption that a policy of 'divide and rule' would be more advantageous than limiting the number of branches in any one district, thus either causing branches to amalgamate or to operate covertly, it was decided to reject this suggestion [that of

[1] Registrar to Ag. C.S., 10 July 1959, S/S 82/81/01.

limiting the number of branches in an area] which was not supported by the Special Branch or the Registrar of Societies.[1]

The Government's policy of 'divide and rule' received a setback almost at once. On 1 August 1959 A.N.I.P. and the U.N.F.P. merged to form the United National Independence Party (U.N.I.P.).[2] Little is known about U.N.I.P.'s actual formation, though it seems likely that A.N.I.P. and U.N.F.P. leaders regarded this as a first step towards African unity, as well as a means of improving their negotiating position with Mukupo's A.N.C. group. In any case, a summit meeting was convened the same day between Mukupo's faction and U.N.I.P.'s leaders to discuss the question of African unity. The meeting included Kalichini, Chitambala, Kalulu, as well as Sykes Ndilia, and Amos Mweemba, both A.N.C., and Mukupo. Invitations were sent to a number of trade unionists, Katilungu, Mwendepole, and Puta, none of whom attended the conference.[3]

The meeting agreed that other political parties should not participate in A.N.C.'s proposed unity conference on the ground that Nkumbula was imposing his own conditions instead of referring the unity issue to a jointly sponsored summit conference. In addition, it was decided that efforts to depose Nkumbula should be continued, in part at least because Kalichini refused to consider accepting any A.N.C. splinter group into U.N.I.P. at that time. Mukupo agreed to remain within A.N.C. for the express purpose of ousting Nkumbula and installing a President acceptable to moderates and extremists alike, who would complete the amalgamation of all African organizations in the country. As a first step Mukupo promised to convene A.N.C.'s National Assembly immediately to remove Nkumbula from office. Mainza Chona, a lawyer recently returned from completing his studies in London, was selected as a suitable candidate to replace Nkumbula as interim President of A.N.C.[4]

On 15 August Mukupo announced that A.N.C.'s National Assembly would meet on 23 August to resolve the split in A.N.C. and to discuss unification with U.N.I.P. Mukupo's action, which

[1] Memorandum on consideration of applications for registration received from new political parties, 27 July 1959, ibid.

[2] Report on A.N.C.'s Annual Conference, 2 October 1959, TS/S 123/01.

[3] M.I.R., August 1959, S/S 123/2/01.

[4] Ibid.; and Report on A.N.C.'s Annual Conference, 2 October 1959, TS/S 123/01.

was supported by Mweemba and A. B. Chisanga, was challenged as unconstitutional by Nkumbula, who called a special meeting of both factions the following day to revoke Mukupo's circular. However, when the matter was put to vote, Mukupo was upheld by eighteen votes to sixteen, and the thirty-six National Assembly delegates convened as scheduled. The Assembly lasted for nearly a week. Feelings ran high as the two factions put their respective cases, with only a conciliatory speech on the 26th by Finess Bulawayo, a Copperbelt provincial official, preventing an open rupture. After a brief adjournment, Nkumbula thanked Bulawayo for his efforts and withdrew the suspension of Mukupo and his colleagues. Chona indicated his willingness to withdraw as a candidate for the presidency, and Nkumbula appeared to have won the day.

On 27 August the Assembly met to discuss union with u.n.i.p. Mukupo proposed that discussions with u.n.i.p. should begin immediately with a committee consisting of five representatives from each of the parties and two independent delegates, presumably representing the trade unions. In addition, he maintained that the presidents of both parties should resign and stand for re-election at the All-African Unity Conference in September. Nkumbula rejected both proposals, arguing that u.n.i.p. had only a few branches, no constitution, and therefore no specific policy, and that until he knew what course the new party would follow talks on unity were impossible. With this Nkumbula instructed the chairman to adjourn the Assembly indefinitely.

Mukupo then took the initiative, issuing notification to the delegates that the Assembly would reconvene the following day to continue its deliberations. When word of Mukupo's action reached Nkumbula, he called on his General Secretary and dismissed him from office. Mukupo's dismissal, however, did not prevent him from assembling seventeen of the thirty-six delegates, who immediately passed a resolution dismissing Nkumbula from the presidency. Though Nkumbula disregarded the Assembly's action as unconstitutional, Mukupo had secured an important tactical victory by isolating Nkumbula as the major obstacle in the way of African unity.[1] Indeed,

[1] M.I.R., August 1959, S/S 123/2/01; also see *Northern News* and *Central African Post* for period 23 August–1 September 1959.

Nkumbula was on the run, and he turned at once, as he had in the past, to the party at large and the African people. A National Assembly, he claimed, was not empowered to dismiss the President. Only a General Party Conference could take such action and this, he blandly announced, would convene on 10 September.[1]

The Two A.N.C.s and the Government's Choice

During the first fortnight of September the leaders of both A.N.C. factions urgently sought to consolidate their respective positions for the General Conference. Nkumbula and Chona departed independently for the Copperbelt;[2] Mukupo visited Eastern Province, distributing anti-Nkumbula pamphlets and attempting, without much success, to rouse the public at political meetings.[3] On the Copperbelt a bitter struggle developed. Chona, accompanied by Bulawayo, held a series of meetings, both private and public, at which Nkumbula was attacked and in one instance his photograph burned. Nkumbula's opponents preceded him almost everywhere and he found local officials unco-operative and in some cases openly hostile. On 2 September he arrived at a public meeting at Ndola only to discover that his name had been excluded from the list of speakers on the police permit, so that he was forced to stand mutely aside. Two days later he tried to cancel a public meeting at Chingola, where he was to debate against Chona, but local A.N.C. officials refused to co-operate and the crowd subsequently shouted anti-Nkumbula slogans in his absence.[4] Government officials reported that Nkumbula appeared to have lost the Copperbelt organization to the Mukupo-Chona group, with the exception of Mufulira and Twapia Township at Ndola. Despite the latter's success in building up a large following on the Copperbelt, Nkumbula, after his initial failures, wisely devoted his efforts to selecting loyal party officials as delegates to the conference.[5]

Tribal considerations assumed an increasingly prominent role as the conference approached. Southern Province remained

[1] *Northern News*, 2 September 1959.
[2] M.I.R., September 1959, S/S 123/8/01.
[3] Ibid., S/S 123/3/01.
[4] Ibid., S/S 123/8/01.
[5] Ibid., DG 58/8/01.

Nkumbula's private stronghold, though he undoubtedly controlled Lusaka and Eastern Province as well.[1] The previous A.N.C.–Z.A.N.C. split had effectively removed Nkumbula's support in Luapula and Northern Province; while in North-Western Province, where nationalist activity only recently had taken root, both A.N.C. and Z.A.N.C.–U.N.I.P. organizers were active and the situation remained confused, partly due to local tribal animosity between the Lunda and Lovale.[2]

Before departing for the Copperbelt, Nkumbula took steps to consolidate his position in Southern Province. Job Michello, the provincial secretary, replaced Mukupo as General Secretary; Amos Sichilaba, A.N.C.'s district secretary in Nkumbula's home area of Namwala, was appointed provincial secretary; and Mrs. Ruth Jere, provincial secretary of the women's league, was raised to national office. A.N.C.'s provincial and district-level officials remained completely loyal to Nkumbula, and every effort was made to encourage delegates to reach Lusaka for the conference. In Monze District alone, where Chona failed even to obtain a hearing, more than 200 delegates and £450 for delegates' fees were produced for the conference.[3]

When the conference opened on 11 September controversy broke out at once over the conditions laid down by Nkumbula for conference delegates. Though A.N.C.'s constitution called for two delegates from each branch, Nkumbula stipulated that each branch was entitled to nominate not less than two and not more than three delegates. That Nkumbula had followed his own directive was obvious: Southern Province's delegation numbered 400; Central Province's, 119; the Copperbelt, 90; Eastern Province's, 22; and Luapula only 4. Barotseland, Northern, and North-Western Province were not represented. In addition, Nkumbula required each delegate to pay a contingent fee of £3. 10s. and to produce a letter of authority signed by two branch officials.[4]

The Mukupo-Chona group had been outmanoeuvred. Armed with the new directives and backed by Nkumbula and hostile Tonga supporters from Southern Province, the con-

---

[1] Report on A.N.C.'s September Conference, 2 October 1959, TS/S 123/01.
[2] M.I.R., March–September 1959, DG 58/6/01, *passim*.
[3] M.I.R., September 1959, S/S 123/7/01.
[4] Report on A.N.C.'s Annual Conference, 2 October 1959, TS/S 123/01.

ference chairman refused to admit Mukupo's followers on the ground that they were not the accredited representatives of branches.[1] Mukupo, Chona, and several colleagues were granted admission, though naturally they refused, claiming, quite rightly, that the delegates' fee had been unconstitutionally levied by Nkumbula to exclude his opponents from the conference. In any case, the Mukupo-Chona group numbered no more than 120 delegates.[2]

With his opponents removed, Nkumbula sought to turn the conference into a major triumph. The opening speaker delivered a lengthy account of Nkumbula's version of the events leading up to the split. Mukupo's convening of the emergency National Assembly on 29 August was referred to as 'callous impertinence', which left Nkumbula no choice but to dismiss Mukupo and all the delegates who had participated. Other speakers echoed the charge of disloyalty against Mukupo and Chona, accusing them of attempting to pack the conference with Copperbelt youths to overthrow A.N.C.'s rightful leader.[3] On 12 September Nkumbula was unanimously re-elected to the presidency.[4]

Meanwhile, the Mukupo-Chona faction made the best of an unfavourable situation by removing several hundred yards to Kabwata's War Memorial Hall. Mukupo sent a lorry to collect U.N.I.P.'s leaders from their conference in Broken Hill in order to decide the next step. Kalichini reiterated U.N.I.P.'s unwillingness to absorb a splinter group of A.N.C.,[5] whereupon it was agreed that the Mukupo-Chona group would elect a new President and continue functioning under the title of A.N.C. Nkumbula would be named the Provincial President for Southern Province, and the issue of which group was the rightful A.N.C. would be settled in court.[6]

National officials were elected the next day, 13 September. Chona became President and Mukupo National Secretary; their respective deputies were Hankie Blackskin Kalanga and Mweemba. Andrew Banda was elected National Treasurer with Mwale as his deputy. Provincial office-bearers were also

[1] M.I.R., September 1959, S/S 123/2/01.
[2] Report on A.N.C.'s Annual Conference, 2 October 1959, TS/S 123/01.
[3] Ibid.   [4] M.I.R., September 1959, S/S 123/2/01.
[5] Ibid.
[6] Report on A.N.C.'s Annual Conference, 2 October 1959, TS/S 123/01.

appointed for all provinces except Barotseland. The conference then gave way to the National Assembly, which held a lengthy planning session. Priority was given to securing recognition as the rightful A.N.C. Chona and Mukupo, who were authorized to negotiate with U.N.I.P. without consulting the National Assembly at each stage, agreed to refuse amalgamation with U.N.I.P. if it involved disposing of A.N.C. The Assembly's principal long-term objective was breaking the Federation, even if the economy should be severely damaged in the process. The usual demands for self-government were voiced, and it was decided to boycott both the Monckton Commission and the 1960 Federal Review. Significantly, plans for positive action were held in abeyance until it was possible to obtain the advice of Kaunda and Sipalo.[1]

The second A.N.C. split produced one somewhat bizarre result. The Government, much to its discomfort, was drawn directly into the political arena, because instead of seeking recognition through court action, Chona's faction turned to the Registrar of Societies. On 14 September the Registrar received notification from the Chona A.N.C. of a change in national office-bearers, and during the following week additional notices were received in respect of provincial office-bearers. By meticulous compliance with the Societies Ordinance, the Chona group hoped to replace Nkumbula's A.N.C., which would be outside the law if, within fourteen days, it did not inform the Registrar of the dismissal of Mukupo, who, legally, remained Nkumbula's General Secretary. On 21 September, nine days after the split, the Chona group approached the District Commissioner, Lusaka, to seek confirmation of the fact that only that A.N.C. which adhered to the Ordinance's requirements for a change of office-bearers would be recognized as the legitimate A.N.C. The District Commissioner pointed out that fourteen days had not yet elapsed, and that in any case the Societies Ordinance was not intended as a means of settling disputes between the factions within a society.[2]

The Registrar confirmed that the Societies Ordinance could not be used to settle an organization's internal dispute over personalities. As he saw it, neither A.N.C. could use the Ordinance

[1] Report on A.N.C.'s Annual Conference, 2 October 1959, TS/S 123/01.
[2] Registrar to Ad. Sec., 24 September 1959, S/S 82/81/01.

to render its rival unlawful. But unhappily for the Government, nothing in the Ordinance could be invoked to prevent either group from continuing as A.N.C., and consequently, any action against the party would inevitably cover both A.N.C.s, a situation the Government found unacceptable. On 23 September Nkumbula's A.N.C. submitted its annual return together with Notice of Change of Office-Bearers to the Registrar.[1] The need for a decision of some kind now became urgent, as both A.N.C.s intensified their competition for power and recognition in Central, Eastern, and Western Province.[2]

After much discussion amongst government officials, during which a clear preference was expressed for Nkumbula's A.N.C.[3] a course of action was decided. The Registrar, while conceding that no means of recognizing one group over another was specifically provided in the Ordinance, proposed that the rejection of Chona's group be based on section 9(d) of the Ordinance, which 'presupposed or implied the existence of a second society calling itself A.N.C. in addition to the one already recognized'.[4] The Government's legal advisers considered that the Registrar, after considering the cases of both A.N.C.s. under his general discretion to demand and to query information from political parties, could only recognize one group and await legal action from the other.[5] The Registrar was reminded that great care was necessary, as Chona himself was a lawyer.[6] To justify his action, the Registrar was forced to interpret the confused events of August and September against the A.N.C. constitution: 'an invidious task'.[7]

Relations between the two factions were especially tense in Lusaka. Nkumbula, who retained the national headquarters in Chilenje, mounted an action-group guard around the building in case the Chona group attempted to capture it by force. Fearing personal assault as well, Nkumbula also extended the guard to his own house. The only physical asset controlled by

<hr>

[1] Registrar to Ad. Sec., 24 September 1959, S/S 82/81/01.
[2] M.I.R., October 1959, S/S 123/2/01, S/S 123/8/01, DG 58/3/01.
[3] A.S.(C.S.) to Registrar, 25 September 1959; Ad. Sec. to C.S., 27 September 1959, S/S 82/81/01.
[4] Registrar to Ad. Sec., 24 September 1959, ibid.
[5] A.G. to Registrar, 30 September 1959, ibid.
[6] Ad. Sec. to C.S., 27 September 1959, ibid.
[7] C.S. to P.C.(E.P.), 3 October 1959, ibid.

Chona's group was A.N.C.'s post box, though this advantage was soon lost when Nkumbula succeeded in having the lock changed. The Chona group, which formed no branches while awaiting recognition from the Registrar, devoted great energy to prose-lytising and propaganda. In late September Chona and Mukupo met members of Lusaka's Euro-African Association who were anxious to discuss a possible merger. Similar overtures were made by Euro-Africans on the Copperbelt; in both cases, Chona was receptive, but postponed the issue until the conflict with Nkumbula was resolved and U.N.I.P. leaders could be present. Chona and his officials also produced a number of pamphlets,[1] which they circulated in early October while Nkumbula was touring rural areas in Southern Province.[2] One such publication, Chona's 'Presidential Address',[3] represented, in many ways, a significant advance over similar nationalist pronouncements of the past two years. Though less militant in tone than the statements of Z.A.N.C.'s leaders in early 1959, Chona's speech was far from moderate and dealt in consider-able detail with the multitude of problems facing Northern Rhodesia's nationalist movement as a whole. Chona argued that Britain's professed policy of granting freedom to dependent peoples in Africa was in danger of breaking down in Northern Rhodesia, which because of its large white immigrant population was a special case. Nothing could be won unless African demands were 'concrete and loud', louder even than those of Ghana and Nyasaland. Failing this, Northern Rhodesia would go the way of Southern Rhodesia and South Africa. Chona also stressed the importance of a Labour victory in Britain's general election; the Labour Party, he maintained, understood the inevitability of majority rule in all African territories. Despite his obvious preference for Labour (he claimed himself to have been a Labour Party member while in Britain), Chona warned against expecting too much. It was not true, he argued, 'that they [Labour] like you more than their fellow nationals living in this country'; Labour was more realistic, not necessarily more trustworthy.[4]

[1] M.I.R., October 1959, S/S 123/2/01.

[2] Ibid., S/S 123/7/01.

[3] Annexure to report on A.N.C.'s Annual Conference, 2 October 1959, TS/S 123/01.

[4] Ibid.

In Chona's view, the role of the nationalist party comprised far more than leading the struggle for African self-government. It was the party's responsibility to concern itself with the broad range of problems facing Africans, and he implied that Africans should judge any nationalist organization on that basis. As for the problems which Africans faced, they were too numerous to elaborate in a single speech.

There is the land dispute within the British South Africa Company; the small number of people who are sent to universities; the removal of the Gwembe people from their homes; the snatching of administrative powers from Paramount Chief Chitimukulu who once courageously refused to meet Welensky—that bitterest enemy of Africa; the high rents for the awful houses in poor and neglected African compounds; the apartheid of establishing African compounds (specially for Africans as Africans) miles away from the town centre; lower Africans' voting rights in municipal elections; Africans' rights for managerial posts and/or training Africans for managerial posts like their fellow Africans in other parts of Africa; Africans' rights to possess freehold land in town as non-Africans; converting Native Trust Lands into native reserves; reducing or even abolishing what are called 'Crown Lands'; abolishing the requirement of carrying identity certificates; making beating by the police or kapasus illegal; compulsory and free education for Africans and not for Europeans alone as at present; etc. etc. etc.[1]

The most significant point about Chona's speech was symbolic. Speeches of this type were common in u.n.i.p. a year later, but in September–October 1959 Chona's address marked the dramatic change which had occurred in nationalist thinking in Northern Rhodesia over the short space of a year. African leaders who had opposed Kaunda's break with a.n.c. in October 1958 now shared z.a.n.c.'s doctrine and looked to Kaunda to lead them in 1960.

Dr. Banda and Kenneth Kaunda are brave men and had brave followers. They deserve our full honour. Even if we did not agree with them, we must remember and glorify them always . . .

We want someone of the nature of Mr. Kaunda—strong, fearless and selfless. The name of Nkumbula should be forgotten—except for his past service . . . We want to begin work soon. 1960 is approaching.[2]

[1] Annexure to report on a.n.c.'s Annual Conference, 2 October 1959, TS/S 123/01.
[2] Ibid.

At this point, October 1959, African unity, though severely strained, was not beyond redemption. Chona's goal, like Mukupo's before him, remained clear. On other occasions Chona disclaimed all political ambition of his own and explained his opposition to Nkumbula purely in terms of the country's great need for a unified African party led by Kaunda.[1] The goal was not Chona's alone; indeed, it was shared, to a greater or lesser extent, by all those who opposed Nkumbula. These men, like Kaunda, Kapwepwe, Sipalo, and their colleagues, had come to realize the limitations of extremist splinter groups. A unified, well-organized and dedicated party of the people would be required for the future, and A.N.C., without Nkumbula, offered the best vehicle for revitalizing the nationalist movement.[2]

In mid-October the latter part of the vision was lost, and with it all hope of complete African unity for the foreseeable future. The Registrar, after both A.N.C. factions had submitted their respective accounts of the split, evaluated each group's case against A.N.C.'s Constitution as it stood at the time of the General Conference of September (at the conference Nkumbula amended the Constitution, giving the President, retroactively from October 1958, power to dismiss, suspend, or reshuffle members of his national executive). Summarizing his findings, the Registrar concluded that 'the only point that emerged clearly from the above [detailed consideration] is that the issue is not one which can be decided fairly under the Societies Ordinance'. Both factions had violated the party's Constitution, so that recognizing the rightful A.N.C. was merely 'a choice of evils'. The Registrar elected to pay less attention to the 'inconclusive struggle for power' in late August and to concentrate instead on the rival conferences of mid-September.

It would seem that although the Chono group objected to delegates' fees and the increased number of delegates summoned, they were quite prepared to attend Nkumbula's meeting if Nkumbula would accept their dubious collection of 'delegates' to add to his probably equally dubious collection. Supposing that Nkumbula was unconstitutional in making it difficult, if not impossible, for them to attend, the question arises whether their hastily summoned rival meeting

[1] M.I.R., October 1959, S/S 123/2/01.
[2] Interview with Kaunda, 9 July 1964.

was constitutional and what authority it had to call itself the National Conference. The National Conference begun in the Nkumbula sponsored gathering, was accepted in a way, as such, by the Chona group. If one must compare breaches of the constitution, the Chona attempt to set up rival Conferences both in August and September must, I think, dwarf the arbitrary action of Nkumbula in, e.g. adjourning the August National Assembly and dismissing the office bearers out of hand.[1]

Thus in the absence of more conclusive evidence, and using A.N.C.'s Constitution to establish the legality of Nkumbula's conference meeting, the Registrar recognized A.N.C. and accepted Nkumbula's list of office-bearers. The only alternative would have been to inform both factions that the issue could not be settled under the Societies Ordinance, which, in fact, was true, and to take no action until A.N.C. had 're-organized itself'. With a tinge of regret, which indicated perhaps that he had not enjoyed his task, the Registrar simply noted that the alternative course of action, however desirable, was out of the question.[2]

A.N.C.'s second split was now complete. At the time it was difficult, for a number of reasons, to estimate the extent and importance of the split. The ensuing contest for official recognition had complicated an already confused situation. No clearcut trade-union reaction to the split emerged, largely because of Katilungu's absence overseas from mid-August to mid-October.[3] U.N.I.P., since its formation in August, had built up its own following, often in those areas most deeply affected by the A.N.C. split. Finally, many Africans—intellectuals, rank and file nationalists, and ordinary party sympathizers alike— had despaired of or simply lost interest in the struggle among African politicians, which in one form or another had persisted for well over a year.

Undoubtedly, the second A.N.C. split had brought in its train a good deal more chaos within A.N.C. than the Z.A.N.C. split of 1958. 'Stupidity and folly could not be more confounded',[4] wrote Sikota Wina from restriction to his brother

---

[1] Annexure to minute by Registrar, RS/1744/1166, 13 October 1959, S/S 82/81/01.
[2] Ibid.
[3] M.I.R., August 1959, DG 58/8/01; November 1959, S/S 123/8/01.
[4] S. Wina to A. Wina, 30 September 1959, A.N.L.W. papers.

Arthur, a student in the United States. S. Wina, possibly the leading nationalist intellectual at this time, dismissed the leadership of both groups out of hand. Nkumbula was finished;[1] Mukupo could only destroy and seemed incapable of creating; Chona, though trained in law, lacked political sophistication and the support of African intellectuals.[2]

Our hope obviously lies elsewhere and all these dramatics are a mere interlude until we get someone else with a sufficiently broad mind and personality to impress himself on the minds of the intellectuals, for the past nine months have proved that after all the intellectuals are still by far the most potent group in Central African nationalism . . . until we get someone enlightened, incorruptible leadership which will be able to persuade not the standard 6 chap but the matriculant and over to join the forces of real nationalism we are doomed to the failure and humiliation that ended the rather flamboyant career of ZAMBIA; to the comic opera which the present Congress so much resembles.[3]

On 22 October, after being released from restriction, S. Wina wrote of the rapidly deteriorating situation: 'Politically, Welensky is winning, if something is not done and done urgently. He is winning not because he is getting African support but because there is *no* African National movement here, literally.' Again, he attacked Chona's leadership, and concluded: 'There is this vacuum to be filled. It is a real crying need. It is no use my working on a monthly paper because as 1960 approaches the Africans will need a weekly reminder and leadership.'[4]

Several days earlier the Registrar, 'as was expected . . . ruled in favour of old Harry and outlawed Mainza and his gang'. Wina continued bitterly:

Of course today we are celebrating Federation Day and everyone is enjoying a public holiday. What we are celebrating I really fail to understand. Is it the death of 51 Africans in Nyasaland? Is it the detention of more than 500 nationalists leaders in the three territories? What is it, Arthur? The measure of our leadership is seen by the fact that there is not even a single demonstration anywhere in Northern Rhodesia. Where are the big protest banners denouncing

[1] S. Wina to A. Wina, 22 October 1959, A.N.L.W. papers.
[2] Ibid., 30 September 1959.
[3] Ibid.
[4] Ibid., 22 October 1959.

Federation? Where are the gatherings re-affirming our faith only in self-determination? . . . One might call the absence of demonstrations a lack of imagination on the part of our so-called leaders. I frankly call it stupidity because the funny thing is that the so-called leaders . . . who form the vanguard of African nationalism here today ought to have known that they should have taken advantage of this 'celebration' to re-state their opposition, not only in the form of demonstrations etc., but by announcing some dramatic new policies which the African people are going to pursue from now on. But then perhaps we are expecting too much from a semi-literate leadership.

In short, the hour is ripe but where is the man?[1]

The Beginnings of U.N.I.P.

In the three months after its formation U.N.I.P. was little more than an amorphous collection of splinter group leaders, joined as time passed by a number of ex-Z.A.N.C. officials returning from restriction to the 'line of rail'. U.N.I.P. did not follow the usual practice of forming and registering branches across the country.[2] Though U.N.I.P. was too poor to mount such an operation, the party's interim leaders, Kalichini and Chitambala, still looked hopefully towards the goal of African unity. From the beginning, they opposed the formation of additional African splinter groups and even went so far as refusing to accept such groups from A.N.C. during August and September 1959.

U.N.I.P.'s early activity was centred largely in Broken Hill, Lusaka,[3] the Copperbelt,[4] Kawambwa District in Luapula Province,[5] and Kasama District in the Northern Province.[6] In other areas, such as Eastern Province, U.N.I.P. appeared only with the return of local ex-Z.A.N.C. restricted persons during September and October.[7] U.N.I.P. meetings in Broken Hill during August were well attended, and in mid-September the organization held a conference simultaneously with A.N.C.'s General Conference in Lusaka. Though U.N.I.P. activity tapered

---

[1] S. Wina to A. Wina, 29 October 1959, A.N.L.W. papers.
[2] M.I.R., August and September 1959, S/S 123 and DG 58 series.
[3] M.I.R., October 1959, DG 58/2/01.
[4] M.I.R., November and December 1959, S/S 123/8/01 and DG 58/8/01.
[5] S.B. to Ad. Sec., 22 September 1959; M.I.R., November and December 1959, S/S 108/4/01.
[6] D.C. (Kasama) to P.C.(N.P.), 17 November 1959, S/S 82/81/01.
[7] M.I.R., September and October 1959, DG 58/3/01.

off along the 'line of rail' during the weeks of intense competition between the two A.N.C.s,[1] in Luapula Province it continued unabated from August to December. Huggins Chewe, formerly Z.A.N.C.'s regional secretary for Luapula Province, returning to Fort Rosebery in mid-August, claimed to have been authorized by Kalichini and Chitambala to organize U.N.I.P. on behalf of Kaunda, Sipalo, and Kapwepwe. Chewe convened two minor conferences almost at once. At the first, attended by a small number of Z.A.N.C. district and branch officials, Chewe proclaimed that U.N.I.P. was already making rapid progress throughout the Territory and that its aim was to secure African government before the end of 1960. The Z.A.N.C. officials, mainly from Kawambwa District, agreed to convert to the new organization as a group. The second meeting comprised some sixty delegates; Chewe reiterated the aims of U.N.I.P., indicated that Kaunda would assume direct control as soon as he was released from prison, and advised that in the meantime local officials should proceed with caution in order to avoid proscription.[2]

As usual, political feeling in the Luapula was particularly intense; both conferences stressed the same general themes. The first was party organization, especially the question of improving party security. Many officials believed that Z.A.N.C's banning of the previous March had been greatly facilitated by the activities of informers who had infiltrated Z.A.N.C.'s organization. Consequently, it was decided that the number of branches per district should be kept to a minimum in order to lessen opportunities for Special Branch penetration, and elaborate plans were discussed at the second conference for guarding leaders, exposing informers, concealing documents and transmitting messages outside the Federal postal system. U.N.I.P.'s provincial executive was to exercise greater control over its constituent organization than had Z.A.N.C. in the past; district and branch level formations, for example, were not to initiate 'positive action' of any kind independently.[3]

The second major theme was the belief that nothing could be achieved, least of all self-government in 1960, without adopting a well-organized policy of violence. Nyasaland's example was

[1] M.I.R., October 1959, DG 58/2/01.
[2] S.B. to Ad. Sec., 22 September 1959, S/S 108/4/01.
[3] Ibid.

cited repeatedly with great envy, and speakers constantly expressed a willingness to sacrifice their lives in the forthcoming struggle. Considerable attention was also given to the necessity of creating an organization capable of carrying out acts of violence; district- and branch-level organizations were authorized to establish action and youth groups to conduct future sabotage actions, as well as a new party security organization known as the Zambia police. The third major theme—which incidentally helps to confirm the veracity of Chewe's claim to be Kalichini's authorized representative—was the stress laid on non-fraternization with A.N.C. Chewe indicated that he was acting on Kalichini's orders, which suggests that the policy of encouraging A.N.C. to put its own house in order, instead of breaking up into small splinter groups, was fairly widespread in U.N.I.P. Relations between Z.A.N.C. and A.N.C., of course, had never been good; indeed, Chewe went so far as to suggest that it had been A.N.C. informers who infiltrated and betrayed Z.A.N.C. at the time of the 1959 general election.[1]

In Northern Province, like Luapula, U.N.I.P. was able to build on the remnants of Z.A.N.C.'s organization, which remained strongest in Kasama District. By November, six U.N.I.P. branches in the District had applied for registration, all heavily staffed by ex-Z.A.N.C. office-bearers. Government field officers in the area expressed opposition to what they believed was the resurrection of Z.A.N.C., organized under a new name by Kalichini on instructions from Kaunda.[2]

Back on the 'line of rail', the Registrar's decision to recognize Nkumbula's A.N.C., announced on 19 October, forced Chona to turn immediately to U.N.I.P. Despite Chona's confidence that the Registrar's ruling could be challenged successfully in court, Chona decided that time was running against the Africans and that the cost of court proceedings would be prohibitive.[3] The Registrar's decision likewise forced U.N.I.P to alter its policy, and three weeks later the two groups convened a conference on unification in order to agree, among other things, on interim office-bearers to lead the new party until Kaunda's release. Rather surprisingly, Chona unseated Kalichini as U.N.I.P.'s

[1] s.b. to Ad. Sec., 22 September 1959, S/S 108/4/01.
[2] d.c. (Kasama) to p.c.(n.p.), 17 November 1959, S/S 82/81/01.
[3] Central African Post, 20 October 1959.

President; Chitambala became Secretary-General and Raphael Kombe Treasurer-General. The other new office-bearers, with the exception perhaps of Gordon Chindele, Vice-President, were relatively unknown, though they included two men, D. C. Mwansa and Ndililia, specifically responsible for territorial propaganda. Kalichini, angered by his defeat, refused to contest any other office and subsequently retired from active politics. Others conspicuous for their absence were Mukupo and Kalulu, the former due to family difficulties, the latter because of his involvement in a business venture. Both pledged their full support to the new organization, though Mukupo, like Kalichini, never held office in a nationalist organization again.[1]

The merger between U.N.I.P. and Chona's A.N.C. put an end to the fluidity which had marked nationalist politics during the previous months and soon revealed more clearly the extent of A.N.C.'s September split. Before long it was apparent that Nkumbula's A.N.C. had, in fact, suffered a severe blow in September and entered a period of marked decline, particularly in Central and Western Province. The hold which Chona and Mukupo established on A.N.C.'s Copperbelt organization in September proved to be a lasting one, a fact which helped explain U.N.I.P.'s rapid growth on the Copperbelt during November and December.[2] Returning from overseas in October, Katilungu expressed alarm at the sudden strength of Chona's new party and sought once again to revive A.N.C., which by November reportedly retained only Mufulira.[3] In December a U.N.I.P. propaganda team toured the Copperbelt and succeeded in creating among Africans an atmosphere of enthusiastic expectation: U.N.I.P., it was said, would soon swing into full action, making 1960 the year of Northern Rhodesia's great showdown. Government officials confirmed a growing measure of unity in U.N.I.P., which they attributed to the urgent desire both among ex-Z.A.N.C. officials and Chona's men 'to be seated firmly on the bandwagon when the driver and his whip, Kaunda and Sipalo, arrive'.[4]

In Central Province A.N.C. was plagued with its usual organi-

[1] Chona to Arthur Wina, 29 November 1959, A.N.L.W. papers.
[2] M.I.R., November and December 1959, S/S 123/2/01 and /8/01; DG 58/2/01 and /8/01.
[3] M.I.R., November 1959, S/S 123/8/01.
[4] M.I.R., December 1959, DG 58/8/01.

zational problems: Nkumbula's erratic leadership and the paralysis this caused among national level officials, who were afraid to act during Nkumbula's lengthy absences; officials working at cross-purposes, because no clear definition of their respective responsibilities existed; misappropriation of party funds at all levels; and a high turnover among lower-level officials. By year's end A.N.C. was almost completely inactive in the province, save for the bitter internal conflicts which raged among its officials. At a joint meeting of action group and branch officials in Lusaka on 7 January 1960, Nkumbula laid the blame for A.N.C.'s weakness on provincial officials, the level hardest hit by the September split, threatening to advise the next National Assembly to do away with the provincial-level organization altogether.[1]

A.N.C.'s organization in North-Western Province had collapsed completely. Nkumbula had appointed the provincial president, Johnathan Ntambo, to a national office at the September Conference, while in November both Hancock Kikombe and Matiya Ngalande, the provincial executive's other two members, defected to U.N.I.P.[2] The situation was little better in Eastern Province, where only three A.N.C. meetings were held during the whole of October. Nkumbula's failure to appear for a promised tour of the province that month only made matters worse.[3] Even in Southern Province, A.N.C.'s traditional stronghold, attendance at public meetings declined; a Livingstone meeting broke up as Nkumbula was speaking, because he refused to name a specific date by which A.N.C. would achieve self-government. Nkumbula began failing again to appear at meetings, and government officials received complaints from Africans about the collection and alleged misuse of party funds. By the end of 1959 U.N.I.P. began to attract limited interest among Africans in several railway towns, particularly in Livingstone.[4]

Thus, A.N.C.'s second split was as decisive in its way as the Z.A.N.C. split of 1958. The careful preparations carried out by Mukupo and his colleagues among A.N.C. provincial officials

[1] M.I.R., November 1959–January 1960, S/S 123/2/01.
[2] M.I.R., November 1959, S/S 123/6/01.
[3] M.I.R., October and November 1959, S/S 123/3/01.
[4] M.I.R., November and December 1959, S/S 123/7/01.

from May through September 1959 resulted in a crippling blow
to A.N.C.'s organization in widespread areas of Northern Rhodesia. The Z.A.N.C. split of 1958, though important for ideo-
logical reasons and because it had been led by outstanding party
leaders, was essentially a split in A.N.C.'s national executive.
The number of lower level officials and party members involved was relatively small, and only several towns and rural
areas were affected. A.N.C.'s second split, though led by men of
less consequence in the movement, was both broad and deep.
A.N.C.'s rebels had carefully prepared a revolt which they hoped
would re-establish African unity. When their bid failed, large
numbers of A.N.C. officials at the provincial, district and branch
levels of the party followed Chona, taking with them A.N.C.'s
physical organization. Viewed in this light the upheavals of
1958 and 1959 represented two stages of a single split: the first
detaching A.N.C.'s most able and militant national leaders; the
second, though concerned with the question of leadership,
splitting away large segments of A.N.C.'s provincial-, district-
and branch-level organization.

One of the major differences between U.N.I.P. and A.N.C.,
which developed during this period and contributed further to
A.N.C.'s decline, arose over the policy to be adopted towards
the Monckton Commission's schedule to visit the Federation
early in 1960 to collect evidence for its report on the Federal
Constitution. Chona and U.N.I.P.'s early leaders all advocated a
total boycott of the Commission by Africans,[1] while A.N.C.'s
first proposal was to make use of the Commission to express
opposition to the Federation.[2] It was for this reason that Katilungu, who when he returned from overseas appeared to think
he would serve on the Commission, renewed his attempts to
build up A.N.C.'s position on the Copperbelt. After considerable
effort, Katilungu persuaded Nkumbula to visit Mufulira, but
with A.N.C.'s officials continuing to advocate co-operation with
the Monckton Commission, defections from A.N.C. to U.N.I.P.
continued unchecked throughout the Copperbelt.[3]

In December Chona made two visits to Luapula Province
from the Copperbelt. Though the province was seething with

[1] M.I.R., November 1959, S/S 108/4/01.
[2] M.I.R., November 1959, S/S 123/2/01.
[3] M.I.R., November and December 1959, S/S 58/8/01 and S/S 123/8/01.

political activity, the plans so vociferously advocated by Chewe in August had not developed significantly. Kawambwa District's thriving organization impressed Chona, but for the most part he was disappointed both by the petty bickering among Luapula's multitude of local officials and by the lack of progress in reorganizing the remnants of z.a.n.c. into the new party. Apart from a number of lively private meetings with officials in Fort Rosebery, Chona's main objective of explaining u.n.i.p. to the people of Luapula was frustrated, largely by the consistent opposition of both the Provincial Administration, whose officers discouraged public meetings, and the local chiefs and Native Authorities. On several occasions, when Chona had failed to obtain the local chief's permission to hold a public meeting, the people became angry with Chona for not going ahead with an unauthorized meeting, and told him to return to the Copperbelt.[1]

The general atmosphere in Luapula, more pronounced even than on the Copperbelt, was one of great expectations for the year 1960. Local officials constantly referred to the progress of other African states towards independence, particularly the Congo and Tanganyika, and in each case the lesson drawn was identical: increased militancy and if necessary extreme violence. In 1960 Africans would have little time for eating and sleeping, it was said; and District Commissioners even less time for drinking tea. Africans would stop paying taxes to a 'foreign government'; identity certificates would be collected and turned in at the Boma; all orders from the central Government and the Native Authorities would be ignored; greetings to touring officers would cease; and the Monckton Commission would be boycotted. Nyasaland's example was held up for imitation, often with considerable emotion: Northern Rhodesia Africans would need to die in 1960, and everywhere they were encouraged not to be afraid. To win the battle against 'foreign government' and Federation, Africans would exhume their dead and call on their unborn children.[2]

Before leaving Luapula Province, Chona appointed a provisional executive which, until the numerous conflicts among Fort Rosebery officials were resolved, was to function in

---

[1] m.i.r., December 1959, S/S 108/4/01.
[2] m.i.r., January 1960, ibid.

Wambwa District under the leadership of Makasa, who was soon for release from restriction. Chona emphasized that the w appointments would last only until U.N.I.P.'s first full-scale national executive meeting in Lusaka on 30 and 31 January 1960. Meanwhile, and perhaps of more lasting importance, Chona succeeded in impressing on local officials the importance of organizing new U.N.I.P. branches and registering them under the Societies Ordinance.[1] U.N.I.P.'s most immediate objective, boycotting the Monckton Commission, gained wide acceptance in Luapula. Agitation among chiefs and Native Authorities to comply with the boycott began almost at once. In addition, though its permanence was difficult to confirm, the Luapula group appeared to have accepted that no militant action of any kind was to be instituted without firm instructions from Lusaka. Thus, by the time Sylvester Chisembele, perhaps the most widely known and respected of Luapula's Z.A.N.C. restricted persons, returned to Fort Rosebery on 8 January 1960, bearing a duplicating machine and 1,000 new U.N.I.P. membership cards, an important advance had been achieved by U.N.I.P. in Luapula. Chisembele sent 500 cards to Kawambwa, began organizing U.N.I.P. branches and appointing delegates to U.N.I.P.'s forthcoming national executive meeting in Lusaka. The new party, though still painfully short of funds, was not lacking in resourcefulness. In Fort Rosebery government suspicions were aroused by the unprecedented number of appeals which were suddenly received from convicted prisoners at the local prison. As it turned out, one Oscar Mulenga, a clerk at the prison, was identified by government officials as an ex-Z.A.N.C. restricted person, planted there by U.N.I.P.'s provincial secretary.[2]

The emergence of U.N.I.P., its attraction for former Z.A.N.C. officials and its affinity to the banned organization, though not unexpected, caused grave concern in the Government. A security report from Luapula Province in September drew from the Chief Secretary the comment: 'I don't like the sound of U.N.I.P.'s ideas—they are learning too fast.'[3] The Governor agreed,[4] and a few weeks later a meeting, which included

---

[1] M.I.R., December 1959, S/S 108/4/01.
[2] M.I.R., January 1960, ibid.
[3] C.S. to Governor, 28 September 1959, S/S 108/4/01.
[4] Governor to C.S., 29 September 1959, ibid.

Roberts, took place at Government House to discuss the growing threat of nationalist parties. The Governor, replying to questions raised by Roberts about u.n.i.p., expressed the Government's concern over the rapid emergence of u.n.i.p., indicating that it might well become necessary to declare a state of emergency in the affected areas in order to detain u.n.i.p.'s leaders. The Governor explained that the Government was contemplating legislation which would provide for detention without the need of first declaring a state of emergency. Difficulties had arisen, however, over the various international conventions regarding such legislation, which would not easily be resolved. The Government had found through its experience with z.a.n.c. the previous March that the pre-emergency provisions, which enabled the Government to restrict leaders for limited periods, were not adequate for curbing the activities of 'dangerous extremists'.[1]

The Government had also been giving consideration to tightening up the Societies Ordinance. Not only was the Government confronted with pressure from certain of its provincial officers, particularly those in Northern Province, to refuse registration to u.n.i.p. under the Ordinance;[2] in September Lusaka's District Commissioner proposed that the Ordinance be amended to prohibit office-bearers of a banned society from holding office in any subsequent society which might appear under a different name.[3] The proposal was taken up by the Administrative Secretary, who suggested to the Registrar that it be included in his list of proposed amendments to the Ordinance.[4] The District Commissioner's proposal then lay dormant for some months, but the opposition of field officers, including the Provincial Commissioner,[5] to registering u.n.i.p. in Northern Province continued to build up until in January 1960 it had become a major issue in the Government.

The Northern Province officials raised several arguments against registering u.n.i.p. Registration would entitle u.n.i.p. to hold public meetings, the most effective way of organizing a political party, and the party's officials would be able to tour

[1] Record of Government House meeting, 22 October 1959, TS/S 123/01.
[2] d.c. (Kasama) to p.c.(n.p.), 17 November 1959, S/S 82/81/01.
[3] p.c.(c.p.) to c.s., 17 September 1959, ibid.
[4] Ad. Sec. to Registrar, 9 October 1959, ibid.
[5] Registrar to Ad. Sec., 22 November 1959, ibid.

around with their registration cards, claiming to the chiefs that the Government approved of the party. Chiefs and Native Authorities reportedly feared U.N.I.P., particularly because it was led by numerous former Z.A.N.C. officials who had caused trouble in the chief's areas in early 1959. Unless action were taken against U.N.I.P., it was argued, the Government could expect wavering loyalties and loss of co-operation from chiefs and Native Authorities, who would not accept registration as anything other than government approval for Z.A.N.C. under a new name.[1] The Provincial Commissioner's view was that ultimately there would be serious disturbances in Northern Province, which would only come sooner if U.N.I.P. were registered.[2]

There were difficulties in meeting the demands of the Northern Province officials. Their opposition to U.N.I.P.'s registration was based on questions of broad policy rather than on the specific activities of U.N.I.P. in Northern Province, and the Registrar pointed out that the arguments raised would apply equally to branches in other provinces where ex-Z.A.N.C. leaders had taken over control. The Government's territorial policy had been to register U.N.I.P. branches. The Registrar feared that if he refused branch registrations in Northern Province and his decisions were appealed, he would then be forced to give reasons for his actions, which would apply equally to those areas where U.N.I.P. branches were already registered.[3] In addition, Special Branch opposed withholding registration from U.N.I.P. on the ground that the more subversive an organization, the more urgent the need to gather information and to use the controlling sections of the Societies Ordinance.[4]

High government officials at the Secretariat were deeply divided on the issue. Though the above points were argued forcefully by the Administrative Secretary in a letter to the Provincial Commissioner in Kasama,[5] the latter maintained his original position, indicating his belief that the central Government lacked bold leadership.[6] The Governor, who visited Northern Province in mid-January, was caught between the

[1] Note by Ag. c.s. for Exec. Co. meeting No. 233 of December 1959, S/S 82/81/01.
[2] Governor to c.s., 27 January 1960, ibid.
[3] Registrar to Ad. Sec., 16 January 1960, ibid.
[4] Ad. Sec. to P.C.(N.P.), 23 January 1960, ibid.
[5] Ibid.   [6] Governor to c.s., 27 January 1960, ibid.

Registrar and Special Branch, on the one hand, and Northern
Province officials on the other. While he appreciated the respective arguments advanced by the Registrar and Special Branch,
the Governor was keenly aware that the Provincial Commissioner faced a grave and fundamental problem involving the
Government's basic policy of backing the chiefs and Native
Authorities against nationalist agitation.[1]

On 4 February a top-level meeting, including the Governor,
the Provincial Commissioner, the Registrar, the Assistant Commissioner (Special Branch), the Commissioner of Police, the
Minister of Native Affairs and the Minister of Legal Affairs took
place at Government House. The Provincial Commissioner
reiterated his position, stressing the importance of retaining the
loyalty of the chiefs, particularly regarding the maintenance of
law and order. Officials of the Provincial Administration, he
argued, had given full support to the chiefs in their opposition
to u.n.i.p., and the chiefs had so far been greatly heartened. The
Provincial Commissioner feared that registering u.n.i.p. would
alienate both the chiefs and the Native Authorities as well as
encourage u.n.i.p.'s growth. He also dismissed the argument
that registration would produce valuable new information about
the party, as the main agitators were already known.[2]

The Assistant Commissioner (Special Branch) submitted a
lengthy memorandum in support of registering u.n.i.p. Immense benefits, he argued, derived from registration: 'it facili-
tates police action to cripple a subversive organization . . . it
provides the best possible insurance against the premature release of persons arrested for detention and against public and
world criticism of the Governor's action in invoking powers to
enable him to deal collectively with the officials of a subversive
organization'.[3] Failure to register a political party raised the
difficulty of producing evidence against the leaders of an unlawful society and prevented the collection of valuable information which enabled the Government to exercise a measure of
control over political organizations. The Assistant Commissioner
stressed that Northern Province was at present the weakest point
in Special Branch coverage of the Territory. Not enough was
known, either about u.n.i.p.'s future plans or about the militant

[1] Governor to c.s., 27 January 1960, S/S 82/81/01.
[2] Record of Government House meeting, 4 February 1960, ibid.   [3] Ibid.

subgroups, such as the action and youth groups, which were attached to existing branches and remained, for the most part, unregistered. In addition, the Assistant Commissioner emphasized the difficulty of reconciling the refusal to register U.N.I.P. in Northern Province with the policy of registering the party in other provinces.[1]

Though the meeting ended somewhat inconclusively, the Registrar and the Special Branch had clearly won the first round. Northern Province officials were instructed to intensify their efforts to convince chiefs and Native Authorities that registration in itself did not amount to government approval for U.N.I.P. Meanwhile, registration of U.N.I.P. branches in Northern Province was to be delayed temporarily until the Registrar had demanded further information from U.N.I.P. concerning its intentions in the North. It was noted that twenty-two applications from U.N.I.P. branches in other provinces were pending and that in these cases registration would proceed.[2]

Thus, in early 1960 the Government's primary concern was to exercise control over U.N.I.P., which was clearly expected to launch a major drive for power during 1960. At the time of the Government House meeting, U.N.I.P. was already beginning its preparations. Kaunda was released from prison on 9 January 1960. On 31 January he was elected to the presidency of U.N.I.P., Chona stepping down to the post of Deputy President. Kaunda's first public statement reflected U.N.I.P.'s determination to force the pace of political advance, setting the stage for a dramatic struggle for power lasting well over two years.

Freedom! All I am asking of Africans of Northern Rhodesia is that they should remain calm and patient; and should prepare themselves for the real non-violent struggle that lies ahead.

The Zambia African Congress was banned, but there is no power to ban our desire to be free, to shape our own destiny. In this struggle for freedom, we will tell the present rulers to realize that the colour of a man should not count; what should count is behaviour . . .

I am determined more than ever before to achieve self-government for Africans in this country. Detentions, imprisonments and rural-area restrictions will only delay, but will not stop us from reaching that goal, which should be reached this year, 1960.[3]

[1] Record of Government House meeting, 4 February 1960, S/S 82/81/01.
[2] Ibid.   [3] Kaunda, *Zambia Shall be Free*, pp. 138–9.

IV

THE UNITED NATIONAL
INDEPENDENCE PARTY

IN January 1960 U.N.I.P.'s situation was critical. Less than a year remained before the Federal Review Conference, which would decide the future of the Federation. The Monckton Commission, which U.N.I.P. had committed itself to boycotting, was scheduled to arrive in Northern Rhodesia in February 1960. U.N.I.P.'s limited organization, supervised by Chona since his merger with Kalichini's U.N.I.P. in November 1959, functioned on a temporary basis, all the various officials, including some of those of the old Z.A.N.C. in some areas, awaiting the return of Kaunda to give firm shape to the new organization. More important, perhaps, U.N.I.P. had almost no funds and lacked sufficient numbers of able and dedicated men prepared to devote themselves to the laborious task of party organization. To Kaunda the primary task was clear: 'When we organize our people, it is important to note that we are building an organization that should not only get us self-government and, ultimately, independence, but an organization sufficiently strong to run our government.'[1] This had been Kaunda's goal since his break with Nkumbula in 1958; now in 1960 and 1961 Kaunda and his colleagues gave form to Northern Rhodesia's first mass political party.

Kaunda was not alone in his preoccupation with organizing an efficient mass party capable of exerting greatly increased pressure on the British Government during 1960. Indeed, one is struck by the emphasis given to party organization from the outset by most of U.N.I.P.'s top leaders. Undoubtedly, Kaunda, Sipalo, and Kapwepwe, all of whom were deeply influenced by experiences overseas,[2] had played a leading part in the growth of this attitude among their colleagues during 1958 and 1959.

[1] Kaunda, *Zambia Shall Be Free*, p. 152.
[2] Kaunda in Britain and India; Sipalo and Kapwepwe in India.

A.N.C.'s lack of organization prior to the 1958 split had been a heavy burden for Kaunda and his colleagues, the more so because Nkumbula's increasingly autocratic leadership prevented them from improving the position. In many ways Z.A.N.C. proved equally frustrating to Kaunda's group, for while they had the freedom to implement their ideas, the rush of events in early 1959, the party's lack of resources and the Government's subsequent ban prevented the emergence of the mass organization envisaged by Kaunda. If anything, the Z.A.N.C. experience, including the Accra Conference of 1958, as well as Kaunda's restriction and imprisonment, only reinforced his determination to build an effective mass party. Meanwhile, for a broad cross-section of African politicians, intellectuals, and trade unionists, the continuing strife in A.N.C. and the humiliating struggle for African unity during the second half of 1959 served to underline the desperate need for a united and well-organized nationalist party. Welensky and the Federal Government had moved from strength to strength since 1957, while African aspirations for self-government and the end of Federation were as far from being realized as ever.

In December 1959 Sikota Wina resigned his post with *African Life*, an African weekly newspaper, and became U.N.I.P.'s international affairs and publicity secretary. Time was running short, he explained in a letter to his brother Arthur, whom he appointed as U.N.I.P.'s official representative in the United States.[1] A new spirit moved men like the Wina brothers, both of whom had a clear understanding of U.N.I.P.'s immediate problems. First, there was the great need for obtaining financial support in the United States, Britain, and other parts of Africa. 'Well you know the story—Nkumbula was so careless a few years ago and has by now completely exhausted African public contributions that it is no longer possible, or even wise for that matter, to raise funds from public meetings.'[2] Even more important, in S. Wina's view, was the need to establish a 'solid administrative entity' which could draw on Pan-African support and which could secure the allegiance of Northern Rhodesia's 'African intelligentsia'. Like most of his colleagues at the time, S. Wina feared that promises of government promotions

---

[1] S. Wina to A. Wina, 7 December 1959, A.N.L.W. papers.
[2] Ibid.

made many leading Africans reluctant to join the forces of nationalism. 'Their main problem is doubt—doubt whether really African nationalism here has got the men who can make it a success or whether they should stick to the rosy side of life which means Government and the u.f.p. It is our job to show them that self determination and African majority rule are not only our goal, but are inevitable.'[1]

Arthur Wina, in accepting his appointment as u.n.i.p.'s United States representative, his first post in active politics, also laid special emphasis on building up an effective mass party. Indeed, in addition to his letter of acceptance to u.n.i.p.'s President,[2] then Chona, A. Wina submitted a lengthy memorandum, 'The Requirements and Tentative Programme of the Northern Rhodesia Representative Abroad', in which he put forward his ideas both on overseas representatives and on matters of general party organization in Northern Rhodesia. What was required was the 'total organization of the people', who, A. Wina argued, 'must be bought by your programme, its seriousness, its certainty of being realized come what may . . .' In such a party the 'intelligentsia and the general population must feel tied together by . . . a sense of national mission of freedom and independence. Whether or not this solid feeling permeates the populace is almost entirely in your [the leaders in Northern Rhodesia] hands.'[3] Wina advocated that 'all efforts must be made to dig the party in and carry out a "grass root" form of organization as has never been done before in Northern Rhodesia'.[4]

A. Wina's memorandum went on to discuss party organization in more detail. Wina asked whether u.n.i.p.'s programme was certain to inspire 'enthusiastic activity and support' and whether it would 'create an atmosphere of confidence among the people'. Did the programme have a realistic 'rallying issue' around which slogans could emerge? In addition, he pointed out the need to organize a system which would enable u.n.i.p. to reach the mass of people at all levels should the party be

[1] S. Wina to A. Wina, 7 December 1959, a.n.l.w. papers.
[2] A. Wina to M. Chona, 14 December 1959, a.n.l.w. papers.
[3] Ibid.
[4] Memorandum on the Requirements and Tentative Programme of the Northern Rhodesia Representative Abroad, u.n.i.p. of n.r., Los Angeles, California, 15 December 1959, a.n.l.w. papers.

prevented by the Government from organizing freely and holding public meetings. When the party did hold public meetings, would 'stage and psychological' techniques be fully utilized? Did the party plan, as Wina put it, to make full use 'for organizational purposes of the now idle Munali [School] boys'?[1]

A. Wina's ideas about party representatives overseas, a field nationalist parties in Northern Rhodesia had not previously exploited, were both interesting and constructive. In addition to the obvious need for representatives to travel, to establish contacts and to publicize the party in their respective countries, Wina made it clear that he expected U.N.I.P. headquarters to keep representatives informed and to supply them with detailed information regarding party policy. He accordingly demanded that he be provided with U.N.I.P.'s programme on economic policy, education, and the Federation. In addition, Wina inquired how far, if at all, U.N.I.P. was prepared to compromise with whites over the question of Federation. If a policy of no compromise was envisaged, a line Wina clearly favoured, he wished to learn the methods U.N.I.P. contemplated to achieve the break-up of the Federation. Finally, Wina indicated that he would not be able to proceed with his duties unless he received sufficient funds on a regular basis.[2] Initially, he requested £20 to begin a Northern Rhodesia news bulletin, a project he eventually launched with funds obtained in the United States.[3]

The exchange between the Wina brothers in December 1959 is less important for what it actually accomplished than for illustrating the high priority given to party organization by U.N.I.P.'s leaders. Significantly, this concern for effective organization persisted among U.N.I.P.'s top leaders, who, shortly after Kaunda's release from prison in January 1960, were active along the 'line of rail' and in Luapula, Northern and Eastern Provinces. In late February, Kapwepwe, S. Wina, and Sipalo toured Luapula Province for the purpose of establishing U.N.I.P. on a firm and more coherent basis. On 19 February they addressed a conference in Chief Milambo's area in Fort Rosebery District, attended by approximately 150 delegates from all over

[1] Memorandum on the Requirements and Tentative Programme of the Northern Rhodesia Representative Abroad, U.N.I.P. of N.R., Los Angeles, California, 15 December 1959, A.N.L.W. papers.

[2] Ibid.

[3] A. Wina to S. Wina, 26 December 1959, A.N.L.W. papers.

Luapula Province. Referring to the formation of provincial, constituency (formerly district), and branch-level committees, S. Wina explained that the electoral principle would be discontinued, because in the past it had resulted in weak leadership at lower levels in nationalist organizations. Executive officials at all levels would be selected by the provincial leaders and approved by u.n.i.p. headquarters. S. Wina then named Luapula's provincial executive, which included both Makasa and Chisembele as provincial president and secretary respectively. Any leader, warned Wina, who showed weakness or disregarded the authority of u.n.i.p. headquarters would be expelled from the party.[1]

One theme repeatedly stressed by all three national leaders, both at the conference and during their subsequent tour of the province, was the need for provincial party officials and their subordinates at lower levels to improve administrative standards. Party membership registers, financial records, and the regular reporting of provincial developments to u.n.i.p. headquarters were singled out as the most essential tasks, all of which required immediate and continuing attention. Kapwepwe, u.n.i.p.'s Treasurer-General, warned that misappropriation of party funds would result in dismissal from u.n.i.p. and formal prosecution. S. Wina directed that applications by branches to hold public meetings should be addressed to the appropriate local authority and that no attempt should be made to coerce the authorities into granting permission.[2]

The three u.n.i.p. leaders remained in Luapula Province to campaign against the Monckton Commission, which visited the area during the first week of March. Though all three leaders experienced difficulty in obtaining permission to hold public meetings, a series of well-attended private meetings in halls and houses was held throughout the province. u.n.i.p.'s immediate objectives—self-government by the end of 1960 and Northern Rhodesia's secession from the Federation—were given wide publicity. The touring leaders promised that u.n.i.p.'s positive-action campaign would begin in September or October 1960 after the necessary preparations had been completed. Meanwhile, the villagers were encouraged to devote their full energy to boycotting the Monckton Commission and building up

[1] s.b. to Ad. Sec., 29 March 1960, S/S 108/4/01.   [2] Ibid.

U.N.I.P.'s strength for the forthcoming showdown with the Government.[1] The assessment of the Luapula tour by government officials in the field was that it had stimulated a marked increase in political activity, that the national leaders had succeeded in tightening their control over the Luapula politicians, and above all that the chiefs and Native Authorities had been severely demoralized by what they regarded as a growing challenge to their authority.[2]

During these early months of 1960 U.N.I.P. made significant advances in other parts of the Territory as well. In Northern Province, as in Luapula, the Government was gravely concerned about the possible effects which might follow the granting of independence to the Congo in June 1960. The Provincial Commissioner, Kasama, reported that in Northern Province 'the sands were running out quite fast'.[3] U.N.I.P. was gradually displacing A.N.C. in the Eastern Province, particularly around Fort Jameson, Katete, and Petauke.[4] The same was true in Lusaka and Broken Hill,[5] while on the Copperbelt the sudden and dramatic increase in U.N.I.P. agitation had roused European fears once again.[6] In those rural areas where U.N.I.P. was active, especially in the two northern provinces, government officials expressed their concern about U.N.I.P.'s growing pressure on schools and subordinate Native Authorities.[7]

U.N.I.P. derived great advantage from the visit of the Monckton Commission, which toured Northern Rhodesia between mid-February and 20 March taking evidence. Rightly or wrongly, Africans associated the Commission with the maintenance of the Federation. The fact that the Commission's terms of reference excluded secession and the question of the break-up of the Federation lent support to U.N.I.P.'s claim that the Commission was merely a device for ensuring the Federation's survival.[8] U.N.I.P.'s plans to boycott the Commission were publi-

[1] M.I.R., March 1960, S/S 108/4/01.   [2] M.I.R., March 1960, DG 58/4/01.

[3] Record of Government House meeting on security matters, 19 April 1960, ibid.

[4] M.I.R., March 1960, S/S 123/3/01 and DG 58/3/01.

[5] M.I.R., March 1960, S/S 123/2/01.

[6] M.I.R., February and March 1960, S/S 123/2/01.

[7] Record of Government House meeting on security matters, 19 April 1960, DG 58/4/01.

[8] For the Commission's terms of reference and itinerary see *Monckton Commission* Cmd. 1148, 1960, pp. 6 and 157–62. For a complete record of evidence collected, by the Commission in N.R. see ibid., Appendix VIII, Vols. I and II.

cized for several months before the Commission arrived.[1] That Africans sympathized with the plan was clear from the disapproval they expressed against a.n.c.'s initial decision to give evidence to the Commission.[2] Thus, at a time when u.n.i.p. was attempting both to extend its influence rapidly throughout the Territory and to develop an effective party organization, the Monckton Commission provided an immediate focal point for widespread political agitation. Unlike constitutional discussions, which were always held in London or Lusaka, remote from the ordinary African, the Commission moved through the country offering an ideal target for local demonstrations.

As u.n.i.p.'s leaders made their initial visits to the various provinces, they were able to rally people to take action against the Commission while at the same time promising further instalments of positive action later in the year. In the event, u.n.i.p.'s boycott proved highly successful.

There is no question in our minds that many more witnesses would have come forward in Northern Rhodesia and Nyasaland to give evidence had it not been for the boycott of the Commission organized by the United National Independence Party and the African National Congress in Northern Rhodesia, and the Malawi National Congress in Nyasaland, and the intimidation with which these boycotts were enforced. The organizations responsible clearly had established a remarkable degree of control.[3]

This was especially true in those areas where u.n.i.p. was building on a nucleus of support. In North-Western Province, for example, Africans failed to observe the boycott. One of the Commission's members made the interesting observation that as the Commission moved west political intimidation declined, many more Africans gave evidence of a much higher standard and yet opposition to the Federation became more pronounced.[4] The Commission member might have carried his conclusions further; what had obviously happened was that most Africans in the other parts of the Territory, where u.n.i.p. support was strong, observed the party's boycott and refused to come

---

[1] m.i.r., November and December 1959, January and February 1960, S/S 123/2/01, /3/01, /4/01, /7/01, 1/8/01; and DG 58/2/01, /3/01, /4/01, /7/01, /8/01.
[2] m.i.r., December 1959, S/S 123/8/01.
[3] *Monckton Commission*, Cmd. 1148, 1960, p. 8.
[4] m.i.r., March 1960, DG 58/6/01.

forward. u.n.i.p.'s leaders could claim with some justification that a hopeful beginning had been made.

The Ban on U.N.I.P. in Western Province

At the end of March 1960, soon after the departure of the Monckton Commission, the newly appointed Secretary of State for the Colonies, Iain Macleod, visited Northern Rhodesia on his way to constitutional discussions which were being held in Nyasaland. The visit marked the beginning of u.n.i.p.'s intensified campaign to secure changes in Northern Rhodesia's Constitution before the Federal Review Conference in December 1960. A speech given by Macleod to a civic luncheon in Lusaka indicated the magnitude of u.n.i.p.'s task. Macleod pointed out that the present Constitution had been in force for only a little more than a year, and though he admitted that it had not satisfied either Europeans or Africans, the Constitution was designed to bring their views together, a process which would require considerable time. 'Let me therefore say again that my colleagues and I have no plans in contemplation to amend the constitution in Northern Rhodesia, although I cannot of course predict the outcome of the Review of the Federal Constitution or guarantee that its result may not entail certain consequential changes in Territorial Constitutions.'[1]

In early April the u.f.p.'s Roberts, who had been greatly heartened by Macleod's assurance, added insult to u.n.i.p.'s injury. Roberts's interpretation of Macleod's statement was that while no change in the Constitution might originate from London, the door had been left open for the Northern Rhodesia Government to 'put forward changes we judge to be timely and correct'. At the Federal Review, he declared, the u.f.p.'s primary objective was to increase local responsibility in government affairs and to prevent the introduction of 'any arrangements which might detract from the participation of Europeans in politics, in Legislative Council or in Government'. On the contrary, Roberts argued that European influence in these spheres should be extended until the time when 'mature and responsible Africans should be encouraged and invited to take a greater share'.[2]

[1] *Northern News*, 30 March 1960.
[2] Text of Roberts's speech at Chalimbana Teacher Training College Field Day, 13 April 1960, GH/S 201/09.

The prospects of U.N.I.P.'s constitutional objectives in Northern Rhodesia looked bleak indeed, the more so compared with Nyasaland, where in April Dr. Banda was released from prison and Macleod announced that Nyasaland's constitutional conference would be held in London during June.[1] Under the circumstances, it was not surprising that as U.N.I.P. strengthened itself and political agitation spread African frustration increased. Clashes between A.N.C. and U.N.I.P. became more frequent after a period of relatively good relations in January and February.[2] Disturbances broke out at a number of African schools during March, which resulted in the Government ordering an official inquiry on the ground that the troubles were politically inspired.[3] By late April the Government, which had become gravely concerned both about U.N.I.P.'s rapid growth in certain areas and its increasing militancy, set about improving its territorial security arrangements. The Government believed that U.N.I.P.'s long-term plans called for a period of intensive organization followed by disturbances in October or November 1960. Despite the apparent breathing-space, the Government feared that the rising tide of agitation in U.N.I.P. together with the threat of disturbances in the Congo might easily spark off violence in Northern Rhodesia at any time. Kaunda himself, it was claimed, had warned about the growing danger of his losing control over U.N.I.P., and Sipalo reportedly predicted that violence would erupt first in Luapula Province.[4] U.N.I.P. now had 127 branches in Luapula Province alone; if the present pace of formation continued there would be approximately 175 branches with over 1,000 office-bearers and 10,000 members by the end of June. The Provincial Commissioner reported that U.N.I.P. had started to concentrate on winning over the Native Authorities by both peaceful persuasion and by intimidation. In Samfya District, an area with nearly 37,000 inhabitants, the Native Authorities had all but lost control. U.N.I.P.'s entire organization in the district was staffed by ex-Z.A.N.C. officials whose declared objective, the Provincial

[1] *Rhodesia Herald*, 4 and 6 April 1960.
[2] *Northern News*, 5 May 1960.
[3] Ibid., 24 March 1960.
[4] Record of Government House meeting on security matters, 19 April 1960, DG 58/4/01.

Commissioner claimed, was self-government in 1960 or violence as in the Congo.[1]

In addition to considering security arrangements, the Government prepared counter-measures for use against U.N.I.P. during the coming months. In rural areas, mainly in the north, U.N.I.P. had been holding unauthorized public meetings inside houses to evade the required permit under the Public Order Ordinance. While U.N.I.P.'s speakers addressed a part of the crowd assembled inside the house, most of the audience stood outside, often in a specially fenced enclosure. Native Authorities were unable to make orders against such meetings, so that amendments to the Public Order Ordinance were considered which would empower the Governor in Council to deal with the situation. In addition, orders had been prepared which would enable Native Authorities to prohibit the addressing of meetings and other activities by U.N.I.P. office-bearers who were not residents in the Authorities' respective areas.[2]

Attention was also given to the Societies Ordinance. Regulating officers throughout the country were urged to intensify their campaign to register new U.N.I.P. branches and to collect information about existing branches and their office-bearers.[3] The aim was to prepare for more effective action against U.N.I.P. officials in the event of the Governor declaring certain U.N.I.P. branches unlawful under section 21 of the Ordinance. The Preservation of Public Security Ordinance was also considered.[4] In government circles at the time there was some sympathy towards the argument that a premature and uncoordinated U.N.I.P. outburst in Luapula or Northern Province, which could be countered by employing all available security measures, might offer the Government positive advantages.[5] Though it was agreed that the present situation had not deteriorated to the point where the Ordinance could be invoked against U.N.I.P., it was assumed that such conditions would arise before the end of

[1] Record of Government House meeting on security matters, 7 May 1960, DG 58/4/01.
[2] Ibid.
[3] Registrar to all P.C.s, D.C.s and Officers Commanding Divisions of N.R. Police, 9 March 1960; Registrar to all P.C.s and D.C.s, 19 April 1960, S/S 82/81/01.
[4] Record of Government House meeting on security matters, 7 May 1960, DG 58/4/01.
[5] Ibid., 19 April 1960.

the year. As a preparatory step and in accordance with the provisions of the Ordinance, it was decided that Colonial Office approval should be sought for possible action under section 3 of the Ordinance, which dealt with the restriction of persons and the control of assemblies.[1]

The disturbances anticipated by the Government erupted almost immediately, not in Luapula or Northern Province, but on the Copperbelt. The most serious incident occurred on 8 May at Ndola, where a mob of Africans, returning home after the police had dispersed an unauthorized U.N.I.P. meeting, attacked a white housewife, Mrs. Lillian Burton, and her two children, who were passing by in their car. The car was stopped, petrol thrown inside and ignited. Mrs. Burton managed to save her two children, but after a grim struggle for life, lasting nearly a week, she died in an Ndola hospital.[2]

The Burton tragedy made a deep and lasting impression on Northern Rhodesians of all races. Initially, the reaction among Europeans and many Africans was one of horror followed by a deep sense of outrage directed mainly against U.N.I.P. and its extremist policies. Copperbelt Europeans, led by the U.F.P. and the Mineworkers Union, called on the Government to ban U.N.I.P. throughout the Territory.[3] For several days rioting and other disturbances continued, European pressure on the Government increased, and on 11 May the Governor, acting under the Preservation of Public Security Ordinance, banned U.N.I.P. in Western Province and declared the party's branches unlawful.[4] The next day orders were published restricting five U.N.I.P. leaders—including Kaunda, who was in London at the time, Kapwepwe, and Sipalo—from entering Western Province.[5]

The Government clearly viewed the disturbances in Western Province as offering an opportunity for weakening U.N.I.P.'s position in the crucial Copperbelt area. 'It seems to me', the Governor wrote to the Chief Secretary, 'that . . . there is just the chance that we may be able to do something in the nature of a cutting operation against U.N.I.P. and its influences in Western Province.' The wave of ill feeling against U.N.I.P., he

---

[1] Record of Government House meeting on security matters, 7 May 1960, DG 58/4/01.
[2] *Northern News*, 9 May 1960.   [3] Ibid., 10 May 1960.
[4] Ibid., 12 May 1960.   [5] Ibid., 13 May 1960.

argued, might facilitate the formation of a strong moderate movement which would seek to exclude u.n.i.p.'s extremists from political affairs. While noting that it was not for the Chief Secretary or himself to engage in the formation of political parties, the Governor felt it might be possible to influence Africans of moderate views without obviously engaging in party politics. The Governor went on to suggest that he might meet Roberts, Moffat, and a representative group of 'responsible' Africans, 'such as Katilungu', in order to discuss the ways and means of dealing with African aspirations and grievances without having 'to resort to the sickening tactics of the political extremists'.[1]

On the advice both of the Chief Secretary and the Minister of Native Affairs, the Governor decided against the proposed meeting.[2] Instead it was agreed that Provincial Administration officers in the Western Province be directed to impress upon responsible Africans, 'through the African Area Housing Boards, the African Mineworkers Union and even the Watch Tower Movement', that the Government sympathized with their aspirations, but not with their methods. In addition, it was believed that successful prosecutions against u.n.i.p. officials in the area might well make Africans listen to their local District Officers and contribute to the emergence of a moderate African pary.[3]

The Government's plan failed to produce any noticeable change in the Copperbelt political scene. In part this was due to the opposition of the Senior Provincial Commissioner, who had been charged with implementing the plan and instructed to report his results in three months' time. The Senior Provincial Commissioner questioned both the wisdom and the practicability of encouraging the formation of a moderate African party[4].

I do not believe myself that we can hit u.n.i.p. out of the field for six just like that, by which I mean that some African party will have as its political platform 'one man one vote' and an African majority in the Cabinet, Legislative Council and the Voters Roll. We have, therefore, to encourage partnership and what the original fabians called the 'inevitability of gradualness'.[5]

[1] Governor to c.s., 18 May 1960, DG 58/8/01.
[2] c.s. to m.n.a., 20 May 1960, ibid.
[3] m.n.a. to c.s., 31 May 1960; m.n.a. to s.p.c.(w.p.), 8 June 1960, ibid.
[4] s.p.c.(w.p.) to m.n.a., 14 June 1960, ibid.
[5] Ibid., 8 July 1960.

The Senior Provincial Commissioner argued that moderate political parties, like the c.a.p., had no future in Northern Rhodesia politics and that at the next election it would be the moderates who joined u.n.i.p., not the other way around. The hope was that liberals, such as Moffat, might gradually come to influence Kaunda and his colleagues to adopt a more moderate course. Meanwhile, the Senior Provincial Commissioner recommended lifting the ban in Western Province, not only because u.n.i.p. might begin to form underground branches, but also because to leave the ban in force for too long would strengthen the white attitude that African nationalism could be contained indefinitely by government controls.[1]

On 13 July the ban was discussed at a high-level meeting at Government House. The Senior Provincial Commissioner's views were hardly considered, and for a number of reasons it was decided to retain the ban at least until September and possibly until the end of the year.[2] The Government believed that the ban had been a severe setback to u.n.i.p. which continued to handicap the party on the Copperbelt.[3] The Burton murder trial and the trials involving u.n.i.p.'s provincial leaders, most of whom were in custody, had not been completed. It was also believed that Katilungu, whose return from the Monckton Commission was imminent, should be given time to re-establish himself firmly in Copperbelt affairs. Finally, the Government wished to demonstrate its willingness to stand behind the firm action it had taken in May,[4] despite the fact that both Kaunda and Kapwepwe had denounced violence and successfully appealed for a period of calm.[5]

Until late June, Kaunda had been overseas visiting the United States[6] and Britain, where for the first time he met Macleod. Their meeting, which took place in May, shortly after the Copperbelt disturbances, was far from successful. The Colonial Secretary indicated that Northern Rhodesia's Constitution would not be altered during 1960, nor would changes

---

[1] s.p.c.(w.p.) to m.n.a., 14 June and 8 July 1960, DG 58/8/01.
[2] Record of g.h. meeting, 13 July 1960, S/S 108/4/01.
[3] Ad. Sec. to s.p.c., 8 August 1960, DG 58/8/01.
[4] Record of g.h. meeting, 13 July 1960, S/S 108/4/01.
[5] *Northern News*, 7 and 26 June 1960.
[6] See *N.R. News Survey*, 11 May 1960, for A. Wina's report of Kaunda's U.S. tour.

be considered until after the Monckton Commission had reported. Macleod rebuked Kaunda for the recent violence in Northern Rhodesia and warned him against continuing U.N.I.P.'s 'misleading' propaganda campaign promising self-government by the end of 1960.[1]

When Kaunda returned to Northern Rhodesia the ban in Western Province actually proved to have advantages for U.N.I.P. After the tumultuous events of May and June, Kaunda was able to call for a period of calm; and U.N.I.P.'s leaders were forced to concentrate their organizing activities in other parts of the Territory. Though U.N.I.P. already controlled both the northern provinces, opposition in Eastern Province from the Native Authorities had limited U.N.I.P.'s influence to Fort Jameson, Petauke, and Katete.[2] In Central Province, with the exception of Serenje District, U.N.I.P. was weak in the rural areas away from the 'line of rail'.[3] A.N.C. remained the undisputed master of Southern Province, while in Barotseland and North-Western Province nationalist activity remained minimal.

For the next two months U.N.I.P.'s leaders devoted their efforts to extending and strengthening U.N.I.P.'s organization. Kaunda toured Northern and Luapula Province, the two areas least responsive to control from U.N.I.P. headquarters. Sipalo swung through Eastern Province; Nalumino Mundia, also a Lozi and U.N.I.P.'s Deputy Treasurer, campaigned in North-Western Province; and Sikota Wina, accompanied by his brother Arthur, who had returned briefly from the United States, toured Southern and Central Province.[4] In July, Kamanga and Kapwepwe attended the inaugural celebrations of the Republic of Ghana, after which Kamanga proceeded to the U.A.R., where he opened U.N.I.P.'s new Cairo office.[5] Kapwepwe remained in Ghana for over a month, attempting to raise funds and making preparations for a new U.N.I.P. office in Accra.[6] Chona, who had only recently returned from a successful fund-raising trip to Liberia, Guinea, and Britain,[7] repre-

[1] *Northern News*, 21 May 1960.
[2] Record of G.H. meeting, 14 December 1960, S/S 98/81/02.
[3] Record of G.H. meeting, 13 July 1960, S/S 108/4/01.
[4] *N.R. News Survey*, 14 September 1960.
[5] R. Kamanga, S/S 201/022.
[6] S.B. to C.S., 22 August 1960, S/S 108/02.
[7] S.B. to Ad. Sec., 9 July 1960, ibid.

sented U.N.I.P. as an observer at the Conference of Foreign Ministers of Independent African States at Leopoldville in August.

Reporting on his visit to Northern Rhodesia in the September number of his news survey, A. Wina was visibly impressed by U.N.I.P.'s energy and progress. He himself had addressed a heavy schedule of meetings, and those officials not actively campaigning in the provinces or travelling overseas were busily engaged at U.N.I.P.'s headquarters. Several committees had been formed to study the country's economic and educational problems and detailed statements of U.N.I.P.'s policy in these areas were being drafted.[1]

U.N.I.P. also sought to win over the chiefs and members of the Native Authorities. A circular with U.N.I.P.'s constitutional proposals attached was issued to all chiefs and councillors in July. The substance of the message was that the chiefs had been stripped of their traditional powers, the African people humiliated and turned into a 'subject race'. While the rest of Africa achieved its freedom, Northern Rhodesia, under a white minority Government, was threatened by the Federation's drive towards independence. The chiefs were being used, albeit unwillingly, to support the European cause. The circular continued: 'Here is a challenge which strikes deep at our racial pride. By all means let us disagree over political ideologies; that is inevitable. But in our fight for equality, there should be no dissenters.'[2] Kapwepwe joined in the campaign from Accra, writing a series of polite letters to leading chiefs in which he addressed them as 'my lord'. Kapwepwe assured the chiefs that they had nothing to fear under a U.N.I.P. Government. To support his assurance he enclosed copies of the *Ghana Government Gazette*, which commented on the growing wealth and increased respect accorded to Ghanaian chiefs since Ghana's independence.[3]

Meanwhile, by mid-September constitutional questions had returned to the forefront of Northern Rhodesia politics. Though

[1] *N.R. News Survey*, 14 September 1960.
[2] U.N.I.P. to all Paramount Chiefs, Senior Chiefs, Chiefs and Councillors, July 1960, author's collection.
[3] Kapwepwe to Paramount Chief of Barotseland; Paramount Chiefs Undi, Chitimukulu, Mpezeni; Chiefs Kasempa, Mwamba, Milambo, Chona, Mapanza, Chikwanda, Kazembe; 8 July 1960, author's collection.

for several months Macleod had been attempting to persuade both Kaunda and Nkumbula to participate in the Federal Review,[1] it was Nyasaland's constitutional conference which set the whole of Central Africa astir. The conference, which placed Nyasaland firmly on the road to African government, was concluded on 4 August 1960.[2] That same week in Lusaka, Kaunda had his first meeting with Governor Hone,[3] who had begun informal soundings in a search for common ground between Northern Rhodesia's various political groups.[4] On 28 September Macleod announced that a constitutional conference for Northern Rhodesia would be convened after the Federal Review early in 1961.[5] Macleod's statement, despite its vagueness, represented something of a victory for U.N.I.P., particularly since it was issued in September, several weeks before the publication of the Monckton Commission's Report. U.N.I.P. clearly regarded it as such. In a letter to A. Wina, Sipalo reported a marked rise in U.N.I.P.'s morale and, more important, in party membership. On 1 October alone, he claimed, more than 160 people, including six Europeans, joined U.N.I.P. directly at party headquarters, while for the Lusaka area as a whole enrolment figures 'shot up by 80%'.[6]

In the case of the Northern Rhodesia Government, the initial effect of the Colonial Secretary's announcement was to force renewed consideration of the existing ban on U.N.I.P. in Western Province. It was clearly recognized that the ban would have to be revoked before the constitutional talks opened in London, but differences of opinion existed over the question of timing. The police and special branch favoured retaining the ban for as long as possible, mainly on the ground that if it were raised such jubilation would follow that U.N.I.P. would regain its old position on the Copperbelt almost at once.[7] A.N.C., it was pointed out, had been drawing larger crowds, and it was suggested once again that Katilungu needed more time to entrench his posi-

[1] *Northern News*, 26 June 1960; *Freedom*, July 1960, p. 18.
[2] *Proposals for Constitutional Change in Nyasaland*, Cmd. 1132, 1960.
[3] *Central African Mail*, 9 August 1960.
[4] Roberts to C.S., 9 August 1960, GHS/S 201/09. In the same letter, Roberts protested against the Governor's meeting with Kaunda.
[5] *Northern News*, 29 September 1960.
[6] Sipalo to A. Wina, 5 October 1960, A.N.L.W. papers.
[7] S.P.C.(W.P.) to Ad. Sec. 4 October 1960, DG 58/8/01.

tion. In addition, there was concern about the effect raising the ban would have on Copperbelt Europeans, especially so soon after the release of the Monckton Commission's Report.[1] Against these arguments, however, the Senior Provincial Commissioner, Western Province, advanced the most telling point: if the Government did not deal with Kaunda now, in due course it might be forced to come to terms with u.n.i.p. in Western Province by the Colonial Secretary.[2]

At a meeting convened by the Governor on 12 October each side advanced its case vigorously. The Governor explained that since the ban had to be lifted in any case, the primary consideration was to get the timing right so as to avoid the impression that u.n.i.p. had forced the Government's hand. For the time being the police and the special branch had their way.[3] The ban was considered again in early November and finally revoked together with the orders against u.n.i.p.'s leaders on 14 November, less than three weeks before the opening of the Federal Review.[4]

U.N.I.P. AT THE CLOSE OF 1960

By late 1960 u.n.i.p. had clearly established its supremacy in nationalist politics and was well on its way to achieving the goals Kaunda had set when he took over u.n.i.p.'s leadership at the beginning of the year. Though u.n.i.p.'s strength varied considerably in different areas of Northern Rhodesia, branches had been established in every province, including Barotseland.[5] The ban in Western Province, far from weakening the party, had encouraged u.n.i.p.'s top leaders to turn their attention elsewhere. With the lifting of the ban in November 1960, u.n.i.p. regained its former strength almost at once.[6] In u.n.i.p.'s two rural strongholds, Northern and Luapula Province, the party had improved its organization and intensified its campaign among chiefs and Native Authorities.[7] u.n.i.p.

[1] s.p.c.(w.p.) to Ad. Sec., also record of g.h. meeting, 12 October 1960, d.g. 58/8/01.

[2] s.p.c.(w.p.) to Ad. Sec., 4 October 1960, ibid.

[3] Record of g.h. meeting, 12 October 1960, ibid.

[4] Exec. Co., 7 November 1960, ibid.; *N.R.G. Gazette*, 11 November 1960.

[5] m.i.r., February 1960, DG 58/1/01.

[6] S. Wina to A. Wina, 1 December 1960, a.n.l.w. papers.

[7] Record of g.h. meeting to consider security threat in n.r., 14 December 1960, S/S 98/81/02.

continued to share Eastern Province with A.N.C., though since August 1960 U.N.I.P. had advanced its campaign deep into Petauke District as a result of Senior Chief Kalindaware lifting the local Native Authority's ban against U.N.I.P.[1] In North-Western Province U.N.I.P.'s strength had increased as well, so much so that Kaunda expressed surprise at U.N.I.P.'s progress in an area which had received so little attention in the past.[2] Far more significant were the changes taking place in Barotseland. Throughout the small Protectorate, government officers agreed that both the prestige and the authority of the Barotse National Government had declined during 1960. At the same time, U.N.I.P. agitation was on the increase and might, it was feared, expand rapidly in the coming months.[3]

Apart from the more obvious forms of political activity, such as public meetings and the publication of propaganda, U.N.I.P.'s efforts during 1960 were devoted to four broad fields. The first was the formation of branches, including youth and women's brigade formations as well as action groups. Second, U.N.I.P.'s top leaders were constantly concerned with the party's financial problems, particularly the raising of funds and the improvement of U.N.I.P.'s internal financial arrangements. U.N.I.P.'s third main field of activity encompassed the diverse and apparently contradictory campaign amongst the Territory's chiefs and Native Authorities. Finally, U.N.I.P. attempted during 1960 to gain control of Northern Rhodesia's African trade union movement, in particular the A.M.W.U.

Organization and Finance

U.N.I.P. followed the pattern of nationalist parties in other African territories by identifying itself with the vision of a new Northern Rhodesia nation, known among U.N.I.P.'s followers as Zambia. All people of any race who accepted the legitimacy of the new Zambia and who were prepared to dedicate their efforts to its emergence were to bear their allegiance directly to U.N.I.P., the embodiment of the new national entity. This commitment was to supersede all others: tribal loyalties,

[1] Kaunda to Kamanga, 2 November 1960, A.N.L.W. papers.

[2] Kaunda to Chona, 2 November 1960, ibid.

[3] General report of the political and security position in the Barotseland Protectorate, 23 September 1960; Ag. Resident Commissioner to M.N.A., 26 September 1960, DG 58/1/01.

regional and economic interests, linguistic differences, allegiance to traditional authorities, religious affiliations and support of minority privileges. U.N.I.P.'s aim was to institutionalize this overriding commitment in an extensive organizational structure, which eventually would cover the entire country and bring each person into as intimate a relationship as possible with the heart of the nationalist movement.[1]

During U.N.I.P.'s first two years its structure remained virtually identical with that of A.N.C. At headquarters level were the President, the national office-bearers and members of the Central Committee, the party's permanent executive. The Central Committee was empowered to call periodic meetings of U.N.I.P.'s chief policy-making organ, the National Council, a body composed of representatives of the party's lower levels as well as members of the Central Committee.[2] Beneath the National Council were seven provincial divisions, coterminous with each of Northern Rhodesia's provinces, except the Barotseland Protectorate, which at the end of 1960 had no recognizable provincial executive. Each province was further subdivided into constituencies and branches, some of which, depending on the area, had formed action groups and youth and women's brigades.

Despite U.N.I.P.'s significant progress during 1960, party organization remained more impressive on paper than in practice. In part this was due to the very expansion which had been so impressive. Branch formation throughout 1960 had been extremely rapid, especially in Luapula and Northern Provinces. During the period March–June 1960 the Government became concerned about the growing number of U.N.I.P. branches which had not applied for registration under the Societies Ordinance. Despite the Ordinance's shortcomings, which had become apparent during the campaign against Z.A.N.C. in 1959, the Government instructed its field officers to concentrate on registering U.N.I.P.'s new branches.[3] Between April and December 1960 the total number of U.N.I.P. branches registered rose from 28 to 482;[4] of these Luapula Province

---

[1] Mulford, *The N.R. General Election, 1962*, p. 41.

[2] *U.N.I.P. Constitution*, n.d. 1960.

[3] Registrar to all P.C.s, D.C.s, and Officers Commanding Divisions of N.R. Police, 9 March 1960; Registrar to all P.C.s and D.C.s, 19 April 1960, S/S 82/81/01.

[4] *N.R.G. Gazette*, April–December 1960, *passim*.

alone accounted for 305 with an estimated membership of 69,000.[1] For the most part U.N.I.P. complied with the Ordinance. Indeed, in some areas the various constituencies began to compete for branch registrations.[2] The certificates provided by the Registrar for each registered branch often proved useful in convincing chiefs that U.N.I.P. had secured, if not government approval, then at least official recognition. U.N.I.P. was less cooperative, however, when the Government sought to register the party's growing number of action groups and youth and women's branches. The advantages of avoiding the registration of such subgroups was obvious to U.N.I.P. Since they could not be called on by the Registrar to supply information under the Societies Ordinance about either their membership or their office-bearers, subgroups were able to supply anonymous party activists and to serve as a second rank of leadership in case U.N.I.P.'s 'orthodox' branches were banned. Nor would U.N.I.P. be forced to raise the £1 per branch registration fee, which was automatically forfeited if branches were declared unlawful under the Societies Ordinance. U.N.I.P. claimed that its various subgroups were non-autonomous bodies, and since in practice most such subgroups were difficult to distinguish from their respective constituency- and branch-level organizations, U.N.I.P.'s contention proved almost impossible for the Government to refute.[3] The Government's position was further weakened by the legal difficulties involved in prosecuting U.N.I.P. branches which failed to comply with the Ordinance,[4] and though U.N.I.P. eventually registered a number of its major youth and women's groups, many more subgroups escaped registration altogether.

Though U.N.I.P.'s branch formation had been most spectacular in Luapula Province, significant progress had been made in every other province except Barotseland by the end of 1960. Branch registration figures for both Western Province (thirty-three) and Northern Province (seventy-seven) were considerably below the actual number of branches;[5] in the first case because of the recent ban on U.N.I.P., in the second because of the

[1] Record of G.H. meeting, 14 December 1960, S/S 98/81/02.
[2] 'Can You Win This Important Competition?' S. Wina to all U.N.I.P. constituency secretaries, Luapula Division, 1 September 1960, A.N.L.W. papers.
[3] Registrar to all P.C.S. and D.C.S., 19 April 1960, S/S 82/81/01.
[4] Legal opinion, 12 March 1960, ibid.
[5] *N.R.G. Gazette*, November 1959–December 1960, *passim*.

Government's policy of delaying branch registration in deference to the opposition of its field officers in the area.[1] In other parts of the Territory, U.N.I.P. had thirty-six registered branches in Central Province, thirteen along the 'line of rail' in Southern Province, eleven in North-Western Province, and ten in the southern half of Eastern Province.[2]

U.N.I.P.'s rapid growth had outstripped its capacity to maintain effective internal communication and co-ordination of party policy. Though the practice of appointing executive members for all branch committees ensured a certain loyalty to the centre, U.N.I.P.'s lower echelons retained great freedom from central control and exercised considerable local initiative. This was less true, of course, on the Copperbelt and in Lusaka than in the more remote rural areas, though in this respect Luapula was something of an exception. Despite its dislike of central control, Luapula's provincial executive kept up a steady stream of correspondence and reports to U.N.I.P. headquarters, in some cases sending copies to U.N.I.P. representatives as far afield as London, Cairo, and the United States.[3] Much party business was conducted in personal letters between friends, particularly in the international sphere, where U.N.I.P.'s representatives complained about the lack of regular information emanating from U.N.I.P. headquarters in Lusaka.[4]

The lack of co-ordination was particularly evident in U.N.I.P.'s financial affairs. The sketchy and ambiguous accounting procedures laid down in U.N.I.P.'s first constitution, together with the limited financial experience of U.N.I.P.'s officials, combined to produce a somewhat chaotic financial situation during the party's first year. Fortunately U.N.I.P. succeeded in raising funds overseas, without which it would have faced certain bankruptcy by late 1960. Membership cards, a main source of local income, were often issued by minor party officials on credit; the funds actually collected at branch, constituency, and provincial levels were never large and seldom reached U.N.I.P. headquarters, either through misappropriation along the way, or because of quite necessary expenses such as house rents and ration money

[1] Registrar to Ad. Sec., 15 March 1961, S/S 82/81/01.
[2] *N.R.G. Gazette*, November 1959–December 1960, *passim*.
[3] See S/S 108/4/01 from mid-1960 for record of correspondence.
[4] Minutes of U.N.I.P. London committee meeting, 6 October 1960, A.N.L.W. papers.

for local officials. Special levies for specific purposes such as a delegation to London, a chiefs' conference at Broken Hill, and legal expenses for U.N.I.P. leaders, fared little better, though one such levy imposed on Copperbelt branches raised enough money to buy U.N.I.P.'s first Land-Rover in March 1960. By June U.N.I.P. had secured an additional Land-Rover, a D.K.W. vannette, both equipped with public-address systems, and furniture for the national headquarters. The total cost of these items was over £2,000, half of which had been paid by July. U.N.I.P.'s only other domestic assistance came from several African Traders' Associations and from certain members of Northern Rhodesia's Indian community, most notably from C. C. Patel, President of Broken Hill's Indian Association, who presented U.N.I.P. with a duplicating machine.[1]

The bulk of U.N.I.P.'s financial assistance came from outside Northern Rhodesia and is extremely difficult to assess accurately. In addition to direct financial transfers, which became more numerous in the second half of 1960, some foreign governments, particularly Liberia, Ethiopia, and Tunisia, provided bursaries for U.N.I.P. officials or members;[2] other governments and private organizations paid travel expenses, including transportation, for visiting U.N.I.P. officials;[3] and in some instances U.N.I.P. received equipment from sources outside the Territory.[4] In the case of funds provided by outside sources, the problem of assessing U.N.I.P.'s support was further complicated, first, by the fact that U.N.I.P. refused to bank its funds locally as a precaution against seizure of funds if the party were banned;[5] and, second, by the practice among U.N.I.P. officials of bringing funds into the country in the form of cash or travellers' cheques.[6]

Despite these difficulties, sufficient evidence exists to support the view that U.N.I.P.'s financial assistance from external sources

[1] The finances of U.N.I.P., 9 July 1960, S/S 108/02.

[2] In addition to the Government's report in July 1960, private letters between U.N.I.P.'s leaders mention specific cases of assistance. Five N.R. students received bursaries to study in Tunisia; Kaunda to Kamanga, 2 November 1960, A.N.L.W. papers.

[3] The finances of U.N.I.P., 9 July 1960, S/S 108/02. Also A. Wina to S. Wina, 25 April 1960 describes Kaunda's tour of the U.S., A.N.L.W. papers.

[4] B. R. Banda to A. Wina, 28 October 1960 confirms that a new Land-Rover from T.A.N.U. had arrived, ibid.

[5] The finances of U.N.I.P., 9 July 1960, S/S 108/02.

[6] S.B. to C.S., 22 August 1960, ibid.

increased significantly after May 1960. U.N.I.P.'s main external sources were the governments of Ghana, Liberia, Egypt, and Ethiopia, as well as T.A.N.U. in Tanganyika and various private groups in Britain and the United States. Though in early 1960 U.N.I.P. made extravagant claims of financial support from a number of sources—including, in addition to those mentioned above, India and Algeria—it seems likely that Ghana was the only major contributor to U.N.I.P.'s coffers during these early months. The extent of Ghana's support is difficult to gauge, though it seems unlikely that the amount approached the figure of £10,000 which U.N.I.P. officials cited on several occasions.[1] Other sources, however, were tapped: Chona obtained funds in Liberia in May,[2] while Kaunda, who visited the United States and Britain about the same time, secured additional assistance.[3] Kapwepwe's extended visit in Ghana provided still more funds,[4] and Chona drew additional support from Liberia in mid-September.[5] In late October, Kapwepwe, this time *en route* to Ethiopia, Cairo, and London, raised more money in Accra, most of which he sent immediately to Kaunda in Lusaka.[6] Funds acquired directly in this way by U.N.I.P. headquarters were put to good use by the party. By October U.N.I.P. had a fleet of eight Land-Rovers, the latest acquisition being a gift from the Tanganyika African National Union.[7]

Chiefs and Native Authorities

One of the cornerstones of the Northern Rhodesia Government's African policy had long been the Native Authority Ordinance, first enacted in 1936 and subsequently strengthened by a series of amendments during the next twenty-five years.[8] The Ordinance created a system of rural African administration which

[1] The finances of U.N.I.P., 9 July 1960, S/S 108/02; and references drawn from private correspondence in the A.N.L.W. papers support these general conclusions.

[2] The finances of U.N.I.P., 9 July 1960, S/S 108/02.

[3] S.B. to Ad. Sec., 28 June 1960, S/S 128/64/01 refers to assistance offered to Kaunda by the A.F.L.-C.I.O. in the United States.

[4] S.B. to C.S., 22 August 1960, S/S 108/02.

[5] Chona to A. Wina, 17 September 1960 and confirmed by Kaunda to Chona, 2 November 1960, A.N.L.W. papers.

[6] Kapwepwe to Kamanga, 24 October 1960, ibid.

[7] Sipalo to A. Wina, 5 October 1960, ibid.

[8] The Ordinance was amended in 1946, 1948, 1951, twice in 1953, 1955, 1957, 1958, and 1960. A similar Ordinance, The Barotse Native Authority Ordinance 1936, applied to the Barotseland Protectorate.

was guided and supervised by European officials of the Provincial Administration. Under the Ordinance, the Government recognized as Native Authorities either individual chiefs, chiefs in council, or councils or other groups of Africans which did not include a recognized chief.[1] Native Authorities were charged with a wide range of local responsibilities, similar in many respects to those of municipal councils, which included the power to make rules and orders in a number of important matters: among them the maintenance of law and order and the movement of Africans to or within the Native Authority's prescribed area. In addition, Native Authorities might make orders—indeed at times they were forced to do so by Provincial Administration officers[2]—for the purpose of enforcing any lawful instructions issued by the Provincial or the District Commissioner.[3] Under the Public Order Ordinance the power to control public assemblies and processions was delegated to Native Authorities recognized under the Native Authority Ordinance. The system of African councils, particularly the African Provincial Councils and the African Representative Council, which the Government had developed during the 1940's and 1950's, rested in large measure on the Native Authority system. When Africans were first elected directly to the Legislative Council in 1959, the Government used the Native Authority system to screen African candidates in 'special' constituencies by requiring such candidates to obtain certificates of approval from two-thirds of their respective constituencies' chiefs.[4] In short, the Native Authority system was the basis for government administration and, more important, for government control of African affairs in the rural areas of Northern Rhodesia.

With the campaign against Federation in the early 1950's and the subsequent rise of African agitation, chiefs and Native Authorities came under increasing pressure, especially after 1958, both from U.N.I.P. and the Government. African national-

---

[1] Native Authority Ordinance, CAP. 157 of 1962, p. 3.

[2] Ibid., pp. 7–9, 14–15.

[3] In the Chisunka area of Luapula Province the Native Authority (N.A.) was 'made' to issue warrants of arrest against U.N.I.P. members who had caused disturbances at Chief Chisunka's court; Notes on N.A.s in Luapula Province prepared by P.C.(L.P.), 4 October 1960, DG 58/4/01.

[4] *N.R. Proposals for Const. Change*, Cmd. 530, September 1960, pp. 28–29.

ist leaders had long understood that strengthening their respective organizations in the rural areas depended upon either winning over the traditional authorities by persuasion or directly undermining both their authority and their ability to maintain law and order. Likewise, the Government, firmly committed as it was to the policy of containing nationalist parties, accepted that 'the key to incipient subversion lies with the chiefs'.[1] The principal objection in 1960 to registering U.N.I.P. branches in Northern Province had been that: 'The branches would, upon registration, acquire in African eyes an aura of respectability and U.N.I.P. influence . . . would undoubtedly increase. . . . The self-confidence of the Chiefs would be adversely affected and security in the Northern Province would be undermined.'[2]

During 1960 U.N.I.P. launched a determined campaign against the Native Authority system. Attempts were made not only to undermine traditional authority but also to win chiefs over to U.N.I.P.'s cause.[3] Admittedly, the former was not always the most effective means of achieving the latter; nevertheless, in certain areas U.N.I.P.'s efforts met with remarkable success. One such area was Luapula Province, where the rise in agitation had forced the Government to enter into 'a more personal commitment with the Native Authorities', and where the tendency had been to back them 'with U.N.I.P. as the "enemy" '.[4] In addition to sending letters to the chiefs, U.N.I.P. leaders often attempted to see chiefs personally for discussions. In September, Kaunda toured Luapula Province and 'swayed' several leading chiefs and Native Authorities in Samfya and Kawambwa District.[5] A more detailed account of U.N.I.P.'s success in undermining Native Authorities in Luapula Province was provided by a District Commissioner who toured Chief Chisunka's area in Fort Rosebery District during September 1960. The District Commissioner, having consulted tour reports of Chisunka's

[1] Tour report no. 4, Chinsali District, N.P., May 1955, N/0001/2/4, Lusaka Archives.
[2] Governor to C.S., 27 January 1960, S/S 82/81/01.
[3] U.N.I.P. to all Paramount Chiefs, Senior Chiefs, Chiefs and Councillors, July 1960, author's collection.
[4] Record of G.H. meeting, 1 July 1960, S/S 108/4/01.
[5] Chiefs Kazembe and Munkanta and the chiefs in the Benangumbo N.A. area, Notes on U.N.I.P. and the N.A.s in Luapula Province, 4 October 1960, DG 58/4/01.

area for the previous ten years, found it difficult to believe that the chief and his assessors had lost so much of their authority in so short a time. The traditional practices of preparing camps for the touring District Commissioner and supplying food and water to his party had not been observed by the local population. Traditional courtesies such as using the title 'Bwana' in addressing the District Commissioner had also been dropped. The District Commissioner continued:

The court work of the Native Authority is appalling. The Senior Assessor, Mwisa, 16 years in his post and who has attended three courses, is a member of U.N.I.P. The senior Kapasu [Native Authority police officer] Tito Mwansa, who has recently completed a six week training course at the D.A.T.C. is suspected of being a member of U.N.I.P. The Chief's sister is an ardent U.N.I.P. member. When these facts became known . . . it is not difficult to realize why, over the last five months, 50% of persons found guilty and fined have not paid their fines, nor has any effort been made to collect or arrest and imprison in default. Many U.N.I.P. members who have appeared before the court have not paid their fines. The Kapasus stated that their lives would be endangered if they were to enforce the court's decision, but they could cite no case in which such an effort had been made and had been met with violence.

The Chief and Assessors were unable to keep order in the court when two cases involving U.N.I.P. adherents were being heard. A stage was reached when a leading U.N.I.P. official, Banabas Mashilipa, alias Chileya, Mundia, Mohomadi Mwabo, Mfula (secretary, Lufubu Branch) stood and remonstrated with the court and told his 'kapasu' (an individual in a black fez) to order all the public outside where U.N.I.P. songs were sung. The public then returned to court. An order by the senior Kapasu, Tito, to clear the court had been ignored just previously. The Agricultural Councillor who was sitting in the court, repeatedly advised the Chief to arrest the ringleaders for contempt but the latter declined to take any action. Had he done so, the two Kapasus present would have been unwilling to enforce the court order nor would they have chosen a more favourable time to effect the arrests.[1]

Chief Chisunka's reaction to the sudden rise of U.N.I.P. agitation was one of bewilderment. His only suggestion to the District Commissioner for restoring the situation was that the police mobile unit should come and take 'the bad people away'. 'With

[1] Tour report no. 13 of Chief Chisunka's area, Fort Rosebery District, Luapula Province, 2 September 1960, DG 58/4/01.

such treacherous support from his assessors and Kapasus [Native Authority police], it is little wonder that the Chief will no longer make a fool of himself by using a traditional authority which cannot be implemented.'[1] The District Commissioner's report alarmed the Provincial Commissioner, who feared that the Chisunka experience might easily become more widespread. Pointing out that Chisunka's area had been both peaceful and well run as recently as May 1960, the Provincial Commissioner stressed, as he claimed he had many times in the past, 'the delicate balance there is in this Province between the power of the Native Authority and the power of U.N.I.P. What has happened in this area could happen equally quickly in any other and it seems necessary to devise some method whereby earlier warning can be obtained.'[2]

U.N.I.P.'s undermining of the Native Authority system, which had succeeded in parts of Northern Province as well,[3] did not have the effect of alienating chiefs throughout the country. On the contrary, when the Chiefs' Council, a body instituted by the Government to represent all the Territory's chiefs, was convened in October to put forward their ideas on constitutional change, the chiefs' proposals differed only slightly from those of U.N.I.P. Like U.N.I.P., the chiefs favoured African majorities in both the Legislative and Executive Councils, though their franchise proposals fell somewhat short of universal adult suffrage. The only other significant point of difference, which the chiefs had conceded under government pressure,[4] concerned the number of officials in the Executive Council and the role of the Chief Secretary during the transition period. As for their own role in politics, the chiefs favoured the creation of a House of Chiefs which, while giving them limited powers, would ensure that they remained above politics. Finally, the chiefs, like U.N.I.P., demanded that Northern Rhodesia's constitutional talks be held before the Federal Review.[5]

---

[1] Tour report no. 13 of Chief Chisunka's area, Fort Rosebery District, Luapula Province, 2 September 1960, DG 58/4/01.

[2] P.C.(L.P.) to D.C., Fort Rosebery District (F.R.D.) (c.c. to S.N.A. and C.S.), 7 September 1960, ibid.

[3] Record G.H. meeting, 1 July 1960, S/S 108/4/01.

[4] M.N.A. to Governor, 21 October 1960, MN/129/10, Vol. I, Box 4348, Lusaka Archives.

[5] Resolutions by N.R. Chiefs on N.R. Constitutional Changes, 18 October 1960, ibid.

Undoubtedly the chiefs had not committed themselves whole-heartedly to u.n.i.p. The future was to bear this out. As a group the chiefs had long been opposed to the Federation, just as for years they had been anxious to see Africans progress in the political field. Seldom, however, had the chiefs expressed such bold ideas with such resolution. This was new. And although it is difficult to interpret this shift of emphasis as a major u.n.i.p. triumph, it undoubtedly worked to u.n.i.p.'s favour. Kaunda was elated by the chiefs' proposals: 'It is all so wonderful', he wrote to Kamanga. 'I pray no pressure will be too strong for them to resist. They have made a very good move and I am sure that they will not be disappointed when we take over.'[1]

U.N.I.P. and the African Trade Union Movement

African trade unionism on the Copperbelt, like the Native Authority system in the rural areas, was a field in which the Government sought to restrict nationalist political influence. Apart from the brief period leading up to the 1956 emergency, the Government's policy of keeping trade-union affairs and politics 'in separate compartments' had been remarkably successful for a combination of reasons.[2] First, the only powerful and wealthy African union in which political influence represented a major threat was the a.m.w.u. Second, the large copper companies, fearing the effect of 'political strikes' on copper production, actively supported the Government's policy. Finally, and perhaps most important, since 1949 the a.m.w.u. had been led by the able and moderate Katilungu, who over the years had himself been committed to maintaining the independence of the African trade-union movement.

Katilungu's willingness to support the Government's aims together with his dominant position in trade-union affairs laid him open to bitter opposition from the more militant political and trade-union leaders, who visualized a close connexion between nationalist political parties and trade unions. When in 1959 Katilungu took a more active interest in politics, his decision to back Nkumbula's a.n.c. only further incensed his enemies, though at the time a.n.c. was still Northern Rhodesia's leading African party. Later, when u.n.i.p. had been formed,

---

[1] Kaunda to Kamanga, 2 November 1960, a.n.l.w. papers.
[2] Ag. Labour Commissioner to Ad. Sec., 10 June 1959, S/S 128/64/05.

opposition against Katilungu gathered momentum, particularly after it became known that he intended to serve on the Monckton Commission in 1960.[1]

At the same time and despite his recent pronouncements about closer co-operation between nationalist parties and trade unions, Katilungu agreed to the concluding of a new 'check-off' arrangement[2] between his A.M.W.U. and the copper-mining companies. In March 1958 the A.M.W.U. made an agreement with the companies which provided that the companies through their pay-roll arrangements would collect union subscriptions for a period of twelve months. The 1958 agreement contained two conditions of primary importance for the relationship between the union and political parties: one condition stipulated that the union's funds, the other that the union's organization, might not be used for any political purposes. In mid-1959, after a careful audit of the A.M.W.U.'s books, the agreement was renegotiated. The copper companies had doubts about renewing the agreement because of the increasing tendency of trade-union leaders to engage in politics.[3] The Government's view was that the 'check-off' system should be continued, despite Katilungu's recent interest in politics and his desire to form a united political party-trade union front in preparation for the 1960 Federal Review. Katilungu, it was argued, was too skilful to become entangled too deeply in politics and would certainly reject any attempt by A.N.C. to get at the A.M.W.U.'s funds.[4]

The 'check-off' agreement was concluded in August 1959; Katilungu was out of the country at the time, and the agreement was signed in his absence by the A.M.W.U.'s General Secretary, Mushikwa.[5] The reason was soon obvious. Under the new agreement the conditions imposed on the union's political activities had been considerably tightened. The companies

---

[1] M.I.R., December 1959, DG 58/8/01.

[2] An arrangement under which the mining companies collected the union dues of individual miners on behalf of the A.M.W.U.

[3] N.R. Chamber of Mines to Sec., Minister of Labour and Mines, 9 July 1959, S/S 128/64/03.

[4] Ag. P.C.(W.P.) to Ad. Sec., 15 July 1959, ibid. The Governor and the C.S. both supported keeping the 'check-off' system, as did the Min. of Labour and Mines, John Roberts; C.S. to Governor 27 July 1959 and Governor to C.S., 28 July 1959, ibid.

[5] C.S. for record, 17 August 1959, ibid.

could terminate the agreement: if the union made either its funds or organization available for political purposes; if the union gave its support to political parties; if a union official or employee joined or supported an illegal society or instigated or supported a political strike.[1] When Katilungu returned in October 1959 he condemned the new agreement and threatened to dismiss Mushikwa, though reportedly Katilungu's anger was 'more than a little feigned'.[2] For the time being at least Katilungu had retained the best of all worlds: he enjoyed the Government's favour; he was free to dabble in politics and to continue to represent himself as the Africans' spokesman for 1960; yet A.M.W.U. funds and patronage remained solely his domain, beyond the reach of nationalist politicians.

It was Katilungu's participation on the Monckton Commission in 1960 which proved to be his fatal mistake. The A.T.U.C.'s annual general conference in December 1959 came out in favour of backing U.N.I.P.'s boycott of the Commission, and though attempts to oust Katilungu from the A.T.U.C. presidency failed, Mwendepole, one of Katilungu's former A.M.W.U. opponents and a 1956 restrictee, was elected A.T.U.C. General Secretary.[3] A second more severe attack on Katilungu occurred at the A.T.U.C.'s general executive meeting in early February, just before Katilungu was due to join the Monckton Commission. Jonathan Chivunga, President of the Union of Commercial and Industrial Workers (U.C.I.W.), a member of U.N.I.P. and an ex-Z.A.N.C. restricted person, was joined by his General Secretary, Albert Kalyati, a militant left-wing member of U.N.I.P., in denouncing Katilungu for accepting his post on the Monckton Commission. Katilungu retaliated by dismissing a number of the smaller unions, including the U.C.I.W., which were in arrears in their A.T.U.C. annual affiliation fees. When the meeting closed only the A.M.W.U. and M.A.S.A. remained in Katilungu's A.T.U.C.[4]

Chivunga and Kalyati, joined now by Mwendepole, who had resigned from the A.T.U.C., immediately formed the smaller unions Katilungu had dismissed into a new organization,

[1] S.O.(C.S.)2 to A.S.(C.S.)1, 28 October 1959, S/S 128/64/03.
[2] M.I.R., October 1959, S/S 128/64/01.
[3] M.I.R. December 1959, ibid., and DG 58/8/01.
[4] S.B. to Ad. Sec., 2 March 1960, S/S 128/64/01.

the Northern Rhodesia Reformed Trade Union Congress (R.T.U.C.).[1] Without the strength of the A.M.W.U. to draw upon, the R.T.U.C. had few resources and represented only a small number of organized workers. Nevertheless, its appearance marked an important turning-point in the campaign to break Katilungu's power in the trade-union movement. Besides serving as a rival organization to the now rather narrowly based A.T.U.C., the R.T.U.C. included a number of militant U.N.I.P. trade unionists, some of whom had received training at the I.C.F.T.U.'s College in Kampala and established overseas contacts with both Western and Communist trade-union organizations.[2] In April 1960, Chivunga and Jonas Ponde, the R.T.U.C.'s Treasurer, a position he formerly held in the A.T.U.C., attended the Positive Action Conference in Accra and visited the I.C.F.T.U. College at Kampala.[3] Later in the year the R.T.U.C. received funds from the Central Council of the Confederation of Trade Unions in Yugoslavia, part of which the R.T.U.C. loaned to U.N.I.P.[4]

Throughout the period of the Government's ban on U.N.I.P. in Western Province, R.T.U.C. officials continued their campaign to undermine Katilungu's position both in the A.M.W.U. and the A.T.U.C.[5] The R.T.U.C. applied for affiliation with the I.C.F.T.U. despite a decided preference for the A.A.T.U.F., but the former organization refused to consider the application until the two African T.U.C.s had been reunited. I.C.F.T.U. attempts at mediation in July 1960 failed to bring the two groups together.[6] By the end of the year the R.T.U.C.'s connexion with U.N.I.P. had

[1] The R.T.U.C. included the U.C.I.W., C.A.R.S., the N.R. Timber Workers Industrial Union and the Food, Drink and Factory Workers Union; S.B. to Ad. Sec., 23 March 1960, S/S 128/64/01.

[2] Chivunga and the R.T.U.C.'s Senior Trustee, Remi Chikonkola, had both been to the I.C.F.T.U. College; S.B. to Ad. Sec., 9 March 1961, S/S 128/64/01. Kalyati had visited Yugoslavia, Czechoslovakia, and Russia and maintained contact with the Yugoslavia Confederation of Trade Unions; S.B. to Ad Sec. 9 March 1960, S/S 128/64/05.

[3] Trade Unions in N.R., 17 October 1961, p. 15, S/S 128/64/01.

[4] Ibid.

[5] The Government became so concerned about the situation that it arranged for Katilungu to be released briefly on 5 April from his Monckton Commission duties in Nyasaland and flown back to the Copperbelt 'to try to stop the rot': A.S.(C.S.)1 to C.S., 25 March 1960; Ad. Sec. to C.S., 30 March 1960; and Ad. Sec. to A.S.(C.S.)1, 5 April 1960, S/S 128/64/01.

[6] Trade Unions in N.R., 17 October 1961, ibid., p. 15.

become increasingly evident. On 25 November, at a meeting convened to discuss Northern Rhodesia's forthcoming constitutional conference, the R.T.U.C. identified itself with U.N.I.P.'s constitutional proposals, promising 'positive action' if Kaunda failed to obtain African majority rule.[1]

In December the struggle reached its climax. Katilungu, shortly after declaring that he had joined forces with A.N.C.,[2] was dismissed from the A.M.W.U. presidency by the union's Supreme Council.[3] Katilungu was replaced by John Chisata, a former A.M.W.U. Mulfulira chairman who had represented the union at the Miners International Federation in Sweden in August 1960. Chisata was joined in office by Mushikwa, despite his part in the 'check-off' agreement, and Redson Namitengo, both comparatively moderate trade unionists who were not openly committed to U.N.I.P.[4]

Katilungu's removal from the A.M.W.U. destroyed his base of power in the A.T.U.C. and smoothed the way for a reunification in early February 1961 of the two opposing T.U.C.s in a new organization, the United Trades Union Congress (U.T.U.C.). The U.T.U.C., which included the A.M.W.U. and M.A.S.A., represented a clear victory for the R.T.U.C. faction. Chivunga was elected President of the U.T.U.C., and Kalyati, Mwendepole and Wilson Chakulya, all former R.T.U.C. officials and members of U.N.I.P., filled the other leading posts. U.N.I.P. was also well represented in the U.T.U.C.'s twenty-seven-member general council and in the Congress's three working committees, one of which was to deal exclusively with political matters.[5]

On the eve of the Federal Review U.N.I.P.'s confidence was running high. In the brief space of a year the party's growth had indeed been phenomenal. Kaunda might well refer to U.N.I.P.'s 'indescribable' support which spread across 'the entire country'.[6] Since April an average of twenty-seven new branches had been registered each month. U.N.I.P. had not only weathered the ban in Western Province but turned it to positive advantage.

[1] s.b. to Ad. Sec., 10 December 1960, S/S 128/64/01.
[2] *Northern News*, 28 October 1960.
[3] Ibid., 12 December 1960.
[4] Ibid., 6 March 1961, Namitengo, however, had been restricted in 1956.
[5] s.b. to Ad. Sec., 9 March 1961, S/S 128/64/01.
[6] Kaunda to Chona, 2 November 1960, A.N.L.W. papers.

Katilungu's power in the trade-union movement had been broken and moves were under way to reunite the two African T.U.C.S. U.N.I.P.'s financial position had been greatly improved. Significant progress had been made among the Territory's chiefs and Native Authorities. A handful of Europeans had joined the party, two of whom had shared U.N.I.P.'s platform at mass rallies.[1] Above all, U.N.I.P. had helped to force significant advances on the constitutional front. The Colonial Secretary had opened the way for a territorial constitutional conference in London. In October 1960 the Monckton Commission's Report had emphasized the 'almost pathological dislike' of the Federation among Africans in the two northern territories as well as the belief held by African nationalists that the Federation had prevented African political advance. Moreover, the Commission had recommended an African majority in Northern Rhodesia's Legislative Council and an unofficial majority in the Executive Council, 'so constituted as to reflect the composition of the Legislature'. It had also called for an immediate declaration by the British Government that these steps would be taken in the near future and suggested that Northern Rhodesia's constitutional conference be held without delay, presumably before the Federal Review.[2]

By contrast A.N.C. had suffered a serious decline during 1960. The party registered only twenty-one new branches during the entire year.[3] In September 1960 Nkumbula was convicted and sentenced to twelve months' imprisonment on a charge of dangerous driving, resulting in the death of an African constable, and leaving the scene of the accident. Pending his appeals to the Northern Rhodesia High Court and the Federal Supreme Court, Nkumbula was freed on bail, which enabled him to lead A.N.C.'s delegation to the constitutional talks in London.[4] But the party was badly demoralized and internally divided.[5] At A.N.C.'s annual conference in September 1960, Nkumbula renewed his attacks on the party's provincial-level officials and appointed a committee to examine each provincial

---

[1] *Northern News*, 1 December 1960. James Skinner, a Lusaka lawyer, and Merfyn Temple, a Methodist minister also of Lusaka, were the two Europeans.
[2] *Monckton Commission*, October 1960, p. 43.
[3] *N.R.G. Gazette*, 12 February, 16 September, 14 October, 9 December 1960.
[4] Extracts from the biography of Nkumbula, 27 November 1962, S/S 201/015.
[5] Ibid.

division's financial affairs. In return, Nkumbula and his executive were severely criticized for failing to visit outlying areas during the year.[1] A.N.C.'s constitutional proposals, produced by the National Assembly for the London talks, were poorly drafted and hopelessly unrealistic.[2] Katilungu's decision in October to join forces with A.N.C., which only hastened his own downfall in the A.M.W.U., made A.N.C.'s situation worse by reducing still further any prospect of increasing the party's influence in trade-union affairs. Once dismissed, however, Katilungu devoted himself full-time to politics, joining A.N.C.'s London delegation and beginning preparations for his own advance in A.N.C.

By 1 December 1960 the stage was set for the bitter struggle over constitutional change which was ultimately to decide the fate of the Federation. The nationalist leaders of all three Federal territories had threatened to boycott the Federal Review unless and until both Southern and Northern Rhodesia's constitutional conferences had been concluded and African majority government introduced in both territories.[3] U.N.I.P. insisted on other conditions as well: first, that Africans should form a majority of Northern Rhodesia's delegation to the Federal Review; second, that the Federal Review's agenda include the issue of immediate secession from the Federation; third, that Joshua Nkomo, the leader of Southern Rhodesia's National Democratic Party (N.D.P.), be admitted to the Southern Rhodesia conference with the other representatives of his party.[4]

In late November, S. Wina, backed by Dr. Banda of Nyasaland, pressed U.N.I.P.'s demands in London. Within several days the Secretary of State for Commonwealth Relations announced that Southern Rhodesia's constitutional conference would be held concurrently with the Federal talks and that Nkomo would be able to lead the N.D.P.'s delegation.[5] Rumours also circulated that Welensky had agreed to discuss the question of secession at the Review.[6] On 1 December Macleod

[1] S.B. to Ad. Sec., 22 October 1960, TS/S 123/01.
[2] A.N.C. Constitutional Proposals to the London Talks of December 1960, ibid.
[3] *Guardian*, 24 October 1960.
[4] S. Wina to A. Wina, 1 December 1960, A.N.L.W. papers.
[5] Ibid., 30 November 1960.
[6] *Northern News*, 30 November 1960.

cabled Kaunda, assuring him that all would be well if only Kaunda came to London for talks and possibly to attend the Federal Review as well. Three days later Kaunda arrived in London, the crucial question of Northern Rhodesia's constitutional conference still unresolved.[1]

[1] S. Wina to A. Wina, 1 December 1960, A.N.L.W. papers.

V

THE NORTHERN RHODESIA
CONSTITUTION, 1962

NORTHERN RHODESIA'S 1962 Constitution evolved in three stages. The first began in December 1960 with the Federal Review and the London Constitutional Conference, ending with the Colonial Secretary's proposals of February 1961.[1] The second, February–June 1961, included the Governor's consultations with the Territory's various political groups in Lusaka and concluded with the Colonial Secretary's presentation of the June proposals.[2] In the third stage, after serious disturbances had occurred in Northern Rhodesia, the British Government reconsidered the June proposals and announced final changes on 1 March 1962.[3]

The Northern Rhodesia Constitutional Conference

The preliminary session of the Federal Review, which opened in London on 5 December 1960, marked the beginning of a new phase in the struggle over the future of the Federation of Rhodesia and Nyasaland. In retrospect it seems remarkable that the Federal Review was ever held at all, let alone with all the Federation's diverse and deeply divided delegations in full attendance. For the British and the Federal Governments the price of this brief victory amounted to nothing less than relinquishing the initiative in the struggle to Central Africa's nationalist leaders. The Federal Review's first task was to discuss problems of procedure and representation for the main Federal talks, which were to be held after a brief Christmas recess. The most contentious procedural issue between the British Government, the Federal Government, and the various political delegations was the question of a time-table for the Federal Review

---

[1] *N.R. Proposals for Constitutional Change*, Cmd. 1295, February 1961.
[2] Ibid., Cmd. 1423, June 1961.
[3] *Hansard*, 1 March 1962, cols. 1340–1.

on the one hand and the constitutional conferences for Northern and Southern Rhodesia on the other. On 4 December, at a meeting between the Colonial Secretary, the Secretary of State for Commonwealth Relations, and the three nationalist leaders, Kaunda, Nkomo, and Banda, the African leaders agreed to attend the Federal Review. In return the British Government agreed to move forward the opening date for the two territorial conferences from January 1961 to 14 December 1960, thus ensuring that both conferences would run concurrently with the Federal Review.[1]

Though this concession succeeded in bringing the African leaders to the conference table, it was not enough to keep them there. On 12 December, joined this time by Northern Rhodesia's chiefs,[2] the nationalist leaders staged a walkout on the grounds that the Federal Review was being used as a delaying tactic and that the British Government was not prepared to grant Africans sufficient representation at the forthcoming territorial conferences. Within hours the British Government postponed both territorial conferences, announcing that they would not be re-scheduled until the situation arising from the walkout had been clarified and the atmosphere for productive discussions improved.[3]

Several days of confused negotiations followed, during which the issue of the timing of the various conferences was finally settled in favour of the African nationalists. On 16 December, after several meetings with the Colonial Secretary, Kaunda led u.n.i.p.'s delegation back to the Federal Review for what proved to be its final session.[4] Southern Rhodesia's conference opened the same day, though Whitehead temporarily excluded Nkomo from Southern Rhodesia's delegation for his part in the walkout from the Federal Review.[5] Banda, satisfied apparently that he had accomplished his main purpose in coming to London, elected to return to Nyasaland.[6] At the Federal Review's last plenary meeting, Duncan Sandys, Secretary of State for Commonwealth Relations, revealed the extent of the tactical victory secured by the nationalists. The Federal Review would not reconvene until after the New Year at a date to be set in

[1] *The Times*, 5 December 1960.   [2] Ibid., 17 December 1960.
[3] Ibid., 13 December 1960.   [4] Ibid., 17 December 1960.
[5] Ibid., 16 December 1960.   [6] Ibid., 17 December 1960.

light of the progress made at the Northern and Southern Rhodesia constitutional conferences. Southern Rhodesia's conference was set to reconvene at Salisbury in late January, while the preliminary round of Northern Rhodesia's conference would begin on 19 December and resume after the Christmas recess on 30 January 1961.[1] The principle that territorial constitutional changes would have to precede any review of the Federal Constitution had been established beyond all doubt. The initiative now lay with the nationalists.

Meanwhile, with the Federal Review quietly shelved for the time being, Welensky turned his full attention to the territorial conferences, particularly to Northern Rhodesia's talks in London, which had clearly become the main field of battle in the struggle over Federation. Since Southern Rhodesia's conference was to be held in Salisbury, the Federal Government was well placed to influence the proceedings; in any case, there was little danger of an African majority being introduced into the colony's Legislative Assembly. Constitutional advance in Northern Rhodesia, however, was quite a different matter. With African majority rule established for Nyasaland, and with Northern Rhodesia's nationalists as firmly committed to breaking the Federation as their counterparts in Nyasaland, the Federation would be unable to survive African rule in Northern Rhodesia.

In an effort to strengthen the Federal Government's position at the London talks, Welensky took advantage of the Christmas recess to demand two concessions from the British Government. The first was an undertaking from the Colonial Secretary that Britain would not give majority rule to Africans in Northern Rhodesia at the present time; the second that the Federal Government be granted direct representation at the Northern Rhodesia talks. Both demands were rejected, though in the case of the second the British Government agreed to allow Federal M.P.s from Northern Rhodesia to join the U.F.P.'s delegation as official representatives. Having failed to obtain concessions from Macleod, Welensky adopted bolder tactics. On 28 January, Northern Rhodesia's U.F.P. delegation, backed by the Dominion Party's representatives, announced their intention of boycotting the Northern Rhodesia talks. Welensky

[1] *The Times*, 19 December 1960.

hoped not only to disrupt Northern Rhodesia's conference but also to circumvent Macleod, whom Welensky deeply distrusted, by making the u.f.p.'s participation in the talks a matter for negotiation between the Federal Government and the British Prime Minister.[1] Welensky's Minister of Law, Julian Greenfield, arrived in London on 30 January for discussions with Macmillan and Macleod, a step reportedly suggested by Sandys, who was in Salisbury at the time.[2] The hope was clearly to delay the Northern Rhodesia conference, possibly until the Federal Review was reconvened and certainly until Southern Rhodesia's talks had been safely concluded.

On 1 February the paralysing effect of the boycott became evident; plenary sessions were cancelled and Macleod called for a series of informal and confidential talks with those delegates who remained in attendance at the conference.[3] The demands of the respective parties could hardly have been further apart. The u.f.p. favoured the maintenance of the principles laid down in the 1959 Constitution and opposed both an extension of the franchise and an increase in African representation in the Legislative Council. The Liberal Party emphasized the importance of providing constitutional machinery which would facilitate a gradual and peaceful transition from European Government to African majority rule in the next five years. The African parties, who had now formed a united front,[4] demanded African majorities in both the Legislative and Executive Councils and an electoral system based on the principle of universal adult suffrage.[5]

As the conference entered its second week the chances for agreement seemed more remote than ever. It was now clear that the u.f.p.'s boycott, together with rumours of possible secession emanating from Salisbury,[6] had forced communications between the white settlers' representatives and the British Government

[1] *Guardian*, 30 January and 2 February 1961.

[2] *Observer*, 29 January 1961.

[3] *Guardian*, 1 February 1961. The u.f.p.-d.p. boycott left ten of the thirty-one conference seats vacant. Delegations in attendance included u.n.i.p.; a.n.c.; Liberal Party; n.r.'s chiefs; representatives of the Asian community and of the independent m.l.c.s.

[4] C. J. Banda (a.n.c.) to Nelson Banda (u.n.i.p.), extract in s.b. to Ad. Sec., 9 February 1961, TS/S 123/01.

[5] *N.R. Proposals for Constitutional Change*, Cmd. 1295, February 1961, pp. 4–6.

[6] *Rhodesia Herald*, 1 February 1961.

outside the walls of Lancaster House. Greenfield met Macmillan twice during the first week, while Macleod, noticeably absent from the Macmillan meetings, continued sterile discussions with the increasingly irritated African and Liberal delegates at the Conference.[1] A second and parallel conference had appeared, one carried on 'behind the scenes in government offices and hotel bedrooms'.[2]

Midway through the second week delegates in attendance at the conference issued an ultimatum calling on Welensky to stop his interference in Northern Rhodesia's talks and demanding that Macmillan cease his private meetings with Welensky's emissary in London.[3] Macleod's answer was that the British Government had a clear obligation to consult the Federal Government about proposed constitutional changes for Northern Rhodesia, although this in no way minimized 'the final responsibility of the British Government for a decision in these matters'.[4] More convincing as an explanation for the delay was the outcome of Southern Rhodesia's conference, where agreement was reached on 7 February on a constitution which fell far short of satisfying African demands. For the time being at least, Nkomo had agreed to a highly restrictive qualified franchise and only fifteen African seats in a sixty-five-member Legislative Assembly.[5] Welensky's bid to delay Northern Rhodesia's conference long enough to secure a satisfactory settlement in Southern Rhodesia appeared to have paid well. Conversely, the position of Kaunda and Nkumbula was severely undermined by Nkomo's acceptance of the Southern Rhodesia plan.[6] If Africans in Southern Rhodesia were prepared to accept only 23 per cent of the proposed seats, an African majority in Northern Rhodesia suddenly seemed less urgent.

The Northern Rhodesia Conference dragged on amid widespread speculation and a growing sense of bitter frustration among the African delegates. Rumours circulated that Macleod was being forced to change his plans for Northern Rhodesia

---

[1] *Rhodesia Herald*, 3 and 6 February 1961.

[2] Ibid., 18 February 1961.

[3] Ibid., 8 February 1961.

[4] *Hansard*, 7 February 1961, col. 187.

[5] *Observer*, 12 February 1961.

[6] Kaunda sharply criticized Nkomo for letting down the people of N.R., *Guardian*, 10 February 1961.

under pressure from Welensky, Sandys and a group of Conservative back-benchers, who for several days had been lobbied by a European Mineworkers' delegation recently arrived from the Copperbelt.[1] Into this tense and uncertain atmosphere Kaunda released his explosive warning that if Welensky and the British Government continued to frustrate the legitimate aspirations of the people of Zambia, the result might well be a mass rising 'which by contrast would make Mau Mau look like a child's picnic'.[2] Back in the Federation, Welensky called up territorial troops in Northern Rhodesia: the conference was now 'teetering on the brink of disaster'.[3]

On 17 February the Northern Rhodesia Conference ended in complete deadlock. The Europeans had clung to their boycott throughout the proceedings, and the African delegates refused to accept Macleod's general proposals, claiming that they were incomplete and failed to reveal essential details on voting arrangements and the racial composition of the legislature. Bitterly denouncing the conference as 'merely a political comic opera, a farce', the Africans complained of being forced to return empty-handed to their supporters in Northern Rhodesia. Indeed, what the delegates themselves knew of Macleod's plan only confused them and bolstered their suspicions that negotiations had, in fact, hardly begun and that further 'tinkering' with the proposals was likely to continue behind their backs.[4] The Colonial Secretary's decision that specific details of the general proposals would be settled in further discussions held by the Governor in Lusaka seemed to Africans to be a particularly ominous sign. Already the 'backstairs' conference conducted on Welensky's behalf by Greenfield appeared to have been more successful than if the u.f.p. had attended the formal conference at Lancaster House.[5]

Despite the ending of the Lancaster House Conference, all the various delegates remained in London, seeking through

[1] *Guardian*, 13, 15, and 17 February 1961. See also *The Times*, 10 February 1961, for report of meeting between Macleod and the Conservative Colonial Committee at which a motion was passed calling on the Government in dealing with N.R. to work within the principles laid down in the 1958 White Paper on constitutional change in N.R. (Cmd. 530). See also *The Times*, 20 February 1961.

[2] *Observer*, 12 February 1961.

[3] *Guardian*, 15 February 1961.

[4] Ibid., 8 February 1961.

[5] *The Times*, 18 February 1961.

last-minute meetings to influence Macleod's final decision.[1] In Salisbury, Welensky called up additional troops in Northern Rhodesia, at the same time indicating his willingness to use force to preserve the Federation.[2] Meanwhile, in Parliament, on 20 February, Macleod announced his controversial 15-15-15 plan for Northern Rhodesia's Constitution.[3]

Macleod's Proposals, February 1961

Macleod's proposals called for a Legislative Council of forty-five elected members, up to six official members and such nominated members as the Governor might appoint on instructions from the British Government. Among the elected members, fifteen would be returned from single-member constituencies, by upper roll voters, fifteen from single-member constituencies by lower roll voters, and fifteen from National constituencies by both rolls voting together. Candidates in National constituencies would be required to qualify for election by obtaining the same prescribed minimum percentage of the votes cast on each roll; their overall support would also be expressed as a percentage figure, calculated by averaging together their respective proportions of votes on the upper and lower rolls. Each of the three sets of constituencies was to extend over the entire Territory; upper roll constituencies concentrated predominantly in urban areas, lower roll constituencies centred mainly in the rural areas.[4]

The intention of the lower roll franchise was to lower the general income and educational qualifications and to add certain categories of voters who held special offices or special qualifications, but who could not comply with the normal income or property-holding requirements (e.g. ex-servicemen and members of Native Authorities). The British Government estimated that approximately 70,000 Africans would be eligible for registration on the lower roll. No major changes were envisaged for the upper roll franchise, except a slight downward adjustment which would qualify between 1,500 and 2,000 additional Africans.

[1] *Observer*, 19 February 1961.
[2] *Guardian*, 21 February 1961; *The Times*, 23 February 1961.
[3] *N.R. Proposals for Constitutional Change*, Cmd. 1295, February 1961.
[4] Ibid., pp. 6–7.

Northern Rhodesia's Executive Council was to consist of three or four officials and six unofficials, including at least two Africans and two non-Africans. In forming the Council, the Governor was to pay due regard to the group which appeared to command the widest support in the Legislative Council. The principle of collective responsibility was maintained.[1]

Detailed suggestions were also put forward for the establishment of an advisory House of Chiefs, and it was proposed that consideration should be given to the inclusion in the Constitution of a Bill of Rights. Finally, in the case of Barotseland, which retained a special relationship with the British Government in constitutional matters, the proposed plan would have to be discussed separately with the Protectorate's Paramount Chief as soon as possible.[2]

Defending his proposals, Macleod claimed that in seeking a middle course the British Government's chief objective was to secure a substantial increase in African representation in Northern Rhodesia's Legislative Council, while still maintaining the principle of 'non-racial' politics by requiring political parties to seek support from both races.[3] By implication, the Monckton Commission's recommendations for a clear African majority, based as they were on a purely racial approach to Northern Rhodesia's development, were rejected. The racial complexities and the intensity of opposing political forces both in Northern Rhodesia and in the wider Federal context had made outright victory to either race out of the question. Yet the very fact that Macleod's proposals represented an attempt to conciliate two profoundly opposed racial and political groups inevitably meant that ambiguities flourished at the expense of both clarity and certainty. Questions of decisive importance in determining the ultimate balance of the races in the new legislature—delimitation of constituencies, the exact method by which National members would be returned, details of the franchise proposals—were deferred for settlement by the Governor after further consultations with political groups in Lusaka.[4]

Macleod's proposals for the National seats were particularly ambiguous. Throughout the negotiations which followed, these

[1] *N.R. Proposals for Constitutional Change*, Cmd. 1295, February 1961.
[2] Ibid., pp. 8 and 12–14.   [3] Ibid., p. 2.   [4] Ibid., p. 9.

arrangements proved not only to be the most contentious issue but also the point which proved most sensitive to political pressure. Under the broad franchise proposals set out in the White Paper, the upper roll was to consist of approximately 25,000 Europeans, 3,000 Africans and 2,000 Asians, thus insuring that the upper roll seats would be mainly European.[1] The fifteen lower roll seats, with an African electorate of approximately 75,000, were certain to be shared exclusively between the African parties.[2] The crux of the proposals lay in Macleod's idea of combining the two rolls in order to return National members. This was far from explicit.

In the 'national' constituencies it would be laid down that to qualify for election a candidate must obtain the *same* prescribed minimum percentage of the votes cast on *each roll*: and that the votes on each of the two rolls would be equalized by averaging the percentage of votes cast on each roll which is secured by each candidate.

This arrangement would achieve the object of securing substantially increased African representation in the Council, while maintaining the principle of a non-racial political approach in which political parties are obliged to seek support from both races. Her Majesty's Government attaches considerable importance to the concept of a group of seats on a 'national' basis as described above, but naturally would be prepared to consider other proposals *which would have a similar result*.[3]

(My italics)

The object was clearly to force National candidates to obtain support from both races. Significantly, this was expressed as the same prescribed minimum percentage of the 'votes cast on each roll', not of the votes cast by each race. Here, then, in the light of the proposed racial composition of the two rolls, was a considerable advantage for the African parties. The upper roll was to be approximately 12 per cent African, while the lower roll was virtually 100 per cent African. Assuming, therefore, that the prescribed minimum percentage was set at 15 per cent, and applying a literal interpretation to Macleod's

---

[1] *N.R. Proposals for Constitutional Change*, Cmd. 1295, February 1961.
[2] Ag. c.s. to all D.C.S, 4 May 1962, MS/2615/37.
[3] *N.R. Proposals for Constitutional Change*, Cmd. 1295, February 1961, p. 7.

words in the White Paper, African candidates in the National seats would be able to satisfy the minimum percentage on the upper roll by obtaining the entire African vote plus only 3 per cent of the European votes. On the other hand, European candidates in National seats would need to obtain the whole of the 15 per cent required on the lower roll from African voters.

It was, in fact, this plan which had been circulated at the London Conference and again by the Governor during the discussions in Lusaka.[1] It was hardly surprising that the Federal Prime Minister was so bitterly opposed to Macleod's proposals, for in them he saw the very real possibility of an African majority in Northern Rhodesia and the far-reaching consequences of such a development both on Southern Rhodesia and on the future of the Federation. Welensky totally rejected Macleod's proposals, claiming that the Federal Government had not been adequately consulted. In Lusaka, Roberts led the U.F.P.'s ministers in resigning from the Northern Rhodesia Government.[2] Rumours that the Federal Government was considering a declaration of independence were not discouraged by Welensky. On the contrary, the Federal Prime Minister threatened to employ all means at his disposal to resist Macleod's or any other plan which resulted in power passing from 'responsible hands' in Northern Rhodesia.[3] Welensky's decision to mobilize troops in Southern Rhodesia also gave rise to speculation, not merely about the Federal Government's intentions, but also about Welensky's dramatic behaviour.[4] Sandys, for one, clearly felt that Welensky's reaction bordered on the irresponsible.[5]

On the other side, the Africans condemned the whole affair; Macleod's plan, the Lancaster House Conference, the British Government, and Welensky.[6] Convinced that eventually they would be denied majority rule, the African leaders protested against the decision to shift the negotiations on details to

[1] Memorandum by the Governor on the Legislative Council, the delimitation of constituencies and the franchise, n.d., circulated to political parties in late March 1961, author's collection.

[2] *Rhodesia Herald*, 22 February 1961.

[3] Ibid., 28 February 1961.

[4] *Rhodesia Herald*, 22 February 1961.

[5] *Hansard*, 22 February 1961, col. 579.

[6] *Guardian*, 18, 20, and 21 February 1961.

Lusaka, where it was feared that the whites would have a considerable advantage.[1] Rather surprisingly and within days of the publication of Macleod's White Paper, the nationalists received still another more severe blow. The Chiefs' Council, which had supported u.n.i.p.'s proposals in October 1960 and whose delegates had joined in the nationalists' walkout from the Federal Review in December, agreed under heavy pressure from the Government to accept Macleod's proposals as an interim measure for Northern Rhodesia's constitutional development.[2]

Thus the representatives of all the various delegations returned to Lusaka frustrated and confused by Macleod's vague proposals. The only group which had not rejected the plan was Moffat's Liberal Party, which suddenly found itself in a particularly favourable position.[3] In the British Government's search for a formula to bridge the gap between the races, the prize had fallen somewhere in the middle. Moreover, the Liberals inherited the Executive Council posts vacated by the u.f.p.[4]

The June Proposals

Under Macleod's proposals the balance of racial and political forces in Northern Rhodesia's legislature would depend solely upon the method adopted for institutionalizing the principle of 'non-racial' political development. The White Paper emphasized that the British Government attached 'considerable importance' to the concept of a group of seats in which candidates were forced to seek support from both races. Macleod's proposed solution had been the National seats, but the White Paper was explicit on the point that other proposals which produced a similar result would be considered.[5]

Welensky, despite his violent outburst in Salisbury, was quick to take advantage of the British Government's receptive attitude. Joined by Greenfield and Roberts at the Common-

[1] *Guardian*, 18 February 1961.

[2] m.n.a. to c.s., 23 February 1961, MN 129/10, Vol. I, Box 4348, Lusaka Archives.

[3] *Rhodesia Herald*, 18 February 1961, and *Guardian*, 4 March 1961.

[4] *Northern News*, 7 March 1961.

[5] *N.R. Proposals for Constitutional Change*, Cmd. 1295, February 1961.

wealth Prime Ministers' Conference during March in London, Welensky presented the British Government with three alternative schemes to Macleod's plan, all modified versions of Northern Rhodesia's 1959 Constitution.[1] More ominous, from the nationalists' point of view, were the 'consultations' which followed; Welensky met Macmillan, Sandys, and even the Colonial Secretary before leaving London in late March.[2] A statement issued by the British Government on 21 March indicated that the representations of the Federal Government would be considered, though only within the 'framework and general spirit' of the February proposals. The statement's rather weak disclaimer that there had been no negotiations between the two governments did little to allay African suspicions back in Lusaka, especially when Welensky announced that he was returning to Salisbury convinced now that Federation would continue.[3]

Though African leaders in Northern Rhodesia protested against Welensky's discussions with the British Government in London, both nationalist parties were fully occupied with pressing problems at home.[4] Nkumbula, having agreed to participate in the Governor's consultations and having launched a campaign to explain the Macleod proposals to his followers throughout the country,[5] was suddenly removed to prison for nine months following the failure of his appeal case to the Federal Supreme Court.[6] Katilungu, who had become A.N.C.'s Deputy National President in March 1961, took over the party's leadership and eventually Nkumbula's seat in the Legislative Council as well.[7] Katilungu, of course, was anathema to U.N.I.P., so that the united front which A.N.C. and U.N.I.P. had formed at the London talks soon broke down completely. Katilungu was also something of a threat to U.N.I.P., partly because he was extremely able and still had supporters in the trade-union movement, but also because unlike most A.N.C. leaders he was a Bemba from Northern Province. Defections

[1] *Northern News*, 6 and 16 March 1961.
[2] *The Times*, 16 and 20 March 1961.
[3] Ibid., 21 March 1961.
[4] *Northern News*, 23 March 1961, and *Week by Week* (A.N.C.), 11 March 1961.
[5] *Northern News*, 7 March 1961.
[6] Ibid., 13 April 1961.
[7] Extracts from biography of Nkumbula, 27 November 1962, S/S 201/015.

from A.N.C. to U.N.I.P. during 1960, together with Nkumbula's personal decline, had left A.N.C. in a pathetic state of disorganization and poverty, a situation which Katilungu had set about remedying as soon as he became Nkumbula's deputy in March 1961. It was then that Nkumbula and Katilungu first established contact with President Tshombe in Katanga, who promised A.N.C. financial assistance and equipment for the campaign against U.N.I.P.[1] Immediately Katilungu became A.N.C.'s acting President he began to strengthen the Katanga link, which by mid-1962 had become invaluable not only to A.N.C. but also to the U.F.P.[2]

Meanwhile, U.N.I.P. was confronted with internal dissension, arising initially at least from the problem of whether or not to accept Macleod's proposals as a basis for further negotiations with the Government. U.N.I.P.'s executive divided into two main schools of thought: one advocating complete rejection of the proposals followed by a dramatic 'positive action' campaign; the other favouring negotiations and a fair trial for the Macleod plan. Though discussions during March 1961 centred on U.N.I.P.'s participation in the Governor's forthcoming consultations, the division in U.N.I.P. ran considerably deeper and raised fundamental differences among the party's leaders. The group which supported co-operation included Kaunda and most of U.N.I.P.'s older leaders, who recognized that the difficulties which Macleod faced in the British Cabinet made it highly unlikely that all U.N.I.P.'s demands could be secured in one step. They also felt that the African people were weary and should not be called upon to face a period of extensive trouble without having first exhausted all reasonable opportunities for further negotiations. The younger group among U.N.I.P.'s leaders, which certainly included the Wina brothers, Sipalo, Mundia, and possibly Kamanga, argued that the African people had never been more ready for action and that it would be a 'betrayal of faith' if U.N.I.P. 'succumbed to the low level of accepting the proposals'. A number of the younger men indicated that they were not prepared to stand as candidates in

[1] Extracts from biography of Nkumbula, 27 November 1962, S/S 201/015; see also S.B. to Ad. Sec., 10 March 1961, TS/S 123/01; *Rhodesia Herald*, 23 February 1961.
[2] Extracts from biography of Nkumbula, 27 March 1962, S/S 201/015; S.B. to Ad. Sec., 26 April 1961, TS/S 123/01.

any election held under the Macleod plan. U.N.I.P., it was claimed, had become so well organized that nothing remained but to 'launch' some kind of militant action: 'The spade work has already been done . . . we have actually reached the limit and if we move from now onwards we cannot move without cracking.'[1]

U.N.I.P.'s younger leaders also questioned whether U.N.I.P. could accept the proposals without sacrificing the party's basic principles. A. Wina, writing from the United States, took the line that co-operation under the Macleod plan meant acceptance of the principle that individuals could be divided into groups of voters and non-voters purely on the basis of wealth, education, and status in the community. In addition, there was the plan's practical result of dividing voters into two racial blocs, Africans being relegated mainly to the inferior status of lower roll voters. The idea, he argued, of equating reason and wisdom with worldly acquisitions was foreign to U.N.I.P.'s tradition; party policy had always been firmly based on the principle of equality of individuals, irrespective of race, wealth, education, or social status. In the event that U.N.I.P.'s executive decided to accept Macleod's proposals, Wina suggested that party candidates for the 'rigged election' be selected through a primary election carried out by U.N.I.P. among all the people of Northern Rhodesia. In this way 'the right of each adult in Northern Rhodesia to choose his own representatives' would be maintained.[2]

Beneath the conflict over the Macleod proposals, which the party kept remarkably well concealed, lay deeper differences over the question of U.N.I.P.'s leadership. This was not the first instance in which Kaunda's leadership was questioned,[3] nor was it the last. There had, of course, always been, as in any nationalist party, a certain amount of friction between 'militants' and 'moderates', and indeed the present difficulties showed this same division. In this instance, however, two additional factors complicated the matter. The first was U.N.I.P.'s policy towards Europeans, which in the light of the Macleod proposals had

[1] S. Wina to A. Wina, 21 March 1961, A.N.L.W. papers.
[2] A. Wina to Sipalo, 28 February 1961, ibid.
[3] Exchange of letters between Kaunda and A. Wina in September and October 1960, ibid.

suddenly become an urgent and potentially explosive problem for the party. The second factor was the marked aggressiveness among several of u.n.i.p.'s provincial groups, which had arisen largely as a result of the party's disproportionate growth in various areas. Where u.n.i.p. was solidly entrenched, such as in Luapula and Northern Province, tension was running high.[1] Given u.n.i.p.'s strength in these areas, together with their remoteness from centres of heavy European settlement, it was hardly surprising that u.n.i.p.'s local officials should have regarded any form of compromise as wholly unnecessary.

Barotseland, which supplied another main wing of u.n.i.p.'s leadership, raised a different problem. u.n.i.p.'s Lozi leaders, steeped as indeed many were in the intricacies of traditional Barotse politics, prided themselves on being a sort of party 'intelligentsia', u.n.i.p.'s most sophisticated politicians. Barotseland itself, however, remained closed to nationalist parties during 1961.[2] The result was that u.n.i.p.'s Lozi leaders, deprived of a base from which to operate and unable to demonstrate convincingly the extent of their tribal support, adopted an extremely aggressive attitude on questions of party policy. In this way men like Sipalo, whose views were particularly extreme, hoped to consolidate their position in the party by taking the lead among urban Africans, many of whom were Lozi migrant workers. In the case of Sipalo this led to persistent rumours that he and his Lozi colleagues were undermining Kaunda.[3] S. Wina, writing to his brother in March 1961, asserted that an open campaign was under way in u.n.i.p. to remove Sipalo at the party's next elections.[4] In May the Press uncovered more convincing evidence of Sipalo's disloyalty which Kaunda made no move to repudiate.[5]

Kaunda, who presided over these and other tensions growing up in u.n.i.p., sought, without tarnishing his image as a militant nationalist leader, to ease the party towards constitutional negotiations and to encourage the policy of multi-racialism.

[1] *Voice of Zambia*, April 1961; Kaunda (on behalf of u.n.i.p.'s National Council) to c.s., 7 April 1961, a.n.l.w. papers; p.c.(n.p.) to Ad. Sec., 17 February 1961, S/S 82/81/01.

[2] m.n.a. to c.s., 29 May 1961, ibid., Vol. III.

[3] *Northern News*, 19 May 1965.

[4] S. Wina to A. Wina, 21 March 1961, a.n.l.w. papers.

[5] *Northern News*, 18 and 19 May 1961.

Macleod's proposals Kaunda referred to as the worst constitution ever offered to a British African territory.[1] He also attacked the Government for its repressive policies in Northern Province and for its dilatory and obstructive attitude towards registering U.N.I.P.'s new branches in the area.[2] Yet by April Kaunda had secured the backing of U.N.I.P.'s National Council to participate in constitutional discussions with the Governor,[3] and the first discreet advances had been made to Northern Rhodesia's European community.[4]

During April and May 1961 the Governor held several rounds of consultations, meeting each of Northern Rhodesia's various political groups separately and maintaining the strictest secrecy over all proceedings. The basis for these discussions was a lengthy memorandum which the Government prepared and circulated in advance to the various parties. Essentially the memorandum provided a more detailed version of Macleod's February proposals, covering the delimitation of constituencies, details of the franchise, and the arrangements for electing the controversial National members. On this latter point the memorandum was explicit; there were to be fifteen National seats and the prescribed minimum percentage, tentatively put at 15 per cent, was to be the same for both rolls.[5]

By early June rumours both in Salisbury and Lusaka of substantial changes in Macleod's plan began to arouse African suspicions. When Sandys visited Salisbury for consultations on the final details of Southern Rhodesia's Constitution, newspapers speculated that he also brought a new Northern Rhodesia plan for discussion with Welensky. To Africans the rumours appeared to be confirmed by the arrival in Salisbury at the same time of Governor Hone, who had just completed his consultations with political groups in Lusaka.[6] Southern Rhodesia's Constitution, which introduced Africans into the Legislative Assembly for the first time, had to be ratified by a referendum set for mid-July. Since Northern Rhodesia's final proposals

[1] Kaunda to Governor, 7 April 1961, A.N.L.W. papers.
[2] Kaunda to c.s., 7 April 1961, ibid., and Registrar to Ad. Sec., 23 March 1961, S/S 82/81/01.
[3] Kaunda to Governor, 7 April 1961, A.N.L.W. papers.
[4] *Northern News*, 13, 17, and 18 May 1961.
[5] Memorandum by the Governor, n.d. March 1961.
[6] *Northern News*, 8 and 10 June 1961.

were due to be announced in June, Africans theorized that majority rule in Northern Rhodesia might well be sacrificed in order to ensure the acceptance of Southern Rhodesia's Constitution as well as the continuation of the Federation.

The strongest indication of a substantial change in the February proposals was given by Roberts, the U.F.P.'s leader in Northern Rhodesia. In an interview with the *Northern News* on 15 June he claimed that under the final plan more weight would attach to the upper roll in the arrangements for electing National members. It was virtually certain, Roberts asserted, that Northern Rhodesia's next Legislative Council would have a white majority, a prediction on which he refused to elaborate, beyond claiming that Africans would be robbed of much of their influence.[1] U.N.I.P. responded immediately: Kaunda cabled a grave warning to the Colonial Secretary predicting 'untold racial strife, chaos and bitterness' if the British Government adopted the 'Welensky-Sandys plan'. Warning the British Government not to confuse U.N.I.P.'s recent co-operation with weakness or moderation, Kaunda threatened to unleash U.N.I.P.'s secret 'master plan', a programme of 'non-violent positive action' aimed at destroying the Federation and securing immediate independence.[2]

By 23 June representatives of the Federal Government and every political party in Northern Rhodesia had gathered in London to exert whatever influence they could on the British Government's final decision.[3] When Macleod presented the Governor's proposals on 26 June, it was clear that the February arrangements for the election of the National members had been significantly altered. The original system of equalizing the votes received by National candidates from each roll had been accepted, but the Governor indicated that because of anxieties expressed by certain of the Territory's political groups alternative proposals had been considered for the minimum percentage requirements in National constituencies.[4]

The first anxiety had been that the original proposals might result in a clean sweep of the National seats by one race, thus making too great a disparity between Africans and Europeans

[1] *Northern News*, 16 June 1961.
[2] Ibid., 17 and 19 June 1961.   [3] Ibid., 22 June 1961.
[4] *N.R. Proposals for Constitutional Change*, Cmd. 1423, June 1961, p. 5.

in the Legislative Council. The Governor believed that if such a disparity should emerge it would be unacceptable at Northern Rhodesia's present stage of development to a wide section of public opinion in the Territory. Hence, four of the seven double-member National constituencies proposed were to return one European and one African member. The fifteenth National seat was to be reserved for Asian and Coloured voters, who would vote together in a Special National constituency extending over the whole country.[1]

The second anxiety was that the minimum percentage requirements might lead to the frustration of National seats, or worse still, to the election of candidates who had obtained only a small minority of the votes cast. To deal with the possible frustration of National seats, the recommendations provided for the holding of one by-election under the same regulations. With regard to candidates returned on a minority vote, the Governor pointed out that the emphasis in the National seats was to be placed on obtaining support from both races, not necessarily on accumulating a majority of the vote.[2] To ensure, however, that candidates had substantial support from at least one section of the community, an additional qualification was introduced which required National candidates to secure 20 per cent of the votes cast on one or other of the two rolls.[3]

Finally, the original minimum percentage arrangements were altered. The Governor explained that under the February proposals a National candidate would have to obtain far more votes from the predominantly African lower roll than from the racially mixed upper roll. This meant that European candidates would be placed at a disadvantage, especially because of the presence on the upper roll of a substantial number of Africans. Moreover, unless the qualifying percentage was set unreasonably high, it might be possible in some National constituencies for an African candidate to qualify solely by obtaining African votes on both rolls, thus defeating the spirit of the Constitution.[4]

The Governor attempted to devise qualifying requirements which would place candidates of both races in a more nearly

---

[1] N. R. Proposals for Constitutional Change Cmd. 1423, June 1961, p. 7; and Hansard, 26 June 1961, cols. 33–34.

[2] Ibid., pp. 6–7.   [3] Hansard, 26 June 1961, col. 34.

[4] N.R. Proposals for Constitutional Change, Cmd. 1423, June 1961, p. 6.

equal position. He suggested that the minimum support required by a candidate should be expressed as $12\frac{1}{2}$ per cent or 400 votes (whichever was the less) of the votes cast by each race in the election. The change was defended on the ground that the inclusion of a specific number had the advantage of providing a set target figure which candidates might use to estimate in advance their chances of securing the minimum support required. Furthermore, the 400-vote option set an upper limit to the number of votes of each race which the candidate would need in order to qualify, without reducing its utility as a measure of racial support. The alternative of obtaining $12\frac{1}{2}$ per cent of the votes cast by each race was included because a low poll or an organized boycott of the election would render the securing of 400 votes impracticable, with the likely result that National seats would be frustrated.[1]

The Governor believed that this complicated formula would give 'practical effect to the principle that national members should be obliged to seek support from voters of both races'.[2] Whether it would produce results similar to those intended by Macleod's original proposals was doubtful. True, it resembled Macleod's plan for a group of seats on a national basis and maintained the obligation on political parties to seek support from both races. The crucial difference in the June plan was that it clearly would not produce increased African representation on anything like the scale visualized either by Macleod in his White Paper or by the Governor in his original memorandum to the parties. Had Macleod's February plan—the same minimum percentage of the votes cast on each roll—been adopted, the probable effect would have been a very substantial increase in African representation through the medium of the National seats. Even if the Governor's subsequent proposal to reserve three or four National constituencies had been included in Macleod's original plan, the maximum increase in African representation through the National constituencies still could have been as high as eleven or twelve of the fifteen seats. Such a result when added to the fifteen African lower roll seats would almost certainly have produced an African majority and probably an African party majority as well.

[1] *N. R. Proposals for Constitutional Change*, Cmd. 1423. June 1961, p. 6.
[2] Ibid., p. 7.

The effect of the Governor's proposals was not simply to ease the position towards parity between the races. In practice, the proposals virtually prevented it. National candidates, faced with the need to satisfy the prescribed requirements, would now find them easier to fulfil on the African side than on the European side, thus giving the advantage to European candidates and parties. For example, if, as was likely, the total electorate in a National constituency comprised approximately 5,000 Europeans and 14,000 Africans, the relevant figures for qualification would be 625 ($12\frac{1}{2}$ per cent) or 400 votes for the European electorate and 1,875 ($12\frac{1}{2}$ per cent) or 400 votes for the African electorate. While in this case all candidates would choose to satisfy the 400-vote option, in percentage terms the European candidate would need to win over only 3 per cent of the African electorate, whereas the African candidate would require votes from 8 per cent of the Europeans. Conversely, in terms of votes, the European candidate would need to convert only one in every thirty-five African voters, while the African candidate would be confronted with winning over one in every thirteen Europeans. There was, therefore, a strong probability that under the new arrangements well over half the National seats would go to Europeans, thus ensuring a white majority in Northern Rhodesia's Legislative Council.

June 1961–March 1962

Africans in Northern Rhodesia angrily condemned the June proposals as a 'betrayal' by the British Government, which under pressure from Welensky had sought to appease the forces of white supremacy in Central Africa.[1] In every respect the June changes worked to the advantage of the u.f.p. In the National seats, more than half of which were now reserved, the 400-vote option clearly favoured the u.f.p. without yielding a similar advantage to the African parties. The introduction of the Special National constituency for Asian and Coloured voters, most of whom would qualify under the higher franchise, severely diminished the prospects of nationalist parties securing upper roll support in the National constituencies. The 20 per cent requirement for National candidates strengthened the u.f.p. against the Liberal Party by ensuring that the latter's

[1] *Northern News*, 28 June 1961, and *Week by Week*, 1 July 1961.

candidates could not succeed in National seats on a small minority of the combined votes of both races.

A brief lull followed Macleod's announcement in the Commons. Kaunda and several colleagues attended a conference of nationalist leaders from dependent African territories in Accra early in July. On 6 July Kaunda returned to London to see Macleod before travelling to Northern Rhodesia for U.N.I.P.'s historic Mulungushi Conference.[1] Speaking to the Conference's 4,000 delegates amid shouts of 'Action Now' and 'Kwacha', Kaunda launched into an impassioned attack on the British and Federal Governments.

They [the British Government] have sold us down the cold river of white supremacy. . . . They are treating us like pieces of dirt. . . . We are being sacrificed on the altar of foreign politics. They gave into Welensky in order to save Whitehead's referendum which means saving Welensky himself and, therefore, saving the Federation at the expense of our political advancement; the very thing successive colonial secretaries have assured us would not happen.

The battle still remains the same. It is not anti-white, but anti-wrong. We have many friends among men of all races. We shall not fight against white racialists and at the same time be racialistic ourselves.

I have repeatedly asked the people of Northern Rhodesia to be patient and non-violent in thought, word and deed. But I have recently had to remove one of these noble words from my vocabulary. It is 'patience'. Welensky refused to be patient and he got what he wanted. We who were patient have been neglected.[2]

Pledging himself 'to strike at the very roots of the British Government in this country', Kaunda claimed that U.N.I.P. would not only reject the June proposals but would wage 'practical, non-violent' war against Welensky's Federation until it was completely destroyed and Africans ruled Northern Rhodesia.[3] Later in the conference, after a day-long closed debate, Kaunda was unanimously granted 'emergency powers' to implement U.N.I.P.'s widely publicized 'master plan'.[4]

The Mulungushi Conference was a resounding personal

[1] C. Kamalondo to A. Wina, 5 July 1961, A.N.L.W. papers.
[2] Kaunda, *Zambia Shall be Free*, pp. 158–9.
[3] *Northern News*, 10 July 1961.
[4] Ibid., 11 July 1961.

triumph for Kaunda, who emerged in a stronger position in the party than ever before. The stirring speeches together with the prospect of immediate action had greatly excited the conference delegates. 'It is agreed by all', S. Wina wrote afterwards, 'that it [the conference] was the biggest affair ever witnessed in the country's history.'[1] Kaunda used his advantage well. Contrary to the plans of U.N.I.P.'s National Council, party elections were held on the conference's final day. The sudden change of plans was the result of an extremely delicate situation created by the behaviour at the conference of Sipalo.[2] On the morning of the final day a move was well under way among conference delegates to remove Sipalo from office, and in the elections that afternoon he was ousted as U.N.I.P.'s Secretary-General and replaced by Chona. Kaunda was returned unopposed and Kapwepwe retained his post as Treasurer-General. Kamanga, who had operated U.N.I.P.'s Cairo office, succeeded Chona as Deputy President, while Aron Milner, a Euro-African from Ndola, became U.N.I.P.'s Deputy Secretary-General.[3] As for Sipalo's downfall, it had been 'purely accidental', due entirely to behaviour he had been warned about repeatedly.[4] The party was sorry to lose him,[5] 'but his appearance that morning was simply revolting and there was no way of saving him'.[6] Kaunda also expressed his regret, indicating that U.N.I.P. would continue to use Sipalo 'somewhere'.[7]

Incidents began immediately after the conference. In Lusaka U.N.I.P. initiated a 'keep sober' campaign and attempted to launch a mass boycott of local beerhalls. Sporadic cases of arson also occurred and minor disorders broke out on the Copperbelt.[8] Anticipating possible government action against U.N.I.P.'s leaders once the 'master plan' was fully in effect, S. Wina and Kapwepwe were hurriedly dispatched to Dar es Salaam.[9] Writing from Tanganyika on 30 July, S. Wina impatiently criticized the beerhall boycotts as simply a repeat of

[1] S. Wina to A. Wina, 30 July 1961, A.N.L.W. papers.
[2] Chona to A. Wina, 12 August 1961, ibid.
[3] *Northern News*, 12 July 1961.
[4] Chona to A. Wina, 12 August and 18 September 1961, A.N.L.W. papers.
[5] S. Wina to A. Wina, 30 July 1961, ibid.
[6] Chona to Kalmalondo, A. Wina, and Kamanga, 18 July 1961, ibid.
[7] *Northern News*, 12 July 1961.
[8] *An Account of the Disturbances in Northern Rhodesia, July to October 1961.*
[9] *Northern News*, 28 July 1961.

the old A.N.C. line of action. 'However', he continued pro-
phetically, 'it was expected that this was merely a "warm up"
and that things of untold magnitude would eventually follow!!'[1]

Early in August serious disturbances erupted in Northern
Province and on the Copperbelt. Within days they had spread
to Luapula Province. By the third week in August the first two
parts of the Preservation of Public Security Regulations had
been applied to Luapula and Northern Provinces. U.N.I.P.'s
branches in both areas were declared unlawful under the
Societies Ordinance and meetings were banned. On the Copperbelt, where the Preservation of Public Security Regulations had
been in force since May 1960, branches of U.N.I.P.'s youth
brigade were declared unlawful.[2] Government reports on
1 September put the number of incidents since 24 July at
901, resulting in 1,400 arrests. Thirty-eight schools had been
burned, 34 in Northern Province alone; more than 60 roads
had been blocked; 24 bridges destroyed or seriously damaged; and 27 deaths had occurred.[3] Among the more than
3,000 persons arrested before the disturbances ended in October,
the Government reported a grand total of 2,691 convictions,
2,158 of which involved known supporters of U.N.I.P.[4]

The disturbances stopped almost as suddenly as they had
begun. In mid-September, following talks in London between
Kaunda and Macleod, the British Government announced its
willingness to consider further representations on the proposed
Constitution, provided that the disturbances ceased immediately.[5] Kaunda returned to Northern Rhodesia and appealed
for an end to the violence.[6] As a result the number of reported
incidents declined sharply in late September, so much so that
by 6 October the Governor announced a substantial withdrawal
of security forces from the troubled areas.[7]

Northern Rhodesia had passed through a major crisis. During
the whole of the 'struggle' for African government, the Territory
never brushed as close to armed rebellion as it had in August

[1] S. Wina to A. Wina, 30 July 1961, A.N.L.W. papers.
[2] *An Account of Disturbances in N.R., July to October 1961*, p. 2.
[3] *Northern News*, 1 September 1961.
[4] *An Account of Disturbances in N.R., July to October 1961*, p. 3.
[5] *Northern News*, 14 September 1961.
[6] Ibid., 22 and 29 September 1961.
[7] Ibid., 3 and 6 October 1961.

1961. The British Government's decision to reconsider the June proposals raised once again not only the question of Northern Rhodesia's future but also the future of the Federation. Coming as it did at the height of the disturbances, Macleod's decision could be regarded as nothing less than a clear U.N.I.P. victory. That, in any case, was the opinion of local Europeans, who, having just recovered from the shock of August's violent outburst, now concluded bitterly that in dealings with the British Government organized violence appeared to pay handsome dividends.[1]

With the Territory's constitutional future in the balance and feelings running high among both Africans and Europeans, it was hardly surprising that the disturbances proved as controversial as they had been dramatic. Most Europeans, the European Press, a number of moderate Africans and the majority of Civil Servants were convinced that Kaunda and his party had wilfully encouraged, planned and executed the violence.[2] Liberal Europeans, a number of government officials and a wide section of Africans believed that African anger and frustration had carried a sincerely non-violent, civil disobedience campaign beyond the control of U.N.I.P.'s leaders.[3] Finally, a relatively small but highly politically conscious group of Europeans and Africans believed that the disturbances had been absolutely necessary, effectively restricted to anti-Government measures and eminently successful.

As is often the case, each interpretation contained an element of truth. The behaviour of Kaunda and his top leaders during late July–early August strongly suggested that U.N.I.P.'s 'master plan' was launched prematurely and largely on the strength of local initiative in the Northern Province.[4] Though Kaunda always repudiated U.N.I.P.'s alleged responsibility for the violence, in other respects his actions were less consistent. Initially he claimed that the disturbances were a spontaneous manifestation of African frustration, arising partly from the constitutional deadlock and partly from the failure of U.N.I.P.'s

[1] *Northern News*, 16 September 1961.
[2] Ibid., August–September 1961, *passim*. Also *An Account of Disturbances in Northern Rhodesia, July to October 1961*, p. 1.
[3] *Northern News*, 28 August 1961.
[4] Asked on 27 July if the outbreak of disorders was U.N.I.P.'s 'master plan', Chona replied 'I really don't know'; *Northern News*, 28 July 1961.

national leaders to implement the party's 'master plan'. Also in the early stages Kaunda called unsuccessfully for a stop to the violence, conceding that the disturbances 'looked organized'.[1] As the disorders continued to spread, however, Kaunda seized the initiative and sought to turn the situation to U.N.I.P.'s advantage. On 18 August he burned his situpa (identity certificate) and announced that the first stage of U.N.I.P.'s 'master plan' had been launched in Northern Province.[2] Later he raised allegations of brutality against the security forces and in a letter to Macmillan demanded that the British Government appoint an impartial commission to inquire into the conduct of the Government's security operations.[3] U.N.I.P. subsequently expanded and elaborated these allegations in its pamphlet, *A Grim Peep Into the North*.[4]

Rather surpisingly, Government records support this same view: that for a time at least U.N.I.P.'s national leaders lost control over the party's lower echelons in the northern provinces and on the Copperbelt. The Chief Secretary, recommending the banning of U.N.I.P. branches, indicated that the Government's evidence showed the disturbances were 'entirely the work of minor U.N.I.P. officials'. In acting against U.N.I.P., the Government was anxious to avoid the allegations which it believed inevitably would follow, particularly from overseas, that it was suppressing the entire party. A suggestion that U.N.I.P.'s Northern Province branches should not be banned until its leaders had been given the opportunity of stopping the violence was dismissed, because it would force U.N.I.P.'s national leaders into an impossible position. If they stopped the violence, they would be accused of having inspired it in the first place; if, on the other hand, they failed, they would be accused of lack of control over their party. Instead, the Government decided to ban U.N.I.P.'s branches in the north, prosecuting as many minor party officials as possible and publicizing simultaneously the extent to which members of U.N.I.P. had been involved in the disturbances. As well as justifying the Government's actions,

[1] *Northern News*, 7 and 10 August 1961.
[2] U.N.I.P. to all Divisional Secretaries, 18 May 1961, A.N.L.W. papers; *Northern News*, 18 August 1961.
[3] *Northern News*, 24 and 28 August 1961; Kaunda to Macmillan, 18 August 1961, A.N.L.W. papers.
[4] *Voice of U.N.I.P., A Grim Peep Into the North*, 17 October 1961.

it was hoped that this course would also bolster chiefs and Native Authorities in the troubled areas, who previously had complained of lack of government support.[1]

The publication of u.n.i.p.'s *Grim Peep Into the North* provoked in the Government an urgent effort to compile its own account of the disturbances, which aimed not merely at refuting the pamphlet's allegations but also at underlining u.n.i.p.'s deep and direct involvement in the violence.[2] This was hardly the impartial commission of inquiry which u.n.i.p. had demanded in August. 'The culprits', u.n.i.p. complained, were to be made, 'judges in their own case.'[3] Indeed, the result was the Government's *An Account of the Disturbances in Northern Rhodesia, July to October 1961*, which, though less flamboyant and containing fewer extreme exaggerations, was no less biased than u.n.i.p.'s *Grim Peep Into the North.*

u.n.i.p.'s allegations, which were based on a visit by Kaunda to Northern and Luapula Provinces in early October, challenged the Government on three main points. u.n.i.p. put the number killed during the disturbances at fifty, compared with the Government's figure of twenty-one, which did not include eight policemen drowned during a security operation in the Chavuma area. Second, u.n.i.p. accused the Government's security forces, which included units of the Federal army, of indiscriminate burning and the 'razing of whole villages to the ground'. Third, the security forces were alleged to have committed 'savage atrocities', including beatings, rape, looting and murder.[4]

The Government's *Account* was a curiously ambiguous document, notable more for its omissions than for the wealth of factual information which it presented. As expected, the *Account* concluded that under difficult, often dangerous, circumstances the security forces had discharged their duties to the best of their ability. It was admitted that while 'many houses were probably burnt accidentally' during the security operations:

At no time has there been any planned campaign by security forces

[1] Exec. Co., 8 August 1961, S/S 57/011.
[2] Ad. Sec. to all p.c.s and d.c.s, 19 October 1961, S/S 208/012.
[3] Chona and Mundia to Governor, 30 October 1961, ibid.
[4] *A Grim Peep Into the North*, 17 October 1961.

to burn houses either as a retaliatory measure, or as a punishment for taking part in disorders, or as a demonstration of a determination to put down violence by stern measures. It is however likely that on one or two occasions the security forces did set fire to houses in circumstances where they considered such action necessary in order to achieve their objective of bringing violence under control and restoring law and order.

There is no substance whatever in the suggestion that the burning of houses by security forces was a deliberate policy.[1]

The highly ambiguous language used by the Government had been necessary, because, in fact, 'the army was responsible for much burning in the Chinsali District, particularly on the Great North Road, and also in Luwingu District . . . as a part of their security operation and a determined effort to put down violence once and for all'.[2] The report of one lieutenant-colonel explained that 'these rigorous counter actions were taken—not in the sense or spirit of spiteful retaliation, but very much more on the lines of harsh and swift justice and also as a deterrent to future action'. His battalion 'did burn houses, both deliberately and accidentally', and the action, he claimed, had been supported both by the police and by officers of the Provincial Administration. 'It was not a nice game of cricket the opposition were playing and therefore a few "Bumpers" were introduced by the visiting eleven.'[3]

The burning of huts was not restricted to the army alone. At Matumba village in Chinsali District, which the Government's account never mentioned, the Mobile Unit cordoned off the village and 'certain houses [forty-four of the village's sixty-four huts][4] were pointed out as U.N.I.P. and burned'. The District Commissioner stated that Matumba village was the worst in his district, that its members had been responsible for the burning of a bus and that as an example 'all U.N.I.P. buildings were to be burnt'.[5] In the case of Mulenga Chenaeka village in Mporokoso District the Government's *Account* was

[1] *An Account of the Disturbances in Northern Rhodesia, July–October 1961*, pp. 71–72.
[2] Notes from reports of persons involved in the operations, S/S 108/012.
[3] Report by Lieutenant-Colonel, 1st Battalion K.A.R., 20 October 1961, ibid.
[4] For record to s.o. (c.s.) 1, 16, November 1961, ibid.
[5] Report on Matumba village, notes from reports of persons involved in operations, ibid.

open and frank. The village had been burned on the orders of Chief Chitoshi, because it had been a constant source of trouble and its inhabitants had refused both to obey Native Authority laws and to acknowledge their chief.[1] Other Native Authorities took similar action in villages where there had been persistent opposition to their rule; the Government explained that in such cases the purpose had been to 'deter lawbreakers' and 'to prevent the spread of violence'.[2]

The Government effectively countered U.N.I.P.'s accusations in five of the seven alleged cases of rape. One soldier was convicted of rape and sentenced to two years' imprisonment. In the other instance the Government claimed to have insufficient evidence to support a charge of rape against three askaris (African soldiers);[3] the opinion of one government official— that the case was one of indecent assault—did not appear in the final *Account*.[4] The Government's handling of the allegations of widespread looting was somewhat disingenuous. 'It would indeed be unlikely', the Government contended, 'that in an operation of this nature the security forces could be held guiltless of taking the stray chicken from deserted villages to supplement their rations';[5] in fact, in two Mporokoso District villages alone twenty-six chickens and four ducks were taken while the police mobile unit was operating in the area.[6] Moreover, as was clearly the case in most reports on hut burning, security forces had often operated on their own, well away from the supervision of responsible officers of the Provincial Administration.[7]

Despite the wealth of evidence presented by the Government, much of it refuting specific U.N.I.P. allegations, Africans plainly rejected the Government's *Account*.[8] It was also criticized by several newspapers, both locally and overseas.[9] Senior government officials in Lusaka had been entirely responsible for compiling and drafting the *Account*, which to them was never

[1] *An Account of the Disturbances in Northern Rhodesia, July to October 1961*, p. 58.
[2] Ibid., p. 71.
[3] Ibid., p. 72.
[4] Notes from reports of persons involved in the operations, S/S 108/012.
[5] *An Account of the Disturbances in N.R., July to October 1961*, p. 72.
[6] Notes from reports of persons involved in the operations, S/S 108/012.
[7] Ibid.
[8] Ag. Chief Information Officer to Ad. Sec., 4 January 1962, S/S 108/012.
[9] *Central African Examiner*, Vol. 5, No. 8, January 1962, p. 7; *The Times*, 5 January 1962.

intended as anything but an answer to U.N.I.P.'s *Grim Peep*. Many of the reports on which the *Account* was based were submitted after the publication of U.N.I.P.'s pamphlet and in response to the Administrative Secretary's circular of 19 October.[1] Thus, it was inevitable that the Government's effort should have resulted in a biased and highly political document, shot through with ambiguities and in the final analysis casting doubt on the general conduct of the Government's security operation. That impartiality was never the Government's main concern became clear beyond doubt during the delicate task of drafting the final Account.

I have endeavoured to be frank enough to resist charges of whitewashing and yet restrained enough to avoid making unnecessary self-inflicted wounds. I hope I have not offended the security forces by gratuitous criticism and at the same time to have disarmed those who will charge us with evasion. . . . I have been mindful of the necessity of avoiding any reference to the central leadership of U.N.I.P., which might present new ammunition to the opposition in Legislative Council, and might embarrass us in impending constitutional negotiations. . . .

You will see therefore, that to balance the damage caused by the security forces, I have had something to say about the damage caused by the law breakers. Similarly, I have detailed the casualties sustained by the security forces as a counterbalance to the casualties inflicted on the law breakers. The inferences which might be drawn from some of the remarks regarding damage in the course of security operations are balanced by an appreciation of the work of the security forces in most difficult circumstances.[2]

By the time the Government published its *Account*, the previous year's disturbances had receded well into the background, replaced now in the centre of the political stage by the final round of constitutional negotiations. The ban against U.N.I.P. in Northern and Luapula Provinces and on the Copperbelt was lifted on 1 November 1961,[3] and the Governor resumed his constitutional discussions with the Territory's various political groups the following week.[4] The British Government's apparent

[1] S/S 108/012, *passim*.
[2] J. E. Maddocks to Ad. Sec., 22 November 1961, S/S 108/012.
[3] *N.R.G. Gazette*, 1 November 1961.
[4] *Northern News*, 7 November 1961.

retreat since the Colonial Secretary's statement in mid-September had been bitterly opposed by the Northern Rhodesia u.f.p. In late September the party's more extreme members formed a militant 'action committee' to 'resist by all possible means' any alterations in the June proposals. This group, which among other things advocated military training for Europeans, work stoppages by the European Mineworkers' Union and civil disobedience against the Government, was particularly critical of the Government's apparent *volte face* towards u.n.i.p. in late October.[1] The lifting of the ban on u.n.i.p. was severely attacked as a confusing and demoralizing blow to the Native Authorities, which had loyally assisted the Government in putting down the recent disturbances.[2]

Meanwhile, behind the scenes Welensky shifted his ground as well, though not in the direction of his party's northern wing. Welensky opposed the creation of the new 'action committee' and sent Greenfield to Northern Rhodesia to discourage any further outbursts of extremism. Government officials believed that Welensky was prepared to give ground on the June proposals; indeed, Greenfield indicated as much to a meeting of the u.f.p.'s 'action committee' in late October.[3] This new flexibility in Welensky's attitude was attributed to a number of factors. The continuing political uncertainty of the previous two years had placed an increasingly heavy burden on the Federal economy, a situation exacerbated by the mobilization of territorial troops each time a new crisis occurred. Welensky had also been concerned over the high proportion of Federal troops which had been required to put down Northern Rhodesia's disturbances. Two such outbursts in the Federation simultaneously would severely strain the Federal forces. On the other hand, Welensky had been heartened by Tshombe's success in Katanga and Welensky believed that Tshombe's example might carry over into Northern Rhodesia, where Katilungu had made a promising start in his campaign to revitalize a.n.c.[4] In September a group of the Copperbelt's European businessmen, also with an eye on Katanga, decided to press the u.f.p. to accept

[1] Report to a.s. (c.s.) 1, 25 September 1961, S/S 119/130/01, and *Northern News*, 27 September 1961.
[2] *Northern News*, 2 November 1961.
[3] Reports to a.s. (c.s.) 1, 5 October and 2 November 1961, S/S 119/130/01.
[4] Ibid.

African leadership of the unofficial members of the Legislative
Council under any new constitution. To this end, co-operation
with moderate, though representative, Africans was urged,
Katilungu being the obvious choice. A moderate and successful
trade unionist, well known among Copperbelt Europeans,
Katilungu had pledged himself to a strong anti-u.n.i.p. line and
announced that a.n.c. was not multi-racial.[1] After the next
election, it was argued, Northern Rhodesia's majority party
would have to be dominated and led by Africans with Europeans exercising a vital influence in the background. Anything
short of this would allow u.n.i.p. to force the pace, and within
two years Northern Rhodesia would be faced with black
nationalist government.[2]

Apparently arguments of this kind advanced by the Copperbelt businessmen had impressed Welensky. In government
circles it was known that Welensky, while still publicly advocating no change in the June proposals, was anxious for a settlement of Northern Rhodesia's Constitution by local agreement,
even if securing such agreement required a somewhat unfavourable adjustment of the minimum percentage arrangements in
the National seats. The changed thinking in Salisbury, however, was not reflected in Lusaka, and Welensky was not prepared to exert his authority against the strong feelings running
in the u.f.p.'s northern wing. Roberts refused to participate in
the Governor's discussions, preferring change in the June proposals by imposition rather than by local agreement.[3]

It was not until the new Colonial Secretary, Reginald Maudling, who had replaced Macleod in October, visited Northern
Rhodesia in December that formal representations were made
by all political parties.[4] It was clear that the British Government
was not open to proposals for extensive changes in the June plan.
Indeed, the parties were warned against expecting any alterations at all. It was no less obvious, however, that having come
this far the British Government could not afford simply to re-
issue the June proposals, and, in any case, the basic point of
contention—the method of electing National members—was

[1] Report to A.S. (C.S.) 1, 18 September 1961, S/S 119/130/01.
[2] Ibid., 30 September 1961.
[3] Report to A.S. (C.S.) 1, 7 November 1961; ibid.; *Northern News*, 7 November
1961.
[4] *Northern News*, 4 December 1961.

well within the scope laid down for representations. Yet since June the chances for agreement between Northern Rhodesia's parties had worsened; Maudling, at his final press conference, admitted that the divergence of opinion was wider even than he had anticipated.[1] The dilemma raised by the Colonial Secretary's failure to bridge the gap between parties in Northern Rhodesia was further complicated during January and February 1962 by disagreement in the British Cabinet, which had long realized that any plan for Northern Rhodesia which produced an African nationalist majority would inevitably mean the end of Federation.[2] Welensky had recently urged the British Government to re-convene the Federal Review Conference in the hope of producing a settlement for Northern Rhodesia which would be compatible with the future survival of the Federation.[3] In late January Lord Lambton, Conservative M.P., revealed that a deadlock over Northern Rhodesia in the British Cabinet had 'very nearly . . . resulted in resignations'.[4] Explaining that Northern Rhodesia's Constitution would be delayed still longer, Lambton claimed that the whole future of the Federation was at stake.[5]

Meanwhile, in early February, Sandys held talks in Salisbury with Welensky and the Governor of Northern Rhodesia,[6] before paying a mysterious and highly controversial week-end visit to Barotseland.[7] 'Dirty Tory Tactics', protested Kaunda.[8] U.N.I.P. had 'every reason to believe that Sandys was here to sabotage Northern Rhodesia's Territorial integrity'.[9] Rumours circulated that the British Government was contemplating the balkanization of Northern Rhodesia to preserve the Federation.[10] African impatience and frustration had reached fever pitch: Kaunda calling on Africans to prepare for a general strike,[11] Nkumbula,

[1] Northern News, 9 December 1961.
[2] Ibid., 24 January 1962.
[3] Ibid., 6 November 1961.
[4] Rhodesia Herald, 23 January 1962.
[5] Ibid., 31 January 1962.
[6] Ibid., 17 February 1962.
[7] Ibid., 19 February 1962.
[8] Northern News, 22 February 1962.
[9] Ibid., 20 February 1962.
[10] Rhodesia Herald, 27 February 1962.
[11] Northern News, 26 February 1962.

released now from prison, demanding the recall of Governor Hone and condemning the growing influence of the Commonwealth Relations Office in Northern Rhodesia's affairs.[1] But the indications were that the Africans had not yet lost the day. Welensky stormed off to London on 27 February after having learned of only half the new proposals.[2]

Compared with the events of late February, the Colonial Secretary's announcement of the British Government's final plan seemed something of an anticlimax. Maudling's only change was in the prescribed minimum percentage arrangements for the election of National members. The contentious requirement, which had stipulated that National candidates must secure $12\frac{1}{2}$ per cent or 400 votes (whichever was the less) of the votes cast by each race, was adjusted to a single figure of 10 per cent of the votes cast by each race.[3] The change, albeit small, was to have vastly important consequences for Northern Rhodesia. The most decisive constitutional negotiations in the Territory's history were over; registration of voters, a complex general election, and eventually African government lay ahead.

[1] *Northern News*, 2 March 1962.
[2] Ibid., 28 February 1962.
[3] *Hansard*, 1 March 1962, cols. 1341.

VI

BAROTSELAND

BAROTSELAND'S most distinctive feature has always been its isolation from the rest of Northern Rhodesia. This was true long before Europeans penetrated into the upper Zambezi valley and remained true both under British South Africa Company rule and later when the British Government assumed direct control over Northern Rhodesia. The ravages of the slave trade were much less severe in Barotseland than in the eastern areas of Northern Rhodesia, and during Livingstone's time Barotseland became noted for its distinctive and highly sophisticated traditional political system in which a powerful King or Paramount Chief reigned over a complex system of councils, comprising not only members of the royal family but commoners as well. Even after the large-scale entry of Europeans, Barotseland remained physically isolated from the growing centres of Northern Rhodesia, Mongu, Barotseland's capital, lying more than 400 miles west of the 'line of rail' and the whole area remaining inaccessible during most of the annual wet season. Apart from the exporting of labour to the Copperbelt and other railway towns, Barotseland's own economy remained inward-looking, almost wholly centred on the vast flood plain which stretches northwards from Sesheke District along the upper Zambezi.

British protection was first extended to the general area of Northern Rhodesia by the Barotse Treaty of 1890, concluded between Lewanika, Paramount Chief of Barotseland, and the British South Africa Company.[1] During the two decades after 1900, when the Company established separate administrations for the eastern and western portions of what later became Northern Rhodesia, Barotseland developed a special relationship with the Company in administrative and judicial matters, which carried over into the period of British administration

---

[1] A copy of the Barotse Treaty is printed in *Africa South*, 414, No. 245.

after 1924.[1] Indeed, at the time of Northern Rhodesia's transfer
from Company rule to the British Government, Barotseland's
special status was explicitly recognized in article 41 of the
Northern Rhodesia Order in Council, 1924. The ensuing years
saw this special position reinforced. When in 1936 the Government established the Native Authority system, the Barotse
Native Government was granted wider powers and a greater
degree of local autonomy than the Territory's other Native
Authorities.[2] Again, in 1953, to allay Barotse fears of Federation, the British Government issued a special Order in Council,
styling Barotseland as a Protectorate within Northern Rhodesia
and reaffirming the rights initially confirmed to the Paramount
Chief in the 1924 Order in Council.[3] In addition, Barotse complaints of a diminution of their Native Authority's *de facto*
powers were satisfied by amendments to the Barotse Native
Courts Ordinance, a concession which, after much discussion,
helped to extract from the Paramount Chief the announcement
that Barotseland would not oppose the implementation of
Federation.[4]

The growth of nationalist agitation which marked the 1950's
in Northern Rhodesia was almost totally absent in Barotseland.
Despite a long history of political intrigue and rivalry between
various sections of the royal family, Barotseland's Government,
unlike many Native Authorities in the Territory, enjoyed widespread support within Barotseland at least until late 1961.
Barotseland's physical isolation was not the only reason for the
marked strength of traditional loyalties; Barotseland's traditional conservatism, a certain communal feeling among its
people, the loss of its young educated elements to the towns and,
above all, widespread vested interest among its *élite*, both commoner and royalty alike, had helped isolate Barotseland from
the forces of militant nationalism.

It was not until the late 1950's that dissatisfaction with the
current ruler was replaced by doubt about the traditional system

---

[1] Historical notes on Barotseland Government (n.d. November 1961), DG
58/1/01.
[2] The Barotse Native Authority Ordinance and the Barotse Native Courts
Ordinance, both of 1936, were made solely for Barotseland.
[3] The Northern Rhodesia (Barotseland) Order in Council, 1953.
[4] Historical notes on Barotseland Government, DG 58/1/01.

of government itself.[1] Both attitudes, of course, reinforced and fed upon one another. The succession of Mwanawina Lewanika to the Paramount Chieftancy in 1948 had been a bitterly contested affair, and it was hardly surprising that Lewanika, who as Paramount Chief had full command over Barotseland patronage, should have had numerous enemies both within the royal family and among various leading commoner families. The Wina brothers, whose father had been excluded from Lewanika's administration after serving as Ngambela (Prime Minister) to his predecessor, were two such examples in u.n.i.p.[2] The younger educated Lozi, who lived on the Copperbelt or along the 'line of rail', shared in the general political awakening of the 1950's and like their colleagues became sceptical of traditional authority and attracted by modern nationalist ideas of democracy. Inevitably it was only a question of time before these new ideas filtered back into Barotseland to infect young relatives and friends. Nor was Northern Rhodesia's postwar development and growing prosperity, particularly along the 'line of rail', shared by Barotseland, a fact which could hardly escape the growing number of Lozi who travelled back and forth between the tiny Protectorate and the railway towns. External influences were growing in other ways as well. Several leading Lozi, notably the Wina brothers, Mundia and Sipalo, had continued their education in other countries, in Uganda, South Africa, Britain, the United States, and India. The appearance in 1959 of the *Central African Mail*, the only newspaper in Northern Rhodesia which catered for Africans and supported nationalist aspirations, had a profound impact generally on African public opinion. In Barotseland, where its only competitor was the Information Department's monthly publication, the *Mail* was widely read and greatly feared by those in authority for its outspoken criticism of the Barotse Native Government.[3] Despite the at first almost imperceptible build-up of these disparate forces during the latter half of the 1950's, government officials were able to note as late as August 1958,

[1] m.i.r., 1959, *passim*; Report on political and security position in Barotseland, 23 September 1960, DG 58/1/01.
[2] *Central African Mail*, 23 October 1962.
[3] Report of political and security position in Barotseland, 23 September 1960, DG 58/1/01; see also *Central African Mail*, 13 September 1960.

the tenth anniversary of Lewanika's accession, that the Paramount Chief's 'stock was continuing to rise'.[1]

Three developments during 1959 marked the beginning of the Barotse Native Government's decline. Following the proscription of z.a.n.c. in March 1959, the central Government restricted Kapwepwe, Kamanga, Chimba, and Nehphas Tembo, four of z.a.n.c's most able and vociferous organizers, to Barotseland. The decision, which had caused considerable concern in Barotseland at the time,[2] was later recognized in the Government as having afforded to nationalists 'an opportunity to subvert previously untouched areas'.[3] In April 1959, for example, it was noted that the z.a.n.c. restricted persons posed 'an ever-growing danger' to Barotseland's 'political scene', so much so that at one point it became necessary to impress upon boys at the Mongu Secondary School, the Protectorate's leading educational institution, the importance of 'Loyalty to the School'.[4]

The second development was the visit of the Paramount Chief to Salisbury in November 1959. Despite the Paramount Chief's acquiescence in the fact of Federation, the majority of Barotseland's indunas and councillors were deeply opposed to Federation. In 1958 the Barotse Native Government had been angered by the Federal Franchise Act and refused to participate in the Federal elections in October that year.[5] The Barotse Native Government also opposed Northern Rhodesia's 1958 constitutional proposals, and it was only after considerable persuasion, by both the Governor and the Colonial Secretary, that the Paramount Chief agreed in December 1958 to advise his people to register on the Territorial voters' rolls.[6] In both cases, the nub of Barotse fears was that the Protectorate's special status with the British Government would be altered. Repeatedly during 1959 the Barotse Native Government expressed its opposition to the granting of dominion status to the Federation, giving this as its main reason for refusing to co-operate in the Federal elections.[7] Self-government in

---

[1] m.i.r., August 1958, DG 58/1/01   [2] m.i.r., April 1959, ibid.

[3] u.n.i.p. in Barotseland, s.b. to Ad. Sec., 22 December 1962, ibid.

[4] m.i.r., April 1959, ibid.

[5] Report of meeting between Welensky and Paramount Chief and Saa Sikalo Council, Mongu, 19 May 1958, N/2190/Box 3513, Lusaka Archives.

[6] m.i.r., August and December 1958, DG 58/1/01.

[7] m.i.r., August and October 1959, ibid.

Northern Rhodesia posed a similar threat in the eyes of the Barotse Government, and by early 1959 there was talk of secession.[1] In the event of either dominion status for the Federation or self-government for Northern Rhodesia, the Barotse National Council advocated that 'Barotseland should remain a separate and true Protectorate under the pure and direct influence of Her Majesty's Government'. The Council also felt that Barotseland should be clearly demarcated on all maps as a distinctive state attached to Northern Rhodesia.[2]

Thus, the Paramount Chief's visit to Salisbury in November 1959, less than a month before the opening of the Federal Review in London, aroused vigorous opposition. When the National Council debated the proposed visit in September, Kwalombota Mulonda, Barotseland's Member in the Legislative Council, warned the Paramount Chief that any dealings with Salisbury might easily be interpreted as implying support for the Federation. In the end the Council approved the trip by the uncomfortably narrow margin of eighteen votes to sixteen.[3] When the Paramount Chief passed through Livingstone on his way to Salisbury, Lozi migrant workers in the town expressed bitter disappointment that he had not stayed at his traditional residence, but with the Provincial Commissioner instead. The crowds which greeted the Paramount Chief were noticeably smaller than usual, and suspicion about the Salisbury visit was reported to be widespread.[4] The same was true in Barotseland itself, where during the next few months rumours circulated that the Paramount Chief had concluded a secret agreement with the Federal Government promising to maintain the Protectorate in the Federation.[5]

By far the most damaging development for the Paramount Chief's prestige during 1959 was the disappearance of Mwana Mulena Akashambatwa, sole surviving adult son of Imwiko, Lewanika's predecessor, and the subsequent discovery of what were thought to have been Akashambatwa's remains.[6] As a result, a host of rumours swept through Barotseland in

[1] M.I.R., April 1959, DG 58/1/01.
[2] M.I.R., October 1959, ibid.
[3] M.I.R., September 1959, ibid.
[4] M.I.R., November 1959, DG 58/7/01.
[5] M.I.R., February 1960, DG 58/1/01.
[6] M.I.R., December 1959, ibid.

December 1959 and during the early months of 1960, alleging without exception that Akashambatwa had been murdered on the instructions or with the consent of the Paramount Chief. The names of the alleged murderers varied in the different versions, though invariably they included prominent councillors. The Government's senior representative in Barotseland, the Resident Commissioner, received a number of anonymous letters accusing the Paramount Chief of complicity in the crime, and in January the Government feared a possible outbreak of disturbances among Africans in Mongu District. Kapwepwe, who was preparing to leave Barotseland at the time after his restriction, sought to capitalize on the popular upsurge of discontent by organizing provincial and district U.N.I.P. committees. The Akashambatwa affair, he asserted, had seriously weakened Lozi loyalty towards their Government; U.N.I.P.'s best path would be to assist the people in overthrowing the Paramount Chief. Kapwepwe was not alone in this design. A number of the Paramount Chief's long-standing enemies converged on Mongu-Lealui: Naluwe Yeta, son of former Paramount Chief Yeta III; Neo Zazu and Mukakani Liatitima, both conspirators against Lewanika on previous occasions; and Walubita, a man of considerable popularity and Lewanika's former Ngambela.[1] By March 1960, however, the danger of an immediate conspiracy had passed, largely because the Barotse Native Government, backed by the central Government, issued a circular reporting on the progress of the investigation and warning purveyors of rumours that they would be liable to prosecution. Nevertheless, the public's attitude—that the Barotse Native Government had been implicated in an unsavoury affair—remained unchanged, a situation the Government feared would ultimately help to swell the ranks of U.N.I.P. in Barotseland.[2]

Apart from a feeble attempt in March 1960 to boycott the Monckton Commission at Mongu, the U.N.I.P. committees formed by Kapwepwe petered out soon after his departure.[3] For the time being Barotseland remained well outside national politics, fully absorbed in its own political problems. The

---

[1] M.I.R., January and February 1960, DG 58/1/01.
[2] M.I.R., February and March 1960, ibid.
[3] M.I.R., March 1960, ibid.

apparent calm, however, was deceptive, for Barotseland's difficulties raised questions of fundamental importance. Indeed, as the year passed it became increasingly evident that the Protectorate was verging on a serious crisis over the potentially explosive question of internal political reform. The problem was all the more urgent in light of the sharp decline in the personal prestige and authority of the Paramount Chief and his Government. Kaunda and Sipalo, who visited Mongu at the end of July 1960, received a rousing welcome from large crowds, which the Government disturbingly noted had included a representative cross-section of African civil servants. A private meeting during the visit was attended by virtually the entire staff of the Barotse Secondary School, and though u.n.i.p.'s support was said to be restricted to this relatively well-educated class, open criticism reportedly was mounting among villagers as well, as evidenced by widespread opposition against a fish-net tax which had recently been imposed by the Barotse Government. In addition, government officials reported a marked reluctance on the part of villagers to perform certain traditional duties, such as the laying of grass at the Ku-omboka ceremony (the annual flood season ceremony which marked the Paramount Chief's move to higher ground outside the flood plain), as well as the customary dancing before the Paramount Chief.[1] Indeed, Barotseland's District Commissioners agreed unanimously in September 1960 that the Barotse Native Government had entered a serious decline which called for urgent reform in the traditional system of government.[2]

Government in Barotseland was both complex and unwieldy. Theoretically, the Paramount Chief was served by the Barotseland Parliament (National Council), a body of about thirty members which met once or twice per year, composed of all the indunas (councillors) living at the capital, Lealui, as well as three representatives (normally the chief, senior councillor and an additional councillor) from each of Barotseland's five District Kutas (councils). A Central Council, comprising only those indunas living at Lealui, met more frequently and itself had an inner cabinet, the Saa Sikalo, in which each induna

[1] Report of political and security position in Barotseland, 23 September 1960, DG 58/1/01.
[2] Ag. Resident Commissioner (r.c.) to m.n.a., 26 September 1960, ibid.

headed a department of Barotseland's administration. In effect, the Saa Sikalo was the Barotse Native Government. Its chief minister, the Ngambela, traditionally a commoner, was the Paramount Chief's leading adviser. Decisions of the Saa Sikalo— both administrative and judicial, for the Council was also the Barotse Supreme Appeal Court—were always referred to, but seldom reversed by the Paramount Chief. Both the National Council and the Saa Sikalo were dominated by the Protectorate's great landholders, who in the past had been Barotseland's major military leaders, but who in 1960 were simply aged and relatively wealthy men with deeply reactionary attitudes and large vested interests in the existing system.[1]

Still another body, the Katengo Council, was the council of the common people. Dating back to the days of the original Paramount Chief Lewanika, the Katengo Council had fallen into disuse until its revival in 1946. Though similar in size to the National Council, five or six members drawn from each district, the Katengo Council's most distinctive feature was that its members were elected by universal male (and in Senanga District female) suffrage with a secret ballot held in each district. Normally the Council met only once each year under the chairmanship of the Ngambela to debate motions and to raise questions for the meeting of the National Council. Motions passed by the Katengo Council and questions which it put down for the National Council had to be approved by the Ngambela before being debated by the higher body, where five Katengo councillors were allowed to take part. In practice, however, the Katengo Council was powerless, and what limited functions it did perform were effectively controlled on the Paramount Chief's behalf by his Ngambela.[2]

At the lower levels in Barotseland's various districts, the Barotse Native Government was represented by District Kutas, each headed by a member of the royal family, with the exception of Mongu-Lealui District's Kuta, which since the late 1940's had been under a senior induna (the Solami) of the Saa Sikalo. Like the Saa Sikalo, District Kutas performed both administrative and judicial functions, and since their member-

---

[1] Brief notes on the form and structure of the Barotse Native Government (n.d. November 1961) DG 58/1/01.
[2] Ibid.

ship for the most part comprised silalo indunas (indunas from the districts' local councils), many of whom were large landholders in their own right, District Kutas also retained a deeply conservative flavour.[1] It was natural that U.N.I.P. should have seized on the issue of reform to advance its position in Barotseland, and equally predictable that the ideas put by Kaunda and Sipalo to the National Council in August 1960 should have shocked and offended both the Paramount Chief and the majority of his councillors.[2] Barotseland faced innumerable problems, and central government officials shared, though for quite the opposite reasons, U.N.I.P.'s concern for major changes in the Barotse Native Government.[3] The entire structure was dominated by the old, the landed, the backward-looking men of Barotseland, while its youthful and growing intelligentsia, whether on the 'line of rail' or in the Protectorate itself, were wholly excluded from the outworn and cumbersome councils of state. There were also serious shortcomings in Barotseland's general administration.[4] In the central area, Mongu-Lealui District, where the population was most densely concentrated and which contained the vast majority of Barotseland's young intelligentsia, 'no effective organ of local government really exists'. Lozi outside the Protectorate had become highly critical of its administration, particularly when returning to Barotseland they encountered difficulties in settling their affairs.[5] Still another feature of Barotse government which had aroused widespread criticism was the Paramount Chief's tendency to extend the influence of the royal family into areas previously reserved exclusively for the common people. This was particularly true in the case of his present Ngambela, who, contrary to all tradition, was a member of the royal family by virtue of his marriage to Lewanika's daughter.[6]

U.N.I.P., in accordance with its national policy of universal

[1] Brief notes on the form and structure of the Barotse Native Government (n.d. November 1961) DG 58/1/01.
[2] Report to Ag. R.C. to S.N.A. (2), 1 October 1960, DG 58/1/01.
[3] Ag. R.C. to M.N.A., 26 September 1960, ibid.
[4] Record of meeting between Ag. R.C. and National Council, 26 September 1960, ibid.
[5] Report Ag. R.C. to S.N.A. (2), 1 October 1960, ibid.
[6] Brief notes on the form and structure of the Barotse Native Government (n.d. November 1961), DG 58/1/01.

adult suffrage and self-government, advocated drastic democratic reforms within Barotseland, as well as a change in its
constitutional status which would make the Protectorate an
integral part of Northern Rhodesia. The central Government's
ideas were less sweeping, designed primarily to modernize
Barotseland to some extent in the hope that u.n.i.p.'s influence
might be kept to a minimum in the area. The reform most
urgently advocated by government officers was the expansion
of the Barotse National Council's membership to include all or a
substantial portion of Katengo councillors. In addition, membership in a reformed National Council might be limited to a
specific period of years with the nominated element of both the
National Council and the Saa Sikalo selected by the Council
itself and not appointed by the Paramount Chief. The Saa
Sikalo, it was suggested, should be divided into separate parts,
one for administration, the other for judicial functions, and the
power of the Paramount Chief to reject both administrative and
judicial decisions should be curtailed. Some Government
officials also believed that the Ngambela should be popularly
elected for a specific period, perhaps five years.[1] Pending these
admittedly major reforms, which, if implemented, would have
had the effect of turning the Paramount Chief into a constitutional monarch, it was widely agreed that some decentraliza-
tion of power to the District Kutas was urgent if the standard of
general administration was to be improved.[2] The Government
believed that these reforms, taken as a whole, would be acceptable not only to Barotseland's young intelligentsia but also in
the long run to u.n.i.p., which, it was argued, probably rightly
at the time, was not intent on overthrowing the Barotse system
as a whole.[3]

As with so much else in Barotseland, reform was a long time
coming. Meanwhile, u.n.i.p., which by late 1960 had clearly
emerged as a major force, stepped up its Barotseland campaign,
a move which raised serious problems for both the Barotse and
the Northern Rhodesia Government. On 4 October 1960 three
u.n.i.p. officials, arriving in Mongu by bus, submitted u.n.i.p.'s

[1] These ideas appeared in official correspondence from September 1960, but
were not noted down together for the record until November 1961, 'Current ideas
on reform of the Barotse Native Government', 21 November 1961, DG 58/1/01.

[2] Ag. r.c. to m.n.a., 26 September 1960, ibid.

[3] Current ideas on reform of b.n.g., 21 November 1960, ibid.

first application to register a branch in Barotseland.[1] The glove
had clearly been thrown down. Only a week earlier, after a
stormy debate, the National Council had rejected by twenty
votes to fifteen a request by the Resident Commissioner that
the Barotse Native Government should apply both 'flexibility'
and 'discretion' in its future dealings with u.n.i.p.[2]
The Barotse Government's reaction to u.n.i.p.'s application
was both immediate and predictable. A delegation called on
the Resident Commissioner to inform him that u.n.i.p. was
totally unacceptable in Barotseland, and further that if u.n.i.p.
organizers entered the Protectorate without the Saa Sikalo's
permission, they would be served with expulsion orders, which,
if disregarded, would be followed up with prosecution. Silalo
indunas throughout Barotseland were to be instructed to refuse
permission for any u.n.i.p. meetings in their respective areas.
The delegation then called on the Northern Rhodesia Government not only to refuse u.n.i.p.'s application but to ban the
party in Barotseland as well![3]

This extremely militant delegation did not genuinely reflect
the full range of attitudes in the National Council, which, in
fact, was deeply divided over the question of Barotse policy
towards u.n.i.p. While most councillors undoubtedly shared the
view that u.n.i.p.'s policy as enunciated by Kaunda and Sipalo
in August was undesirable for Barotseland, not all were prepared to conclude that u.n.i.p. should necessarily be rigorously
excluded from Barotseland as a matter of policy. This group,
which comprised well over a third of the Council's members,
pointed out that u.n.i.p. had considerable attraction for many
Lozi living on the Copperbelt or along the 'line of rail', and
that for this reason it was unrealistic to believe that Barotseland
would isolate itself from u.n.i.p. influence indefinitely. In short,
the Barotse Native Government would be forced at some stage
to learn to live with u.n.i.p.[4] The more militant group, led as
they were by the Paramount Chief and the Ngambela, had
quite different ideas. Indeed, the Paramount Chief believed
that:

[1] Ag. R.C. to S.N.A. (2), 7 October 1960, DG 58/1/01.
[2] Ibid.
[3] Ibid.
[4] Ibid.; and record of meeting between the Ag. R.C. and the National Council,
26 September 1960, DG 58/1/01.

Malozi who emigrated from the Protectorate and openly identified themselves with a political party or benevolent and patriotic society whose professed policy was inimicable [*sic*] to his Government and whose real aim was the destruction of traditional authority and seizure of power within the Protectorate, automatically surrendered their rights within the Protectorate. Although their parents and relatives remained in the Protectorate as loyal, law abiding citizens, their erring sons and daughters should, in customary law, be considered outlawed.[1]

The Resident Commissioner supported the Paramount Chief and recommended that u.n.i.p.'s application be refused. Despite the fact that the National Council had rejected his suggestion for a flexible policy towards u.n.i.p., the Resident Commissioner indicated that since the Barotse Government was entitled both to make its own policy for Barotseland and to apply it, government officers in the Protectorate would loyally back the Barotse authorities.[2] In Lusaka, however, the central Government, fully occupied with the Federal and territorial constitutional conferences, delayed taking a decision on the Barotseland problem.

Thus by early 1961 the issue of reform in Barotseland, difficult enough in itself, had been further complicated by the broader problem of opening Barotseland to nationalist political organizations. Though the Barotse Government's main legal argument against the registration of u.n.i.p. branches—that the Societies Ordinance was *ultra vires* the Barotse agreements with the British Government—was thought in Lusaka to be incorrect,[3] Barotseland's special position in Northern Rhodesia made it particularly risky for the Government simply to overrule the Paramount Chief and his Council. A central government decision to register u.n.i.p.'s branches would not in itself have opened the Protectorate to unrestricted nationalist penetration. Under the Barotse Native Authority Ordinance the Barotse Government was provided with extensive powers to control both public meetings and the movement of persons within the Protectorate. Rather, the heart of the Government's dilemma lay in the fact that any move it made to recognize u.n.i.p. would

---

[1] Record of discussion between R.C. and Paramount Chief, R.C. to S.N.A. (2), 1 October 1960, DG 58/1/01.

[2] R.C. to S.N.A. (2), 7 October 1960, ibid.

[3] U.N.I.P. branches in Barotseland, Attorney-General to Registrar, March 1961, S/S 82/81/01, Vol. III.

alienate the Paramount Chief at a time when the Government
hoped not only to reform Barotseland, and therefore in effect to
strengthen it against U.N.I.P., but also to induce the Barotse to
accept voluntarily the constitutional changes planned for
Northern Rhodesia as a whole.[1] Meanwhile, A.N.C. had applied to register a branch in the
Mankoya District on the eastern border of Barotseland.[2] The
Minister of Native Affairs, writing at the height of the crisis over
the Macleod proposals and shortly before constitutional discussions were due to begin with the Paramount Chief, advised
that 'this is clearly not the time to back an action which, however explained, would be seen by the Lozi as our taking sides
with their critics'.[3] As a result A.N.C.'s application was refused,
largely because it was felt that any political organization in
the Nkoya area would stir up long-standing secessionist agitation among a subject tribe (the Nkoya) against the Barotse
Government. Indeed, it was doubtful if the Mankoya application had the support of A.N.C. headquarters.[4] U.N.I.P., on the
other hand, had now submitted several more branch applications, and the Government, keenly aware that its A.N.C. refusal
could not be taken as setting a precedent for Barotseland,
delayed taking a decision on U.N.I.P.'s branches once again.[5]

Continuing uncertainty over Northern Rhodesia's Constitution forced a postponement of the discussions planned for
April with the Paramount Chief, now known officially as the
Litunga of Barotseland.[6] In late May U.N.I.P. began pressing
for the registration of its Barotseland branches and again the
Minister of Native Affairs pleaded for further delay. While
agreeing it was 'axiomatic' that the Litunga and his councillors would have to become more flexible on the question of
political activity in the Protectorate, the immediate problem
was one of 'timing'. Barotseland had not yet agreed to the
Macleod plan, and the Litunga, who had been under virulent
attack from the nationalists, was 'understandably touchy at the
moment'. The minister indicated that recently he had frankly

[1] S/S 82/81/01, Vol. III, March 1961, passim.
[2] R.C. to Registrar, 26 January 1961, ibid.
[3] M.N.A. to C.S., 13 March 1961, ibid.
[4] Registrar to C.S. 11 February 1961, ibid.
[5] C.S. to M.N.A., 11 March 1961; C.S. to Registrar, 25 March 1961, ibid.
[6] Brief notes on the form and structure of the B.N.G., DG 58/1/01.

explained the position to Sipalo, who had agreed that under the circumstances U.N.I.P. would be unwise to press registration too energetically against the Litunga's wishes.[1]

The interests of both U.N.I.P. and the Government were well served by this somewhat curious compromise. Under the provisions of the Societies Ordinance, an organization which had lodged its application with the Registrar was entitled to continue operating freely until the Registrar actually rejected the application. The Government, on the other hand, quite apart from the advantages of avoiding an immediate conflict with the Litunga, obtained from the branches' application forms most of the information required for security purposes by the special branch.[2] Thus, U.N.I.P. was able to organize what it came to call 'unofficial' branches in Barotseland, while in June 1961 the Barotse National Council unanimously rejected the idea that any political party should be registered in the Protectorate.[3] The Government continued to stall, though not with a particularly easy conscience. One Barotseland District Commissioner questioned the Government's policy, arguing that it seemed difficult to justify discrimination against U.N.I.P. in Barotseland when it was a lawful organization elsewhere in the Territory. In due course an election would be held, and U.N.I.P. would expect to be able to campaign freely in the Protectorate. It was far better, he asserted, that U.N.I.P.'s branches should come out into the open.[4] The Government ignored these arguments, which, oddly enough, it had employed with some force itself during 1960 in favour of registering U.N.I.P. branches in the Northern Province.

Before long, however, Northern Rhodesia's political situation had been radically transformed, upsetting the mutually acceptable arrangement between U.N.I.P. and the Government over political activity in Barotseland. The June 1961 proposals had provoked a new militancy in U.N.I.P. Gone was the reasonable attitude which U.N.I.P. had displayed during the constitutional discussions with the Governor in April and May. When in August disturbances broke out in the north and on the

---

[1] M.N.A. to C.S., 25 May 1961, S/S 82/81/01. Vol. III.
[2] M.N.A. to C.S., 27 November 1962, ibid.
[3] Barotse National Council meeting, 16 June 1961, ibid.
[4] D.C. (Senanga) to R.C., 18 May 1961, ibid.

Copperbelt, the Government quickly took advantage of the situation to reject U.N.I.P.'s long-standing applications for branch registrations in Barotseland. Altogether, six U.N.I.P. branches in the Protectorate were refused registration. Supporting his action, the Registrar argued that U.N.I.P.'s part in the disturbances indicated that it was an organization which would disrupt peace and good government in accordance with section eight of the Societies Ordinance. Since the Barotse Native Government, which together with the central Government was responsible for maintaining law and order in Barotseland, had advised against registering U.N.I.P.'s branches, the Registrar considered, rather suddenly it seemed, that the Litunga's views could not be ignored. Moreover, under the Barotse Undesirable Persons Rule orders had been made against Kaunda, Sipalo, and Mundia, which prevented them from entering Barotseland and which the Barotse Government had no intention of revoking. The Registrar also cited U.N.I.P.'s obvious connexion with the Barotse Anti-Secession Society, an organization for reform-conscious Lozi residing outside the Protectorate which Mundia had formed in late 1960.[1]

Nor could U.N.I.P. continue following a soft-line policy in Barotseland. In part this was due to U.N.I.P.'s Lozi leaders, who realized that their future influence in the party would depend largely upon their ability to demonstrate extensive personal support in the Protectorate. More important, perhaps, was the obvious strengthening of secessionist ideas in Barotseland itself. In September 1961 the Barotse Native Government submitted a petition to the British Government requesting Barotseland statehood, a proposal the Resident Commissioner attempted unsuccessfully to discourage during an eight-day session of the Saa Sikalo. At the same time, the Litunga invited the Katengo Council to debate his own proposal that Barotseland should be reconstituted as a fourth state in the Federation. Neither U.N.I.P. nor the central Government lightly dismissed the Litunga's growing interest in secession. To an aged ruler who felt his régime besieged from all sides, secession was the all too obvious panacea for all Barotseland's ills. What is more, by November 1961 the U.F.P. had begun to take an active interest in Barotse politics. There was 'interference', in the words of the

[1] Registrar to C.S., 13 September 1961, S/S 82/81/01. Vol. III.

Resident Commissioner, by a lawyer from one of Salisbury's law firms.[1]

The pressure on the Barotse Native Government from all quarters was obviously on the increase. The Barotse National Society, a semi-political organization formed in the mid-1950's, continued to advocate reform. The more extreme Barotse Anti-Secession Society was joined by a new group, the Barotse Patriots, which urged the immediate appointment of 'an independent commmission of enquiry into the growing unrest in Barotseland so that peace could be restored before it becomes too late'. The Resident Commissioner, reporting on the Barotse Patriots, indicated that in his view the new organization's line genuinely reflected informed opinion within the Protectorate. The Resident Commissioner himself favoured the appointment of a one-man commission to inquire into the internal administration of Barotseland.[2] Ultimately the Litunga accepted the Resident Commissioner's proposal and the Government appointed Sir Charles Hartwell to conduct the inquiry.[3] This course, the Resident Commissioner believed, had the great advantage of keeping things quiet in Barotseland for six months to a year, by which time the composition of Northern Rhodesia's next Government would be known and Barotseland's relationship to Northern Rhodesia might more sensibly be re-examined.[4]

It was at this juncture that Sandys paid his mysterious visit to Mongu in February 1962.[5] Against the background of the previous few months, it was hardly surprising that Sandys's visit should have been viewed with the utmost suspicion both by U.N.I.P. and A.N.C., not to mention the numerous Barotse, both within and outside Barotseland, who favoured reform and closer ties with the future Zambia. At the time, Northern Rhodesia was awaiting Maudling's announcement of the Territory's final constitutional proposals, and the nationalists had learned the previous June not to underestimate the flexibility of the British Government when it came to dealings with

[1] R.C. to Perm. Sec. (M.N.A.), 17 November 1961, DG 58/1/01.
[2] Ibid.
[3] The Litunga later refused to co-operate with Hartwell, Ad. Sec. to Perm. Sec. (M.N.A.), 8 December 1961, ibid.
[4] R.C. to Perm. Sec. (M.N.A.), 17 November 1961, ibid.
[5] *Rhodesia Herald*, 19 February 1962.

the Federal Government in Salisbury.[1] Whether U.N.I.P.'s
claims, that the British Government was considering a Federal
plan for balkanizing Northern Rhodesia and attaching the
'line of rail', the Copperbelt, and Barotseland to the Federation, were well founded or not is impossible to say. That the
rumours deeply stirred nationalist fears and were widely
believed by Africans seems undeniable.[2] Indeed, the future was
to give a measure of credence to African fears about Barotseland.

Meanwhile, with the announcement of Northern Rhodesia's
final constitutional proposals on 1 March 1962, the Government began preparations for an October general election. As
will be shown in greater detail later, the prospect of a general
election in which all the Territory's political groups were encouraged to participate necessitated a marked change in attitude on the part of the Government towards nationalist parties.
When U.N.I.P. agreed in early March to consider participating
in the election, one of its conditions was that all bans against
political activity throughout Northern Rhodesia be lifted
immediately to ensure that political parties were provided with
equal opportunities to organize and campaign during the
election period.[3] U.N.I.P.'s demands were raised again when
R. A. Butler, the British Government's newly appointed
Minister for Central African Affairs, visited Northern Rhodesia
in mid-May.[4] Registration of voters, which had begun in early
April, had got off to a slow start, particularly in Barotseland,
where after a full month only nine Africans had registered on
the lower roll.[5] U.N.I.P. delayed the launching of its own large-
scale registration campaign, partly to induce the Government to
extend the registration period into July, and partly to ensure
that its demands of early March were met.[6] During Butler's
visit the Governor was obliged to give the British minister a
general assurance 'that legitimate political activity would be
permitted throughout the Territory'. Officers of the Provincial
Administration were instructed to ensure that the Governor's

[1] Sipalo to A. Wina, 20 January 1962, A.N.L.W. papers.
[2] *Northern News*, 20 and 22 February 1962.
[3] Ibid., 6 March 1962.
[4] *The Times*, 22 May 1962.
[5] Mulford, *The N.R. General Election, 1962*, p. 53.
[6] Ibid., p. 52.

assurance was carried out. Chiefs who refused to co-operate, either by favouring one political party over another or by refusing parties the freedom to campaign, e.g. hold public meetings, would have their powers to regulate such activities in their respective areas withdrawn.[1]

The opening of Barotseland to nationalist political parties was now inevitable. In the registration of lower roll voters Barotseland continued to lag far behind all other areas in Northern Rhodesia; in early June the number of lower roll voters actually registered amounted to only 9 per cent of the Government's original estimate for the area.[2] Shortly afterwards, however, under pressure from the Government, the Litunga agreed to encourage registration, so that by the end of the period 69 per cent of Barotseland's estimated lower roll electorate had been registered.[3]

In July, following negotiations between the Barotse Native Government on the one hand and U.N.I.P., A.N.C., and government officials on the other, the Litunga reluctantly agreed to open Barotseland to all political parties.[4] Later that month Kaunda, Kamanga and the two Wina brothers held the first nationalist political rally in Barotseland's history. The Barotse Government and U.N.I.P. were at last on an equal footing in the Protectorate. U.N.I.P. immediately dispatched its band and several small campaign teams to Barotseland.[5] The battle for Barotseland was on; within three months the power of the ballot box would irrevocably settle the Protectorate's future.

[1] Extracts from conferences with P.C.s, May 1962, S.O. (N) 3 to Under Secretary (U.S.), 10 September 1962, MN 129/10, Vol. I, Box 4348, Lusaka Archives.

[2] New claims for registration—position as at 4 June 1962, MS 2615/37, Lusaka Archives.

[3] Position as at 11 July 1962, ibid.

[4] R.C. to Ag. Perm. Sec. (M.N.A.), 8 September 1962; and 'U.N.I.P. in Barotseland', S.B. to Ad. Sec., 22 December 1962, DG 58/1/01.

[5] *Northern News*, 19 July 1962.

VII

THE DRIVE FOR POWER:
THE 1962 GENERAL ELECTION

THE year 1962 was one of dramatic changes in Northern
Rhodesia. The introduction of the final version of the
Macleod Constitution in March 1962 broke the year-old
stalemate, confronting political parties and the Government
alike with the prospect of immediate and far-reaching political
change. The general election, set for late October 1962, less
than seven months away, was to bring the first significant
electoral confrontation between Europeans and Africans in the
Territory's history. Before then thousands of new voters had to
be registered, constituencies delimited and administrative
arrangements implemented for one of the most complicated
elections ever held in a British dependency. Restrictions on
political organization in the Territory had quickly to be lifted
in order that all parties might compete for power on an equal
footing.[1] The parties themselves faced the challenge of organizing for a massive campaign effort which was to stretch from
the beginning of the registration period in April through the
general election in October to the by-elections and the formation of a new Government in December 1962.[2] Briefly, and for
the first time, Africans and Europeans shared a common political arena. Europeans heard articulate Africans put their own
case for self-government, while African nationalists were forced
to sound their ideas against a pessimistic and frightened white
community. This was to be Northern Rhodesia's first truly
national election campaign, unfolding across the entire country

[1] Extracts from conferences with p.c.s in May 1962, s.o. (n) 3 to u.s., 10
September 1962, MN 129/10, Vol. I, Box 4348, Lusaka Archives.
[2] Under the 1962 Constitution, if the general election failed to produce results
in the National constituencies, by-elections were to follow automatically in approximately six weeks. In the event, this proved necessary; by-elections were held in ten
of the fourteen National seats on 10 December 1962 and the new Government was
formed six days later.

and dominated by vital national issues—the future of the Federation, African majority rule and the future of relations between the races. The outcome, on 16 December 1962, was Northern Rhodesia's first African Government, an abrupt and irrevocable climax to the struggle for power which European settlers had initiated fifty years before.

The 1962 Constitution was a purely transitory instrument designed to achieve a delicate compromise between two profoundly opposed racial and political groups while securing their co-operation in the critically important step from minority to majority government. Under such a Constitution it was inevitable that ambiguities should flourish at the expense of both clarity and certainty. As early as February 1961, answering criticisms that the constitutional proposals assured neither an African nor a European majority, Macleod had pointed out: 'If one were to seek to find . . . a non-racial approach to this problem, one cannot, at the same time, build an assured majority into the structure.'[1] What was true for a racial majority applied even more to a party majority. Indeed, ambiguities had advantages, for they offered to all parties both the possibility of winning the election and the means of justifying electoral participation. The upper and lower rolls were certain to produce near-racial parity and approximately equal representation for both U.N.I.P. and the U.F.P., thus ensuring that neither race would be deprived of significant influence in the new legislature. Beyond this, the National seats, which had been given prominence, particularly because they embodied the Constitution's non-racial concept, held out the prospect of victory to any party which could attract 10 per cent support from voters of the opposite race.

The Constitution's electoral arrangements presented political parties with a dual challenge. The first was to mobilize traditional supporters, Africans or Europeans, who predominated on one or other of the two rolls. Since no party could command majority support among voters of both races or both rolls, it was essential initially to dominate either the fifteen upper roll or fifteen lower roll seats. The National seats presented the second and more complex challenge. In order to win a National seat a candidate had to secure 10 per cent of the votes cast by

[1] *Hansard*, 21 February 1961, col. 514.

each race and 20 per cent of the votes cast on one or other of the two rolls. The winner was then determined by averaging together the candidates' percentage support on both rolls.[1] Thus to satisfy the 10 per cent requirement parties were forced to appeal to (or even to form electoral alliances with) racial and political opponents without alienating, and this was the delicate aspect, traditional party supporters or introducing intolerable internal strains in the party. Somehow within the framework of the new Constitution parties had simultaneously to mobilize their traditional followers and to secure multi-racial support. From March onwards it was this dilemma which set the tone of pre-election politics in Northern Rhodesia.

PRE-CAMPAIGN POLITICS

It was perhaps paradoxical that U.N.I.P., the party which throughout the constitutional negotiations had opposed the various sets of proposals most vigorously, should in the end have been the party most deeply affected by the new Constitution. On 5 March U.N.I.P.'s National Council accepted the final proposals provisionally and agreed, subject to five conditions,[2] to participate in the election. A massive task now faced the party. In December 1960 at the time of the first constitutional discussions, U.N.I.P. had been a rapidly growing, inadequately organized national movement. During the lengthy and arduous negotiations which followed, U.N.I.P. leaders had become increasingly aware, particularly after the 1961 disturbances, of the need for more widespread and effective organization:[3] first, to obtain their demands; second, to fight a major election; and, finally, to prepare U.N.I.P. for assuming control of the

[1] Section 38, The Northern Rhodesia (Constitution) Order in Council 1962, 30 August 1962.
[2] The conditions were: (a) that the delimitation commission consist of 'independent' unbiased members; (b) that if any National seat could not be filled by election, it should not be filled by nomination; (c) that bans be lifted from political organizations and leaders; (d) that the Federal Review be postponed until a representative Government was formed in Northern Rhodesia; (e) that the general election be held before October. Resolution of the National Council on the new Maudling Constitution, 5 March 1962, author's collection.
[3] Circular to members of U.N.I.P. Central Committee on party reorganization, 12 December 1961, author's collection.

government.[1] Between April and July 1962 nearly 100,000 new
African voters had to be registered and taught the complicated
voting procedures called for under the new Constitution.[2] Lower
roll voters in particular had to be mobilized for a convincing
demonstration of U.N.I.P. solidarity and ascendancy among
African parties. At the same time there was U.N.I.P.'s European
campaign to organize. Any serious attempt to attract European
support would require both the creation of a new, less-militant
U.N.I.P. image as well as the exercise of effective control over all
party echelons in order to prevent the violent outbursts and
clashes with A.N.C. which had alienated Europeans in the past.

In March and April 1962 U.N.I.P.'s leaders initiated an
extensive reorganization of the party. The need for such reform
was first raised by Kaunda in a confidential circular to U.N.I.P.'s
Central Committee in December 1961.[3] The circular which
received the committee's unanimous endorsement called for a
number of reforms which were subsequently developed for
implementation by a three-man subcommittee composed of
Lewis Changufu U.N.I.P.'s Transport Secretary, H. Dingiswayo
Banda, U.N.I.P.'s recently appointed Director of Youth, and S.
Wina.[4] The purpose of the reorganization, according to Kaunda's
circular, was to improve U.N.I.P.'s ability to launch either 'the
third stage of the master plan or an election campaign'.[5] The
old organization of divisions, constituencies and branches was
not only 'cumbersome', but, more specifically, it ran too close
to the Government's provincial structure and failed to bring
both the top and subsidiary leadership into close enough contact with the 'common man'.[6] The subcommittee's report
admitted that complaints had been voiced at lower levels in the
party about 'bureaucracy', 'top-heaviness' and the lack of

[1] As early as December 1960 Kaunda sought advice from Commander Fox-Pitt
and Lord Listowel about the problems U.N.I.P. would face with the civil service
when Africans assumed control of the Government; Listowel to Fox-Pitt, 26
December 1960, Emanuel collection.
[2] For a description of registration, and voting procedures under the 1962 Constitution see Mulford, *The N.R. General Election, 1962*, pp. 52–84.
[3] Circular to members of U.N.I.P. Central Committee on party reorganization,
12 December 1961, author's collection.
[4] Party Re-Organization Proposals, n.d., submitted as Appendix 'F' to U.N.I.P.'s
National Council meeting, 5 March 1962, ibid.
[5] Circular to U.N.I.P. Central Committee, 12 December 1961, ibid.
[6] Party Re-Organization Proposals, submitted to U.N.I.P. National Council,
5 March 1962, ibid. Interview with Kaunda, 9 July 1964.

dynamic leadership from above. By March 1962 it was the
election campaign which had taken precedence rather than the
master plan. U.N.I.P.'s aim was to create an organization which
effectively reached 'the common man [in] the most unapproach-
able village in our country'.

Let every man have a feeling—genuine—that each married man in a
family is some sort of chairman; each woman some sort of secretary
and each first born some sort of treasurer, in their organization
linking up with the neighbouring families, then the village unit,
branch, constituency, the region and then the full party and finally
the country as a whole.

With an efficient and powerful party in motion and a powerful
parliamentary set-up, it is possible to sandwich a civil service that
may—in the initial stage—not be considered loyal. . . . An organization of this nature would make all Zambians vigilant in safe-
guarding their hard-won National Independence.[1]

U.N.I.P.'s reorganization, however, was not undertaken solely
to improve the party's contact with the 'common man' or to
reduce the burden of work on headquarters officials. Kaunda
was also anxious to establish more effective control over the
party's lower echelons, particularly the youth brigade, which
had played such a dominant and independent role in the 1961
disturbances. The subcommittee's report made only an oblique
reference to the problem, noting that it was common knowledge
that the 'strain of the master plan has somehow impaired the
smooth administration of the party' and proposing that youths
might only become members of the brigade after joining the
main body of the party.[2] Other evidence, apart from the subcommittee's report, suggests that Kaunda attached considerable
importance to the delicate problem of exercising closer control
over the party apparatus.[3] Kaunda's behaviour when the 1961
disturbances first broke out gave the unmistakable impression
that U.N.I.P.'s top leadership had lost control over large parts
of the party's Luapula and Northern Province organizations.[4]

[1] Party Re-Organization Proposals, submitted to U.N.I.P. National Council,
5 March 1962, author's collection.
[2] Ibid.
[3] Kaunda, K., and Morris, C., Black Government, Lusaka, 1960, pp. 99–103.
[4] See pp. 201–2.

Government reports at the time support this view,[1] as does the Government's *Account of the Disturbances* which was produced in October–November 1961.[2] Commenting early in 1962 on U.N.I.P.'s capacity for locally initiated action in Samfya District (Luapula), the District Commissioner noted: 'At the time of the troubles [1961] it was apparent that even District U.N.I.P. officials were unable to control their people . . . youth leaders ignored the advice and guidance of their own political leaders, who had advocated non-violence and restraint.'[3]

In November the Central Committee issued a circular to all divisional treasurers which aimed at improving procedures for the collection of local donations and subscriptions.[4] The same month, Kaunda appointed H. D. Banda, one of U.N.I.P.'s most militant and able political organizers, as Director of Youth and instructed him to bring the youth brigade up to the standard of U.N.I.P.'s most effectively organized divisions.[5] In April 1962 in conversation with the Acting Chief Secretary, Kaunda indicated that he had considerable trouble controlling parts of Northern Province, where he could not allow the party's minor officials to select their own local leaders.[6]

U.N.I.P.'s reorganization involved three major changes. First, the party's eight provincial divisions were abolished and the provinces subdivided into twenty-four regions covering the entire Territory. Western and Luapula Province were divided into four and two regions respectively, while all other provinces, including Barotseland, were each divided into three regions. Full-time regional organizing secretaries, who bore sole responsibility for party activities and for constituency and branch-level groups in their respective areas, were appointed by and made responsible to U.N.I.P.'s Central Committee.[7]

Secondly, the youth and women's brigades were brought more closely into the party. As noted earlier, members of the

[1] Ex. Co., 8 August 1961, S/S 57/011.

[2] *An Account of the Disturbances in Northern Rhodesia, July to October, 1961*, pp. 73–74.

[3] D.C. (Samfya) to P.C. (Luapula), 16 January 1962, DG 58/4/01.

[4] Circular to all divisional treasurers, 17 November 1961, A.N.L.W. papers.

[5] S.B. to Perm. Sec. (C.S.), 25 April 1963, GHS/S, 108/015.

[6] Ag. C.S. to Ad. Sec., 28 April 1962, S/S 82/81/01, Vol. III. At this stage, with registration in progress and the election only a few months away, conversations of this kind were not unusual.

[7] Party Re-Organization Proposals, submitted to U.N.I.P. National Council, 5 March 1962, author's collection. Also see *U.N.I.P. Constitution*, April 1962.

two brigades were required to join the main body of the party. While both brigades were the responsibility of their respective directors at U.N.I.P. headquarters, and though each had its separate organization running parallel to that of the main party, brigade officials at regional, constituency and branch levels were brought under closer supervision of the main party's officials at each of the three levels. U.N.I.P.'s new constitution was specific on the point that 'the brigades shall not take any separate action on political matters', and the regional youth organizer, a major figure now in the youth brigade's hierarchy, was required to perform his duties 'in consultation with' the regional organizing secretary.[1]

Finally, U.N.I.P.'s National Council was made more representative. Whereas the Council had previously numbered about fifty members, it was now expanded to include seventy-two elected delegates, twenty-four regional secretaries and the party's leaders at the national headquarters. Each region's delegation comprised, in addition to the regional secretary, one elected delegate from the main body of the party and one from each of the two brigades.[2]

Thus by cutting each division into roughly three regions and by concentrating the responsibility for organizing the Territory in the hands of the twenty-four regional secretaries, a much more intensive party organization was achieved. These structural changes, however, were probably less important than the attention given to training the men who would take over the newly created regional posts. Between late 1961 and April 1962 U.N.I.P.'s former division secretaries attended training courses in Ghana organized by Sipalo, U.N.I.P.'s representative in Accra.[3] In addition, Banda, who had begun building the youth movement into a formidable cadre during 1962, initiated courses in both Ghana and East Africa for leading youth brigade officials,[4] who, as regional youth secretaries, would be second in command of the new regional organizations.[5]

---

[1] Party Re-Organization Proposals, submitted to U.N.I.P. National Council, 5 March 1962, author's collection. Also see *U.N.I.P. Constitution*, April 1962.
[2] Ibid.   [3] Sipalo to A. Wina, 20 January 1962, A.N.L.W. papers.
[4] 'The Youth Brigade of the U.N.I.P.', 8 April 1963, GHS/S 018/105.
[5] Each regional headquarters included the regional secretary, treasurer and publicity secretary as well as the regional youth and women's secretaries; *U.N.I.P. Constitution*, April 1962.

With two important exceptions, U.N.I.P.'s reorganization was carried out both swiftly and effectively. The first exception was in Luapula Province, where U.N.I.P.'s notoriously independent provincial organization refused to accept the new reforms and clung tenaciously to the existing system.[1] The streamlining of U.N.I.P.'s organization made many lower-level officials redundant and forced them to reintegrate themselves in lower echelons of the party's hierarchy. Luapula was not only U.N.I.P.'s most fiercely independent division, it was also the most highly organized and one of the most heavily populated areas in Northern Rhodesia. A multitude of minor officials, full-time politicians, fanatically committed to the nationalist struggle, reigned over their respective precincts in the Luapula.[2] There was no way of moving them; and having demonstrated on more than one occasion in the past both a remarkable degree of local authority and frightening capacity for independent action, the Luapulists were wisely allowed to retain their traditional organization for the duration of the election period.[3]

The other exception concerned the youth brigade. While brought under closer control at various levels within the party, the youth brigade had also been greatly strengthened and with its own vertical line of command was actually more autonomous as a national unit. In December 1961, shortly after his appointment, Banda issued a circular emphasizing that the youth brigade was a separate body in the party and instructing youth brigade officials to maintain their membership registers independently from those of the main party. In addition, Banda indicated that youth brigade branches should be registered separately under the Societies Ordinance.[4] U.N.I.P.'s 1962 constitution institutionalized the new national appointment of Director of Youth and provided a more clearly defined role for the movement.[5] Though the youth brigade was subordinated to the main party at all levels, there clearly was reluctance in

[1] 'The Youth Brigade of the U.N.I.P.', 8 April 1963, GHS/S 108/015. Also, interview with Kaunda, 9 July 1964.
[2] Report P.C. (Luapula) to Ag. Perm. Sec. (M.N.A.), 23 January 1963, DG 58/4/01.
[3] Interviews with Luapula and headquarters officials, September–October 1962; Mulford, *The N.R. General Election 1962*, p. 90.
[4] 'The Youth Brigade of the U.N.I.P.', 8 April 1963, GHS/S 108/015.
[5] U.N.I.P. Constitution, n.d. March–April 1962, p. 17, author's collection.

some areas to relinquish local control over what in the past had usually been an appendage of u.n.i.p.'s various lower-level formations. In Northern Province the regional secretary stressed that both brigades would remain firmly under the supervision of the main party. In Luapula Province party leaders warned that any youth brigade official who failed to liaise with constituency-level officials would be dismissed. Youth leaders were also reminded that brigade accounts were to be submitted through the main party. In July 1962 Luapula's division president (Luapula continued to use u.n.i.p.'s old titles) announced that while the youth brigade would be responsible for implementing positive action campaigns, another purely local group, the u.n.i.p. Workers, would ensure that the brigade carried out its instructions.[1]

The most serious conflict over the youth brigade occurred at Lusaka in May 1962. Lusaka's constituency executive insisted on retaining control over its own youth brigade, refusing to accept the new regional youth secretary on the grounds that Banda had failed to consult the executive about the new appointment. After securing the acquiescence of the Central Committee to deal with the matter himself, Banda suspended the executives of the constituency and four of its branches, nominated new constituency officials and announced dates for the election of new branch office-bearers.[2] The Lusaka incident provided a striking illustration of Banda's growing strength in the party as he sought, with increasing success during 1962, to develop the youth brigade into the militant vanguard of u.n.i.p.'s new organization.

Banda, who was directly responsible to u.n.i.p.'s President, could not have reformed u.n.i.p.'s youth movement without Kaunda's active support. u.n.i.p., and a.n.c. before it, had always had youth and action groups which until 1962 had largely been the responsibility of u.n.i.p.'s constituency- and branch-level organizations. Kaunda had always been particularly sympathetic to the problems faced by young Africans in Northern Rhodesia. Indeed, he himself had felt the frustrations of working under an older, more moderate leader, and in 1958, when Kaunda revolted against Nkumbula, one of the dissident

---

[1] 'The Youth Brigade of u.n.i.p.', 8 April 1963, GHS/S 108/015.
[2] Ibid.

group's long-standing complaints was that A.N.C. had failed to satisfy its more youthful and militant elements. The leadership of both Z.A.N.C. and U.N.I.P. was notable for its youthfulness, and both organizations placed heavy emphasis on recruiting young people. It was not, apparently, until the disturbances of 1961 that Kaunda fully recognized that a militant and loosely organized youth movement brought dangers as well as advantages to the party. Nevertheless, Kaunda maintained his previous attitude that the nationalist party, as father of the nation, was obliged to include young people in its ranks and to train them as future leaders of the new Zambia. Kaunda never considered repressing U.N.I.P.'s youth groups; instead, he sought to consolidate them, to provide them with a constructive role which, while absorbing restless energy, utilized their willingness to serve.[1]

In appointing Banda Director of Youth, Kaunda had chosen a man more than equal to the task. Banda combined several outstanding qualities for his new post. An ardent (possibly fanatical) nationalist, Banda had been a long-standing advocate of the need for militant subgroups in nationalist parties and had himself had considerable experience with such groups in A.N.C., Z.A.N.C., and U.N.I.P. He was a tireless political organizer and one of the major contributors of ideas for U.N.I.P.'s reorganization. But perhaps his greatest asset was the widespread popularity Banda enjoyed among U.N.I.P.'s more youthful members. Banda had been active in politics since 1954, both on the Copperbelt and in his home area of Eastern Province.[2] In A.N.C. Banda had always been one of the party's young militants, active both in the boycotts of the middle 1950's and in the group led by Sipalo which worked to oust Nkumbula in 1957. In 1958 Banda followed Kaunda into Z.A.N.C., serving as provincial president for Western Province until he was restricted for eight months in 1959. Banda was imprisoned twice after the formation of U.N.I.P., once for six months in 1960 for taking part in an illegal meeting, and again for nine months in 1961 for sedition. After his appointment as Director of Youth, Banda travelled extensively in Europe and Africa, often with Kaunda,

[1] Interview with Kaunda, 9 July 1964.
[2] Banda's original home was Zithonga village, Lundazi District, Eastern Province.

and a close personal relationship, undoubtedly the basis of
Banda's rather special position in u.n.i.p., appeared to take
shape between the two leaders.[1]
Shortly after u.n.i.p.'s reorganization, Kaunda revived its
campaign for European support, which had been disrupted by
the disturbances in 1961. Though it was not until much later
that u.n.i.p. launched its major effort to attract Europeans,
Kaunda began in June to hold private-house meetings with
Europeans.[2] By now the party had a few European members
who provided part-time assistance and several white supporters
who gave the party limited financial backing.[3] u.n.i.p.'s most
illustrious European member was Sir Stewart Gore-Browne, one
of the Territory's early settlers who had served as a leading figure
in the Legislative Council for nearly two decades. In April
1962 Gore-Browne accompanied Kaunda to New York to give
evidence before the United Nation's Committee on Colonialism.[4] James Skinner, a Lusaka lawyer originally from Dublin,
acted as u.n.i.p.'s legal and campaign adviser[5] while Reverend
Merfyn Temple, a Methodist minister also from Lusaka, who
had supported various liberal multi-racial groups for many
years, became one of the party's leading campaigners for European support.

Though u.n.i.p. clearly hoped to increase its European support for the election campaign in October, no change was
made on major points of party policy to make it more acceptable to whites. u.n.i.p. remained rigidly opposed to the Federation and firmly committed to its complete destruction. Despite
u.n.i.p.'s willingness to contest the election, the party had not
accepted the new Constitution as a satisfactory arrangement for

[1] This picture of Banda is a composite, drawn both from the author's field work
in Northern Rhodesia and from 'The Youth Brigade of the u.n.i.p.', 8 April 1963,
GHS/S 108/015. The youth brigade paper tended to overplay Banda's more
militant characteristics, but provided much valuable factual information about his
past activities.
[2] u.n.i.p.'s first public attempt to court Europeans was a large multi-racial
cocktail party at Kitwe's Edinburgh Hotel on 24 June; *Northern News*, 25 June
1962.
[3] This point is based on field research. The persons in question have not authorized the author to use their names.
[4] *Rhodesia Herald*, 11 April 1962.
[5] In July, Skinner prepared u.n.i.p.'s *Election Worker's Handbook* (30 July 1962),
an impressive and extensive electioneering guide which was distributed to party
officials at all levels.

African political aspirations. Nothing short of universal adult suffrage, a government fully representative of the African people and, in due course, the granting of independence would satisfy the party. Europeans were offered the opportunity to share in the building of a new democratic Northern Rhodesia based on majority rule and individual rights, rather than minority privilege.[1]

U.N.I.P. had no monopoly on political change during the period leading up to the 1962 election. Northern Rhodesia's other political parties were also in a state of flux during late 1961 and 1962. The U.F.P. began to address itself to the problem of attracting African support as early as September 1961.[2] As noted previously, Welensky discouraged the militant 'action committee' formed in September by the U.F.P.'s northern wing to resist further changes in the June constitutional proposals.[3] Behind the scenes Welensky adopted a somewhat more accommodating attitude,[4] largely, it would seem, as a result of pressure exerted by a group of realistic Copperbelt businessmen, who argued that the European unofficials in Northern Rhodesia's next Government should be led by a moderate African with widespread popular support. Katilungu, A.N.C.'s acting President, was the obvious choice; experienced in trade-union affairs, moderate politically and deeply opposed to U.N.I.P. If in the next election Europeans voted for the U.F.P. in upper roll constituencies and for Katilungu's A.N.C. in the National seats, European dominance could be maintained through a U.F.P.– A.N.C. coalition Government.[5]

Such ideas were premature in late 1961, and, in any case, if they had aroused interest among U.F.P. leaders, any prospect of developing a closer liaison with A.N.C. was suddenly shattered with the death of Katilungu in a road accident in November.[6] Thus for the second time in nine months A.N.C.'s leadership changed hands; Edward Mungoni Liso, the party's National Chairman, became acting President,[7] and Job Michello,

[1] U.N.I.P.'s *Policy*, released on 15 June 1962, author's collection.
[2] S.O. (C.S.) 2 to A.S. (C.S.) 1, 18 September 1961, S/S 119/130/01, Vol. I.
[3] S.O. (C.S.) 2 to A.S. (C.S.) 1, 5 October 1961, ibid.
[4] Tucker to A.S. (C.S.) 1, 7 November 1961, ibid.
[5] S.O. (C.S.) 2 to A.S. (C.S.) 1, 18 September 1961, ibid.
[6] *Northern News*, 10 November 1961.
[7] Ibid., 15 November 1961.

A.N.C.'s National Secretary, inherited Katilungu's seat in the Legislative Council.[1]

During his brief presidency Katilungu had done a great deal to revitalize a declining A.N.C. Once elected to the Legislative Council, Katilungu set about establishing contacts with European businessmen and improving A.N.C.'s feeble organization. Unlike Nkumbula, who devoted most of his energies to Southern Province, Katilungu was active on the Copperbelt and in both Northern and Luapula Provinces, where in August he sought to capitalize on the ill feeling which U.N.I.P.'s role in the disturbances had caused among chiefs and Native Authorities.[2] Relatively detailed party accounts were produced for the financial year ending 30 June 1961,[3] and A.N.C.'s circulars and publications became both more frequent and better in quality.[4] By mid-August Katilungu claimed that he had launched A.N.C. campaigns throughout the country. Gwembe, Kalomo, Serenje, Mwinilungu, Chadiza, and Lundazi Districts, areas closed to A.N.C. for many years, were opened to the party once again.[5] A.N.C.'s financial position had also improved, largely due to the efforts of Katilungu and Berrings Lombe, Deputy National Secretary, to maintain the party's lucrative relationship with Tshombe.[6] A.N.C.'s 1961 financial statement showed a contribution of £10,000 from Katanga, most of which had been used for the purchase of vehicles.[7] Attendance at A.N.C.'s annual conference in late September rivalled that of U.N.I.P.'s Mulungushi conference the previous July. Katilungu delivered an impressive presidential address, and the persistent bickering among party officials which had plagued A.N.C. in the past was noticeably absent.[8]

In November the U.F.P. organized the Northern Rhodesia Build-A-Nation (B.A.N.) campaign, the party's first major effort

[1] *Rhodesia Herald*, 13 January 1962.

[2] *Week by Week*, 3 June and 5 August 1961.

[3] A.N.C. accounts for the year up to 30 June 1961, appendix to report on A.N.C.'s annual conference, 28 October 1961, TS/S 123/01.

[4] Circular to Chiefs and People of N.R., 16 August 1961, ibid.

[5] *Week by Week*, 12 August 1961.

[6] Memorandum from British Consulate, Elisabethville, to the Federal Minister of External Affairs, Salisbury, 31 July 1961, TS/S 123/010.

[7] A.N.C. accounts for the year up to 30 June 1961, appendix to report on A.N.C.'s annual conference, 28 October 1961, ibid.

[8] Report on A.N.C.'s annual conference, 28 October 1961, ibid.

to gain African support since the formation of the Federation eight years earlier.[1] The need for attracting African support had now gained relatively wide acceptance in the u.f.p., except among the party's more militant Copperbelt organization. At the u.f.p.'s annual congress in late November, where Welensky launched the new campaign, six u.f.p. branches— Lusaka Rural, Fort Jameson, Choma, Chisamba, Monze and Broken Hill—introduced a resolution demanding that recruitment of Africans be treated as the party's first priority.[2] For years the u.f.p. had claimed that Federation rested on the two principles of partnership and government by responsible men irrespective of race. Africans, of course, had rejected the u.f.p.'s version of partnership since the beginning, and government by responsible men had come to mean nothing more than government by Europeans and those few Africans whom Europeans judged had reached their own standards of education and wealth. Even among those Africans who had attained 'European standards', the u.f.p. had never attracted more than a mere handful, most of whom were better known for their love of 'civilized comfort' than for their distinctive political abilities.

Having sponsored the b.a.n. campaign, the u.f.p. then sought to detach itself and to represent the programme as virtually a public service, well removed from partisan politics.[3] For a number of reasons, which should have been obvious to the organizers, the u.f.p.'s continuing involvement was ludicrously evident.[4] Indeed, the b.a.n. organization appeared to be exactly what it was, a well-endowed but atrociously organized u.f.p. front. The whole affair was a dismal failure and within a few months the b.a.n. campaign had closed its offices.[5]

[1] *Northern News*, 27 November 1961. The first b.a.n. campaign was launched in Southern Rhodesia a few months earlier.

[2] Ibid., 25 November 1961.

[3] Letter to the *Central African Post*, 23 February 1962, from the chairman, Lusaka branch of the b.a.n. campaign.

[4] The names on the b.a.n. campaign's executive committee read like a u.f.p. 'roll of honour' for the Federation; minutes of meeting of n.r. Division of the b.a.n. Committee, Kitwe, 12 December 1961. u.f.p. personnel organized and staffed the b.a.n. campaign in most areas and the two organizations often shared the same offices and passed out each other's literature; circular 211, 29 November 1961. Attempts were made to organize courses for Africans at which Federal ministers and other leading lights of the u.f.p. gave lectures; circular HRD/1775, 18 December 1961. These materials were attached to a file on 'European Politics', S/S 119/130/01.

[5] *Northern News*, 28 June 1962.

Perhaps the most striking demonstration of the U.F.P.'s utter failure to attract Africans was provided by the 1962 Federal election, which Welensky suddenly called for in April apparently with the aim in mind of strengthening his mandate to carry on the fight to save the Federation. Both nationalist parties in Northern Rhodesia boycotted the election. In the Territory's two 'special' African seats, the two successful candidates, both of whom supported the maintenance of Federation and campaigned under the name of the National Republican Party, a U.F.P. 'front' organization, were elected on the lowest percentage poll ever recorded. From a total electorate of more than 4,000, the two new African Federal M.P.s accumulated between them a total of forty-seven votes, most of which had reportedly been extracted from members of the candidates' extended families.[1]

When Nkumbula was released from prison in January 1962, he stepped into a political situation radically different from the one he had left in April 1961. Though A.N.C. was not in a position to challenge U.N.I.P.'s ascendency among Africans, Katilungu's leadership, together with the financial support received from Katanga, had done much to reverse A.N.C.'s previous decline. Moreover, Nkumbula resumed leadership of a party which, in European eyes, had become increasingly moderate and responsible. A.N.C. had accepted the constitutional proposals of June 1961;[2] it had disassociated itself from the militant forces of Pan-Africanism;[3] friendly relations had been established with Tshombe's Government in Katanga;[4] and, above all, A.N.C. had not been involved in the 1961 disturbances. Equally dramatic were the changes in European politics. In this respect Tshombe's régime had made a deep impression on Northern Rhodesia's Europeans, who could hardly miss the fact that in Tshombe Welensky and Nkumbula shared a common friend.[5] The apparent lesson of Katanga was

---

[1] The two successful candidates in the election, which was held on 27 April 1962, were Edward Mukelabai and Dixon Konkola, who in N.R.'s election headed yet another U.F.P. front organization, The Central African Peoples Union (C.A.P.U.). The percentage poll was 1.37 per cent. *Central African Examiner*, May 1962, p. 19.

[2] *Northern News*, 17 July 1961.

[3] Ibid., 6 June 1962.

[4] Extracts from Nkumbula's biography, 27 November 1962, S/S 201/05; see also *Observer*, 29 July 1962.

[5] S.O. (C.S.) 2 to A.S. (C.S.) 1, 18 September 1961, S/S 119/130/01. Vol. I.

that given rich economic resources, such as copper, and adequate financial power, Europeans might retain control over the country long after they ceased to hold the majority in the Legislative Council. To the U.F.P., Katanga represented far more than merely a buffer against the African nationalist states to the north; Tshombe's régime was the only African Government to date which had resisted both the onslaught of Pan-Africanism and the subtle influences of Communism.

The collapse of the B.A.N. campaign coupled with the Federal election results left the U.F.P. with no illusions about its ability to attract African support independently. Some form of co-operation with an African group now seemed inevitable, but to whom could the party turn? Had he lived, the most logical choice would have been Katilungu. Now there was only Nkumbula, an uncertain and unappetizing possibility so far as the Europeans were concerned. Nevertheless, on 1 March 1962 the U.F.P.'s caucus issued instructions that on no account were U.F.P. leaders to speak out in public against A.N.C.[1] By June the seeds of a U.F.P.–A.N.C. alliance had been sown.[2]

Finally, there was the Liberal Party, which in association with government officials had been governing Northern Rhodesia since the U.F.P.'s resignation in February 1961. Essentially, the Liberal Party was one man, Sir John Moffat. The Moffat Resolutions of 1954,[3] together with Moffat's theories about the 'movement of power' in Northern Rhodesia from Europeans to Africans, constituted the basis for all Liberal policy on political and constitutional issues. Moffat argued that the 1962 Constitution provided Europeans with their last opportunity to establish a genuine and effective partnership with the African. Since 1953 Africans had been gaining power steadily at the expense of European dominance until, under the 1962 Constitution, complete European control was no longer possible. Yet Moffat claimed that the Constitution was also designed to prevent the immediate introduction of African majority rule, favouring, through the device of the National

[1] s.o. (c.s.) 2 to a.s. (c.s.) 1, 2 March 1962, S/S 119/130/01. Vol. I.

[2] Roberts told a u.f.p. committee meeting in the Copperbelt in June that he had seen Nkumbula and felt that many people underrated him. Nkumbula, said Roberts, was being 'very Tshombe like'; s.o. (c.s.) 2 to a.s. (c.s.) 1, 12 June 1962, ibid.

[3] Leg. Co. *Debates*, 29 July 1954.

seats, the emergence of a moderate, multi-racial Government. Moffat believed that such a Government would provide both a valuable period of training for responsible African nationalists as well as the opportunity for peacefully negotiating Northern Rhodesia's independence constitution.[1]

Though Moffat viewed the Liberal Party's role as purely transitory, lasting little more than five years, the party suffered from several serious weaknesses. As a multi-racial party in a racially polarized society, the Liberals never attained more than a handful of European and African members. In April 1962 the Liberals had only fifteen registered branches in the Territory and less than a hundred active members.[2] Thus it lacked the necessary reservoir from which to draw party leaders, organizers, candidates and money. The Liberal Party consistently overestimated its appeal to Africans as well, usually pointing to its performance as the c.a.p. in the 1959 election when the party secured three Legislative Council seats, mainly on the strength of African votes. Moffat's subsequent claims that his party had proved its ability to attract Africans in 1959 disregarded the special circumstances of the 1959 election.[3] z.a.n.c. boycotted the election, and a.n.c. nominated candidates in only one of the three constituencies which the Liberals won.[4] The truth was that to Africans Moffat's party simply represented a lesser evil than the u.f.p.

Moffat himself tended to be somewhat doctrinaire, lacking both colour and the common touch. Widely respected in Northern Rhodesia's European community, Moffat did not enjoy the trust of most African politicians.[5] Nor was his party free from internal strife, much of which revolved around Moffat's approach to practical political problems. One such conflict occurred early in 1962 over the question of Liberal

[1] This summary of Moffat's position is taken from speeches given during the 1962 election campaign and from an interview with the author on 19 October 1962.
[2] *Central African Post*, 4 April 1962.
[3] *Rhodesia Herald*, 6 March 1962; interview with Moffat, 19 October 1962.
[4] *Northern News*, 28 February 1959.
[5] Moffat's role at the Victoria Falls Conference of September 1951, his ambivalent position during the campaign against Federation, the ideas he expressed on the Crown land issue in 1951, and the feeling among Africans that Moffat had quietly withdrawn his promised support for u.n.i.p. and a.n.c. during the 1961 constitutional conference, all contributed to a loss of confidence in Moffat among African nationalist politicians.

co-operation with the African nationalist parties in the general election. Moffat, who wished to avoid involvement in the rivalry between A.N.C. and U.N.I.P., refused to consider co-operating with either party unless they first united, a completely impracticable suggestion at best. On the other hand, Moffat's Vice-President, Reverend Colin Morris, favoured an immediate alliance with U.N.I.P., arguing that the new Constitution made it essential that U.N.I.P. not be isolated from the European community during the coming election. Morris accordingly began private discussions with Kaunda, first to explore the possibility of an election alliance, and, failing that, to propose an arrangement between a private group of Europeans and U.N.I.P. On 12 March the conflict between Moffat and Morris became public. Despite the fact that Moffat himself had known about Morris's talks with Kaunda, the Liberal executive publicly dissociated itself from Morris's activities and he subsequently resigned, followed shortly afterwards by the party's able young secretary, Denis Acheson.[1]

For months Moffat maintained his neutrality between the two African parties, insisting all the while that the Liberals would be happy to form an alliance with a united nationalist movement.[2] By insisting, as he did, that the split between U.N.I.P. and A.N.C. was simply a long-standing quarrel over the division of 'political plums' between the parties' leading personalities,[3] Moffat revealed both a fundamental misunderstanding of nationalist politics and a strong streak of paternalism. In the end Moffat's policy was to prove a major blunder. The one party founded on the principle of multi-racialism appeared either unable or unwilling to give practical effect to the crux of its policy. More important perhaps, Moffat had offended the leadership of both African parties and seriously weakened his position for future negotiations with U.N.I.P.

Registration of Voters[4]

The decision to hold the general election in late October, before the rains set in, committed the Northern Rhodesia Government

[1] *Northern News*, 6, 9, and 12 March 1962.
[2] *Central African Daily News*, 28 June 1962.
[3] *Northern News*, 7 May 1962.
[4] For a more detailed account of the registration of voters, see Mulford, *The N.R. General Election, 1962*, pp. 50–75.

to a rigid time-table which originally allowed only eleven weeks—9 April to 30 June—for the registration of voters.[1] The Government envisaged a total electorate of approximately 30,000 upper roll voters, 90 per cent of whom were to be Europeans, and approximately 70,000 lower roll voters, virtually all of whom were to be Africans registering for the first time.[2]

A large and well-balanced registration, closely approximating the figures which the Government had set, was particularly important to the successful operation of the 1962 Constitution. As a result, the Government adopted a vigorous and positive policy towards registration.[3] A massive 'Register Your Vote' programme was mounted by the Information Department, and political parties were encouraged to organize campaigns of their own.[4]

The 1962 Constitution introduced a complicated two-tier qualified franchise system. All voters, regardless of the roll on which they were registered, had to possess four general qualifications: literacy in English; age of 21 years; two years' continuous residence in the Federation; and citizenship of the Federation or of the United Kingdom and Colonies, or the status of a British Protected Person by virtue of connexion with Northern Rhodesia. Persons who satisfied these conditions were then required to qualify under one of the two sets of 'additional qualifications' for upper and lower roll voters contained in the Schedule to the Northern Rhodesia (Electoral Provisions) Order in Council, 1962. Generally speaking, the 'additional qualifications' enabled the voter to qualify on the basis of income, education or property as well as on the basis of the voter's position in his respective community.[5]

Registration figures at the end of the first month fell far below the Government's expectations. With less than two-thirds of the registration period remaining, new registrations on the upper and lower rolls together amounted to only approximately 14 per cent of the Government's target figure. Re-registrations, which were conducted by post and applied mainly

[1] Ad. Sec. to all p.c.s and d.c.s, 22 March 1962, MS/2615/37.
[2] *N.R. Proposals for Constitutional Change*, Cmd. 1295, February 1961, p. 8.
[3] Ad. Sec. to all p.c.s and d.c.s, 22 March 1962, MS/2615/37.
[4] Interview with Chief Electoral Officer (c.e.o.), 29 August 1962.
[5] Northern Rhodesia (Electoral Provisions) Order in Council, 1962, 30 March 1962.

to European upper roll voters, showed more hopeful progress.[1]
Two factors accounted for the poor results of the first month.
First, the Federal election, held on 27 April, had led the
Northern Rhodesia Government to postpone its publicity
campaign until early May.[2] Second, both African parties had
also delayed their respective campaigns until after the Federal
election, A.N.C. through sheer lack of preparation, U.N.I.P. in part
at least because it had not completed its reorganization.[3] The
result was that the Government came under increasing pressure
to extend the registration period into July.[4] The African parties
in particular argued that the Government's decision to postpone the Information Department's campaign was especially
damaging to their election preparations, because most of the
Territory's 70,000 new voters were lower roll Africans.[5] The
pattern of the first month's lower roll registrations supported
the African parties' contention. Though the figures for the
entire country were low, those for major urban areas, where
newspaper circulation and contacts among Africans were
extensive, indicated that Africans were aware at least that
registration had begun. In rural areas, however, the figures
were very depressed indeed. South-Western electoral area
topped the list with only 464 registrations in an estimated
electorate of 3,600, while Barotseland, with eight registrations
out of an estimated 3,800 potential voters, occupied the bottom
—though admittedly the apparent indifference of the Lozi was
due more to the obstinacy of the Litunga than to the absence
of government publicity.[6]

The Government at first withstood the demands, but by
early May it was evident that unless registrations increased
markedly in coming weeks, the Government would be forced

[1] Voters registered in the four weeks ending 7 May 1962, 9 May 1962, MS/
2615/37.

[2] Ad. Sec. to all p.c.s and d.c.s, 22 March 1962, MS/2615/37.

[3] In mid-April S. Wina resigned as U.N.I.P.'s Director of Elections as a result of a
speech he made in Salisbury which caused a furore throughout the Federation. Wina
had announced that it was U.N.I.P.'s intention, after achieving power, to declare
Welensky a prohibited immigrant in Northern Rhodesia as the first step in a
campaign to demoralize the white man in Central Africa; *Central African Post*, 9
April 1962; *Northern News*, 11, 14 and 17 April 1962.

[4] Ag. c.s. to all p.c.s and d.c.s, 4 May 1962, MS/2615/37.

[5] *Central African Post*, 9 April and 14 May 1962.

[6] Voters registered in the four weeks ending 7 May 1962, 9 May 1962, MS/
2615/37.

to grant the desired extension, thereby risking the conduct of elections in the November rains. Immediate steps were taken to improve the situation. District Commissioners were instructed to give special priority to registration, and those whose districts were in areas with low enrolment figures were asked to examine the local situation with a view to increasing registrations at once. In rural districts emphasis was placed on ensuring that registration officers were available over wider areas and especially in all major centres of population.[1] The Government also liberalized the residence requirement for new applicants. Whereas previously the applicant had to have resided in an electoral area continuously for three months immediately prior to his application, the Government's amendment provided that a person who had lived in any electoral area for any continuous period of three months and who, during the three months immediately preceding his application, had been continuously in the Territory but had removed from one electoral area to another, was eligible to register. Similarly, a person who had maintained his home or employment in any electoral area while absent from the Territory for some temporary purpose was also eligible to register under the amended provision.[2] Though impossible to calculate, the number of potential voters affected by the change must have been considerable. In any event, the amendment's double purpose was clear. First, it accommodated persons such as school teachers, migrant workers and civil servants, a significant proportion of whom were on the move at any given time. Second, and more in line with the Government's drive to register new voters, the amendment took cognizance of the fact that the majority of such persons were Africans who were likely to qualify as lower roll voters.

By late May the Government's campaign was in full operation. Registration figures showed a dramatic rise. New 'claims' totalled 8,391 for the week ending on 26 May (1,972 upper roll and 6,419 lower roll).[3] The next week the figures remained steady,[4] but by mid-June the weekly total for new 'claims' had

[1] Ag. c.s. to all p.c.s and d.c.s, 4 May 1962; c.e.o. to all p.c.s and d.c.s, 9 May 1962, MS/2615/37.
[2] c.e.o. to all d.c.s for distribution to registering officers, 10 May 1962, ibid.; *Central African Post*, 11 May 1962.
[3] *Central African Post*, 30 May 1962.
[4] New claims for registration—Position as of 4 June 1962, MS/2615/37.

climbed first to 10,188 (11 June) and then to 11,672 (18 June), over 2,000 more 'claims' than during the entire month of April.[1] By the first week of June the Government was satisfied with the progress of registration in urban areas. Upper roll figures were particularly heartening. For the Territory as a whole, new upper roll 'claims' were only 1,269 below the target figure, and every town, except Mufulira, was either approaching or had reached the Government's estimates.[2]

Lower roll registrations remained approximately 28,145 below the adjusted estimate of 62,000. Breakdowns by electoral areas indicated that the trouble lay in rural areas. New claims in Luapula, Northern, Eastern, North-Western, and Barotseland all fell below 31 per cent of their respective estimates, with Barotseland still showing an astonishingly low figure of 9 per cent.[3] A week later the figures had improved. New upper roll claims exceeded the estimate, while lower roll registrations for the Territory advanced by nearly 8,000, an increase of 23 per cent over the previous week. Rural electoral areas, however, continued to lag behind with an average increase for the week of approximately 12 per cent.[4]

U.N.I.P. was the only party which staged a significant drive to register new voters. Registration was treated as the citizen's duty. Circulars were sent out to all branches and instructions on registration procedures and suggestions for the organization of the campaign. Nine pamphlets in the vernaculars and in English were distributed to constituency- and branch-level groups, and U.N.I.P. officials toured their respective areas with teams, encouraging and instructing potential voters.[5] Indeed, it soon became evident that U.N.I.P. was organizing registering schools, particularly in towns, where instruction in completing the registering form was given to party members whose only disability was insufficient literacy in English.[6] Under the Electoral Provisions Order in Council, 1962, the test of literacy for registration was the applicant's ability to complete 'in his

[1] Position as of 11 June and 18 June 1962, MS/2615/37.
[2] Position as of 4 June 1962, ibid; C.E.O. to all D.C.s, 5 June 1962, ibid.
[3] Position as of 4 June 1962, ibid.
[4] Position as of 11 June 1962, ibid.
[5] *Northern News*, 9 April 1962; interviews with S. Wina, 9 September 1962, and Mundia, 15 October 1962.
[6] *Northern News*, 6 June 1962; *Broken Hill Observer*, 15 June 1962.

own handwriting, in English and without assistance, such form for registration as may be prescribed.'[1] By June U.N.I.P.'s schools were operating on a large scale. That some of their products, however, were not sufficiently literate became painfully evident when occasionally an applicant began filling in the required information on the wrong line of the form, not realizing the mistake until it was pointed out by the registering officer.[2] Likewise, in Chingola registering officers caught African women cribbing after it was noticed that they had the answers written upside down on the upper part of their breasts. Evidently they were discovered in a moment of difficulty, looking down, and the red-faced officers concerned complained of being placed in a highly delicate situation.[3]

The literacy issue proved highly contentious. The U.F.P. attacked U.N.I.P.'s registration schools and demanded that the Government outlaw them. Complaining of a 'tremendous vote fiddle', Roberts maintained that 25 per cent of the voters on the rolls were illiterate and therefore not entitled to vote.[4] The Government's view was that the Electoral Provisions did not prevent such preparations; indeed, government officials saw little difference between the student studying before his school examinations and the aspiring voter practising before his attempt to register. As with the student, who was entitled to his certificate even if unable to pass the examination a second time, so it was with the claimant who had completed his registration.[5] The U.F.P., however, persisted with its allegations,[6] causing the Government considerable irritation and anxiety, until September when the Government's position was upheld in the High Court.[7]

Apart from its complaints against U.N.I.P., the U.F.P. took little

[1] N.R. (Electorial Provisions) Order in Council, 1962, 30 March 1962.
[2] Interview with C.E.O., 20 September 1962.
[3] *Northern News*, 27 June 1962.
[4] *Northern News*, 7 June 1962.
[5] Interview with C.E.O., 26 November 1962.
[6] *Northern News*, 1 September 1962.
[7] Judgement in the matter of an application by Mustard Simukonda for leave to apply for orders of mandamus and certiorari, and in the matter of the hearing of an objection by Mustard Simukonda under section 20 of the Legislative Council Ordinance by the Magistrate at Luanshya on 11 August 1962, Ndola High Court, 20 September 1962. For a full account of the literacy issue and the above judgement see Mulford, *The N.R. General Election 1962*, pp. 57–60.

interest in the registration of new voters, instead devoting its efforts to the re-registration of voters already on the rolls.[1] Nor did the Liberals organize a registration drive, mainly because the party lacked funds and voluntary assistance from its rank and file members.[2]

A.N.C. showed little sign of having a well-organized registration campaign. Yet among the rural electoral areas, those traditionally regarded as A.N.C. country (Southern, South-Western, Livingstone, and part of Eastern) consistently showed the highest percentage figures of actual compared with estimated registrations. In addition, South-Western, Livingstone, and Southern were the first of the rural areas to reach their respective targets, Southern more than doubling its estimated electorate by the end of registration. While it was true that Livingstone and Southern both had relatively low estimates, it was still an unexpected pattern and not the last time during the election period that A.N.C. surprised political observers.[3]

Nkumbula raised a number of criticisms against the Government's conduct of registration. He alleged that the Government had appointed a number of Nyasa registering officers who were allowing their countrymen easy access to the rolls. In the 1959 election, he claimed, seventy-three Nyasas had voted in Eastern Province alone.[4] In June Nkumbula complained that proof of identity was not rigorously enforced, and later in the month he accused the Government of appointing known members of U.N.I.P. as registering officers and allowing them to register voters in U.N.I.P.'s headquarters. The only allegation Nkumbula attempted to support with evidence was his accusation that registering officers were sympathetic towards U.N.I.P. applicants. He cited the low registration figures in A.N.C.'s Mufulira stronghold, compared them with the higher figures in Kitwe and Luapula Province and concluded that the reason for the divergence was that registering officers in Mufulira insisted that applicants read the declaration on the application

[1] *Northern News*, 14 May 1962.
[2] Interview with Moffat, 19 October 1962.
[3] New claims for registration—Position as of 4, 11, 18 June and 11 July 1962, MS/2615/37.
[4] *Central African Post*, 9 April 1962.

as a kind of literacy test.[1] Although this particular complaint did not stand up to examination, it was undoubtedly true that some Nyasas qualified for the vote illegally and that a small number of voters, mainly on the Copperbelt and in Lusaka, qualified by evading identity and literacy requirements.[2] The steady rise in new registrations up to 18 June became a flood in the final two weeks of the month. Whereas in early June new 'claims' averaged approximately 10,000 per week, in the last two weeks they poured in at the rate of nearly 3,000 per day.[3] The final figures, including re-registration, surpassed Government estimates on both rolls: 129,093 voters had registered—37,152 on the upper roll and 91,941 on the lower roll.[4] Only a few electoral areas—Mufulira, Northern, and North-Western—failed to achieve their respective targets for new claims on both rolls. Barotseland finished the registration approximately 1,300 voters below its estimate on the lower roll, while Luanshya, Luapula, South-Western, and Northern all fell slightly short of their respective goals on the upper roll.[5]

The African parties had good reason to be satisfied both with the enlarged lower roll electorate and with the surprising number of Africans who had qualified for the upper roll: 7,321 compared with the Government's estimate of 3,000, or approximately 20 per cent of the upper roll.[6] The Liberals also welcomed the increased proportion of Africans on the upper roll, not only for the advantage the party hoped to reap in upper roll constituencies, but also because the party's prospects of satisfying the 20 per cent requirement on the upper roll side in National constituencies appeared to be much improved. On the other hand, the u.f.p. had grounds for concern. While African registrations on the upper roll as a whole formed only 20 per cent of the total, there were some areas, notably rural areas such as Barotseland, Northern, and South-Western, where the

---

[1] *Central African Post*, 25 June 1962. The allegation concerning u.n.i.p. registering officers referred to James Skinner, u.n.i.p.'s legal adviser, who was appointed a registering officer in his capacity as a lawyer, and nothing in the regulations prevented him from registering voters in u.n.i.p.'s headquarters.

[2] This point is based on field research in n.r. between August and December 1962.

[3] New claims for registration—Position as of 11 July 1962, MS/2615/37.

[4] *Report of the Delimitation Commission*, 3 September 1962, p. 2.

[5] New claims for registration—Position as of 11 July 1962, MS/2615/37.

[6] Records of racial breakdowns in constituencies, n.d., October 1962.

proportion of upper roll African voters would be closer to 50 per cent. Moreover, with African lower roll registrations 31 per cent above the expected level, all European National candidates who sought to obtain 10 per cent African support were confronted, in terms of votes, with a much more formidable task.

Provisional registers were compiled at great speed and published in late July to enable the delimitation Commission to begin its work. Because the provisional registers were based on the 1959 electoral areas and the existing 'ordinary' and 'special' constituencies, the registers served little purpose to the parties beyond providing a general guide to registration patterns in the Territory. Detailed campaign plans were impossible to formulate until the delimitation of new constituencies, electoral areas and polling districts had been completed.

Delimitation of Constituencies[1]

Delimitation of constituencies under the 1962 Constitution was a particularly formidable task. The terms of reference in the Northern Rhodesia (Delimitation Commission) Order in Council, 1962, set out the rules for delineating, in a single delimitation, three separate sets of constituencies, each extending over the whole Territory and each based on different principles. The upper roll delimitation was based on the total number of voters registered under the higher franchise, while the lower roll constituencies were based on total adult African population.[2] In delimiting constituencies, the number of upper roll voters in each upper roll constituency was to be as nearly equal to the 'electoral quota'[3] as was reasonably practicable; the number of adult Africans included in each lower roll constituency was to be as near to the 'population quota'[4] as reasonably practicable. In order to take account of means of communication, geographical features, population distribution and administrative boundaries, the number of voters in an upper or

[1] For a more detailed account of the delimitation of constituencies, see Mulford, *The N.R. General Election, 1962.*

[2] Northern Rhodesia (Delimitation Commission) Order in Council 1962, 4 July 1962. These figures were based on Labour Department statistics. The first African census was not produced until 1963.

[3] The number obtained by dividing the total number of upper roll voters by fifteen.

[4] The number obtained by dividing the total number of adult African inhabitants by fifteen.

a lower roll constituency might vary above or below its respective quota by 25 per cent in urban constituencies and $33\frac{1}{3}$ per cent in rural constituencies.[1]

In addition to the separately based, double-roll delimitation, the National constituencies were formed by combining upper and lower roll constituencies in such a way as to reflect the numerical difference, nearly 1 :3, between the Territory's upper and lower roll electorates. The delimitation of National constituencies was governed by the use of an 'average ratio' figure.[2] The ratio between the number of upper roll voters and the number of lower roll voters in any given National constituency was not to vary excessively from the 'average ratio', and the total number of voters (upper and lower roll) included in the constituency could not be less than one-tenth of all registered voters in the Territory.[3]

Besides these principal rules for delimitation, six additional provisions were set out in the Order. Every upper roll rural constituency was either to be coterminous with a lower roll constituency or to consist of two or more complete lower roll constituencies. Similarly, each urban lower roll constituency was either to be coterminous with an upper roll constituency or to consist of two or more complete upper roll constituencies. National constituencies were to be composed of two or more complete constituencies, any of which could be either an upper or lower roll constituency. The four National constituencies whose upper roll/lower roll ratios varied least from the 'average ratio' were designated as the 'reserved' National constituencies and required to return one European and one African member. Barotseland, in the case of the lower roll delimitation, was not to be included with any other part of Northern Rhodesia. Finally, every constituency was to comprise a single area of territory with the important exception of those which bordered on the Katanga pedicle.[4]

The Commission had first to determine the 'electoral' and 'population' quotas, the permissible limits of variation in urban and rural, upper and lower roll constituencies, as well

---

[1] N.R. (Delimitation Commission) Order in Council 1962, 4 July 1962.
[2] The proportion of total upper roll voters to total lower roll voters.
[3] *Report of the Delimitation Commission*, 3 September 1962, pp. 2–3.
[4] N.R. (Delimitation Commission) Order in Council 1962, 4 July 1962.

as the 'average ratio' and minimum electorate for National constituencies. To calculate the 'electoral quota' for upper roll constituencies, which worked out to 2,477, the Commission utilized the total number of upper roll voters registered as of 31 July (37,152) and simply divided it by 15. This figure permitted variation limits of from 1,858 to 3,096 for urban constituencies and from 1,651 to 3,302 for rural constituencies.[1]

The figures required for the lower roll delimitation were more difficult to ascertain. It was decided that the official statistics of population and labour in the Territory as of 1 December 1961 should be used to estimate current adult population in small individual areas. From these figures the Commission derived its final estimate of 1,275,768 for the whole of Northern Rhodesia. Accordingly, the 'population quota' for lower roll constituencies was 85,051, giving permissible variation limits of from 63,788 to 106,314 for urban constituencies and from 56,701 to 113,401 for rural constituencies.

Before computing the 'average ratio' for National constituencies, it was necessary to deduct, from the total registration figures for the upper and lower rolls respectively, Asian voters and those Coloureds who had not elected to vote in an ordinary National constituency. These deductions left the following totals:

Upper roll	37,152	Lower roll	91,941	Total	129,093
Asian & Col.	1,928	Asian & Col.	28	Asian & Col.	1,956
Net	35,224	Net	91,913	Net	127,137

Thus for the purpose of delimiting a National constituency, the 'average ratio' between upper and lower roll voters in the national electorate was 1:2.609. The minimum electorate for any given National constituency was 12,714 voters.[2]

A number of technical problems complicated the Commission's task. On the basis of registration figures alone, upper roll rural constituencies would have been unmanageable if minimal deviations from the 'electoral quota' were observed. In these constituencies the Commission decided to sacrifice narrow margins of deviation from the 'electoral quota' and to include

[1] *Report of the Delimitation Commission*, 3 September 1962, pp. 1–3.
[2] Ibid.

peri-urban areas in order to reduce the constituencies' size. However, under Northern Rhodesia's three-tier delimitation, a problem in one set of constituencies inevitably had repercussions elsewhere. For example, an excessive deviation from the 'electoral quota' in an upper roll constituency necessitated greater deviations from both the 'population quota' of certain lower roll constituencies and the 'average ratio' of the National constituency. Furthermore, reducing the size of upper roll rural constituencies automatically multiplied their number, a development which was bound to affect the lower roll delimitation, because unless an upper roll rural constituency was coterminous with a lower roll constituency, it had to be formed by a grouping of lower roll constituencies. In spite of these difficulties, however, the Commission felt that smaller upper roll constituencies justified both wider deviations from the various quotas and the inclusion of peri-urban areas in rural constituencies, as well as the unavoidable effects on the lower roll delimitation.[1]

National constituencies had their own awkward problems. The African parties, and probably the Liberals as well, favoured the formation of one or more National constituencies consisting entirely of rural areas. While the terms of reference stipulated that National constituencies might consist of any combination of two or more complete upper or lower roll constituencies, in practice, the distribution of voters between urban and rural areas made purely rural National constituencies impracticable. The resulting divergence between a constituency's balance of upper and lower roll voters and the 'average ratio' of 1:2.609 would have been too wide. As a working rule, the Commission adopted the figure of 25 per cent as the widest permissible variation from the 'average ratio', with the result that all National constituencies had to be formed either by joining rural and urban constituencies, or by combining urban constituencies only. In the final delimitation, only one National constituency, Kafubu, comprised exclusively urban constituencies.[2]

The lower roll delimitation produced nine completely rural constituencies, four urban constituencies, three of them on the Copperbelt, and two semi-urban constituencies. Electorates in

[1] *Report of the Delimitation Commission*, 3 September 1962, pp. 1-3. [2] Ibid.

the rural constituencies ranged between 5,191 in South-Western and 1,271 in Barotseland West, while urban electorates all exceeded 14,000 voters, except Copperbelt West, which included a large section of the sparsely populated North-Western Province.[1]

On the upper roll the Commission delimited four rural and eleven urban constituencies. The rural constituencies, except Northern Rural, converged on the 'line of rail' where the vast majority of their respective electorates were concentrated.[2] Though the upper roll was predominantly European, in Northern Rural and Southern Rural, African voters outnumbered Europeans by 1,363 to 493 and by 909 to 697 respectively. In urban upper roll constituencies, African voters formed on the average only 13 per cent of the electorate, although in Chingola the figure was as high as 22 per cent. Certain urban constituencies (Roan, Luanshya/Kansenji, Broken Hill, Lusaka West, and Livingstone) had small concentrations of Asian and Coloured voters which, when combined with the African group, formed a substantial non-European bloc. In Lusaka West this group comprised 34 per cent of the electorate, while in both Livingstone and Luanshya/Kansenji it formed slightly under 30 per cent.[3]

The table below summarizes the upper and lower roll delimitations. In addition to indicating the number of voters in each upper and lower roll constituency, the table also shows the number of voters of the opposite roll included in each constituency.

In delimiting National constituencies, the Commission gave special consideration to transport and communication facilities, with the result that five of the seven National constituencies swept outwards from the 'line of rail' along the Territory's main rural roads. Every National constituency, except Kafubu, included huge rural areas, and in both Chambeshi and Luapula National constituencies urban and rural areas were separated by the Katanga pedicle. Table 2 below, which summarizes the National delimitation, shows the upper and lower roll

[1] *Report of the Delimitation Commission*, 3 September 1962, pp. 1–3.
[2] Ibid.
[3] Records of racial breakdowns in constituencies, n.d., October 1962. All percentage figures in this paragraph are approximate.

Table 1

UPPER ROLL AND LOWER ROLL CONSTITUENCIES

Upper roll constituency	Lower roll constituency	Electorate		
		Upper roll	Lower roll	Population
	1. Barotseland West	209	1,271	92,718
	2. Barotseland East	440	1,456	73,476
	3. South-Western	1,057	5,191	74,474
1. Southern Rural		1,706		
	4. Eastern	618	3,112	98,367
	5. South-Eastern	302	2,876	87,466
	6. Lusaka Rural	1,614	3,420	73,008
2. Eastern Rural		2,534		
	7. Muchinga	392	3,248	92,048
	8. Northern	724	4,555	97,098
	9. Bangweulu	761	5,124	97,839
3. Northern Rural		1,877		
	10. North-Western	243	1,951	78,257
	11. Copperbelt West	2,161	6,395	71,197
4. Western Rural		2,404		
5. Chingola		2,467	6,137	
6. Mufulira		2,743	2,732	
7. Kitwe East		2,734	3,220	
8. Kitwe West		2,565	6,868	
	12. Copperbelt Central		18,957	93,345
9. Roan		2,358	3,705	
10. Luanshya-Kansenji		2,382	5,746	
11. Ndola East		2,397	5,508	
	13. Copperbelt East		14,959	89,686
12. Broken Hill		2,608	4,182	
13. Lusaka West		2,877	8,564	
14. Lusaka East		2,693	2,151	
	14. Midlands		14,897	89,585
15. Livingstone	15. Southern	2,807	4,539	67,204
		37,152	91,941	1,275,768

Table 2

SEVEN NATIONAL CONSTITUENCIES

National constituency	National electorate			Ratio (number of lower roll voters for each upper roll voter)	Variation from average ratio
	Upper roll	Lower roll	Total		
KABOMPO comprising: Chingola (ur) North-Western (lr) Copperbelt West (lr)	4,832	14,482	19,314	2.997	0.388
LUAPULA comprising: Mufulira (ur) Northern (ur) Bangweulu (lr)	4,187	12,409	16,596	2.964	0.355
KAFUBU* comprising: Ndola East (ur) Luan./Kansenji (ur) Roan (ur)	6,583	14,957	21,540	2.272	0.337
CHAMBESHI* comprising: Kitwe West (ur) Kitwe East (ur) Muchinga (lr)	5,661	13,323	18,984	2.353	0.256
LOWER KAFUE* comprising: Broken Hill (ur) Lusaka West (ur)	4,823	12,741	17,564	2.642	0.033
LUANGWA* comprising: Lusaka East (ur) Lusaka Rural (lr) South-Eastern (lr) Eastern (lr)	5,022	11,550	16,572	2.300	0.309
ZAMBEZI comprising: Livingstone (ur) Barotseland W. (lr) Barotseland E. (lr) South-Western (lr)	4,116	12,451	16,567	3.025	0.416
Total electorate and average ratio in National constituencies	35,224	91,913	127,137	2.609	—

* Designated in accordance with the Commission's terms of reference as a constituency which shall return one African member and one European member to the Legislative Council.

constituencies which comprised each National constituency, as well as the size of each National constituency's upper and lower roll electorates and its 'average ratio'.[1]

THE CAMPAIGNS

It is exceedingly difficult to characterize Northern Rhodesia's 1962 general election campaign.[2] Indeed, though one speaks of a single campaign, in practice there were actually three campaigns—upper roll, lower roll and National—all fought simultaneously in several sets of constituencies, yet each markedly different with a pace and style of its own. On the one hand was the National campaign, something of a paradox in itself. That it was the focal point of the entire election was clear beyond doubt. It was the National constituencies which provided Africans and Europeans with their first experience of a common political arena, and it was the National seats which were to exercise a decisive influence on the ultimate balance of racial and party forces in the new legislature—all this despite the rather curious fact that although success depended on capturing only a few hundred votes from both races, eight National seats were never filled.[3] The National campaign itself was, in the final analysis, an image-building contest, conducted around several national issues by a mere handful of leading party spokesmen, most of whom were not themselves candidates for National seats.[4] In sharp contrast, the upper and lower roll contests were little more than exercises in racial mobilization. Here the currency of well-established political traditions—militant solidarity, loyalty to race and party, 'civilized standards', self-determination and political and economic survival—was ruthlessly employed by the various party organizations. For if it was true that the final outcome of the election would be decided in the National seats, it was no less axiomatic that to succeed a party had first to dominate either the upper or the lower roll constituencies.

Party preparations had begun almost immediately after the

---

[1] *Report of the Delimitation Commission*, 3 September 1962, p. 5.
[2] For a more detailed account of the election campaigns, see Mulford, D. C., *The N.R. General Election, 1962*, pp. 85–145.
[3] *Northern News*, 12 December 1962.
[4] Only Moffat contested a National seat, *Northern News*, 10 October 1962.

announcement of the Constitution on 1 March, and although it
is impossible to date the formal opening of the campaign, it was
certainly well under way by nomination day on 9 October.
Party organization for the campaign depended largely on the
overall strategy a party adopted in the various sets of constituencies. Though all parties were confronted with mobilizing
support in their respective racial spheres, attempts to attract
voters of the opposite race fell into two broad categories: one a
direct appeal undertaken independently by a single party; the
other an election alliance between two parties, each committed
to support the other's candidates in the National constituencies.

u.n.i.p., which mounted a completely independent effort,
launched its European campaign in June and its Barotseland
offensive in July,[1] all the while maintaining among lower roll
voters generally the momentum of the party's registration
drive. u.n.i.p.'s only flirtation with the idea of an election
alliance occurred in September with the Liberal Party.[2] Most
of u.n.i.p.'s top officials believed that there was little to be gained
by contracting debts with other political groups simply to
enhance u.n.i.p.'s short-term electoral prospects. If u.n.i.p. lost
the election, Britain could not long delay further constitutional
changes, which could only work in u.n.i.p.'s favour. Perhaps the
most convincing argument for an independent campaign,
apart from doubt about Moffat's ability to deliver 10 per cent
of the European vote to u.n.i.p. in the National constituencies,
was the view that u.n.i.p. should use the general election to test
the entire electorate, especially the Europeans. The party had
not contested previous elections, and not unnaturally its
leaders were anxious, irrespective of the number of seats secured,
to demonstrate u.n.i.p.'s overwhelming support throughout the
Territory. An election arrangement with another party would
tend to blur the election result, thereby lessening its significance
as an indicator of u.n.i.p. power.[3]

u.n.i.p. staged by far the most massive and well-organized
campaign of the election. On the lower roll u.n.i.p.'s main

[1] *Northern News*, 25 June and 19 October 1962.
[2] Interview with Moffat, 19 October 1962.
[3] Interviews with S. Wina, 4 September 1962, and with Kaunda, 16 October
1962.

objectives were to mobilize support, to acquaint its supporters with their respective candidates (both lower roll and National), and to teach its voting members, most of whom had not voted before, how to mark lower roll and National ballot papers. As early as June U.N.I.P. held a special election seminar for its regional officials, who together with lower roll candidates bore the main burden of the lower roll campaign.[1] In July Skinner's *Election Worker's Handbook*, which dealt with all aspects of election procedure and organization, was distributed to party officials at all levels. The handbook called on U.N.I.P.'s regional secretaries to organize fifteen-member election committees in each constituency to assist in the campaign effort. In addition, U.N.I.P.'s regular regional level organization was charged with forming and supervising branch election committees to which were assigned the tasks of house-to-house canvassing as well as lower roll and National voting instruction.[2]

As a rule, U.N.I.P.'s regional-, constituency- and branch-level organizers put extensive efforts into their work. Canvassing records and registers of voters requiring postal ballot papers were kept by many. Every lower roll voter in the Territory received a white voter's card from U.N.I.P. which listed in the voter's lower roll and National constituencies, his polling district and U.N.I.P.'s three candidates, the latter being a matter of particular importance, because official ballot papers provided no party designation for candidates. By far the most time and effort of U.N.I.P.'s organizers were devoted to instructing voters in the marking of the various types (eleven in all) of ballot papers. U.N.I.P. instruction teams, equipped with ballot papers of the appropriate colour showing the local candidates' names, followed up the Information Department's film show and instruction sessions with door-to-door lessons in how to vote. In urban areas night sessions to coach local U.N.I.P. members were held by branch election committees.[3]

U.N.I.P.'s upper roll and National campaign organization was separate and markedly different from the party's lower roll

---

[1] Interview with Vernon Mwanga, Regional Youth Secretary at the time in Choma, 21 September 1962.

[2] *Election Worker's Handbook*, 30 July 1962.

[3] Based on field research in Northern Rhodesia between August and December 1962.

arrangements. Constituency election committees, whose main function was to canvass support from Europeans, Asians, and African 'intellectuals' (upper roll voters), were organized for upper roll and National constituencies together. In part the composition of these groups reflected the totally different challenge of the upper roll and National campaign. The committee's chairman and secretary, unlike the equivalent body for lower roll constituencies, had only to be party members, not officials, and the primary consideration governing their appointment was possession of 'a good standard education'. Only the committee's election agent was a regional level official. The nine additional members were ideally to be equally representative of Europeans, Africans, and Asians, and the handbook stressed that the African members should be upper roll voters able to approach and converse easily with Europeans and Asians.[1]

The most far-reaching effect of u.n.i.p.'s decision to campaign for European support was Kaunda's attempt to create a new party image. u.n.i.p.'s European campaign, which had opened at the Edinburgh Hotel at Kitwe in late June,[2] reached its peak in the third week of October. Until the week before polling day, when the u.f.p. unleashed a virulent propaganda attack on u.n.i.p., no other party matched the ingenuity and sheer intensity of u.n.i.p.'s National campaign.[3] Only u.n.i.p.'s top officials were closely involved, and when Kaunda announced u.n.i.p.'s nominations well over half of the party's forty candidates, particularly those in the National constituencies, were men whom Europeans had not previously associated with the party.[4]

These were u.n.i.p.'s 'new' men, carefully recruited by Kaunda from Northern Rhodesia's 'respectable African community' and, by virtue of their candidacy, tentatively incorporated into u.n.i.p. immediately beneath the party's central committee level. For a long time Kaunda had discreetly emphasized u.n.i.p.'s desperate need for technically qualified

[1] *Election Worker's Handbook*, 30 July 1962.

[2] *Northern News*, 25 June 1962.

[3] Based on field research and observation in Northern Rhodesia between August and December 1962.

[4] *Northern News*, 10 October 1962; see also Mulford, *The N.R. General Election 1962*, p. 93.

Africans as the hour of Zambia's birth approached. Though most of the 'new' men had supported U.N.I.P. since the beginning, and several had secretly assisted the party in many situations, it was not until 1962, when the prospect of power was near, that Kaunda persuaded them to take a more open and active part in the party affairs.[1] A highly qualified team of candidates not closely identified in European eyes with U.N.I.P.'s past was essential in both the upper roll and National constituencies. But as Kaunda assembled his 'new' men, he was keenly aware that many of U.N.I.P.'s most loyal and experienced organizers, those most deserving of the spoils of victory, were anathema to Europeans and had somehow to be kept in the background during the election period. Admittedly, blending the 'new' men together with the 'old guard' was a delicate manœuvre in which Kaunda was greatly assisted by the new Constitution. Its rigorous requirements, and Kaunda stressed this point among his lower-level officials, demanded not only multi-racial support but also an efficient election machine, staffed by experienced professionals capable of carrying the burden of Northern Rhodesia's complicated election.[2]

Three broad themes ran through U.N.I.P.'s European campaign. The first was a direct appeal to make common cause with U.N.I.P. in the building of a new and prosperous Northern Rhodesia. Kaunda opened nearly all of his almost nightly multi-racial meetings with the observation that for the first time in the Territory's history Europeans and Africans were breaking out of their respective racial shells and listening to one another. Though Kaunda believed that the development of a genuine multi-racial society was inevitable, he argued that the time for actively fostering it had arrived. 'Men do not live in the past; they live in the present and plan for the future'—and the future lay with U.N.I.P., whose 'hand of friendship' was extended to Europeans 'now'. Europeans were promised a useful and secure future. Kaunda rejected what he termed 'the short-term view' of racial co-operation—that whites were required only for their technical knowhow. U.N.I.P. wished Europeans to remain in Zambia purely because they were human beings, children of the same God, who shared with Africans the same

[1] Interviews with Kaunda, 16 October 1962 and 9 July 1964.
[2] Ibid.

inalienable rights to life, liberty, and security of person and property.[1]

A second theme of u.n.i.p.'s National campaign, which, though less pronounced, was probably of greater long-run importance, was the party's attempt to explain itself. A constant and determined effort was made to present u.n.i.p.'s policy. Perhaps u.n.i.p.'s leaders assumed that because Europeans were relatively well educated and comparatively wealthy they would be intensely concerned with the whole spectrum of proposed policy; or it may have been that u.n.i.p. felt compelled to demonstrate to whites that it could both conceive and express the kinds of ideas required for the governing of Northern Rhodesia. Thus, while other parties produced only brief manifestoes, u.n.i.p. issued a sixty-page booklet with detailed statements of the party's position.[2]

Europeans in Northern Rhodesia, as in most of Southern Africa, were almost wholly unaware of the nature of African nationalism and mass African political movements. The majority had immigrated to Northern Rhodesia only in the past decade and had since been subjected to a steady diet of propaganda about Africans, particularly African politicians, from white friends, the u.f.p., and the European Press. Kaunda was aware of this and took great care in providing lengthy and informative answers to European questions at public meetings, often with such wit and vigour that he won considerable sympathy and admiration from his white audience. This was especially true when Kaunda traced the history of African opposition to the Federation. The British Government's disregard for African opposition to the Federation; the complete failure of Partnership; the sacrifice of Northern Rhodesia's interests and wealth to Southern Rhodesia; and the long and cheerless struggle of Kaunda and many of his colleagues against minority rule and Federal domination, were brought skilfully to the attention of Europeans, many of whom had never before listened to the arguments behind the African position.

At other times Kaunda discussed the difficulties involved in

[1] Material in this paragraph has been drawn from the considerable number of speeches Kaunda gave to European audiences between late September and 30 October 1962. The author attended many of the meetings, which as a rule were inadequately reported by the Press.

[2] *U.N.I.P. Policy.* issued 15 June 1962, author's collection.

organizing a mass nationalist movement, often in the face of
government opposition and always without sufficient funds and
trained personnel. He attempted to convince Europeans that
non-violence was far more difficult to organize and implement
than a policy of violence, especially when the people were as
frustrated as Africans had become over the past decade. Unem-
ployment, the demoralizing influences of poverty, the painful
forces of social change, the physical size of Northern Rhodesia
and u.n.i.p.'s lack of adequate means of communication and
transportation all were singled out as contributing to the
nationalist leader's difficulties. Kaunda argued that the worst
of u.n.i.p.'s struggle to establish itself was past, and though he
conceded that mistakes had been made during these formative
years, u.n.i.p. had become fully recognized as the party of the
people. Its organization was more effective, its personnel more
experienced and able; yet u.n.i.p.'s tremendous drive, idealism,
and potential for creative innovation had not been compromised.
These were considerable achievements, though Kaunda carefully emphasized u.n.i.p.'s awareness of the new and challenging
problems which lay ahead.[1]

The third major theme of u.n.i.p.'s campaign was its attack
on the u.f.p.–a.n.c. alliance, which since nomination day had
come into the open.[2] Unlike the lower roll campaign, where
a.n.c. was the primary target, the brunt of u.n.i.p.'s attack was
directed against the u.f.p. Here, claimed Kaunda, was an
example of dishonesty and irresponsibility unparalleled in
Northern Rhodesia politics. Kaunda repeatedly challenged
Europeans to apply the norms of responsible action to their own
leaders. The u.f.p.'s power was nearly broken, yet in a desperate
bid to retain its influence, the u.f.p. had adopted a course
which if successful could only lead to instability and bloodshed.
Kaunda condemned both parties for consummating a marriage
of pure convenience in which neither partner held anything in
common but the desire for power and the wish to destroy u.n.i.p.
Europeans were graphically reminded of the gulf which formerly separated Welensky and Nkumbula, neither of whom,
and this was particularly dishonest in Kaunda's opinion, would

---

[1] Material in the foregoing paragraphs has been drawn from Kaunda's speeches
to European audiences between late September and 30 October 1962.
[2] *Northern News*, 10 and 17 October 1962.

admit to their deceit. Despite Kaunda's public commitment to
abide by the 'will of the electorate', it was obvious that U.N.I.P.
would never accept a U.F.P.–A.N.C. minority victory. Europeans
were encouraged to exercise a measure of foresight, for in the
long run, Kaunda claimed, such a 'fly by night' arrangement
could not survive.[1]

Unlike U.N.I.P., the U.F.P. and A.N.C. did not organize independent National campaigns. Instead, they formed a limited
kind of election alliance whereby in several National constituencies each party nominated only one candidate and instructed their respective supporters to cast the second of their
two National votes for the allied party's candidate.[2] The
alliance was the best-kept secret of the election. Roberts and
Nkumbula had first discussed the possibility of co-operating in
June.[3] Several weeks later a visiting trade commission from
South Africa encouraged U.F.P. leaders both in Salisbury and
on the Copperbelt to pursue the idea. In a lengthy memorandum the trade commission argued that African government in
Northern Rhodesia was inevitable and that rigid resistance to it
on the part of Europeans would, in the long run, only work to
the advantage of U.N.I.P. The commission urged the U.F.P. to
use its decisive influence in the October election to establish in
power the African leader of its choice. Nkumbula was clearly
the commission's first preference, and it confidently concluded
that if the U.F.P. backed A.N.C. and formed a coalition Government led by Nkumbula, Northern Rhodesia would enjoy both
peace and stability, particularly if Nkumbula took strong action
to break the power of U.N.I.P. It was even suggested that an
A.N.C.–U.F.P. victory in October might well lead to the evolution of a powerful 'Entente Cordiale' of Katanga, Northern and
Southern Rhodesia, South Africa, and the Portuguese territories.[4]

Though a number of U.F.P. leaders had favoured closer links

[1] Material in this paragraph has been drawn from Kaunda's speeches to
European audiences between late September and 30 October 1962. Kaunda's
commitment to abide by the election results was given in U.N.I.P.'s *Our Future*,
8 October 1962.

[2] *Northern News*, 10 October 1962; U.F.P. public meeting, Ndola, 12 October
1962, author's collection.

[3] S.O. (C.S.) 2 to A.S. (C.S.) 1, 12 June 1962, GHS/S 119/130/01.

[4] Memorandum on the thinking of the South African Trade Commission,
13 July 1962, ibid.

with A.N.C. for a number of months, the attitude of the South African trade commission appeared to strengthen the hand of the pro-A.N.C. group in the U.F.P.'s caucus, which by mid-July was being won over to the idea of forming some sort of election alliance with Nkumbula.[1] Just what sort of alliance was not certain. On 20 July Welensky met Nkumbula in Broken Hill,[2] and early in August Roberts discussed the problem with Sykes Ndilila, A.N.C.'s publicity secretary for Central Province.[3] Meanwhile, the U.F.P. conducted soundings amongst its own supporters. One of the party's M.L.C.s, who discreetly canvassed European miners on the Copperbelt, first about the alliance and then about the possibility of forming an A.N.C.–U.F.P. coalition Government, reported a surprising amount of support for the idea.[4]

In the negotiations which followed absolute secrecy was essential if U.N.I.P. and the Liberals were not to be stampeded into forming their own election arrangements. In the event the alliance was not revealed until nomination day, and even then the extent of A.N.C.–U.F.P. co-operation was unclear. In Kafubu and Luwangwa National constituencies, where each party nominated only one candidate, it was obvious that a pact had been formed, but in Chambeshi and Lower Kafue the position was somewhat confused. In Chambeshi, A.N.C. had only an African candidate, while the U.F.P. nominated a full team, one African and one European. Lower Kafue was exactly the reverse: the U.F.P. had a single European candidate and A.N.C. both an African and European.[5] More perplexing still, the U.F.P. had apparently formed a separate election pact in Zambezi National constituency with the Barotse National Party, a newly created royalist party with U.F.P. backing.[6]

The chief objective of the A.N.C.–U.F.P. alliance was, of course, the defeat of U.N.I.P. To this end the U.F.P. and A.N.C. were prepared to co-operate, despite their diametrically opposed policies and traditions. Beyond this, however, their intentions diverged, inevitably weakening the alliance and

---

[1] s.o. (C.S.) 2 to A.S. (C.S.) 1, 12 July 1962. GHS/S 119/130/01.
[2] S.B. to Ad. Sec., 11 August 1962, ibid.
[3] S.B. to Ad. Sec., 7 August 1962, ibid.
[4] s.o. (C.S.) 2 to U.S., 13 August 1962, ibid.
[5] *Northern News*, 10 October 1962.
[6] *Northern News*, 18 October 1962.

laying it open to serious differences of interpretation. A.N.C. aspired to the role of an independent third force in the new legislature, while the U.F.P. intended not merely to create an anti-U.N.I.P. bloc, but also to secure a clear majority over both African parties together. The disadvantage of election pacts was that if they worked correctly, both parties gained seats together. Thus, for the U.F.P. to achieve an absolute majority over the African nationalist bloc in the Legislative Council, it had either to trick A.N.C. out of one or two seats or to form an alliance with a third group. This was the reason for the U.F.P.'s pact with the B.N.P. in Zambezi, despite the fact that A.N.C. controlled Southern Province. It also suggests attempted deception as the explanation for the appearance of the extra A.N.C. and U.F.P. candidates in Lower Kafue and Chambeshi respectively.

During the course of the campaign, A.N.C. and the U.F.P. drew closer together. At first both parties refused to acknowledge their co-operation,[1] but by the last week of the campaign the question of whether or not an alliance existed had become an irrelevant game of semantics to which both allies paid less and less attention. The Copperbelt U.F.P. transformed the alliance into a supra-party organization, the United Anti-U.N.I.P. Movement (U.A.U.), which openly assisted A.N.C. with its canvassing and publicity campaigns.[2] On 22 October the U.F.P.'s European candidate in Lower Kafue withdrew from the campaign, a move which confirmed the existence of a pact in that constituency and greatly improved the chances of the remaining A.N.C. and U.F.P. candidates.[3] The U.F.P. issued voting instruction leaflets showing the names of U.F.P. and A.N.C. candidates side by side with no mention of the fact that one was A.N.C.[4] For the Copperbelt wings of both parties the alliance came to mean much more than simply a temporary and informal electoral arrangement. A.N.C.'s Kitwe officials boldly discussed grandiose schemes for a powerful Northern Rhodesia-Katanga

[1] *Central African Mail*, 16 October 1962.
[2] Ibid., 23 October 1962, and *Northern News*, 11 October 1962. Interview with Derek Sparrow, U.F.P. Federal M.P. and member of the U.F.P. Copperbelt regional committee, 6 December 1962. Interview with Roy Horrell, A.N.C.'s European adviser, formerly a U.F.P. organizer in Southern Rhodesia and author of A.N.C.'s election manifesto, 17 December 1962.
[3] *Central African Mail*, 23 October 1962.
[4] Published by the U.F.P.'s Electors Association and released in the last week of October 1962, author's collection.

Federation under the leadership of Nkumbula and Tshombe
with the whites of both territories playing a supporting role,
and top leaders of both parties began seriously to consider the
possibility of coalition government in the event that together
they secured a majority of the Legislative Council seats.[1]
The alliance with A.N.C. enabled the U.F.P. to concentrate its
campaign almost exclusively on upper roll voters. Though the
U.F.P.'s position amongst Europeans could not seriously be
challenged, Roberts faced the rather difficult task of mobilizing
whites for a show of strength in upper roll constituencies, while
at the same time he prepared whites to vote for A.N.C. candidates
in several National constituencies. Indeed, it made little sense
for the other parties to organize extensive upper roll campaigns,
except in those few constituencies where the racial composition
of the electorate warranted such an effort. The significance of
the upper roll contest lay not so much in the party results—for
on the whole they were readily predictable—as in the racial
breakdown of the vote and the degree of white solidarity
demonstrated by the U.F.P.

The U.F.P. nominated fourteen upper roll candidates, one of
whom was an African, and supported A.N.C.'s nominee in the
fifteenth constituency, Northern Rural. U.N.I.P. supported
European independents in three upper roll constituencies and
in eleven others nominated its own candidates—seven Africans,
two Europeans, an Asian, and a Euro-African. The Liberals
and A.N.C., both of whom had difficulty inducing candidates to
stand, contested twelve and six seats respectively.[2]

U.F.P. victories were assured in all eight Copperbelt constituencies as well as in Broken Hill, Lusaka West, Livingstone,
and Eastern Rural; largely because African upper roll voters
never comprised more than 22 per cent of the electorates in the
urban constituencies and 30 per cent in Eastern Rural and
Western Rural.[3] Only three upper roll constituencies offered the
prospect of a close contest. Lusaka East, despite its predominantly European electorate, could not be rated a safe seat,

[1] Interviews with Sykes Ndilila and Gordon Chindele, A.N.C. Kitwe office,
17 October 1962; memorandum on A.N.C.–U.F.P. co-operation by the U.F.P.
election sub-committee, n.d., November 1962, author's collection.
[2] *Central African Mail*, 9 October 1962, and *Northern News*, 10 October 1962.
[3] Records of racial breakdowns in constituencies, n.d., October 1962, author's
collection.

because the party's central election committee, disregarding opposition from its local branch organization, nominated an African, Gabriel Musumbulwa, formerly the U.F.P.'s Minister of African Education.[1] In the other two constituencies, Northern Rural and Southern Rural, the delimitation had produced electorates with substantial majorities of African voters.[2]

The U.F.P. believed that upper roll Africans in Northern Rural had been alienated from U.N.I.P. by the previous year's disturbances and would support the more moderate A.N.C. Thus instead of nominating its own candidate, the U.F.P. lent one of its own supporters from Kasama, V. A. Shone, to stand for A.N.C. Shone was well known amongst the constituency's European voters, approximately 500 in number, and if 30 per cent of the Africans supported him U.N.I.P. would be defeated. U.N.I.P., however, placed the most outstanding of its 'new' men, John Mwanakatwe, in Northern Rural.[3] Originally from Chinsali District, Mwanakatwe had a distinguished record in government service, first as an education officer and later as the first African secondary-school principal in the Territory. In June 1961 Mwanakatwe was appointed an assistant to the Commissioner for Northern Rhodesia in London, one of the few senior posts in the Civil Service to be held by an African. Apart from Kaunda himself, Mwanakatwe was U.N.I.P.'s most widely respected candidate among Europeans, especially those in the Provincial Administration.[4] The U.F.P.'s plan was further frustrated by the presence of a Liberal candidate, and, in the end, Mwanakatwe convincingly demonstrated U.N.I.P.'s solidarity in the north, winning a few European votes as well.[5]

Southern Rural, radically different from its northern counterpart, produced the closest contest of the election. The delimitation of Southern Rural was especially important, for it included substantial areas in which U.N.I.P., A.N.C., and the U.F.P. could

[1] *Northern News*, 5 and 6 October 1962. In the end Musumbulwa won the constituency easily by a majority of nearly 1,200 votes out of the 2,445 votes cast; *Northern News*, 31 October 1962.

[2] Africans outnumbered Europeans by 1,363 to 493 in Northern Rural and by 909 to 697 in Southern Rural; records of racial breakdowns in constituencies, n.d., October 1962.

[3] *Northern News*, 10 October 1962.

[4] This point together with the general analysis offered in the paragraph is based on field research in Northern Rhodesia, August–December 1962.

[5] *Northern News*, 1 November 1962.

each muster considerable support. Covering an area approximately equal to the whole of England and Scotland, the constituency included Barotseland, where U.N.I.P. was rapidly gaining strength amongst upper roll Africans,[1] and most of Southern Province, A.N.C.'s traditional stronghold. In addition, its eastern end took in the towns of Kalomo and Choma, where a number of European railway workers lived, as well as the large European farming community west of the 'line of rail' from Pemba down nearly to Livingstone. Equally important was the racial composition of Southern Rural's electorate: 52 per cent African, 41 per cent European, and 7 per cent Asian. Slightly over half the Africans were in Barotseland, the remainder being either in the African farming areas of Southern Province or in the small railway towns.[2] The relatively high franchise qualifications meant that most of Southern Rural's African voters were Civil Servants or school teachers, groups in which U.N.I.P. held an edge over A.N.C., though a substantial number of well-to-do African farmers in Southern Province had also qualified and would certainly support A.N.C. Among European voters, many were farmers, and practically all Europeans, together with the Asians, were concentrated along the 'line of rail'.

The four main parties and the R.R.P. all nominated candidates, though the real contest was between U.N.I.P., A.N.C., and the U.F.P. U.N.I.P.'s candidate, Dr. Nalumango, was the son of a Barotse induna and another of U.N.I.P.'s 'new' men. A.N.C., confident of its African support in Southern Province, attempted to win the crucial Asian vote by nominating G. H. Patel, an Indian businessman from Pemba. The U.F.P. nominated a local farmer of South African origin, J. J. Burnside, in the hope that European voters, many of whom were from South Africa, would not defect to the more militantly white supremist R.R.P.[3] Results in Southern Rural confirmed one of colonialism's oldest and over-used maxims—'divide and rule'. Though Africans had clearly rejected the U.F.P. and both nationalist parties together amassed 787 votes to the U.F.P.'s 588, it was Burnside who captured the seat, 97 votes in front of U.N.I.P.'s Nalumango. As in

[1] Ag. R.C. to Ag. Perm. Sec., 8 September 1962, DG 58/1/01.
[2] Record of racial breakdowns in constituencies, n.d., October 1962.
[3] *Northern News*, 10 October 1962.

the upper roll campaign generally, Europeans stood solidly
behind the u.f.p., giving only 38 votes to the r.r.p.[1] For u.n.i.p.,
which had counted on a victory to match its triumph in the
north, the loss of Southern Rural was a heavy blow and a particularly painful price to pay for its bitter rivalry with a.n.c.[2]

Nkumbula's alliance with the u.f.p. was nothing less than a
frank admission that a.n.c. could not hope to challenge u.n.i.p.'s
superiority on the lower roll. Indeed, once nominations revealed
Nkumbula's collaboration with the champions of Federation, it
was an open question whether or not a.n.c. would suffer a total
eclipse on the lower roll. In addition, there was the link with
Tshombe which, for all its financial advantages, could not help
but tarnish Nkumbula's image as a nationalist leader in Northern Rhodesia. Though a.n.c. could never have hoped to draw
even with u.n.i.p. on the lower roll, after nomination day only
two lower roll constituencies, Southern and South-Western,
could be counted as reasonably safe a.n.c. seats.

Both constituencies were in Southern Province, long a.n.c.'s
leading stronghold, but also one of the strongest anti-Federation
areas in Northern Rhodesia.[3] u.n.i.p. naturally attempted to
exploit this by publicizing a.n.c.'s alliance with the u.f.p.,[4] but
both time and political traditions in the area worked to Nkumbula's advantage. In South-Western, which Nkumbula himself
contested, the main voting strength lay with villagers in the
farming areas west of the 'line of rail'. Voters in Southern were
more concentrated, the majority living either in Livingstone or
in one of the small railway centres.[5] Nkumbula and John Banda,
a.n.c.'s National Secretary and candidate in Southern, both
ignored u.n.i.p.'s accusations regarding the alliance or simply
treated them as lies. Both men also sought to emphasize local
issues in their campaigns. Nkumbula, whose home was in Namwala in South-Western, hardly needed to devote his time to the

[1] *Northern News*, 1 November 1962.
[2] The analysis of Southern Rural as a whole is based on field research in Northern Rhodesia, August–December 1962.
[3] This was particularly evident at the chiefs' meeting following the election in
Monze; minutes of the meeting of Southern Province chiefs, 2 November 1962,
MN 129/10, Vol. I, Box 4348, Lusaka Archives.
[4] 'Congress Marries u.f.p.', *Voice of U.N.I.P.*, October 1962.
[5] Record of racial breakdowns in constituencies, n.d., October 1962.

local campaign, while Banda responded to U.N.I.P.'s attack by
reminding voters that its candidate in Southern, Hezekiah
Habanyama, another of U.N.I.P.'s 'new' men, had been a
member of the Gwembe Native Authority in 1958 when it co-
operated with the Government's resettlement scheme in the
Lake Kariba area.[1] Moreover, U.N.I.P.'s well-established reputation in Southern Province, carefully nurtured by years of A.N.C.
propaganda, made it extremely difficult in the space of three
weeks to convince already sceptical voters that A.N.C. was col-
laborating with the U.F.P.

A.N.C. won both the southern seats easily, though Banda's
majority was not nearly as large as Nkumbula's.[2] Part of the
reason for Banda's less-spectacular victory undoubtedly lay in
the fact that Southern included many more urban voters, who,
because of their proximity to the 'line of rail', learned of A.N.C.'s
alliance with the U.F.P. A.N.C. resignations over the alliance
were more numerous in the towns where newspapers, regular
public meetings, and European political activity constantly confirmed the alliance's existence. Once Africans in more remote
areas of Southern Province understood what Nkumbula had
done, many opposed further co-operation with the U.F.P. This
was borne out after the election, when Nkumbula's actions were
attacked within the party.[3] For the moment, however, A.N.C.
had demonstrated that even with a less efficient electoral
machine it still controlled Southern Province.[4] What was less
certain was A.N.C.'s strength outside its provincial stronghold.

Certainly A.N.C. had no chance in the three constituencies
which covered the heart of U.N.I.P. country in Northern and
Luapula Provinces. Indeed, a U.N.I.P. official in Fort Rosebery
expressed surprise when he learned that U.N.I.P. would face
opposition candidates in Bangweulu, Northern, and Muchinga.[5]
A.N.C. nominated candidates in all three constituencies, while
the U.F.P., again resting its hopes on U.N.I.P. disaffection in the

[1] Biographies of candidates, N.R.G. press release 713, 11 October 1962.
[2] *Northern News*, 1 November 1962.
[3] Letters to the editor, *Central African Mail*, 16, 23, and 31 October and 6 November 1962.
[4] The analysis of Southern and South-Western is based on field research in N.R., August–December 1962.
[5] Interview with U.N.I.P. constituency secretary, Fort Rosebery, 9 September 1962.

North, contested Northern and Muchinga. U.N.I.P. nominated National office-bearers in all three seats: Bangweulu, which included U.N.I.P.'s rebellious Luapula division, was given the honour of returning Kaunda himself; Kapwepwe contested Northern, which contained his home district of Chinsali; and Aaron Milner, a Euro-African from Southern Rhodesia and U.N.I.P.'s Deputy National Secretary, stood in Muchinga.[1] As expected, U.N.I.P.'s organization in the north was particularly intensive; opposition candidates in all three constituencies found it difficult to campaign freely, and for the most part they were hardly seen in their respective areas. The results confirmed U.N.I.P.'s overwhelming strength in the area. In all three constituencies the U.F.P. and A.N.C. together accounted for only 423 votes out of a total of 11,342. That U.N.I.P.'s northern organization was the most efficient in the Territory was borne out by the strikingly low proportion of spoiled ballot papers in the three constituencies: 3.1 per cent compared with an average of 4.3 per cent on the lower roll as a whole.[2]

Nor could U.N.I.P. be seriously challenged on the Copperbelt, where nearly half the Territory's lower roll voters were concentrated in three predominantly urban constituencies.[3] Nevertheless, a bitter party contest developed on the Copperbelt. U.N.I.P.'s candidates were all important party figures: S. Wina (Copperbelt West), a man of immense popularity and one of the most able of all U.N.I.P. leaders; Alexander Grey Zulu (Copperbelt Central), one of U.N.I.P.'s five National Trustees; and John Chisata, successor to Katilungu as President of the powerful A.M.W.U.[4] A.N.C.'s candidates were no match for U.N.I.P.'s, though, with considerable assistance from the Copperbelt U.F.P., A.N.C. managed to mount an impressive publicity campaign. Feelings ran high between the nationalist parties, and sporadic violence, provoked as often by A.N.C. and the U.A.U. as by U.N.I.P.'s militant youth brigade, broke out regularly after mid-October.[5]

The most striking feature of the campaign was U.N.I.P.'s intensive effort to mobilize the Copperbelt's African population.

---

[1] *Northern News*, 10 October 1962.
[2] Ibid., 1 November 1962.
[3] *Report of the Delimitation Commission*, 3 September 1962, p. 4.
[4] *Northern News*, 10 October 1962.
[5] Ibid., 16, 27, and 29 October 1962.

U.N.I.P. hoped to demonstrate dramatically that A.N.C.'s power on the Copperbelt had been utterly destroyed. At U.N.I.P.'s mass rallies, which attracted huge crowds every week-end, Nkumbula was attacked and his alliance identified with the preservation of Federation. How could a self-respecting nationalist party, which had fought against Federation since 1948, suddenly form a 'marriage of convenience' with the Federalists? Every U.N.I.P. candidate, and even several A.N.C. officials who had resigned in protest over the alliance, alleged that Nkumbula had simply sold himself to the highest bidders —Tshombe and Welensky. U.N.I.P.'s youth brigade also played a prominent role in the campaign, constantly harassing A.N.C.'s organizers in the African townships and pulling down the posters of U.N.I.P.'s competitors. The brigade also did much of U.N.I.P.'s canvassing and assisted in the publicity campaign by painting 'Vote U.N.I.P.' and 'U.N.I.P. is Power' on literally hundreds of road signs, on houses and schools, and at one-mile intervals on most of the Copperbelt's main roads.[1]

On the Copperbelt, unlike Southern Province, A.N.C. could not ignore its alliance with the U.F.P., especially since the U.F.P.'s European candidates openly admitted that an 'understanding' had been reached between the two parties in National constituencies.[2] A.N.C.'s Copperbelt officials were themselves more open about the alliance than their colleagues in other areas, visualizing a form of co-operation which would result in an A.N.C.-U.F.P. coalition Government led by Nkumbula. At the same time, they spoke of developing closer relations with Katanga.[3] A.N.C. resignations on the Copperbelt were heavy and a number of the party's disillusioned supporters wrote angry letters to the Press.[4] Attendance at A.N.C. meetings, even in the party's Mufulira stronghold, declined markedly towards the end of October, and voting results in the three constituencies emphatically demonstrated that the Copperbelt A.N.C. was little more than a group of active officials. Out of a total vote of 41,076, A.N.C. candidates secured only 3,001 votes. Zulu and

[1] This account of the Copperbelt campaign is based on field research in the Copperbelt during October 1962 and is a composite of interviews with minor officials, newspaper reports and attendance at various U.N.I.P. and A.N.C. rallies.
[2] *Northern News*, 17 October 1962.
[3] Interview with Chindele and Ndilila, Kitwe, 17 October 1962.
[4] Letters to the editor, *Central African Mail*, 16 and 23 October 1962.

Chisata won their seats with majorities of over 11,000, while
against S. Wina A.N.C. could muster only 225 votes.[1]

In the six lower roll constituencies of Eastern, South-Eastern,
Lusaka Rural, and the two Barotseland seats, which formed an
almost continuous belt across the middle of Northern Rhodesia,
results were somewhat uncertain. U.N.I.P.'s prospects in all six
seats were considerably better than A.N.C.'s, but several factors
made prediction difficult. Both Eastern Province constituencies
had once been A.N.C. areas, and though U.N.I.P. had made impressive gains since 1960, its organization was still relatively
new. There had also been considerable feeling against U.N.I.P.
amongst chiefs in Eastern Province after the 1961 disturbances.[2]
Lusaka Rural, nearly 300 miles long, included likely U.N.I.P.
supporters east of both Lusaka and Broken Hill, but the constituency's southern arm, which extended deep into Southern
Province, contained nearly half its total electorate.[3] Midlands,
in which a large group of Tonga-speaking Lenje people occupied the rural areas west of Broken Hill, brought Elijah
Mudenda, one of U.N.I.P.'s most talented 'new' men, up against
Michello, A.N.C.'s popular National Secretary.[4] Finally, the outcome in both Barotseland seats was uncertain simply because
neither A.N.C. nor U.N.I.P. had been allowed to organize freely
in the area until three months before the election.

A.N.C.'s victory in Lusaka Rural, one of the most surprising
results of the election, was its only triumph in the six uncertain
seats. In a contest between the national chairman of both
parties, U.N.I.P.'s Solomon Kalulu, a Catholic and former headmaster, was defeated by Edward Liso, one of A.N.C.'s 'old guard'
leaders. Liso wisely set about consolidating his supporters in
Lusaka Rural's southern arm, all of whom were well removed
from the 'line of rail'[5] busily engaged in planting their crops and
not receptive to stories of an A.N.C.-U.F.P. alliance. To this
nucleus Liso added A.N.C.'s not inconsiderable support in

[1] *Northern News*, 1 November 1962.
[2] When Kaunda visited Eastern Province in December 1961, Chief Mpezeni
at first refused to see him. Record of meeting between Kaunda and the Ngoni
Native Authority, 28 December 1961; S.B. to P.C. (E.P.), 11 January 1962, S/S
108/3/01.
[3] Record of racial breakdowns in constituencies, n.d., October 1962.
[4] *Northern News*, 10 October 1962.
[5] Record of racial breakdowns in constituencies, n.d., October 1962.

Lusaka, where he had lived for over ten years. In the end he
defeated Kalulu by approximately 545 votes in a poll of 2,695.[1]
In Midlands, Eastern, and South Eastern U.N.I.P. won by
comfortable margins, though A.N.C. managed on the average to
secure about a third of the votes cast. Eastern, like Midlands,
was won by one of U.N.I.P.'s 'new' men, Wesley Nyirenda, a B.A.
Honours graduate of London University and principal of the
Monze Secondary School. U.N.I.P.'s Deputy President, Kamanga, won South-Eastern (which included his home area), after
becoming a candidate at the last moment before nomination
day.[2] On the afternoon of 8 October a suspended sentence imposed on him in late September for entering Southern Rhodesia
as a prohibited immigrant was withdrawn on appeal, and
U.N.I.P.'s youth leader, Banda, agreed to stand down in favour
of his superior.[3]

The U.F.P.'s strategy of preventing a U.N.I.P. majority by
limiting its success on the lower roll depended upon defeating
U.N.I.P. in the two Barotseland constituencies. Suspecting A.N.C.'s
weakness in Barotseland and hoping to fragment the legislature's
African bloc generally, the U.F.P. formed and assisted the B.N.P.
which, with the Litunga's blessing, nominated candidates in
both constituencies. In Barotseland East, F. L. Suu stood against
A. Wina, who recently only had returned from the United
States. Suu, who was seventy years old, had been administrative
secretary to Yeta III and a close friend of Wina's father, who in
those days had served as Yeta's Ngambela. When Yeta was succeeded by the present Litunga, both Wina's father and Suu had
been excluded from Lewanika's administration. The Wina
family remained staunch enemies of the Litunga, but Suu had
recently regained favour at the royal court and had been a
member of the Barotse delegation which held constitutional
discussions in London in April 1962. U.N.I.P.'s other candidate
in Barotseland was Mubiana Nalilungwe, also a Lozi and one of
U.N.I.P.'s 'new' men who had recently resigned his teaching post
at Munali Secondary School. His B.N.P. opponent, Griffiths
Mukande, had been Treasurer of the Barotse Native Government and reportedly was particularly close to the Litunga. The

[1] *Northern News*, 1 November 1961.
[2] Ibid.
[3] Ibid., 9 October 1962.

other two candidates were Isaac Singulwani (A.N.C.), a son-in-law of the Litunga, and Boswell Akombelwa (Liberal).[1]

The main issues of the Barotseland campaign were the Litunga's overriding concern to maintain his traditional authority and the question of Barotseland's secession from Northern Rhodesia. When the B.N.P. was formed in June 1962, its major objectives were 'to protect, defend and preserve the protectorate status of Barotseland as well as the Barotseland Kingship, and to fight for the separation of Barotseland from Northern Rhodesia'.[2] In September the Litunga had grave second thoughts about his earlier decision to allow political parties into Barotseland, largely because of U.N.I.P.'s rapid growth in the Protectorate since July. In addition, the Federal Government intensified its efforts to encourage secessionist groups in Barotseland, so much so that in September the Resident Commissioner had no doubt 'that the Federal Government was making promises of financial and other forms of support to the Barotse Native Government'. Not only was Barotseland encouraged to seek some sort of special relationship with the Federation, attempts were also made to persuade the Litunga to ban U.N.I.P. activity in the area altogether.[3] Then in early October, shortly after a Colonel Sinn of Angola had visited the Caprivi Strip, came a curious secret report that one Soba Cambungo, a chief in the Portuguese administration, had visited the Litunga in late September, bearing a letter from the Portuguese administrator at Ninda. In the meeting which followed between the two chiefs, Cambungo reportedly claimed that he had been sent by the Portuguese authorities to find out the Litunga's feelings about the forthcoming election and to inquire whether the Litunga would be interested in Portuguese protection![4]

U.N.I.P. was highly suspicious of the Litunga, particularly since the mysterious visit of Duncan Sandys and Godwin Lewanika (U.F.P. Federal M.P. for Luwangwa Special Electoral District) to Mongu in February 1962, during which the Litunga had submitted his application to the British Government for the right to secede from Northern Rhodesia, though not from the

---

[1] *Central African Mail*, 23 October 1962.
[2] *Northern News* 18 October 1962.
[3] Ag. R.C. to Ag. Perm. Sec. (M.N.A.), 8 September 1962, DG 58/1/01.
[4] Ag. R.C. to Perm. Sec. (M.N.A.), 2 October 1962, ibid.

Federation. U.N.I.P. had protested at the time against what it regarded as an underhand plan to save the Federation by balkanizing Northern Rhodesia.[1] Though the British Government indicated shortly afterwards that it would be unwise for Barotseland to be separated from Northern Rhodesia, U.N.I.P.'s suspicions and the Litunga's fears remained as intense as ever.[2] Though the Litunga did not officially declare his support for any party in the Barotseland campaign, it was well known that he and a number of his indunas supported the B.N.P. The U.F.P., assuming that any traditional party which had the blessing of the Litunga would be a powerful force in Barotseland, provided financial assistance and Land-Rovers for the B.N.P.[3] What the U.F.P. apparently failed to realize was that the B.N.P. was a political party in name only. Indeed, it never launched a recognizable election campaign at all. Nor had the U.F.P. paid sufficient attention to the pattern of registration in Barotseland. The Litunga's failure to encourage registration until June resulted in a lower roll dominated largely by educated commoners who were critical of the Litunga's Government. In addition, the registration of indunas and village headmen fell far short of the Government's original estimates, so that a large sector of the Litunga's supporters played no part at all in the election.[4]

U.N.I.P. launched a widespread and intensive campaign, canvassing practically every voter in the Protectorate, though concentrating on the great clusters of voters along the Zambesi River and the great flood plain.[5] A. Wina and Nalilungwe, both extremely popular in Barotseland, insisted on the Protectorate's continued inclusion in Northern Rhodesia, though they pledged that U.N.I.P. would not interfere either with the Litunga's personal position or with the protectorate status of Barotseland. Grandiose promises of more schools, agricultural development centres, roads and even a railway from Lusaka to Mongu were also made by U.N.I.P.[6] When the results were announced, U.N.I.P. surprised everyone except itself, dramatically sweeping Barotse-

---

[1] *Rhodesia Herald*, 26 and 27 February 1962.
[2] Ibid., 6 March 1962.
[3] *Central African Mail*, 23 October 1962.
[4] Interview with D.C. (Sesheke), 23 November 1962.
[5] Record of racial breakdowns in constituencies, n.d., October 1962.
[6] *U.N.I.P. Policy*, issued 15 June 1962.

land and depriving all other candidates of their respective deposits. Suu collected only sixty-five votes against A. Wina, while in Barotseland West, not one of Nalilungwe's opponents scored over seventy votes. Barotseland's electorate had administered a stunning defeat both to their ruler and to the U.F.P., and they had voted not only for U.N.I.P. but to remain a part of Northern Rhodesia.[1]

The impact of U.N.I.P.'s European campaign was difficult to assess. Certainly its general effect was favourable, but whether it would gain European votes on polling day was quite another question. U.N.I.P. drew sizeable European crowds at its meetings during the campaign's early weeks and stimulated considerable discussion amongst whites, many of whom, though previously supporters of the U.F.P., seriously questioned the realism of voting for the party again. Despite substantial European dissatisfaction with the U.F.P. and the general level of its campaign, few Europeans would risk openly committing themselves to U.N.I.P., even amongst their friends. While it was not generally recognized (though it could not seriously be denied), intimidation was as prevalent amongst Europeans as it was in the African community. To be sure, Europeans, for a host of reasons, could employ more subtle forms, but the effect was strikingly similar.[2]

Attitudes towards the Liberal Party and A.N.C. only heightened European indecision. The Liberal cause was regarded as utterly futile, and little respect remained for A.N.C., in part at least because Nkumbula appeared intoxicated on television one evening, which only emphasized what most Europeans already knew.[3] Yet white attitudes towards A.N.C. showed a curious duality; while refusing to support the party directly, they displayed rather smug approval of the U.F.P.'s alliance and the control which this implied over A.N.C. The result was that the alternatives facing Europeans were farther apart than they first appeared, because most Europeans saw that a vote for the Liberals or A.N.C. would be wasted. Yet for those who had

[1] *Northern News*, 1 November 1962.
[2] These general observations, as well as those in the paragraph below, are based on field research in N.R., August–December 1962.
[3] The author observed Nkumbula's performance on 23 October 1962.

always supported the U.F.P., it was precisely these two alternatives which were easiest to contemplate. The reorientation involved in a shift from the U.F.P. to U.N.I.P. was practically inconceivable to most Europeans, certainly far more agonizing than shelving doubts about the U.F.P. Thus, if it was true that as the campaign entered its final week there was a substantial floating vote amongst Europeans, part of which U.N.I.P. might reasonably have expected to gain, it was equally true that they were floating considerably closer to the U.F.P. shore and that they were particularly vulnerable to appeals from their traditional masters.

The U.F.P. saved its major effort for the campaign's final ten days. Not only were some Europeans in a state of indecision at the time, but many more were critical of the U.F.P.'s apparent lack of vigour in matching U.N.I.P.'s intensive campaign.[1] Once European confusion and frustration had been given ample rein, the U.F.P. struck its most decisive blows. Welensky entered Northern Rhodesia for a whirlwind tour of the Territory's major towns,[2] and the party released what in retrospect proved to be the campaign's most devastating propaganda. Particularly damaging was a small U.F.P. brochure entitled 'You Have Been Warned', a concise and inflammatory document cleverly designed to summarize the Europeans' worst fears, which quoted U.N.I.P.'s own leaders to drive the points home.[3] The producers knew their audience. The brochure's brutal frankness stunned Northern Rhodesia's complacent whites and fanned the fears sparked off by the U.F.P.'s earlier propaganda. Welensky's dynamic presence and skilful oratory completed the closing of European ranks. Almost overnight Europeans seemed to have come to one mind in their fear of U.N.I.P. and their renewed confidence in the U.F.P.

Against these tactics U.N.I.P. appeared to be defenceless. Its campaign funds were depleted, its leaders exhausted and discouraged. In a dramatic speech (which no Europeans except the police heard) at Lusaka on 28 October, Kaunda wept with frustration before 15,000 of his followers. He accused Welensky of undoing U.N.I.P.'s work and leading Europeans down a path

[1] Letters to the editor, *Northern News*, 15–25 October 1962.
[2] For reports of speeches see *Northern News*, 19, 20, 26, and 27 October 1962.
[3] See Mulford, *The N.R. General Election 1962*, pp. 116–17.

with nothing but disaster at its end. He pointed to the immense distance U.N.I.P. had come; its people had suffered rustication, imprisonment, poverty, and even death, yet they were prepared to forget the past and to start afresh with Europeans in building a nation where Welensky had failed. U.N.I.P. had already demonstrated its willingness in its campaign, but even this, claimed Kaunda, had been distorted and belittled by Welensky and the European Press. Kaunda admitted his temptation to forget the Europeans and to turn only to the black man (here the crowd expressed its approval), but he knew that, under God, this was not right, that such a policy held no future for the new Zambia.[1]

Thus, at the end of the National campaign, Europeans and Africans appeared as fundamentally divided as ever. The European parties had not made a significant appeal directly to Africans, and U.N.I.P.'s European campaign had faltered in the final week. The Liberal Party, apart from Moffat's own meetings, had been a dismal failure. Public attention returned to the U.F.P.–A.N.C. alliance, which it was generally agreed provided the only reasonable prospects for results in the National constituencies. Even so, this was a guarded optimism, for while sufficient numbers of U.F.P. Europeans might follow their party's instructions, it was widely believed that A.N.C. had destroyed itself and would fail to command even 10 per cent of the African vote. On 30 October, after a record poll of 88.8 per cent, the country awaited the results of its decision.[2]

POST-ELECTION POLITICS AND THE FORMATION OF GOVERNMENT

The general election results produced a dramatic balance of political forces in Northern Rhodesia's newly elected Legislative Council. In the upper and lower roll constituencies results were much as expected. The U.F.P. swept thirteen of the fourteen upper roll seats,[3] all except Southern Rural by large

---

[1] Notes on U.N.I.P. rally in Lusaka, 28 October 1962.

[2] *Northern News*, 2 November 1962.

[3] In Livingstone, the death of U.N.I.P.'s candidate necessitated a by-election, which the U.F.P. won on 10 December 1962.

majorities, and U.N.I.P. won Northern Rural. On the lower roll
U.N.I.P. won twelve seats to A.N.C.'s three.[1] The table below
summarizes results on the upper and lower rolls, showing both
the number and the percentage of valid votes received by each
party.

Table 3
SUMMARY OF VOTING

Party	Total valid votes	Percentage valid votes	seats
Upper Roll			
U.F.P.	21,558	70.5	13
U.N.I.P. (and independent candidates with			
U.N.I.P. support)	6,034	19.75	1
Liberals	1,541	5.0	—
A.N.C.	1,025	3.4	—
R.R.P.	65	0.2	—
Independent (Unsupported)	337	1.15	—
	30,560	100	14
Lower Roll			
U.N.I.P.	59,648	78.2	12
A.N.C.	16,268	21.3	3
U.F.P.	183	0.2	—
B.N.P.	136	0.2	—
Liberals	83	0.1	—
	76,318	100	15

In the National contest, the A.N.C.–U.F.P. alliance operated
successfully in both Luangwa and Lower Kafue, giving each
party two additional seats. Ten National seats were frustrated,
because no candidate succeeded in satisfying all three minimum
percentage requirements. The Special National seat (Asian)
was won by a U.N.I.P.-supported independent.[2] The table
below indicates the Legislative Council's racial composition
and the state of the parties after the general election.

U.N.I.P. and the U.F.P. had both convincingly demonstrated
their dominance among African and European voters respectively. The U.F.P. obtained 70.5 per cent of the total upper roll
vote and something over 90 per cent amongst Europeans.

[1] *Northern News* 13 October, 1 and 2 November 1962.
[2] *Northern News*, 2 November 1962, and *Central African Post*, 9 November 1962.

Table 4

LEGISLATIVE COUNCIL

Racial and Party Composition of Elected Members
following the General Election

	U.N.I.P.	U.F.P.	A.N.C.	Total
Europeans		13	1	14
Africans	12	2	4	18
Asians	1			1
Euro-Africans	1			1
State of parties	14	15	5	34

U.N.I.P.'s portion of the upper roll vote (19.75 per cent) corresponded approximately to the proportion of Africans on the upper roll. On the lower roll U.N.I.P. administered an overwhelming defeat to A.N.C., a victory all the more significant when it is realized that nearly two-thirds of A.N.C.'s support was confined to Southern Province and the relatively narrow strip of country running north-east along the Great East Road. A.N.C.'s candidates lost their deposits in six of the fifteen contests, while in the three seats which U.N.I.P. lost its candidates managed to secure a quarter of the votes cast.[1] Apart from Southern Province, U.N.I.P. clearly controlled the entire country.

One of the election's most striking features was the complete destruction of Moffat's party. Liberal candidates were all defeated, twenty-eight of the thirty losing their deposits, and the party as a whole won less than 5 per cent of the total vote. Too severely crippled to contest subsequent by-elections, the Liberal Party disbanded on 5 November, encouraging its former supporters to lend their support to U.N.I.P.[2]

But it was the National constituency results which most dramatically affected the outcome of the election. On the strength of the four seats in Luangwa and Lower Kafue, the U.F.P. eased past U.N.I.P. into the majority position in the Legislative Council, and A.N.C., with five decisive seats, held the balance of power, a position of immense influence, far exceeding A.N.C.'s expectations and radically disproportionate to the party's actual strength in the country.[3]

[1] *Northern News*, 2 November 1962, and *Central African Post*, 9 November 1962.
[2] Press statement by executive of the N.R. Liberal Party, 5 November 1962, author's collection.
[3] *Northern News*, 2 November 1962.

Results in Luangwa and Lower Kafue were also important, because they were the only instances in which members of one race voted for candidates representing a significant section of the opposite race.[1] That is not to say that Europeans and Africans refused to vote for each other's candidates purely on racial grounds. Party discipline was also an important factor.[2] In many instances U.F.P. African candidates and U.N.I.P. Europeans obtained more than 90 per cent of the votes cast by their racial opposites, but their failure in most cases even to secure 5 per cent support from their own races seriously weakened their respective claims to represent their own people.[3] Apart from the two successful pacts, every National candidate was rejected by one or both of the two races. Not one of U.N.I.P.'s fourteen National candidates obtained 5 per cent of the European vote and eleven failed even to register 3 per cent. African rejection of the U.F.P. was even more striking; apart from Kafubu and Chambeshi, where the alliance, though unsuccessful, raised the U.F.P.'s African support to 5 per cent, U.F.P. candidates never obtained more than 1.7 per cent of the African vote.[4]

The results provoked the claim, particularly amongst U.N.I.P. and the Liberals, that voting in the National seats had been purely racial. In a strict sense this was not true, for Europeans and Africans had voted in large numbers for candidates of the opposite race, even in the 'open' seats where voters were not required to support an African and a European. Yet in a more important respect U.N.I.P.'s claim was entirely justified and raised a significant political question. The vast majority of Europeans and Africans voted for *their own* parties' candidates of the opposite race—candidates who were not representative of their respective racial groups.[5] Thus, it was extremely difficult to determine what constituted racial voting, as opposed to party voting, and whether, in fact, voting generally had been along

[1] Charts for ascertaining results of election in National constituencies, 2 November 1962, author's collection.

[2] For a more detailed analysis of the importance of race and party discipline in voting in National constituencies, see Mulford, *The N.R. General Election 1962*, pp. 147–64.

[3] Charts for ascertaining the results of election in National constituencies, 2 November 1962, Kabompo, Chambeshi, Kafubu, author's collection.

[4] Ibid., all National constituencies.

[5] Ibid.

racial lines. If, however, the question of representativeness was brought in, as indeed it must be when political parties represent racial groups, then voting was obviously racial. In effect, most Europeans refused to vote for African candidates who obviously represented the African people, and instead voted for 'black' Europeans. Africans, on the other hand, refused to support the genuine representatives of the European community and instead voted for their own parties' 'white' Africans.[1]

'They're all wild about Harry'. So read the caption of a newspaper cartoon depicting Northern Rhodesia's political crisis on the day after the election results were known. The cartoon portrayed Nkumbula as a smiling bride, flanked on either side by the prospective grooms, Kaunda and Roberts, both kneeling and clutching huge bouquets.[2] Despite the picture of obvious pride, Nkumbula's position was far from enviable. Co-operation with the u.f.p. had carried two serious liabilities: alienation of a.n.c.'s traditional support once the extent of Nkumbula's link with the u.f.p. was fully appreciated; and closer involvement with the u.f.p. over the course of the campaign than Nkumbula himself dared to admit, especially in Lusaka and on the Copperbelt.

The crux of a.n.c.'s immediate problem was not so much which way to turn, but how to maintain its 'fulcrum' position throughout the period leading up to the by-elections in the National constituencies, which had been set for 10 December. Deviation from the middle ground would have meant negotiating a coalition Government before the possibility of maximizing a.n.c.'s power had been fully exploited. Outright rejection of the u.f.p. would inevitably have destroyed all hope of a.n.c. gaining European support in the by-elections. Equally undesirable, any further move towards the u.f.p. would have undermined a.n.c.'s already limited African support, not to mention the possibility of provoking serious violence between the two nationalist parties.[3] Thus, to Nkumbula the path ahead, though fraught with subtle dangers, seemed obvious. He had first to play for time, continually stressing a.n.c.'s crucial middle position. Next, he had to maintain the u.f.p. electoral alliance,

[1] Charts for ascertaining results of election in National constituencies, 2 November 1962, all National constituencies.
[2] *Lusaka Advertiser*, 2 November 1962.   [3] *Northern News*, 3 November 1962.

while at the same time encouraging both his suitors to expect
an A.N.C. coalition after 10 December. Finally, giving success
in these risky plans, Nkumbula hoped to improve his future
bargaining position by gaining additional National seats in the
by-elections.
Nkumbula's chances of maintaining his position were doubtful at best. Neither U.N.I.P. nor the U.F.P. could afford to concede six weeks' neutrality to A.N.C., and both immediately
made determined efforts to win over Nkumbula. A series of
separate meetings took place between Nkumbula and his
suitors, one with Kaunda lasting eight hours through the
night.[1] Hundreds of cables urging the nationalist leaders to
come together poured into the parties' headquarters, though
Nkumbula characteristically insisted that those he received
were half for coalition with U.N.I.P. and half against.[2] During the
early days of November Nkumbula refused to be pinned down,
first demanding that Kaunda publicly condemn Communism
and intimidation and then that Roberts denounce Federation.
Kaunda dismissed Nkumbula's demands on the grounds that
such a statement would imply past support for Communism and
intimidation, while Roberts refused to comment publicly at
all.[3] On 3 November the Governor announced the resignation
of the Liberal ministers and the appointment of an official
caretaker Government to run the country until the by-elections.[4]
But the pressure on Nkumbula increased. On 8 November a
meeting of the Territory's Council of Chiefs interviewed both
nationalist leaders and unanimously called on the African
parties to come together before the by-elections.[5] A previous
meeting of Southern Province chiefs in Monze had instructed
its delegates to the Council in Lusaka to bring U.N.I.P. and
A.N.C. together against the hated Federation.[6] The chiefs'
Lusaka declaration and their marked sympathy for Kaunda's
tactics of reconciliation placed Nkumbula in an embarrassingly
difficult position, particularly when Kaunda publicly ordered

[1] *Northern News*, 2, 3 and 5 November 1962; *African Daily News*, 3 November 1962.
[2] *Central African Post*, 5 and 11 November 1962.
[3] *Northern News*, 2, 3, 5, and 6 November 1962.
[4] Ibid., 5 November 1962.
[5] Ibid., 9 November 1962.
[6] Minutes of meeting of Southern Province chiefs, Monze, 2 November 1962, ibid.

U.N.I.P. members across the country to make common cause with A.N.C. supporters.[1] Meanwhile, A.N.C.'s Copperbelt wing, which was securely under U.F.P. influence, protested bitterly against co-operating with U.N.I.P. and threatened to split away to join the U.F.P.[2] A flurry of contradictory statements were issued by A.N.C. officials, and rumours of A.N.C. M.L.C.s defecting to U.N.I.P. circulated widely. Towards mid-November it was obvious that Nkumbula faced a growing crisis within his own party; if disintegration were to be avoided, a positive move of some kind could not be postponed.

The problems involved in forming a coalition with the U.F.P. were formidable, to say the least. Apart from the thorny question of timing, which was rapidly slipping from Nkumbula's control, three major obstacles stood out: A.N.C.'s long-standing commitment to destroy the Federation; A.N.C.'s policy of universal suffrage; and the risk of complete annihilation in the ensuing political aftermath. Agreement with the U.F.P. over the Federation question (e.g. dissolution of political ties with economic links remaining) might have greatly strengthened Nkumbula's short-term position ('Harry the Federation killer' was suggested as a possible by-election slogan). Universal suffrage he would have gladly shelved, but ultimately political destruction was virtually certain as long as U.N.I.P. remained.

Immediate coalition with U.N.I.P. would have helped restore A.N.C.'s image as a respectable African nationalist party, intent on breaking the Federation and establishing representative African government. It would also help prevent further disintegration in A.N.C., except perhaps on the Copperbelt. Disadvantages, however, were not difficult to find. A.N.C. would negotiate from a weaker position than it might reasonably have hoped to command after the by-elections. Nor could the risk of political destruction be ruled out; A.N.C. would be the weaker partner in any coalition, its men assigned to the less important Executive Council posts, and U.N.I.P. would undoubtedly continue to undermine A.N.C.'s position in the country.

Finally, there was A.N.C.'s link with Tshombe and extensive financial backing to consider. While A.N.C. had openly supported

---

[1] Notes on U.N.I.P. rally, Lusaka, 11 November 1962, author's collection.
[2] Interview with Ndilila, Kitwe, 13 November 1962; *Northern News*, 13 November 1962.

Katanga's secession for over a year, U.N.I.P. had been intensely hostile to Tshombe. This was reinforced by U.N.I.P.'s involvement in the Pan-African Freedom Movement for East, Central, and Southern Africa (P.A.F.M.E.C.S.A.), which at its Addis Ababa meeting in February 1962 had decided to shift the main thrust of its activities from the newly independent Tanganyika to Northern Rhodesia.[1] At the same meeting Kaunda had been elected President of the Pan-African organization which during U.N.I.P.'s election campaign had provided both political and financial assistance.[2]

The respective positions of both U.N.I.P. and the U.F.P. were not without their difficulties. The U.F.P. was seriously burdened both by lack of agreement amongst its leaders and by its Federal connexion. A.N.C.–U.F.P. co-operation had been particularly close on the Copperbelt, so that it was not surprising that the Copperbelt U.F.P. was prepared to go considerably further with A.N.C. than the Lusaka-Broken Hill group, which, because it included Roberts, was responsible for the negotiations with Nkumbula. A memorandum issued by the Copperbelt group in November proposed extensive electoral and governmental co-operation with A.N.C. and set out immediate measures to establish the alliance on a firmer basis. Given sufficient time, money and effort, the Copperbelt U.F.P. believed that A.N.C. could be expanded and strengthened to compete with U.N.I.P.[3] Concessions would be necessary, particularly on Federation. There was talk of renaming the Federation and of moving its capital from Salisbury; some were prepared even to consider fundamentally altering political links between the territories. Once A.N.C. had been 'revitalized', the more extreme elements in the Copperbelt group were prepared, indeed anxious, to unleash their new charge on to U.N.I.P., which presumably would be destroyed in the ensuing violence and governmental repression.[4]

The Federal question was indeed the crux of the U.F.P.'s dilemma, though it was not as simple as the Copperbelt wing supposed. Quite apart from the Federation's future, the U.F.P.

---

[1] Cox, R., *Pan-Africanism in Practice*, London, 1964, pp. 55–65.

[2] *Rhodesia Herald*, 15 March 1962; *Central African Post*, 4 May 1962.

[3] Memorandum of the U.F.P. Copperbelt election subcommittee on U.F.P.-A.N.C. co-operation, n.d., November 1962, author's collection.

[4] Interviews with Sparrow, 6 December 1962, and Cecil Burney, U.F.P. M.P. for Luanshya/Kansenji, 15 November 1962.

was a Federal party whose real leader was the Federal Prime Minister. This handicapped Northern Rhodesia's U.F.P. during its negotiations more than any other single factor. In reality, the kind of Federal alterations required to capture Nkumbula were beyond the reach of the Northern Rhodesia leaders, and no one knew this better than Roberts himself. Welensky was prepared, and actually offered, to concede to Nkumbula the senior ministerial post and half the Executive Council seats in a U.F.P.–A.N.C. coalition, but he never considered serious compromise on the Federation.[1] Besides, the U.F.P.'s more responsible leaders recognized that coalition with A.N.C. had little value if it provoked serious territorial disturbances and destroyed Nkumbula's following.[2]

U.N.I.P. bitterly resented its failure to defeat the U.F.P. and the necessity of turning to A.N.C. Courting Nkumbula would have been unpleasant at the best of times; that his power derived from an alliance with the U.F.P. made matters worse. Kaunda was determined to swallow this distasteful pill immediately and employed every available means, including his P.A.F.M.E.C.S.A. presidential office, to win over his 'mis-directed friend'.[3] The resentment provoked by U.N.I.P.'s compromise manifested itself in a sharp reaction against Europeans, who, because they had rejected U.N.I.P. and supported the A.N.C.–U.F.P. alliance, were seen as the source of U.N.I.P.'s difficulties.[4] U.N.I.P.'s lower-level officials and ordinary members had been led to believe during the election campaign that Europeans were being converted. When the full extent of U.N.I.P.'s rejection became evident, a wave of disillusionment and contempt swept through the party.[5] Kaunda was in no position to stem this reaction, which caused Europeans considerable alarm,[6] and wisely let it vent itself. Gradually the sting of rejection subsided, though U.N.I.P. never resumed its extensive European campaign of October.

[1] Interview with Welensky, Salisbury, 20 November 1962.

[2] The above paragraphs are set against the background of the author's field research during the post-election period in N.R., November and December 1962.

[3] Interview with Kaunda, 3 November 1962.

[4] *Central African Mail*, 6 November 1962.

[5] *Report on General Election Outcome by the Director of Elections to the National Council of U.N.I.P.*, 10 and 11 November 1962, author's collection.

[6] *Northern News*, 12 November 1962.

Meanwhile, pressure on Nkumbula began to force his hand. On 11 November he hinted that a coalition with u.n.i.p. after the by-elections was likely, announced that a.n.c.'s final decision would be taken at the party's National Assembly later that week and called for a stop to the anti-a.n.c. and anti-Katanga feeling in u.n.i.p.[1] Two days later, following several u.n.i.p. claims that the coalition was settled, Nkumbula angrily denied any commitment and pointed out the grave differences separating the two parties. 'Our policy is moderate and democratic while those of u.n.i.p. aim at a one-party system. Their whole history is marred by intimidation and violence on a massive scale. Their ties with the Pan-African-Casablanca bloc with its communist backing are well known.'[2] In addition, Nkumbula cancelled the National Assembly, claiming that the way for negotiations was still open. On 14 November, however, it was reported that a.n.c. had been admitted to p.a.f.m.e.c.s.a.[3] The u.f.p., sensing a.n.c.'s shift, raised a new demand for the formation of a National Government in which the u.f.p. would hold three of the six ministerial portfolios.[4]

Later that same day Nkumbula announced that he had again changed his mind: 'coalition with u.n.i.p. was inevitable', though it was not to occur until after the by-elections. He accused the u.f.p. of 'cheating' and putting unfair pressure on him.[5] Reaction from the Copperbelt was immediate: Lombe, a.n.c.'s Deputy National Secretary, withdrew his allegiance from Nkumbula, claiming that the Copperbelt would 'go it alone' unless the President retracted his coalition statement. Lombe then departed for Katanga, where he planned to ask Tshombe to redirect a.n.c.'s financial aid. Nkumbula retaliated by dismissing Lombe as a.n.c.'s prospective candidate in Chambeshi.[6]

On 16 November, three days before nomination day, Kaunda and Nkumbula issued a joint statement confirming

[1] *Northern News*, 12 November 1962.
[2] Ibid., 14 November 1962.
[3] Ibid., 15 November 1962.
[4] *Central African Post*, 14 November 1962.
[5] *Northern News*, 15 November 1962.
[6] Ibid., 16 November 1962; s.o. (c.s.) 2 to a.s. (c.s.) 1, 22 November 1962, S/S 119/130/01, notes strong opposition of Copperbelt a.n.c. to proposed coalition with u.n.i.p.

their intention to form a coalition and calling on their respective supporters to cease hostilities. Together they assured all minorities of their place in Northern Rhodesia and denounced Communism, intimidation, violence, and racial bitterness.[1] Yet Nkumbula still clung doggedly to his earlier position that the final decision on coalition would be taken after the by-election. Speaking at a week-end rally at Lusaka, he taunted: 'I have the key in my pocket to form a coalition, but the key is still there.' At the same time, at a Mufulira meeting addressed by Frank Stubbs, A.N.C.'s Luapula European candidate, 4,000 Africans voted unanimously against any further alignment with U.N.I.P. or any other party until after the by-election.[2]

U.N.I.P. remained in a precarious situation, despite Nkumbula's public commitment. Kaunda, in addition to the original compromise involved in turning to A.N.C., was forced to make further concessions. One of Nkumbula's chief concerns in co-operating with U.N.I.P. was the maintenance of his profitable Katanga connexion. Twice in early November Nkumbula visited Elisabethville before confronting U.N.I.P. with his Katanga demands: an assurance against hostile Katanga politics; a tripartite meeting with Tshombe before the coalition was formed.[3]

While A.N.C.'s first demand might have been quietly satisfied, U.N.I.P.'s Pan-African affiliations and previous Katanga policies ruled out consideration of the second. At the time of the joint A.N.C.–U.N.I.P. declaration, however, Nkumbula forced the issue by informing the Press, in Kaunda's presence, that a meeting with Tshombe had been arranged. Kaunda reacted quickly, refusing to confirm the meeting, but emphasizing that as President of P.A.F.M.E.C.S.A. he was empowered to meet any African leader.[4] He immediately took the initiative and secretly arranged a private meeting with Tshombe at Kitwe on 18 November. This was done without the consent of U.N.I.P.'s central committee; Kaunda's only colleague at the three-hour meeting was his Kitwe regional secretary. A.N.C. had been caught by surprise, and the following day Nkumbula rushed to Kitwe to meet Tshombe.[5]

[1] *Northern News*, 17 November 1962. [2] Ibid., 19 November 1962.
[3] Ibid., 7 and 17 November 1962. [4] Ibid., 17 November 1962.
[5] Ibid., 19 and 20 November 1962.

Despite the obvious concession of meeting Tshombe, the Kitwe confrontation was a considerable *coup* for Kaunda. By reassuring the Katangese President, Kaunda had removed a major barrier to coalition without seriously compromising U.N.I.P.'s position, either within or outside Northern Rhodesia. He emphasized repeatedly that he had acted as P.A.F.M.E.C.S.A. President, not as U.N.I.P.'s leader, and that the discussions had centred on Pan-African problems. This was probably true, but in the process Tshombe's fears were mollified and his anger over A.N.C.'s P.A.F.M.E.C.S.A. membership softened.[1]

With by-elections only three weeks away, Nkumbula continued, amid considerable confusion and speculation, to utilize his 'fulcrum' position. Short of actually reversing his decision, he still maintained considerable leverage in his dealings with U.N.I.P. Nkumbula's most powerful lever was A.N.C.'s attempt to renew the U.F.P. alliance for the by-elections, a move Kaunda tried desperately to prevent. On 20 November, Nkumbula and Liso, together with Mbiu Koiniange, the P.A.F.M.E.C.S.A. Secretary-General, who had come to Lusaka at Kaunda's request, and two attractive members of A.N.C.'s women's league, departed for East Africa to meet Nyerere and Kenyatta. From East Africa Nkumbula and his team were scheduled to proceed to London, far away from U.F.P. pressure and persuasion.[2]

Outwardly, the U.F.P. displayed a striking lack of concern over Nkumbula's behaviour. Though it was impossible to discover if Nkumbula had actually committed himself to both sides, his removal from Northern Rhodesia did not prevent the re-establishment of A.N.C.–U.F.P. electoral co-operation. This time, however, the U.F.P. took greater care to cover itself against A.N.C. betrayal. Electoral pacts with A.N.C. were not easily discernible when nominations closed on 19 November. The U.F.P. had both an African and a European candidate in every National constituency except Zambezi, where the U.F.P.'s candidate again appeared to align himself with the B.N.P.'s African. Apart from Chambeshi, where A.N.C.'s African candidate, Ndilila, was disqualified for violating nomination procedure, A.N.C. also nominated full teams in each constituency. Nevertheless, there was evidence of A.N.C.–U.F.P. co-

[1] *Northern News*, 17 November 1962.
[2] Ibid., 21 November 1962.

operation in four of the five National constituencies. In Zambezi
the U.F.P.'s candidate reached an understanding with Michello,
who was widely regarded in European circles as a possible
A.N.C. deserter. In Chambeshi the U.F.P. formed a pact with
Lombe, who, though standing under the A.N.C. banner because
of Ndilila's disqualification, had challenged Nkumbula's
leadership the week before. In Kabompo it was rumoured that
A.N.C.'s European candidate would, if elected, cross over to the
U.F.P.[1] Finally in Luapula Frank Stubbs publicly committed
himself to resign from A.N.C. if Nkumbula formed a coalition
with U.N.I.P.[2]

Meanwhile, Nkumbula arrived in London and took immediate advantage of his position to grasp the initiative once again.
Discovering that an individual approach to the Central African
Office would not succeed, Nkumbula cabled Kaunda asking
him to come to London to join in demanding a new Northern
Rhodesia constitution. This time the response was Kaunda's,
and he left Lusaka on 26 November amid offers by A.N.C. to
pay half his London air fare![3]

Once in London, Kaunda and Nkumbula came closer
together than ever before. Several joint meetings were held with
Butler in early December, and Nkumbula reaffirmed his
decision to form a coalition with U.N.I.P. It was inconceivable,
he claimed, that after a twenty-year struggle he should stand in
the way of African government in Northern Rhodesia. Of
course, he added, his decision was subject to ratification by
A.N.C.'s National Assembly after the by-election.[4] Back in
Lusaka, one of A.N.C.'s European candidates, Frank Stubbs,
refuted Nkumbula's London statements, pledging himself to
have 'no further dealings with A.N.C.' if it turned 'extremist' and
formed a coalition Government with U.N.I.P. However, Stubbs's
partner at the meeting, Francis Chembe, already a M.L.C. on the
strength of A.N.C.–U.F.P. co-operation, defended the proposed
coalition, arguing that A.N.C. would act as a moderating influence on U.N.I.P.[5]

[1] s.o. (c.s.) 2 to A.s. (c.s.) 1, 15 November 1962, S/S 119/130/01; *Northern News*,
20 November and 8 December 1962.
[2] *Northern News*, 4 December 1962.
[3] Ibid., 27 November 1962.
[4] Ibid., 1 and 5 December 1962.
[5] Ibid., 4 and 8 December 1962.

As polling day drew near, two of the Territory's three political leaders remained outside the country. The by-election campaign was scarcely noticed amid the flurry of top-level political activity. U.N.I.P., which again nominated a full team of candidates in the National seats, organized several small African rallies, but adopted a 'take us or leave us' attitude towards Europeans.

What future relationships exist between Europeans and Africans depends entirely on what line Europeans adopt towards the formation of an African Government. 'There comes a tide in the affairs of men, which, if taken at the flood, *leads on to fortune.*' It was high tide in Northern Rhodesia on 30th October 1962. Europeans missed it. The tide is ebbing fast, but there is still a chance for some of you to launch one last cockle shell.[1]

Kaunda and Nkumbula returned to Northern Rhodesia the day before polling, both claiming that Butler had committed the British Government to granting Northern Rhodesia a new constitution before the end of 1963. Though Nkumbula was clearly committed to U.N.I.P., confusion and rumours of revolt surrounded others in his party. At a meeting in Nkumbula Square at Mulfulira, Stubbs again rallied a 3,500-strong A.N.C. crowd unanimously to oppose any U.N.I.P. coalition.[2] In the country generally there was wide agreement that Northern Rhodesia would soon have an African Government, provided A.N.C. was not torn apart in the next round of polling and negotiation. This was a possibility which even Nkumbula refused to deny.[3]

In the by-elections A.N.C. startled the country by securing, mainly on the strength of U.F.P. support, two additional National seats, Michello in Zambezi and Stubbs in Luapula. Changing from October, A.N.C. voters almost unanimously rejected their U.F.P. allies, except in Chambeshi, where A.N.C. failed to command 10 per cent of the African vote. Europeans again rejected U.N.I.P., though its share of the European vote (3.3 per cent) was somewhat larger than in October. By contrast, seven of the

---

[1] *U.N.I.P. Christmas Message to Europeans,* issued 8 December 1962, author's collection.
[2] *Northern News,* 10 December 1962.
[3] Ibid., *Central African Mail,* 11 December 1962.

nine U.F.P. candidates received less than 1.3 per cent of the African vote, the other two scoring 2.2 per cent and 6.7 per cent respectively.[1] The following table indicates the final party and racial composition of the Legislative Council.

Table 5

LEGISLATIVE COUNCIL

Racial and Party Composition of Elected Members

	U.N.I.P.	U.F.P.	A.N.C.	Total
Europeans		15	2	17
Africans	12	1	5	18
Asians	1			1
Euro-Africans	1			1
State of parties	14	16	7	37

The final by-election results were released on 12 December. That same day A.N.C. convened its crucial National Assembly meeting for the final decision on coalition with U.N.I.P.[2] A number of delegates, mainly from the Copperbelt districts, were violently opposed to co-operating with U.N.I.P. and threatened to make a 'last-ditch' stand. Nkumbula's handling of the meeting was a tribute to his political agility. Accompanied by Kaunda, he marched into the assembled meeting and posed three questions in rapid succession: how many favour African government; how many want African government now; how many are behind me? Most hands went up in answer to each question, and Nkumbula abruptly departed with Kaunda for Government House![3]

Before their first meeting with the Governor the African leaders had not reached agreement between themselves and were therefore advised to return to Government House when they had achieved a settlement. On 13 November Kaunda and Nkumbula met the Governor twice after individual meetings with their respective executives and a long discussion at Nkumbula's house the previous evening. When no announcement was made that day speculation and rumours arose that a 'hitch' had developed. Both African leaders denied the rumours, and

[1] *Northern News*, 13 December 1962; Charts for ascertaining the results of by-elections in National constituencies, 12 December 1962.

[2] *Northern News*, 13 December 1962.

[3] Interview with Roy Horrell, A.N.C.'s European adviser, 17 December 1962.

the Government explained that the delay was caused by the Governor having to deal with two leaders instead of one.[1] In fact, more than one 'hitch' developed in the negotiations. The first was A.N.C.'s demand for half the six ministries, despite the fact that it had only seven as against U.N.I.P.'s fourteen Legislative Council seats. The claim for three portfolios was originally raised by Ted Cousins, A.N.C.'s European M.P. for Laungwa, in early November as a condition for co-operating with U.N.I.P.[2] Though at the time Kaunda brusquely rejected the demand, he found Nkumbala's position a good deal stronger after the by-election. The Constitution explicitly required at least two members of the Executive Council to be European and two others to be Africans.[3] Nkumbula had the only two Europeans between both parties, Cousins and Stubbs, a situation which virtually fulfilled his demands.

Nkumbula's position, however, was somewhat undermined by Stubbs's reluctance to co-operate with U.N.I.P. Stubbs had made his own position particularly uncomfortable by the rigid anti-U.N.I.P. stand he assumed during the by-election campaign.[4] As a result he had acquired not only sufficient U.F.P. European support to succeed but an acutely troubled conscience as well. If Stubbs had refused to disregard his electioneering pledge, Northern Rhodesia would have been deprived of an exclusively African party Government and Nkumbula of portfolio parity with U.N.I.P. On Friday, 14 December, Stubbs hurried to Mufulira to consult his supporters.[5]

Meanwhile, a third 'hitch' had developed in the distribution of portfolios. U.N.I.P. demanded the crucial Ministries of Local Government and Social Welfare, African Agriculture and African Education. Nkumbula was offered the Ministry of Transport and Works. This Nkumbula adamantly refused, reportedly expressing his unwillingness 'to talk to roads and bridges', and insisted instead on the portfolio of African Education.[6] On 15 December Stubbs returned to Lusaka, having

[1] *Northern News*, 13 and 14 December 1962.

[2] *Central African Post*, 2 November 1962.

[3] Part 2, sec. 8(ii), *The Northern Rhodesia (Constitution) Order in Council 1962*, 1 September 1962.

[4] *Northern News*, 10 December 1962.

[5] Ibid., 15 December 1962.

[6] Interview with C. E. Cousins, 18 December 1962.

decided to 'serve the interests of the country'; U.N.I.P. acceded
to Nkumbula's demand and the Governor announced the
formation of Northern Rhodesia's first African Government.[1]

Ministers		Parliamentary Secretary
K. D. Kaunda (U.N.I.P.)	Local Government and Social Welfare	A. G. Zulu (U.N.I.P.)
H. M. Nkumbula (A.N.C.)	African Education	C. J. Banda (A.N.C.)
S. M. Kapwepwe (U.N.I.P.)	African Agriculture	E. K. Mudenda (U.N.I.P.)
R. C. Kamanga (U.N.I.P.)	Labour and Mines	J. M. Mwanakatwe (U.N.I.P.)
F. N. Stubbs (A.N.C.)	Transport and Works	F. B. Chembe (A.N.C.)
C. E. Cousins (A.N.C.)	Land and Natural Resources	J. E. Michello (A.N.C.)
	Finance	A. N. Wina (U.N.I.P.)

Officials	Chief Whip
Chief Secretary	S. Wina (U.N.I.P.)
Finance	
Native Affairs	
Justice	

In selecting U.N.I.P.'s ministers and parliamentary secretaries,
Kaunda made a clear distinction between seniority in the party
and technical qualifications.[2] His ministers were chosen strictly
on the basis of party seniority; Kapwepwe and Kamanga were
both early U.N.I.P. officials and important national office-
bearers. The distribution of parliamentary secretary posts was
governed primarily by technical qualifications. Zulu was a
U.N.I.P. National Trustee and A. Wina had been U.N.I.P.'s
United States representative, but Mwanakatwe and Mudenda
had officially joined U.N.I.P. less than six months before and
neither had held party offices. The appointment of S. Wina,
U.N.I.P.'s national publicity secretary, as Chief Whip immediately provoked a wave of speculation that he had been demoted
in the party heirarchy. Within three weeks, however, S. Wina
was appointed Parliamentary Secretary for Local Government
and Social Welfare and Zulu was tranferred to the Ministry of
Native Affairs. At the same time, A.N.C.'s Liso was appointed
Parliamentary Secretary to the Chief Secretary, making A.N.C.
a party with no backbenchers.[3]

---

[1] *Northern News*, 15 December 1962; *Central African Daily News*, 15 December
1962.
[2] Interview with Merfyn Temple, 17 December 1962.
[3] *Central African Mail*, 31 December 1962.

VIII

THE ACHIEVEMENT OF POWER

TWO years had elapsed between Northern Rhodesia's
constitutional conference and the formation of the coalition Government. By any standard the Territory's
political metamorphosis had been phenomenal. Yet even before
the Government had been formed both U.N.I.P. and A.N.C. had
raised demands for a new constitution based on universal adult
suffrage and the granting of independence to Northern Rhodesia outside the Federation.[1] U.N.I.P. in particular, despite its
participation in the election, had consistently emphasized its
unqualified rejection both of the 1962 Constitution and its
underlying principles.[2] Thus, even as the new Government took
office, the days of Northern Rhodesia's 'fancy franchise' and
'three tier' electoral system were clearly numbered.[3]

In spite of its short life, the 1962 Constitution had played an
important role in Northern Rhodesia's transition. Quite apart
from the Constitution's failure to satisfy the Territory's various
political groups, the Constitution's most outspoken critics attacked it on the grounds that it was unnecessarily complex, un-
intelligible to the common voter and a nightmare to administer.
Though all three criticisms were to some extent justified,[4] more
important points were often overlooked or forgotten. By late
1960 Northern Rhodesia's political situation had reached a
critical stage. The belief that breaking the Federation depended

[1] *Northern News*, 6 December 1962.
[2] *U.N.I.P. Policy*, issued 15 June 1962.
[3] *Northern News*, 6 December 1962.
[4] A strong case may be made against the criticism that the Constitution was
incomprehensible to ordinary voters. Though they did not fully understand the
complicated electoral arrangements (especially the delimitation of constituencies
and the qualifying percentages) it was obvious in the election that voters knew how
to record support for the candidates of their choice. Except amongst lower roll
voters in two National constituencies, the proportion of spoiled ballots remained
well under 9 per cent in all constituencies, a tribute both to the political parties
and to the Government Information Department. Analysis of Polling, N.R. General
Election 1962, Secretariat, 3 November 1962, author's collection.

upon seizing power in Northern Rhodesia had gained wide acceptance amongst the Territory's nationalist leaders,[1] and African opposition was both effectively organized and militant. Events in the Congo had vividly underlined the risks of transition from white to black Government. Central Africa's whites looked increasingly to Northern Rhodesia as the test for their future, and Welensky rightly perceived that the last fight to preserve the Federation lay not in the long-delayed Federal Review Conference, but in Northern Rhodesia's Constitution and the 1962 general election.[2] Like his African opponents, Welensky had adopted a rigidly uncompromising position and attempted to bolster Northern Rhodesia's European community for the 'showdown' with the British Government. Finally, there was Macleod's own personality, particularly his belief that a constitutional formula might be devised which, while ensuring African political advance, would not be rejected outright by the Territory's Europeans.[3] That Northern Rhodesia's political groups had all been induced to participate in the elections was a factor of immense significance, largely attributable to the delicate compromise achieved within Macleod's original constitutional framework. This political fact alone deserves precedence over the whole range of technical criticisms.

True, the Constitution had failed to achieve the 'non-racial' political approach explicitly encouraged by its design. Election results in the National constituencies clearly indicated that while Europeans and Africans voted for each other's candidates, both had refused to support those candidates who genuinely represented the opposite race. Though party allegiance played an important role in this rejection, it would be incorrect to conclude that party loyalties overrode racial considerations. No amount of support for a party's candidates of the opposite race could conceal the fact that voting on both sides had been racial. Political parties in Northern Rhodesia were firmly based on racial lines, and voters saw parties as organizations representing one or other of the two races, irrespective of the race of the

---

[1] Sipalo to A. Wina, 5 October 1960; Kaunda to A. Wina, 1 November 1960; S. Wina to A. Wina, 1 December 1960, A.N.L.W. papers.

[2] Welensky, Sir Roy, *Welensky's 4,000 Days*, pp. 310–55, *passim*.

[3] *N.R. Proposals for Constitutional Change*, Cmd. 1295, February 1961.

parties' respective candidates. A vote for U.N.I.P. candidates of either race was a vote for African government, while support for the U.F.P. expressed a preference for white government and the continuation of Federation. Yet the Constitution had brought Northern Rhodesia's races into contact. To some extent they had shared a common political arena, and the Territory's political parties had joined in an electoral contest the effect of which was to give the stamp of legitimacy to Northern Rhodesia's crucial step from minority white to majority black government. In short, for all its weaknesses the Constitution had softened the impact of African government.

What in one sense had been a limited success was in another sense a serious and perhaps dangerous failing. For in easing the introduction of African government, the Constitution had failed to produce a conclusive election result. Both African parties held power, each regarding itself as Northern Rhodesia's legitimate nationalist movement. U.N.I.P., with approximately 60 per cent of the total vote and 37 per cent of the Legislative Council's seats, had been forced to share ministerial posts equally with A.N.C., which had won a mere 16 per cent of the total vote and controlled only 19 per cent of the legislature's membership. The U.F.P., long the Territory's only significant political force, and still the party with the largest single bloc of seats, found itself suddenly and apparently irrevocably stripped of power. The stage was set for a stormy interlude of interparty rivalry and intrigue, which could only deepen as the next and final round of constitutional negotiations approached. It was hardly surprising under these conditions that the U.N.I.P.–A.N.C. coalition produced neither stable nor productive government. Treating the coalition as a temporary expedient necessitated by an unsatisfactory constitution,[1] both parties decided at the outset to restrict their co-operation exclusively to members of the Government.[2] There was to be no merging of the two parties, and in the country generally they instituted a precarious state of mutual toleration between their respective supporters.[3] By late January, before the Legislative Council's first session was two

[1] *Northern News*, 20 December 1962.
[2] U.N.I.P. rally at Twapia Township, Ndola, 2 December 1962. Interview with Horrell, 17 December 1962.
[3] *Central African Mail*, 8 January 1963.

weeks old, relations between U.N.I.P. and A.N.C. had deteriorated sharply, warning of the more difficult times to come.[1]

The Coalition Government

Instability was the coalition's greatest weakness. From the outset it was plagued by the constant threat of dissolution, largely
because of the continuing uncertainty which surrounded A.N.C.'s
position. Unlike Kaunda, who regarded the 1962 election as but
one step towards full independence, Nkumbula apparently
viewed the election as A.N.C.'s greatest triumph. After nearly
five years of playing a secondary role in nationalist politics, it
was said that the sudden acquisition of power appeared to have
'gone to his head'.[2] In his own judgement, Nkumbula had
achieved both his major political goals in a single *coup*:African
government for Northern Rhodesia, and the virtual end of
Federation. Indeed, Nkumbula disclaimed all interest in his
prospects for the Territory's next election.[3] Even as he joined
the Government, Nkumbula promised the U.F.P. that he would
reconsider its co-operation proposals should the U.N.I.P.-A.N.C.
coalition fail to run smoothly,[4] and within two weeks he con-
fided to his European lawyer that the coalition had little chance
of surviving.[5]

Nor was the U.F.P. prepared to acquiesce in its role as the
opposition party. As early as January the U.F.P.'s Copperbelt
branches forced the convening of a Territorial Central Executive meeting which Welensky agreed to attend. The Copperbelt
M.P.s, arguing that the end of Federation was a foregone conclusion, proposed that the U.F.P. be dissolved and that the
Northern Rhodesia wing, under a new name, form an alliance
with A.N.C. A new coalition Government might then be formed,
led either by Nkumbula or, if he refused, by Michello or Lombe,
in which the key posts would all be held by Africans with Europeans acting as their advisers. As usual, Welensky was able to
dissuade the dissidents from forcing a showdown within the
party, but his influence was clearly on the wane.[6] Within days

---

[1] *Central African Mail*, 22 January 1963.
[2] 'A.N.C. in N.R. 1963', 15 August 1963, DG/123/01.
[3] s.o. (c.s.) 2 to A.s. (c.s.) 1, 21 January 1963, S/S 119/130/01.
[4] Ibid., 17 December 1962.
[5] Ibid., 18 December 1962.
[6] Ibid., 21 January 1963.

after the meeting the rebels, as they were soon called, began surreptitiously to attempt to break the coalition.

The u.f.p.'s rebel group included six Copperbelt m.p.s as well as the members from Livingstone and Southern Rural. Their first move was to appoint Norman Coates, m.p. for Kalilushi, to befriend and gain information from a.n.c.'s Stubbs, who since becoming a minister in the coalition Government had been ostracized by whites on the Copperbelt.[1] Nkumbula actively encouraged the rebels, meeting privately with their representatives on a number of occasions in February and March.[2] In mid-February Nkumbula claimed that he could bring several u.n.i.p. m.p.s into the new alignment, including both Wina brothers, Kamanga, Nyirenda, and possibly Mudenda,[3] and soon afterwards rumours began to circulate of an imminent break-up of the coalition Government.[4] By this time Welensky had given his blessing to the rebels' efforts and one of the large copper companies reportedly pledged financial support to the new group once it had emerged successfully.[5] Reports from Barotseland indicated that the u.f.p. was active there as well, playing on the Litunga's fears of u.n.i.p., encouraging secessionist groups and spreading the rumour that the existing Government would soon be replaced by an a.n.c.-European coalition.[6]

By March the rebels had got themselves into difficulties. The announcement in late February that the Legislative Council would resume its session on 12 March led the rebels to attempt to force Nkumbula's hand.[7] Originally they had pledged themselves to join Nkumbula as soon as he produced a Legislative Council majority composed of his own party and various elements of u.n.i.p. and the u.f.p.[8] But Nkumbula's tendency to delay matters roused the rebels' suspicions, particularly since he never managed to organize direct negotiations which in-

[1] s.o. (c.s.) 2 to a.s. (c.s.) 1, 31 January 1963.
[2] Ibid., 19, 22, and 27 February, 4 March 1963.
[3] Ibid., 19 and 28 February 1963. The only confirmation of u.n.i.p. m.p.'s attending joint a.n.c.-rebel meetings concerned the Wina brothers, who were reported to have attended a meeting at the house of Kalilushi lawyer David Houston-Barnes on 20 February; ibid., 28 February 1963.
[4] Central African Mail, 9 March 1963.
[5] s.o. (c.s.) 2 to a.s. (c.s.) 1, 27 February 1963, S/S/ 119/130/01.
[6] Sec. (r.c.) to Ad. Sec., 5 March 1963, ibid.
[7] s.o. (c.s.) 2 to a.s. (c.s.) 1, 9 March, ibid.
[8] Ibid., 31 January 1963.

cluded the suspected U.N.I.P. defectors.[1] More serious perhaps were the news leakages which exposed the rebels' activities to public view, and reports in early March that Nkumbula's own Parliamentary Secretary, C. J. Banda, was preparing to cross over to U.N.I.P.[2] On 13 March Kaunda dealt the rebels a further blow by issuing a statement in which he indicated that he had been aware all along of Nkumbula's activities and categorically denied that any U.N.I.P. M.P.s had been swayed by A.N.C.'s overtures.[3]

Far from breaking the coalition, the rebels very nearly destroyed the U.F.P. Lacking decisive leadership and distrusting Nkumbula's motives, the rebels, despite frequent contacts with Nkumbula, failed to act on their plans during April and May.[4] Meanwhile, Roberts attempted to resist the drift towards A.N.C., first by seeking advice from the Governor on the Territory's next constitution,[5] and second by changing the party's name to the National Progress Party (N.P.P.).[6] Roberts rightly judged that the party was passing through a crisis of identity. Confronted with exclusion from the present Government and aware that Europeans would never again hold power exclusively in Northern Rhodesia, the U.F.P. was forced to define a new role for itself in Northern Rhodesia politics, unless its members were to join African political parties and resign themselves to acting in minor advisory capacities behind the scenes. As early as mid-April Roberts had been told by the Governor that Kaunda, despite a public commitment to the contrary, favoured a new constitution which reserved a bloc of seats for Europeans.[7] Not long afterwards Roberts gave Kaunda an assurance that he could never agree to lead a party which wished to join A.N.C., while Kaunda, for his part, indicated that he hoped Europeans would be given twelve reserved seats in a legislature of approximately sixty members.[8] Thus, by late May

[1] s.o. (c.s.) 2 to A.s. (c.s.) 1, 19 and 22 February 1963. S/S/119/130/01.
[2] Ibid., 12 March 1963; *Central African Mail*, 9 March 1963.
[3] *Northern News*, 13 March 1963.
[4] Report on the U.F.P. Territorial Committee Meeting, s.o. (c.s.) 2 to A.s. (c.s.) 1, 30 April 1963; also s.o. (c.s.) 2 to A.s. (c.s.) 1, 1 and 8 May 1963, S/S/119/130/01.
[5] Governor to c.s., 10 April 1963, ibid.
[6] s.o. (c.s.) 2 to A.s. (c.s.) 1, 30 April 1963, ibid; *Northern News*, 30 April 1963.
[7] Governor to c.s., 10 April 1963, ibid.
[8] s.b. to P.s. (c.s.), 14 May 1963, ibid.

Roberts could offer the N.P.P. the promise of a continuing, if markedly less important, role in Northern Rhodesia politics. But Roberts had also been assisted in his efforts to preserve a European party by a plan which he presented on behalf of Welensky to the N.P.P.'s caucus meeting on 25 May. The meeting was something of a showdown between Roberts and the rebels. Afterwards, fewer M.P.s were prepared to cross over to A.N.C.,[1] and less than a week later Nkumbula himself suddenly appeared to lose interest in a merger with the Europeans.[2] The two developments were not unrelated, and neither augured well either for U.N.I.P. or for the coalition Government.

In January 1963 Welensky, together with two Federal colleagues and a Copperbelt M.P., met A.N.C.'s Lombe in Kitwe to discuss the possibility of forming a new African party with which Europeans could safely co-operate. Welensky complained bitterly about Nkumbula's 'breach of faith' in joining the U.N.I.P. coalition Government and suggested that Lombe form a new group, the Mukuba National Party, to replace Nkumbula's A.N.C. For his part, Welensky pledged U.F.P. support for such a group, promising in addition to endeavour to persuade Tshombe to allocate to the new party funds he had previously reserved for A.N.C.[3] The optimism of the rebel group, together with Nkumbula's apparent willingness to co-operate with them, led Welensky to postpone his Mukuba plan. Once it became apparent, however, that the rebels were not capable of taking decisive action and that Nkumbula was simply playing the rebels off against his coalition partners, Welensky unfolded a new plan to assist A.N.C.'s anti-Nkumbula faction.[4]

The faction was not new in A.N.C. Its chief figures, Michello and Lombe, had opposed the coalition with U.N.I.P. from the beginning and been highly critical of Nkumbula's handling of the 1962 election campaign. After the formation of the Government, Nkumbula's preoccupation with his power to make or break the Government, his total neglect of A.N.C.'s lower echelons, his insincere and abortive negotiations with the U.F.P. rebels, provided Michello and Lombe with a growing body of

[1] s.o. (c.s.) 2 to a.s. (c.s.) 1, 25 May and 6 June 1963, *Northern News*, 30 April 1963.
[2] Ibid., 10 June 1963.
[3] s.b. paper, 'a.n.c. in n.r. 1963', 15 August 1963, DG 123/01.
[4] s.o. (c.s.) 2 to a.s. (c.s.) 1, 25 May and 6 June 1963, S/S 119/130/01.

discontented supporters in the party. In addition, A.N.C.'s
financial position had become critical. Despite the large contributions received from Tshombe for the general election, by
June 1963 A.N.C. was in debt to the tune of approximately
£24,000. Much of the Katanga money had been squandered,
some on personal items for top officials, such as cars, clothing
and housing, and a still larger amount on a fleet of fifty vehicles
for the election campaign, forty-one of which, largely because of
poor maintenance and irresponsible driving, were no longer in
running order. The plethora of funds in late 1962 and the growing rift in A.N.C. during 1963 had discouraged the collection and
forwarding of funds by the lower-level formations to A.N.C.'s
headquarters. The result, painfully obvious to the party's senior
officials regardless of their personal attitudes towards the coalition, was that A.N.C. in its present condition could not hope to
contest another election during 1963 or even early in 1964. Nor,
in the minds of the anti-Nkumbula group, could A.N.C. hope to
recover as long as Nkumbula continued to dominate the
organization.[1]

Several moves were made in April and May 1963 to reduce
Nkumbula's control over A.N.C.'s day-to-day operation. Early
in May, following a series of national executive meetings,
A.N.C.'s publicity bureau issued a new allocation of duties for
headquarters officials which made it clear that the President's
responsibility for general administration had been transferred
to the National Secretary, Michello. Policy matters were to be
decided jointly by the President, the National Secretary, and the
National Chairman. If they failed to reach agreement, the
matter then was to be submitted to the national executive,
summoned from now on by the National Secretary instead of
the President. At about the same time fifteen prominent A.N.C.
members formed a small reform committee named the Mukuba
Pressure Group, which allied itself with the party's anti-
Nkumbula faction. The Mukuba Group, whose members were
businessmen, Civil Servants and school teachers from Central
and Southern Provinces, submitted preliminary proposals for
reform to A.N.C.'s national executive in late May. In addition to
changes at headquarters level, the Mukuba Group recommended a major reorganization of A.N.C.'s lower echelons,

[1] 'A.N.C. in N.R. 1963', 15 August 1963, DG 123/01.

which would divide the Territory into smaller, more manageable units and improve both the recruitment and control of youth groups. The practice of drinking amongst party officials on duty was condemned, and A.N.C.'s top leaders were urged to tour rural areas more regularly and to be more receptive to the problems of ordinary A.N.C. members. At first Nkumbula agreed to the new ideas, but a short time later, sensing the move to reduce his authority in the party, he changed his mind.[1]

Meanwhile, the connexion between the Mukuba and anti-Nkumbula groups on the one hand, and Welensky and the N.P.P. on the other, began to take shape. In early June, John Kalenga, A.N.C.'s Administrative Secretary, who had resigned from U.N.I.P. after being attacked with a petrol bomb in December 1962, and A.N.C.'s Financial Adviser, A. N. Banda, both members of the anti-Nkumbula faction, travelled to Paris with six Katangese officials to visit Tshombe.[2] From Paris the two A.N.C. officials went to London to meet Nkumbula, who in addition to attempting to raise funds for A.N.C. in Britain tried unsuccessfully to see Tshombe in Paris.[3] When Kalenga and Banda returned to Northern Rhodesia in late June the special branch reported that Tshombe had promised to donate £100,000 to A.N.C., provided that two conditions were met. The first was that A.N.C. would be reorganized on efficient lines; the second that Nkumbula be stripped of the dictatorial powers vested in his office of National President. The money, which had been transferred to the Bank of Rhodesia and Nyasaland, reportedly by the Federation's High Commissioner in London, was to be released to A.N.C. only when the above conditions had been fulfilled.[4] Although the person or group responsible for releasing the funds was never specifically identified, the evidence strongly suggests that the decision was left to Welensky. Welensky had promised the anti-Nkumbula group to use his influence with Tshombe to divert Katangese funds reserved for Nkumbula to Michello and Lombe.[5] In May, claiming that he had a plan for A.N.C., Welensky had successfully discouraged the N.P.P.'s

[1] 'A.N.C. in N.R. 1963', 15 August 1963, DG 123/01.
[2] S.B. to P.S. (C.S.), 20 June 1963; British Consulate, Elisabethville, to P.S. (C.S.), N.R.G., 6 July 1963, TS/S 123/01.
[3] S.O. (C.S.) 2 to A.S. (C.S.) 1, 19 June 1963, S/S/ 119/130/01.
[4] S.B. to P.S. (C.S.), 2 August 1963, GH TS/S 123/01.
[5] 'A.N.C. in N.R. 1963', 15 August 1963, DG 123/01.

rebels from carrying on further negotiations with Nkumbula.[1] In July, shortly after the return of Kalenga and A. N. Banda, the Mukuba Pressure Group, which like Michello and Lombe favoured co-operation with Europeans, submitted a lengthy and extremely professionally prepared memorandum on A.N.C.'s reorganization to the party's national executive. In addition to the measures proposed by the Mukuba Group in May, there were new proposals which obviously aimed at depriving Nkumbula of his dictatorial powers in the party.[2] Finally, in early July, Kalenga himself placed an order with a local motor firm for seventy-five Land-Rovers valued at £80,000.[3]

Unlike earlier groups which had attempted to depose Nkumbula, the Michello-Lombe group sought only to reduce Nkumbula's power, first by effectively transferring responsibility for party administration to A.N.C.'s National Secretary, and second by depriving the President of his authority to appoint and dismiss officials at all levels of the party hierarchy.[4] Unfortunately for the Michello group, Nkumbula learned of the Tshombe transaction in mid-July and summoned an emergency meeting of A.N.C.'s national executive, where he claimed that Michello, Kalenga, and A. N. Banda had been bribed and were conspiring with the U.F.P. in Salisbury to remove him illegally from office. Michello and his colleagues, suddenly forced on the defensive, responded by declaring that the 'Supreme Action Council', a body Nkumbula denied existed, had already suspended the President and summoned a National Assembly for early August to elect new national office bearers.[5]

The confrontation took place on 3 August. With elections only a matter of months away and the funds from Tshombe beyond his immediate grasp, Nkumbula sought to restore party unity. He proposed that a steering committee be formed along the lines suggested by the Mukuba group to supervise A.N.C.'s finances and administration, while the President retained con-

[1] s.o. (c.s.) 2 to A.s. (c.s.) 1, 25 May and 6 June 1963, S/S 119/130/01.
[2] Memorandum on A.N.C. organization for more effective action, n.d. July 1963, TS/S 123/01. The name 'Mukuba' was originally suggested by Welensky in January; 'A.N.C. in N.R. 1963', 15 August 1963, DG 123/01.
[3] 'A.N.C. in N.R. 1963', 15 August 1963, DG 123/01.
[4] Memorandum on A.N.C. organization for more effective action, n.d. July 1963, TS/S 123/01.
[5] 'A.N.C. in N.R. 1963', 15 August 1963, DG 123/01.

trol over party policy. Nkumbula also agreed to appoint three members of the Mukuba group to A.N.C.'s national executive. These plans were approved by the National Assembly, which passed a vote of confidence in both Nkumbula and Michello. The Assembly also resolved that written reports be prepared on A.N.C.'s 1962 election expenditures, which were said to have totalled approximately £57,000, and on the recent fund-raising activities of Kalenga and Banda.[1]

But the compromise achieved by the National Assembly was shattered that same afternoon. As Michello left the meeting he was assaulted by a group of pro-Nkumbula youths. Michello resigned as National Secretary, followed by Kalenga, Banda, and the leading figures of the Mukuba group. Nkumbula's efforts to persuade Michello to return to his post failed, and on 5 August Michello announced the formation of his own party, the People's Democratic Party (P.D.C.).[2]

Meanwhile, the Government was urgently pressing ahead with its plans for an early election under a new democratic constitution. In June the Governor warned Kaunda that with the introduction of universal suffrage the staging of the next election would be a long and difficult task, probably impossible to accomplish before the end of the year.[3] Preparations began in early July immediately after Kaunda and Nkumbula had met with Butler, First Secretary of State, at Victoria Falls for discussions on the new constitution.[4] Writing for advice on the timing of the election to the Governor of Kenya in mid-July, the Chief Secretary indicated that U.N.I.P. was 'desperately anxious' to hold elections before the end of 1963. A.N.C., with its financial difficulties and internal strife, was 'much less enthusiastic about elections and finds all sorts of things to hold things up to May 1964'. Since Northern Rhodesia was to have its new constitution by September or October, the timing of the election depended upon the administrative problems involved. U.N.I.P.'s demands for speed had to be balanced, the Chief Secretary wrote, against the problem of ensuring that the election was run well and appeared fair. 'The coalition', he con-

[1] 'A.N.C. in N.R. 1963', 15 August 1963, DG 123/01.

[2] Ibid.; *Northern News*, 6 August 1963.

[3] A.S. (C.S.) 3 to Ad. Sec., 25 June 1963, MS/2615/37/3, Vol. II, Box 4353, Lusaka Archives.

[4] C.S. to Ad. Sec., 8 July 1963, ibid.; *Central African Mail*, 29 June 1963.

cluded, 'has been most useful, but as time passes its advantages grow less and its disadvantages increase.'[1]

The 1964 Constitution

In mid-July Kaunda began to apply pressure for the granting of a new constitution. Speaking at Mpika he publicly threatened for the first time to break the coalition Government.[2] A.N.C.'s internal difficulties and subsequent split in August only made the Governor's problem more urgent. Before a new constitution could be introduced, however, the question of Barotseland's integration into Northern Rhodesia had to be resolved. While Barotseland had been opened to political parties before the 1962 election, the Litunga steadfastly refused to compromise the Protectorate's special political position in any way. Indeed, in late December 1962 he attempted to restore Barotseland's isolation from the territorial political arena once again by announcing to the District Commissioner, Sesheke, that political meetings had been allowed only for the duration of the election period and that in the future political parties would not be allowed to organize freely or to establish permanent offices in Barotseland.[3]

In January 1963 senior officials from the Central African Office in London met with the Chief Secretary and the Minister of Native Affairs to discuss the strategy to be employed towards Barotseland during the next round of constitutional negotiations. The British officials were anxious to negotiate a new omnibus Barotse agreement which would replace all previous agreements and undertakings between the British Government and Barotseland. So far as the British Government was concerned, Barotseland's future clearly lay with Northern Rhodesia. At a meeting on 26 January it was agreed that the ultimate aim was to integrate Barotseland into Northern Rhodesia. It was recognized that the British Government's ability to sustain its earlier agreements with Barotseland would diminish as independence approached.[4] Meanwhile, it was decided that further

---

[1] c.s. to Governor (Kenya), 13 July 1963, MS/2615/37/3.
[2] *Northern News*, 17 July 1963; s.o. (c.s.) 2 to a.s. (c.s.), 18 July 1963, S/S 119/130/01.
[3] s.b. to Ad. Sec., 31 December 1962, confirmed by u.s. with r.c., 25 January 1963, DG 58/1/01.
[4] Record of Discussions about Barotseland, 26 January 1963, ibid.

attempts should be made to institute political reforms which would produce a more representative Government in Barotseland. If this could be accomplished within the next six months, the way would be cleared for the conclusion of a new Barotseland agreement which could be included as part of Northern Rhodesia's next constitution. If the Litunga continued to press for secession, the British Government would ultimately be forced to issue a blunt statement that should Barotseland break its long-standing links with Northern Rhodesia the Protectorate would be left to face the consequences of its own isolation.[1]

The Government's first step was to re-form the Barotse National Council to include twenty-five elected members. In late May the Barotse Native Government issued an order dealing with the election of members to the National Council, and elections were set for late July. All adult men and women resident and registered as taxpayers in Barotseland were qualified to vote. Candidates for the election, who also had to be registered residents of Barotseland, were required to submit nomination papers signed by seven qualified voters residing in the candidates' respective constituencies. In addition, candidates had to satisfy the District Kuta in their constituencies that they were qualified for election.[2]

As the election approached U.N.I.P. mounted an effective campaign, nominating candidates for each of the twenty-five seats. The Minister of Native Affairs took up once again the thorny question of registering U.N.I.P. branches in Barotseland,[3] and District Commissioners encouraged their Kutas to accept U.N.I.P.-sponsored nominations.[4] Though the Litunga again protested violently against the registration of U.N.I.P. branches, claiming that such an action was in breach of all existing treaties and agreements between the British Government and Barotseland, this time he was overridden.[5]

The National Council elections proved to be a major turning-point in Barotseland politics. U.N.I.P. nominated candidates in all twenty-five seats, seven of them unopposed. U.N.I.P.'s major opposition came from independents, fifty-three of whom con-

[1] Record of Discussions about Barotseland, 26 January 1963, DG 58/1/01.
[2] B.N.G. Order No. 28, 28 May 1963, ibid.
[3] M.N.A. for the Record, 2 July 1963, ibid.
[4] Telephone conversation between M.N.A. and R.C., 2 July 1963, ibid.
[5] P.S. (M.N.A.) for the Record, 3 July 1963, ibid.

tested eighteen seats.[1] Feelings ran high during the ensuing campaign, particularly towards the end of July, when the Litunga visited London for discussions with the British Government on Barotseland's future. Indeed, during the Litunga's absence the Provincial Administration feared a conspiracy amongst a group of the more progressive indunas, backed by certain U.N.I.P. elements, to depose either the Litunga or his Ngambela.[2] The Government took special precautions to prevent such a move,[3] and both Kaunda and A. Wina instructed U.N.I.P.'s Mongu office that on no account should there be trouble in Barotseland.[4] In the end the conspiracy never materialized, and in early August U.N.I.P. won all twenty-five National Council seats.[5]

In September a conference was held with the Litunga at Victoria Falls to attempt to secure at least tentative agreement on the future status of Barotseland. The Litunga and his indunas refused to compromise on the question of Barotseland's special status, which had been most recently reiterated by Macleod while Colonial Secretary in April 1961.[6] As stated then, no constitutional change affecting Barotseland could be made 'without full consultation and the consent of the Litunga and National Council'.[7] On this occasion the Litunga refused to agree to anything more than the holding of the general election in Barotseland.[8] This enabled the British Government to proceed with plans for the new Constitution, the broad features of which were known by the end of September. Press reports drawn from 'informed quarters' revealed that a general election would be held on 20 and 21 January 1964, under a constitution based on universal adult suffrage. The Legislative Council, renamed the Legislative Assembly, was to be expanded to seventy-

---

[1] Position in Barotseland after nominations, 25 July 1963, DG 58/1/01.

[2] See correspondence between 11 and 29 July 1963, ibid. The chief U.N.I.P. figure in the plot was Mundia.

[3] R.C. to P.S. (M.N.A.), 18 July 1963, ibid.

[4] Ibid., 26 July 1963.

[5] Central African Mail, 17 August 1963.

[6] Ibid., 14 September 1963. In fact, the Litunga demanded that Barotseland be established as a High Commission territory with its boundaries drawn to include what in his view was Barotseland's original area of jurisdiction—all of North-Western Province, most of Southern Province and half the Copperbelt; ibid., 31 August 1963.

[7] Northern News, 19 April 1961.

[8] Central African Mail, 14 September 1963.

five members, of whom sixty-five were to be elected in main roll constituencies by African voters and ten in reserved roll constituencies by European voters.[1] Asian and Euro-African persons were to be allowed to choose at the time of registration the roll on which they wished to vote. The Constitution was also to provide for the replacement of the Executive Council with a Cabinet consisting of a Prime Minister and not more than thirteen ministers with portfolios. These were to be assigned by the Government on the advice of the Prime Minister, although the Governor would retain responsibility for defence and external affairs, together with the usual reserved powers. The Constitution was also to contain a Bill of Rights setting forth certain fundamental rights and freedoms of the individual and ensuring protection from discrimination on the ground of race. To strengthen these provisions, the Constitution would provide for the establishment of a Constitutional Council to review any legislation referred to it by not less than seven members of the Legislative Assembly. If such legislation were deemed by the Council to be inconsistent with the Bill of Rights, the legislation could be delayed for six months.[2]

The 1964 Election

There was never much doubt about the outcome of Northern Rhodesia's pre-independence election. The introduction of universal adult suffrage was bound to benefit the party with the most extensive and efficient territorial organization. Despite the weaknesses of the coalition Government, u.n.i.p. was stronger than ever, while a.n.c. and its recent offspring, the p.d.c., were both highly disorganized and bordering on bankruptcy. Unfortunately for Nkumbula and Michello, the British Government was anxious to push ahead as quickly as possible with plans for a January general election.

u.n.i.p. was the only political party which organized a territory-wide registration campaign in preparation for the election. Kaunda encouraged voters of all races to register; at many registration stations, particularly in the towns and in

[1] *Central African Mail*, 28 September 1963. A memorandum for the leaders of the political parties, 'The New Constitution and Election Arrangements for a General Election in January 1964', was circulated by the Chief Secretary on 28 August 1963; MS/2615/37/3, Vol. II, Box 4353, Lusaka Archives.
[2] Northern Rhodesia (Constitution) Order in Council, 1963.

marginal areas such as Southern Province, U.N.I.P. teams took the name of each applicant who supported the party. These lists later served as a valuable guide both for placing candidates in constituencies and for canvassing operations.[1] Meanwhile, A.N.C. and the P.D.C. continued their feud, which by this time was less concerned with policy differences than it was with which of the two rivals could secure the Tshombe funds. In mid-August, Michello and several of his colleagues flew to Spain to plead their case before Tshombe, who at that time was staying in Barcelona. Also in the P.D.C. group was Roy Horrell, formerly Nkumbula's European adviser and go-between with Welensky.[2] When Michello and his party returned to Northern Rhodesia on 6 September, after having visited London and Dakar, the group reportedly possessed £1,350 in traveller's cheques and 300 copies of a cyclostyled letter to appeal for funds from abroad.[3]

Michello then convened the P.D.C.'s inaugural conference, during which he claimed that financial aid had been promised to the new party by a 'certain man', provided that the present leadership of A.N.C. was reorganized and the two parties merged once again. That Michello's claims were not merely empty words was borne out by the fact that before the end of September the P.D.C. had taken delivery of thirty-eight new and second-hand vehicles from two of Lusaka's main automobile dealers, making a small down payment in cash and negotiating the balance by postdated cheques payable before the end of October.[4] In early October the P.D.C. acquired seventeen additional second-hand vehicles, but by this time both dealers had threatened that unless a cash payment were made soon the automobiles would be repossessed.[5]

A.N.C. faced serious financial problems as well. At the end of August, its debts were estimated to be approximately £34,000, and the party's movable assets were being seized and sold under

[1] Mulford, D. C., 'Some Observations on the 1964 General Election', *Africa Report*, February 1964, p. 14.

[2] s.b. to p.s. (c.s.), 21 August 1963, GHS/S 119/016.

[3] Ibid., 30 September 1963. It was not clear where Michello obtained these funds; press reports at the time claimed that he had been unsucceessful with Tshombe; *Central African Mail*, 31 August 1963.

[4] s.b. to p.s. (c.s.), 30 September 1963, GHS/S 119/016.

[5] s.b. to p.s. (c.s.), 10 October 1963, GHS/S 119/016.

writs issued by the High Court.[1] Proceeds from the public auction of twelve A.N.C. vehicles hardly made a mark on the party's debts. More than a dozen Lusaka business firms to which A.N.C. owed over £12,000 also brought actions against the party.[2] To raise the additional funds, Nkumbula imposed a direct levy on A.N.C. members, but this was a source the old leader had exhausted in the past, and in any case only a small portion of such funds ever reached the national headquarters in A.N.C.'s organization.[3] Nkumbula also sought assistance from Tshombe, first by letter and then by paying a personal visit to Tshombe in Europe. However, Tshombe, who in September had written a letter to Kaunda offering to act as 'peacemaker' in Northern Rhodesian politics, reportedly refused all pleas for aid not only from A.N.C. but also from the P.D.C.[4]

The one objective which A.N.C. and the P.D.C. shared at this time was to force the British Government to postpone the general election until at least May 1964 after the end of the annual wet season. Michello met with the Governor on 18 September to complain about the iniquities of the Government's registration plans and demanded that the election be postponed on the ground that the British Government had pledged in February 1961 that it would not allow any elections to be held in Northern Rhodesia during the rains. Pointing out that it had taken three months to register 120,000 new voters in 1962, Michello argued that the Government's plans to register more than 1,000,000 voters in two weeks were completely unrealistic and could not hope to achieve an equitable registration.[5]

Nkumbula and Roberts were also critical of the Government's plan for registration. Nkumbula, of course, simply wanted registration and the election postponed in order to gain time to replenish A.N.C.'s coffers and to restore some measure of coherent organization to the party.[6] Roberts complained about a number of procedural weaknesses which he believed would open the 'whole registration setup . . . to a mammoth fiddle'.

[1] S.B. to P.S. (C.S.), 4 September 1963, TS/S 123/02; *Central African Mail*, 31 August 1963.
[2] S.B. to P.S. (C.S.), 12 September 1963, TS/S 123/02.
[3] Ibid., 4 September 1963.
[4] *Central African Mail*, 31 August, 21 September, and 5 October 1963.
[5] Record of meeting at G.H., 18 September 1963, GHS/S 119/016.
[6] *Central African Mail*, 21 September 1963.

He also attempted to persuade the Chief Secretary to agree to a system of automatic re-registration for upper roll Europeans, 15 per cent of whom Roberts contended would be outside the country on holiday or business trips during the two-week registration period.[1]

The Governor and Chief Secretary disregarded all such demands and registration proceeded on schedule during the two-week period 23 September to 6 October. With the introduction of universal adult suffrage, the government officials were anxious to achieve as large a registration as possible, though they did not go so far as to accept a proposal Kaunda made in June that voters' rolls should be abolished altogether. Indeed, the Central Registering Officer had indicated at the time that there were more than 3,000 registered white aliens in the territory, approximately 5,000 white South Africans, and several thousands of alien Africans, all of whom would be able to vote if restrictions on registration were dropped. 'Would Roberts be overjoyed to know that long-haired fabians had marched in and exercised their votes—and would the Litunga be pleased to know that gangs of P.O.Q.O. types from South Africa and Z.A.P.U. chappies from Southern Rhodesia had knocked his candidates into a cocked hat by the exercise of a democratic right?'[2]

In the event the new Constitution set only minimal requirements for prospective voters.[3] The Territory was divided into 1,500 areas (each containing approximately 1,000 prospective voters) to validate the registration of the vast numbers of new voters. The Government also launched a massive publicity campaign, and in the two-week registration period, 1,379,804 on the main roll and 23,981 on the reserved roll claimed their votes. Almost to a man Asians and Euro-Africans followed U.N.I.P.'s instructions and registered with Europeans on the reserved roll.[4]

During November the Delimitation Commission divided Northern Rhodesia into sixty-five main roll and ten reserved

[1] Roberts to Governor, 18 September 1963, MS/2615/37/3, Vol. II, Box 4353, Lusaka Archives.

[2] Memorandum on General Election, Central Registering Officer to C.E.O., 1 July 1963, MS/2615/37/3, Vol. II, Box 4353, Lusaka Archives.

[3] The Northern Rhodesia (Constitution) Order in Council, 1963.

[4] Mulford, D. C., 'Some Observations on the 1964 General Election', *Africa Report*, February 1964, p. 14.

roll constituencies. The main roll constituencies, fifteen of which were based on urban areas, had electorates of approximately 21,000 voters, while the reserved roll constituencies contained between 1,800 and 2,900 voters apiece. Because of the disproportionate concentration of Northern Rhodesia's European population along the 'line of rail', urban voters predominated in all the reserved constituencies, despite the fact that five of the ten constituencies stretched hundreds of miles into the country.[1] Perhaps the most significant feature of the reserved roll was that Asian and Euro-African voters, most of whom sympathized with U.N.I.P., formed approximately 10 per cent of the reserved roll electorate. In several constituencies the non-European proportion was considerably higher (Ndola, Broken Hill, Luangwa, Midlands), though nowhere did it exceed 18 per cent.[2]

By November A.N.C.'s financial situation was critical. In the High Court a Northern Province trader instituted an action concerning alleged A.N.C. debts against the party's three ministers in the coalition Government, Nkumbula, Stubbs, and Cousins.[3] Further approaches to Tshombe in October had failed and Nkumbula was clearly casting about for some means of securing funds to fight the coming election.[4] Unity talks were held with the P.D.C., but Michello's terms—that P.D.C. supply two-thirds of the candidates in safe A.N.C. seats in return for financial support from the P.D.C.—were flatly rejected by Nkumbula.[5] In any case, the P.D.C., although in a stronger financial position than A.N.C., was itself short of funds, because Michello had never gained access to Tshombe's famous £100,000. Nkumbula also met with U.N.I.P.'s leaders reportedly to discuss a merger of the two parties, but Kaunda insisted on the complete dissolution of A.N.C. and would accept Nkumbula only as a regular U.N.I.P. member without special privileges or a party office.[6]

In November there was a marked deterioration in the general

[1] *Report of the Delimitation Commission*, 29 November 1963.
[2] Mulford, D. C., 'Some Observations on the 1964 General Election', *Africa Report*, February 1964, p. 14.
[3] *Central African Mail*, 1 November 1963.
[4] Ibid., 15 November 1963.
[5] Ibid., 29 November 1963.
[6] Ibid.

security situation. Undoubtedly, this was partly due to the upsurge in rural political activity which during the past few months
had accompanied the reconstituting of Northern Rhodesia's
Native Authority Councils to include a larger elected element.[1]
When it became clear that U.N.I.P. would dominate the new
elected positions in most areas and with the new system of rural
District Councils being introduced during late 1963,[2] Northern
Rhodesia chiefs, despite repeated assurances from U.N.I.P.'s
national leaders, expressed anxiety about their future status
under an independent African Government.[3] Certainly, the
chiefs' experiences with the first reconstituted Native Authority
Councils appeared to confirm these fears. In North-Western
Province, U.N.I.P.'s elected councillors refused to co-operate with
either the chiefs or the District Commissioner. In a meeting of
the finance committee, for example, the U.N.I.P. councillors
passed a resolution that the Native Authority should purchase
ten Land-Rovers for the elected councillors and consider a
sitting fee for them of £30 per month.[4] Similar instances of
friction between U.N.I.P. councillors and the traditional elements
of Native Authority Councils occurred in other areas as well.[5]
Violent clashes between the supporters of the three African
parties also became more frequent,[6] while on the Copperbelt
attempts were renewed to heal the split in the A.M.W.U. which
had plagued the African trade union movement for nearly a
year.[7] On the constitutional front, there were rumours of delays
which the Press attributed to renewed intransigence on the
part of the Litunga.[8]

    In late November the first reports appeared of an A.N.C.-
P.D.C. plan to sabotage the general election, despite the earlier
collapse of negotiations to merge the two parties.[9] It was also
rumoured that Tshombe was making preparations to return to

[1] Political Situation series, DG 58/1/01 to DG 58/8/01, June–September 1963.
[2] *Central African Mail*, 7 September 1963.
[3] Ibid., 8 November 1963.
[4] D.C. (Solwezi) to P.C. (N.W.P.), 30 November 1963, DG 58/6/01.
[5] P.C. (N.W.P.) to P.S. (M.N.A.), 2 December 1963, ibid.; also A.S. to U.S., 19 July 1963, DG 58/4/01.
[6] *Central African Mail*, 25 October and 1 November 1963; *Northern News*, November 1963, *passim*.
[7] *Central African Mail*, 15 November and 6 December 1963.
[8] Ibid., 1 November 1963.
[9] Ibid., 22 November 1963.

Katanga, and at least one version told of plans for the re-creation under Tshombe of a huge Lunda empire sweeping from north-east Angola across the north-western corner of Northern Rhodesia and into Katanga.[1] In a more practical vein, Nkumbula was suddenly confronted with difficulties amongst his own ministers and parliamentary secretaries. Cousins, who for many months had been critical of Nkumbula's leadership, was expelled from A.N.C. and two weeks later joined U.N.I.P.[2] On 17 December, three days before the close of nominations, Banda, A.N.C.'s Director of Elections, resigned and fled to Dar es Salaam. 'I have lost confidence in your leader-ship', Banda wrote to Nkumbula, and 'I am disappointed with the way you are conducting the elections'. He continued:

Every time I have been appointed to do a job, you have always made it a point to interfere. . . . You have been interested more in your Southern Province. . . . You have lost the confidence of the world leaders, including your old friend Tshombe. . . . I had wanted to stay on with you to the end. But your artificial courage is baseless. . . . Last Friday, in my house, you admitted to me that you as a leader were finished as long ago as 1958 and that if Congress won more than seven seats, 'we'll be lucky'.[3]

Nkumbula's situation was desperate. In addition to A.N.C.'s financial difficulties, Nkumbula faced a deep-seated conflict in the party over the assigning of prospective candidates to safe A.N.C. constituencies.[4] This was the issue which provoked Banda's resignation, for despite the poor quality of most A.N.C. aspirants, there simply were not enough safe constituencies to distribute amongst A.N.C.'s national office bearers and provincial level officials. Nor in seeking to co-operate or to merge with another group could Nkumbula hope to negotiate from a posi-tion of strength. He had nothing to offer except the purely negative threat that in those constituencies with both A.N.C. and P.D.C. candidates they would inevitably split the anti-U.N.I.P. vote.

[1] *Central African Mail*, 29 November and 28 December 1963.
[2] Ibid., 13 December 1963.
[3] *Central African Mail*, 20 December 1963.
[4] Interviews with A.N.C. regional officials, Lusaka and Ndola, January 1964; Report on nomination days by the C.E.O., 30 December 1963, MS/2615/37/3, Vol. II, Box 4353, Lusaka Archives.

As nomination day, 20 December, drew near, it was clear that U.N.I.P. would dominate the sixty-five seats on the main roll. The only question of interest was how U.N.I.P. would fare in those areas where A.N.C. had shown strength in the 1962 election; Southern Province; west of the railway in Central Province; Mufulira town; and Mwinilungu District in the north-west corner of the Territory.[1] Nkumbula defiantly declared that 'broke or not, A.N.C. will fight the election'.[2] Meanwhile, U.N.I.P. was having its own problems placing candidates in early December. When Kaunda announced U.N.I.P.'s proposed list of candidates, the A.M.W.U. and the U.T.U.C. both complained bitterly of insufficient representation for Northern Rhodesia's African trade-union movement.[3]

Immediately before nomination day A.N.C. and the P.D.C. settled their differences and merged once again, a move which further complicated both parties' already confused nomination plans.[4] In fact, actual nominations suggested that no merger had taken place at all: A.N.C. and P.D.C. candidates found themselves competing in a number of constituencies, while U.N.I.P. candidates were left unopposed in twenty-five of the sixty-five main roll seats.[5] Nkumbula immediately petitioned the Government to reopen nominations, charging that a number of A.N.C.-P.D.C. candidates had been prevented from submitting their nomination papers by groups of U.N.I.P. 'thugs'. Several such cases had, in fact, occurred, and the Governor agreed to accept further nominations and to allow withdrawals on 28 December. Government officials also knew that the signatures on a number of A.N.C.-P.D.C. candidates' nomination papers had been forged, but since returning officers had already accepted the nominations, they could not be withdrawn.[6] Not surprisingly Nkumbula failed to take advantage of the situation. Although by shifting a number of candidates he reduced to four the number of constituencies in which A.N.C. and the P.D.C. were opposed,

[1] Mulford, *The N.R. General Election, 1962*, p. 190.
[2] *Central African Mail*, 13 December 1963.
[3] Ibid.
[4] *Central African Mail*, 20 December 1963; Report on nomination days by the C.E.O., 30 December 1963, MS/2615/37/3, Vol. II, Box 4353, Lusaka Archives.
[5] *Northern News*, 23 December 1963.
[6] Report on nomination days by the C.E.O., 30 December 1963, MS/2615/37/3, Vol. II, Box 4353, Lusaka Archives. The only course of action which was open in such cases was to bring the matter to court. In several instances this was done.

he failed to produce the additional candidates required to make up a full team. When nominations closed for the second time, U.N.I.P. nominees remained unopposed in twenty-four main roll seats.[1] As in the 1962 election U.N.I.P. fielded a formidable team of candidates. Thirteen of U.N.I.P.'s fourteen incumbents sought re-election, and two of the party's top national leaders, Chona and Mundia, contested seats for the first time. In the previous election they had been barred from standing by the electoral regulations because both were serving suspended prison sentences. This time, because Chona was still serving a suspended sentence, the order in council was amended to enable him to stand.[2] But the most significant feature of U.N.I.P.'s slate was the great influx of candidates from the party's regional level organization. In 1962 Kaunda had sought European support by presenting candidates not associated by Europeans with U.N.I.P.'s past. Not one of U.N.I.P.'s loyal organizers from below headquarters level had been selected then, and although several of U.N.I.P.'s national office bearers had won seats, so had a number of men who were not 'old guard' politicans.[3] In 1964 the picture was radically different. Over a third of U.N.I.P.'s sixty-five main roll candidates were regional level officials; eight had been U.N.I.P. representatives overseas; and fourteen were national office bearers or held official posts at Freedom House in Lusaka. The new pattern was even more apparent in the allocation of constituencies. With the exception of three regional secretaries in Southern Province, junior party officials were given safe seats.[4]

The 1964 election lacked the colour and excitement which had marked the general election of October 1962. With nearly half the main roll seats uncontested, the final result was a foregone conclusion. Apart from mobilizing its massive support throughout the country and explaining to the many disappointed voters in the uncontested constituencies why they were

[1] *Northern News*, 30 December 1963.

[2] The Northern Rhodesia (Electoral Provisions) (No. 2) Order in Council, 1963; Report on nomination days by the C.E.O., 30 December 1963, MS/2615/37/3, Vol. II, Box 4353, Lusaka Archives.

[3] Mulford, *The N.R. General Election, 1962*, p. 93.

[4] Mulford, D. C., 'Some Observations on the 1964 General Election', *Africa Report*, February 1964, pp. 14–15.

not able to use their newly acquired votes, u.n.i.p. directed its main campaign efforts to the marginal areas such as Southern Province, Mulfilira, and parts of Central, Eastern and North-Western Province. u.n.i.p. held most of its mass rallies in these areas, and during the course of the campaign a number of bloody conflicts occurred between supporters of the rival parties.[1] In many instances u.n.i.p.'s top national leaders played only a limited part in the main roll campaign, instead devoting considerable time to assisting the party's European and Asian candidates in reserved roll constituencies.[2]

Meanwhile, Nkumbula intensified his efforts to have the election postponed. In early January, after his demands for a postponement had been flatly rejected by the Governor, Nkumbula accused the Government of favouring u.n.i.p. and of 'fixing' nominations to ensure the destruction of a.n.c. Nkumbula called for the immediate removal of the Governor and announced that unless a.n.c.'s demands were met he would launch a 'master plan' to prevent the holding of the election.[3] Apparently, there was a good deal more to Nkumbula's threats than ever came out in the Press. Nkumbula, Michello, and Liso visualized disturbances on the order of those which had occurred during 1961 in Northern Province. Roadblocks were to be thrown up in Southern Province, trains derailed, tribal animosities stirred up, and arms smuggled into the Territory for the killing of u.n.i.p. candidates. In September a.n.c. had assisted ex-Katangese gendarmes to obtain Northern Rhodesia passports to facilitate their movement to Spain to see Tshombe. Now a.n.c. was said to be organizing ex-gendarmes to come to Northern Rhodesia to help launch the party's 'master plan'.[4] One report even went so far as to claim that a private farm in Northern Rhodesia with its own airstrip was being prepared to provide cover for arms and ex-gendarmes.[5] Even if the reports were true, which for the most part appeared to be doubtful, the

---

[1] *Central African Mail*, 3, 10, and 17 January 1964; *Northern News*, 1–20 January 1964, *passim*.

[2] Analysis in this paragraph is based on field research in Northern Rhodesia during the 1964 campaign.

[3] *Central African Mail*, 3 January 1964; Circular to all Divisional s.b. Officers, 6 January 1964, TS/S 123/01.

[4] Circular to all Divisional s.b. Officers, 6 January 1964, TS/S 123/01.

[5] Record of discussions between Kaunda and Governor, 8 January 1964, ibid.

important question was whether A.N.C. itself was well enough organized to initiate any kind of 'master plan'. If the party's election campaign was any indication, the answer was clearly negative. The Government took no chances, however, and put both the army and the police on the alert for possible trouble before the two-day poll.[1] In the event A.N.C.'s 'master plan' never amounted to anything more than an empty threat. Indeed, the party appeared to become more and more demoralized with every week that passed. Several A.N.C. candidates resigned and began campaigning for U.N.I.P., and Nkumbula, in his last press interview before the poll, seemed to have resigned himself to A.N.C.'s imminent defeat.[2]

The reserved roll, particularly the European voters, posed the more interesting if less significant challenge of the campaign. In the 1962 election the N.P.P., then the U.F.P., had secured almost universal support from Northern Rhodesia's whites, despite U.N.I.P.'s intensive year-long European campaign. Except for the short-lived anti-European reaction which had swept U.N.I.P. after it had been rejected by whites in 1962, U.N.I.P. had not given up its campaign for European acceptance and support.[3]

The N.P.P., campaigning under the slogan 'experience counts', nominated ten reserved roll candidates—nine of them former members of the Legislative Council. The crux of the N.P.P.'s claim for support lay in the argument that Europeans who identified themselves with an African nationalist governing party could never hope to represent their community adequately or to influence the course of government policy. Although the N.P.P.'s maximum strength in the new Legislative Assembly would be limited to ten seats, the party's leader, John Roberts, continually emphasized the importance of the Constitutional Council which could be brought into action on the initiative of only seven legislators. Roberts argued that the fundamental principle of democracy was the two-party system, and that it was the N.P.P.'s task to play the role of the constructive opposi-

[1] *Central African Mail*, 17 January 1964.
[2] *Zambia News*, 12 and 19 January 1964.
[3] *Report on General Election Outcome by the Director of Elections to the National Council of U.N.I.P.*, 10 and 11 November 1962, author's collection.

tion in Northern Rhodesia. Roberts justified a purely racial opposition on the grounds that the party represented the minority group which held economic power in the country— a group which only incidentally happened to be European. For the next few years, Roberts contended, a u.n.i.p. government would need the experienced advisers offered by the n.p.p.; and it was preferable that these men should be free to advise publicly and independently of u.n.i.p.'s party whip.[1]

u.n.i.p. contested all ten reserved roll seats. Its most outstanding European candidates, though well known, were all relatively new to u.n.i.p.: C. Cousins (Luangwa); Richard Sampson (Midlands), former mayor of Lusaka, and a u.n.i.p. member for less than a year; and the former leader of the Liberal Party, Sir John Moffat, who stood in the important Ndola seat.

u.n.i.p.'s ministers and parliamentary secretaries campaigned vigorously for non-African support, promising 'representation in government' in return. It was far better, Kaunda argued, to influence government policy from the inside; u.n.i.p. would listen more readily to friends within the Government than to a single racial bloc across the aisle. He stressed Northern Rhodesia's need to move forward as one nation, not two nations in one, and he promised publicly to abolish the reserved seats before the Territory achieved independence. But Kaunda also warned Europeans that he simply could not continue to seek their support indefinitely unless he achieved concrete results in this election. Already many of his supporters had lost faith in the white man, he warned, and there was constant pressure on u.n.i.p.'s leadership to ignore Europeans altogether.[2]

Europeans were clearly in a state of indecision during the campaign. However, u.n.i.p.'s reserved roll meetings were relatively well attended, while the n.p.p. was hard pressed to attract an audience of fifty.[3] As polling day approached it was impossible to predict with any certainty whether Europeans would continue to support the n.p.p., swing towards the wave of the future, or abstain from voting altogether, thereby greatly im-

[1] Notes from public meetings, January 1964, author's collection; *Zambia News*, 15 January 1964.
[2] Notes from public meetings, January 1964, author's collection.
[3] *Central African Mail*, 17 January 1964.

proving U.N.I.P.'s reserved roll prospects, especially in those constituencies with large numbers of Asian and Euro-African
voters.

Northern Rhodesia's leading European newspaper headlined
the general election result as 'Kaunda's Greatest Triumph'.[1]
U.N.I.P. had both mobilized and controlled its overwhelming
African following in the country; maintained its prodigious
party organization intact; and secured the electoral support of
nearly a third of Northern Rhodesia's Europeans. On the main
roll, U.N.I.P. achieved its predicted victory without difficulty,
securing fifty-five of the sixty-five seats in an overall percentage
poll of 94.3. The popular vote—which gave U.N.I.P. 69.6 per
cent of the votes cast and A.N.C. 30.5 per cent—did not provide
a true picture of U.N.I.P.'s strength in the country, because the
twenty-four uncontested seats would all have been won by
U.N.I.P. with substantial majorities.

Nevertheless, A.N.C.'s ten seats represented something of a
setback to U.N.I.P., which had organized a major campaign
effort in A.N.C. areas. The results suggested that A.N.C.'s strength
in the country, or conversely African opposition to U.N.I.P.
generally, bore little relation to the strength and efficiency of
A.N.C.'s party organization. As in 1962, A.N.C. was clearly a
tribally-based party deriving its greatest support from the
Tonga-speaking groups in Central and Southern Provinces,
together with marked support amongst the Lunda of Mwinilungu District in the North-West. The fact that A.N.C. won
Chisamba constituency south of Broken Hill, and amassed noteworthy support in Lusaka (approximately a third of the total
votes cast) and in parts of Eastern Province, suggested that
U.N.I.P.'s future policies were likely to meet with opposition in
these areas, irrespective of A.N.C.'s fate as a political party.
U.N.I.P.'s great strength, on the other hand, was on the Copperbelt, in Barotseland, in parts of Eastern Province, and amongst
the Bemba-speaking people of both Northern and Luapula
Provinces. Most A.N.C. candidates in these areas lost their
deposits. U.N.I.P. also registered two impressive new victories
over A.N.C.; one in Mulfulira, long A.N.C.'s only Copperbelt

[1] *Northern News*, 23 January 1964. A full record of the results may be found in
Central African Mail, 24 January 1964.

stronghold; and the other in Livingstone, where Chona secured
U.N.I.P.'s only seat in Southern Province by a majority of 489
votes out of 19,841 votes cast.

On the two polling days Europeans turned out in relatively
large numbers, recording an average poll of 73 per cent. When
the votes were counted U.N.I.P. failed to win a single reserved
seat. European voting patterns, however, were radically different from the 1962 election; U.N.I.P. candidates fell short of
victory in Luangwa and Ndola by only 70 and 120 votes respectively. A swing of under 400 votes would have brought U.N.I.P.
four reserved seats. U.N.I.P. captured 35.2 per cent of the reserved roll vote and the N.P.P. 63 per cent. Compared to the
1962 election, and making allowances for the considerable
Asian and Euro-African vote which U.N.I.P. received, U.N.I.P.'s
European support had increased approximately nine- or tenfold
in less than fifteen months.

Despite U.N.I.P.'s failure to win a single reserved seat, Northern Rhodesia's European community had been divided for the
first time.[1] With the U.F.P.'s virtually unanimous control of the
white community in previous elections reduced in 1964 to less
than two-thirds support on the reserved roll, Roberts could
hardly claim that the N.P.P. held a clear mandate for preserving
the ten reserved seats after independence. Indeed, had it not
been for the *coup d'état* in Zanzibar on 12 January and the army
mutiny a week later in Tanganyika, U.N.I.P. might well have
won several reserved seats. Europeans were particularly shaken
by the violence in Tanganyika, which occurred on the first of
Northern Rhodesia's two polling days, and by the initial
rumours that Nyerere had disappeared.[2] They were well aware
of the close friendship between Kaunda and Nyerere, and many
whites believed that Kaunda had fashioned his leadership of
U.N.I.P. on Nyerere's example in Tanganyika. That Nyerere had
now apparently lost control undoubtedly worked to Kaunda's
disadvantage amongst the European voters. Nevertheless, in the
long run U.N.I.P.'s failure to win reserved seats probably
strengthened Kaunda's position. Having demonstrated significant European support without actually winning the seats,

---

[1] U.N.I.P. did have one European M.P. James Skinner, who was elected in one
of the main roll seats in Lusaka.

[2] *Northern News*, 21 January 1964.

Kaunda could not fulfil his campaign pledge to remove the reserved seats before independence without his action affecting U.N.I.P. M.P.S.[1]

As soon as U.N.I.P.'s majority was confirmed, Northern Rhodesia's Governor invited Kaunda, as the country's first Prime Minister, to form his new Government.[2] Kaunda's parliamentary party was much changed from 1962, when half of U.N.I.P.'s fourteen legislators held no party offices of any kind, a number having officially joined the party only a short time before. In 1964 the 'old guard' predominated; more than two-thirds of U.N.I.P.'s fifty-five Members were professional politicians—twenty-two regional-level officials, fourteen national office bearers or headquarters officials, and eight former overseas representatives.

In selecting his thirteen Cabinet ministers Kaunda drew heavily on this group. Distributing the portfolios among them, however, was not an easy task, in part at least because U.N.I.P. had become a genuine national party encompassing all of Northern Rhodesia's various political and economic, linguistic and regional groups. Whereas in 1962 with only three ministerial posts to fill Kaunda had simply appointed in addition to himself the two most senior men in the party, this time he was faced with the problem of balancing U.N.I.P.'s various factions. It was not simply a question of militants and moderates, or the 'old guard' against the 'new' men. There was also the need to balance linguistic and tribal groups to allay the fears of domination by the militant Bemba-speaking North which many of U.N.I.P.'s other leaders shared. Kaunda also wished to promote to Cabinet positions several of U.N.I.P.'s most highly qualified 'new' men such as Mwanakatwe and Mudenda, who had served as parliamentary secretaries in the coalition Government, but who had not had time to build up a firm political base either in the party or in the country generally. There were also the trade unionists to consider, not to mention the men whose strongest claims to a Cabinet post were loyalty to Kaunda and long service to the nationalist movement. At one point during the negotiations U.N.I.P.'s Lozi leaders threatened to withdraw from the party altogether, unless they were granted

[1] *Zambia News*, 12 January 1964.
[2] *Northern News*, 23 January 1964.

what they regarded as adequate representation in the new Cabinet. In the case of one appointment Kaunda was threatened with physical violence if he refused to assign one of U.N.I.P.'s most militant and long-standing leaders to a certain ministerial post.[1]

In the end Kaunda formed a well-balanced and extremely capable Government.[2] Seven of his ministers had gained experience in the coalition Government as ministers or parliamentary secretaries. Amongst the other appointments, all except Banda and Kalulu had either been outside the country in 1962 or barred from standing for election then because they were under suspended prison sentences. Northern Rhodesia's major linguistic groups and provinces (except North-Western Province) were all represented; four ministers, including Kaunda, were from the Bemba-speaking North; four were Lozi from Barotseland; three were from the Nyanja-speaking Eastern Province; two were Tongas from the South; and one was a Soli from Central Province.[3] Balance was also achieved in the four most important posts below the Prime Minister. Kapwepwe, a militant nationalist and a Bemba, held the powerful portfolio of Home Affairs. A. Wina, a Lozi, was given the Ministry of Finance, where he had been the Parliamentary Secretary in the coalition Government. The Education portfolio was assigned to Mwanakatwe, a Bemba with moderate political views and one of U.N.I.P.'s most able 'new' men in 1962. Banda, U.N.I.P.'s militant Director of Youth and a Ngoni from Eastern Province, became Minister of Housing and Social Development, which included responsibility for the country's youth programmes.

The other ministers who had served in the coalition Government included Kamanga (Transport and Communications), U.N.I.P.'s Vice-President and a Chewa from Eastern Province; Alexander Zulu (Commerce and Industry), also from Eastern Province; A. Wina (Health) from Barotseland; and Mudenda (Agriculture), a Tonga from the South who, like Mwanakatwe,

---

[1] This account of the difficulties which Kaunda faced during his Cabinet negotiations was obtained from a reliable source whom the author is not at liberty to name.

[2] *Central African Mail*, 24 January 1964.

[3] The various tribal-linguistic groups were as follows: Bemba—Kaunda, Kapwepwe, Chimba, Mwanakatwe; Lozi—S. Wina, A. Wina, Sipalo, Mundia; Nyanja—Kamanga, Banda, Zulu; Tonga—Chona, Mudenda; Soli—Kalulu.

had joined U.N.I.P. in 1962 and was thought of more as a skilled technician than a politician.

Six members of the Cabinet had no previous experience in government. Sipalo, who had recovered from the severe burns he had suffered in a petrol-bomb attack in December 1962, was named to the Ministry of Natural Resources. Chimba, who was given the important position of Minister of Labour and Mines, had only recently returned from Cairo, where for several years he had added considerably to his reputation as one of the most militant of all U.N.I.P.'s leaders. His appointment dismayed both white Civil Servants and Northern Rhodesia's European business and mining groups. Kalulu was named to Land and Works after a year of intensive party work following his defeat in the 1962 election. Mundia and Chona, both of whom had been barred from election in 1962 by the electoral regulations, were assigned the portfolios of Local Government and Justice respectively. Party professionals also dominated U.N.I.P.'s sixteen parliamentary secretary appointments; twelve were party officials, eight of them seasoned organizers who held positions below headquarters level at the time of the election. The others included two prominent trade unionists, Chisata and Chivunga, as well as U.N.I.P.'s only European M.P., James Skinner.

Thus, Northern Rhodesia's first African party Government was sworn into office, setting the stage for Zambia's final step to independence. The country accepted the result of the election calmly. The mass exodus of Europeans so often predicted by white politicians in the past never occurred. A.N.C. stripped now of the power it had enjoyed during the days of the coalition, and the N.P.P. fell to quarrelling over the title of official opposition. The P.D.C. disappeared from the scene completely, Michello resuming his old position in A.N.C. Only the final Constitution remained to be settled before October. Kaunda had set the date of Zambia's independence even before the general election. The date he selected—24 October 1964—symbolized Zambia's future as well as its past, for it marked not only the nineteenth anniversary of the United Nations, but also the date on which six years earlier Kaunda had led his followers from A.N.C. to the Zambia African National Congress.

IX

CONCLUSION

NORTHERN RHODESIA'S independence Constitution, which was agreed upon in May 1964, introduced a republican form of government when Zambia became an independent nation in October 1964. Important as this change undoubtedly was, the basic characteristics of Zambian politics had been set during the period between 1957 and 1964. The changes which occurred during these years were fundamental; indeed, in Northern Rhodesia's political context at that time the changes might well be regarded as revolutionary. In the short space of five years, the Territory's African electorate had virtually mushroomed from eleven voters to nearly a million and a half. White minority rule, the reality of power for more than fifty years, was reversed in favour of African majority government in the short space of four years. What for the past decade had been a poorly organized African nationalist movement was transformed in less than two years into a mass nationalist political party, organized to mobilize the African people and to achieve and exercise political power. African leaders, who in the past were obscure to the European community and harrassed by the Provincial Administration, suddenly achieved prominence, first becoming national figures and later ministers or parliamentary secretaries in the new Government.

National consciousness amongst Africans in Northern Rhodesia had clearly emerged well before the Territory's transition to African government in the late 1950's. Africans—the progressive, who taught school or were active religious leaders; the uneducated, who were drawn to the towns and mines; and even Africans in rural areas who resented the new order of the white men—had long resented white domination. Initially, Africans had simply resisted the general conditions of life under which they lived. It was not until after World War II that these protests began to give way to a broader African identity which manifested itself in the political consciousness of being *African*, a Northern Rhodesia African. This marked the emergence of African nationalism in Northern Rhodesia and clearly represented a response to the white settlers' drive for power. The crucial stimulant was the threat of amalgamation between Northern and Southern Rhodesia. In the late 1940's, during the struggle over Federation, Africans remained adamant in resisting what they regarded as nothing less than an alternative and more subtle form of amalgamation. This struggle, in which Africans saw their deeply held feelings as well as their future political interests blatantly overridden by white politicians and the British Government, did more than any other single development to kindle African national consciousness.

That Northern Rhodesia's first surge of African nationalism rested almost wholly on the issue of Federation was revealed by the rapid decline of that surge after Federation had been imposed in 1953. A.N.C. failed to build a strong organization during its early years, partly because it lacked the resources, partly because its leaders were preoccupied with the struggle against Federation, and also because in the period leading up to 1953 A.N.C. had not needed an organization to reach the African people. Once Federation had been imposed, A.N.C.'s situation changed. Africans appeared resigned to the fact of Federation, and A.N.C.'s leaders were confronted with the harsh realities of organizing a mass political party in Northern Rhodesia. The leadership was slow to take up the challenge. A.N.C. underwent a marked deterioration; its leaders were discouraged, its former followers disillusioned by A.N.C.'s failure to prevent Federation. Many provincial, district, and branch leaders turned their attention to community political activities in their respective local areas. Many participated in local African societies or in the Government's system of Urban Advisory and African Provincial Councils. A number turned to trade-union affairs as well, and a few remained active in the periodic meetings of the African Representative Council.

The hard core of A.N.C.'s leaders, however, faced up to the bleak challenge of organizing a more effective political party. They faced a vast country whose sparse population was concentrated along the railway and in several far-flung areas, a country with only one railway line, fewer than half a dozen

major roads, and an extremely primitive communications network. They faced tribal and linguistic diversity, tribally mixed
populations on the Copperbelt and in the railway towns, and
perhaps most important a psychological attitude of subservience
amongst Africans, the result of fifty years of white domination.
These, however, were not the only obstacles. A.N.C.'s leaders
also lacked equipment and funds, which would have to be
drawn, initially at least, from sources which had already
financed the unsuccessful campaign against Federation. Finally,
as they worked and sought to draw upon the limited pool of
trained Africans, A.N.C.'s leaders ran up against the hostility of
the white 'establishment', which controlled both the Government and the economy.

These were the years during which Kaunda was A.N.C.'s
General Secretary. Before August 1953 he had organized
Northern Province, travelling from place to place by bicycle,
giving speeches and entertaining village gatherings by playing
his battered guitar. In the period after 1953, A.N.C.'s resources
for organizing the whole territory were little better than those
Kaunda had in Northern Province. The first signs of a revival
of significant political activity came with the boycotts of 1955
and 1956. Nkumbula and Kaunda had both served prison terms
during the interim, and Kaunda had come out of prison with a
new view of the kind of leadership which would be required
for the future. Not long afterwards Kapwepwe and Sipalo returned to Northern Rhodesia from overseas, and Kaunda gained
his valuable training in political organization with the Labour
Party in Britain.

Meanwhile, the Federal Government's drive for dominion
status began to take shape, as did the British Government's
apparent willingness to acquiesce in whatever political advantages Welensky managed to seize. By mid-1957 the Federal
Government's disregard for African opinion, not to mention
African political aspirations, had also emerged into the harsh
light of reality during the struggle over the Constitution Amendment Act and the Federal Franchise Act. In the end, the
African Affairs Board, which had been established under the
Federal Constitution, was destroyed, and Africans in both
northern territories were left with no illusions about Welensky's
objectives in Central Africa.

This point, mid-1957, marked the beginning of Northern
Rhodesia's transition to African government. The Governor
had begun discussions, admittedly not with the African nationalists, on Northern Rhodesia's Constitution, which had not been
changed since 1953. On the African side, A.N.C.'s young militant
leaders had begun their efforts to push Nkumbula along a more
extreme path. The first effective A.N.C. youth groups had been
formed by Sipalo, and Kaunda, fresh from his experience in
Britain and greatly inspired by Nkrumah's success in Ghana,
threw himself into reforming the party and organizing for
practical action.

A.N.C.'s demands for parity of representation between the
races in the Legislative Council were well known, as were the
Governor's views on control and guided political development
for Northern Rhodesia. Governor Benson's attitude was not
insignificant, because in conducting his soundings and in planning for a new constitution in 1958, he looked to the Moffat
Resolutions of 1954 for his basic position. Although as a practical
matter the Moffat Resolutions might be viewed as at best little
more than a pious hope and at worst as a plan for indefinitely
delaying African rule, their intent was unmistakably clear. The
objective of policy in Northern Rhodesia was to remove from
each race the fear that the other might dominate for its own
racial benefit and to move forward towards a franchise with no
separate representation for the races. Until that objective was
reached, there was to be a short 'period of transition' during
which 'special arrangements' were to be made in the Legislative
and the Executive Councils to ensure that no race could use
either the preponderance of its numbers or its more advanced
stage of development to dominate the other. During the transition, which was clearly regarded as a temporary phase, the
balance on contentious issues was to be held by the British
Government.[1]

The Benson Constitution, despite its many failings and the
fact that it was rejected by Kaunda and his colleagues, established beyond doubt that Northern Rhodesia was commencing
on a period of transition. Arrangements for the gradual elimina-
tion of the distinction between 'ordinary' and 'special' voters,
together with the prospect over the years that more and more

[1] Leg. Co. *Debates*, 29 July 1954; see also pp. 56–7.

Africans would qualify to vote, strongly suggested that African control was only a matter of time. How much time the Constitution did not explictly indicate, though at one point during the negotiations a period of ten years was mentioned. Nor was the Constitution explicit about where the transition might ultimately lead. The immediate objective was to encourage the development of non-racial politics, whatever that might mean, and political parties which cut across racial lines. Benson had, however, spelled out the mechanics of the process, and in accepting these the whites, for all practical purposes, had accepted that a transition was under way in which African influence would inevitably grow. Kaunda and his colleagues, of course, rejected the Constitution, and understandably so, because the only acceptable solution for them, with dominion status for the Federation a possibility in 1960 and with only one constitutional change scheduled for Northern Rhodesia before then, was immediate self-government. Kaunda never disputed the need for a period of transition, but it had to be a transition which Africans rather than the white settlers controlled. To Europeans, who had no intention of giving up power in the foreseeable future, such a resolution in effect represented no transition at all.

The Benson Constitution failed because it sought to find the middle ground between Europeans and Africans when, in fact, no meaningful middle ground existed. Instead, it provoked in A.N.C. the split between Nkumbula and Kaunda which had been building up for more than a year. Z.A.N.C., after it had established its position, and A.N.C. went their separate ways, Z.A.N.C. boycotting the election in an effort to destroy the Constitution and to force the Government's hand. Benson, finding himself threatened with the impending failure of his Constitution, and the first of Northern Rhodesia's transition elections, was forced to act to save his position. In doing so he gave Kaunda the advantage he was never to lose.

By the time of the next round of constitutional negotiations, which began in late 1960, the political situation in Central Africa had undergone significant change. Nyasaland had been promised African majority rule in July, the Monckton Commission had recommended African majorities in both the Legislative and the Executive Council in Northern Rhodesia, and

Kaunda had taken over the leadership of u.n.i.p. and built it into the most powerful and militant nationalist political party in Northern Rhodesia's history. The party, which had been banned on the Copperbelt in May 1960, controlled the Copperbelt, Northern and Luapula Provinces, Broken Hill and Lusaka, and parts of Eastern and Central Provinces. u.n.i.p. had also made inroads into Barotseland and North-Western Province. Kaunda was clearly in a position to negotiate from strength when the constitutional talks opened in London in December 1960—a fact which was dramatically confirmed when the British Government, under pressure from the Africans, agreed to postpone the Federal Review and to hold the territorial conference first.

The negotiations leading up to Northern Rhodesia's 1962 Constitution, the Constitution itself and the elections held under it, brought Northern Rhodesia through the most crucial stage of its transition to African government. Macleod's great strength as a Colonial Secretary during the negotiation was that he sensed where the middle ground between Europeans and Africans lay, and then was able to produce a constitution which neither side could afford to reject, though both refused to accept it. The June proposals, in which Macleod was forced by the British Cabinet to compromise on his February proposals, failed to strike the necessary balance between u.n.i.p. and the u.f.p., and the disturbances which followed in Northern Province pointed up how high the price of failure in Northern Rhodesia could be. In the end, after Maudling's changes in March 1962, all Northern Rhodesia's political groups were induced to participate in elections under the new Constitution. This political fact alone was of the greatest significance and warrants precedence over the wide range of technical and other criticisms made of the Macleod Constitution at the time.

The 1962 election was the turning-point in Northern Rhodesia's transition, not only because the election resulted in the Territory's first African Government, but also because the vast majority of Europeans remained in the Territory and accepted African rule. The period of nearly two years which had elapsed since Macleod first made his constitutional proposals had witnessed important changes among both Europeans and Africans. During the election the two races had shared, partially

at least, a common political arena. The effect, albeit small, was
to be a lasting one. u.n.i.p., as has been pointed out, was deeply
influenced by the experience. When in 1964 u.n.i.p. had not
required European support to win the election, the party contested every reserved seat and mounted a major campaign for
European support. The same was true of the European community. Whereas in 1962 whites had refused to support u.n.i.p.,
in 1964 approximately a third of the Territory's European voters
elected to support u.n.i.p. candidates.

The greatest weakness of the 1962 Constitution was its failure
to produce a conclusive election result. The coalition Government was ridden by political manœuvring and rent with internal dissent. With Cabinet posts divided between two parties
fewer men who would hold important posts in the Zambian
Government had the opportunity to gain valuable experience
during the period of transition. Worse still, the coalition was
unproductive, and its a.n.c. elements behaved irresponsibly,
consistently threatening to break the coalition and join the
u.f.p. in what could only have been a disastrous and short-lived
partnership. By May 1963 the coalition for all practical purposes had ceased to be effective and the problem of instituting
Northern Rhodesia's next step to independence became urgent.

u.n.i.p. took sole control over the Government for the first
time in January 1964, nine months before the granting of independence. European elected members had been eliminated
from the Cabinet, although one of u.n.i.p.'s parliamentary
secretaries was a European. Except for the change to republican
status and the departure on 24 October of the Governor,
Northern Rhodesia's transition was completed by early 1964.
By any standard the change had been eminently successful. It
had been accomplished without serious economic or political
dislocation. African political aspirations had been met and
Europeans had elected to remain in an independent Zambia.

Looking back over the period 1957–64, one is struck by the
clear and consistent relationship between constitutional arrangements and the development of political parties. In the short
space of five years Northern Rhodesia had three general elections, each held under different constitutional and electoral
arrangements. The Benson Constitution brought to a head the
conflict within a.n.c., and the 1959 election campaign witnessed

the first organized attempt by a militant nationalist party to boycott a national election. Though Z.A.N.C. was banned before it could build an effective national organization, the militant spirit, the objectives, and the dedication to professionalism which were Z.A.N.C.'s never died. Its successor, U.N.I.P., which had captured important elements of A.N.C. in late 1959, was built up under the shadow of Welensky's drive for dominion status in the 1960's. By early 1961, when Macleod produced his White Paper, it was evident that the white settlers' bid for power had been deflected from its previous course. For the first time, U.N.I.P. and the U.F.P. were on an equal footing. The struggle over the 1962 Constitution and the elections held in October that year significantly influenced U.N.I.P.'s development. The party reorganized itself in April 1962 in order to contest a general election held under the complicated electoral arrangements provided for in the 1962 Constitution. U.N.I.P. launched a massive European campaign, absorbed a new group of educated Africans into the ranks of its leadership, organized to reach thousands of new voters and to preserve central control over the entire party structure.

It would be a mistake, however, to ascribe too much weight to the relationship between constitutional arrangements and party development in Northern Rhodesia. After all, A.N.C. responded to the 1959, 1962 and 1963 Constitutions quite differently from Z.A.N.C. or U.N.I.P. Other factors were at work as well: the Native Authorities and the Government's policy of using them to combat the growth of nationalist parties in rural areas; the Government's administrative arrangements for controlling nationalist parties, particularly security arrangements and the Societies Ordinance; Government policy towards the African trade-union movement and the relationships between trade unions and African political parties; external influences, such as the actions of the Federal Government, developments in the Congo, contacts with other African states, the growth and spread of Pan-Africanist ideas and organizations, and the relations which developed, or failed to develop, between these groups and nationalist parties in Northern Rhodesia.

The Native Authorities during the 1950's provided the Government's major bulwark against national penetration in the rural areas. Chiefs and their councils were little more than an extension of the Provincial Administration down to the village level. Although the Native Authorities were responsible for their respective areas, the fact that they were subject to the control of the Provincial Administration inevitably resulted in the Native Authorities being used to carry out the central Government's policy of discouraging the growth of nationalist organizations. Thus, the chiefs and their councillors were often placed in the uncomfortable position of directly opposing a nationalist party which their people supported. Since theoretically the Native Authorities controlled access to their respective areas and were responsible for the maintenance of law and order, it was natural that U.N.I.P. and A.N.C. should have viewed the Native Authorities as the major obstacle to gaining control of the rural areas. Almost from its inception U.N.I.P. sought with varying degrees of success to undermine the Native Authority system. By mid-1961 U.N.I.P. had gained control over large areas of both Northern and Luapula Provinces, while in the rest of the country, except in Southern Province, it had gained enough influence at least to be able to intimidate the chiefs and their councillors.

U.N.I.P. was particularly responsive to the Societies Ordinance, which required political parties to register their branches with the Government. The main function of the Ordinance from the Government's point of view was to facilitate the collection of information regarding the strength, organization, structure, and financial resources of nationalist parties, so that plans for controlling or banning a political party could be kept in constant readiness. The information thus secured could also be used to improve the chances of successful prosecution against 'objectionable' nationalist politicians. In practice, however, the Societies Ordinance encouraged branch formation, because parties, and even regional divisions within the parties, attempted to compete in registering new branches. In addition, the Ordinance contributed to the development of more sophisticated organizational techniques in U.N.I.P., both in regard to the creation of youth and action groups, which were usually not registered and therefore were not as amenable to government control, and also in regard to arrangements for the securing and holding of party funds. More elaborate forms of communication between U.N.I.P.'s organizers were also evolved, and in registering branches U.N.I.P. often created 'front organizations', submitting the names of office-bearers who were not the major figures in the constituency- or branch-level organization.

U.N.I.P. never ceased to regard the Societies Ordinance as an offensive and unjustified burden, in part because the party was required to pay £1 for each branch it registered. Nevertheless, the Ordinance imposed a measure of discipline on the party. U.N.I.P. officials all over the Territory were required to keep records of their respective formation's membership, changes in office-bearers, and records of financial transactions. Such information, which under the terms of the Ordinance could be requested periodically by the local District Commissioner, was also sent by regional, constituency, and branch organizations to U.N.I.P.'s headquarters in Lusaka, where it was available to help co-ordinate party activities.

The town-based African trade-union movement, like the Native Authorities in the rural areas, was another area in which the Government sought to prevent nationalist penetration. The policy was strongly supported by the copper-mining companies, as well as by Katilungu, whose long reign over the African trade-union movement was an important factor in keeping African political parties out of trade-union affairs. By 1957 Katilungu had become the target of the more militant leaders of A.N.C., but it was three years before they successfully ousted him from the A.M.W.U. After Katilungu's removal, U.N.I.P. came to depend less on the militant but financially weak U.T.U.C. and formed a closer relationship with Chisata's A.M.W.U. Katilungu's control over the African trade-union movement, however, had deprived Kaunda of a powerful weapon as well as of an important source of potential financial support, both during Z.A.N.C.'s boycott of the 1959 election and later during U.N.I.P.'s struggle to build itself up as quickly as possible into a formidable political organization. The lack of financial support to U.N.I.P., which was explicitly forbidden under the terms of the A.M.W.U.'s 'check off' agreement with the mining companies, was a particularly serious disadvantage. Nevertheless, U.N.I.P. always commanded wide support amongst the A.M.W.U.'s membership, and many of its officials held regional-, constituency- or branch-level positions in U.N.I.P.

U.N.I.P.'s and A.N.C.'s contacts with outside groups differed

markedly in both range and extent. Kaunda had always maintained regular correspondence with various sympathetic groups
in London and the United States, while Nkumbula had never
devoted himself, with the single exception of his relationship
with Tshombe, to developing and maintaining support for his
movement outside Northern Rhodesia. The sharp contrast between the two leaders came out clearly when, shortly after the
A.N.C.-Z.A.N.C. split, they both attended the Accra Conference
in December 1958. Kaunda used the opportunity well, staying
behind in Ghana for several weeks to establish contacts in the
then capital of Pan-Africanism. The investment paid handsome
dividends, both politically and financially, when Kaunda
emerged from prison in 1960 to assume the leadership of U.N.I.P.
Kaunda also maintained close touch with Kenyatta and
Nyerere, and established an affiliate status with P.A.F.M.E.C.S.A.
when it was formed. Later, Kaunda became the organization's
President and in 1962 received valuable financial support for
the general election. After the 1962 election, Kaunda again
used P.A.F.M.E.C.S.A.'s 'good offices' to bring Nkumbula into the
coalition Government.

This book, in addition to establishing a detailed account of
party development during Northern Rhodesia's transition to
African government, has attempted to present and to analyse
the underlying relationships between constitutional and electoral arrangements, elections, the administration of African
affairs, and the administrative arrangements for controlling
nationalist political parties, on the one hand, and African
political parties on the other. While it is evident that party
organization and development, particularly in the case of
U.N.I.P., as well as political tactics and party leadership, were
directly affected by the above factors, it is extremely difficult to
be exact in determining which factors specifically influenced
which aspects of politics and political parties.

In addition, as in the case of all politics everywhere, personalities also played a crucial role in the formation and development
of political parties. U.N.I.P. bore Kaunda's stamp as clearly as
A.N.C. reflected the leadership of Nkumbula. Because Kaunda
had served so many years as Nkumbula's General Secretary,
and had suffered from the frustrations of weak organization and
ineffectual leadership, when Kaunda formed his own party he

devoted almost fanatical attention to the details of effective organization. His two experiences in prison made a deep and lasting impression on Kaunda as a leader. He disciplined himself, refined his ideas of leadership, and intensified his devotion to the task at hand. Nkumbula, on the other hand, lacked Kaunda's discipline and concern for the mechanics of political organization. Prison for Nkumbula was a trial, whereas for Kaunda it had been a time of rejuvenation.

As the years passed Nkumbula, despite his great natural gifts for politics, was content to allow A.N.C. to remain a poorly organized, tribally based political movement. Kaunda matured, sharpened his political sensitivities and devoted all his energies to building a modern and efficient party of the people. He pulled together Northern Rhodesia's diverse tribal and linguistic groups, merged them in his party and in the highest council of the land. Kaunda offered leadership to Northern Rhodesia's whites as well; for over two years before independence he devoted much of his energies to securing lasting support from Northern Rhodesia's Europeans. When Zambia achieved independence in October 1964, Kaunda became President of all the people, white and black alike, leader of one of Africa's great political parties and the hope of the new nation of Zambia.

SELECT BIBLIOGRAPHY

Published Material

A. *Books*

Allighan, Gary, *The Welensky Story*, Cape Town, 1962.

Barber, William J., *The Economy of British Central Africa*, Stanford, 1961.

Barnes, John A., *Politics in a Changing Society: A Political History of the Fort Jameson Ngoni*, Cape Town, 1965.

Brelsford, W. V., *The Tribes of Northern Rhodesia*, Lusaka, 1957.

Chandos, Oliver, Lyttleton Viscount, *The Memoirs of . . .*, London, 1962.

Clegg, Edward, *Race and Politics: Partnership in the Federation of Rhodesia and Nyasaland*, London, 1960.

Coillard, Francois, *On the Threshold of Central Africa*, London, 1897.

Colson, Elizabeth, *The Plateau Tonga of Northern Rhodesia: Social and Religious Studies*, Manchester, 1962.

Cunnison, I. G., *The Luapula Peoples of Northern Rhodesia: Custom and History in Tribal Politics*, Manchester, 1959.

Davidson, J. W., *The Northern Rhodesian Legislative Council*, London, 1948.

Epstein, A. L., *Politics in an Urban African Community*, Manchester, 1958.

Epstein, A. L., *The Administration of Justice and the Urban African*, London, 1953.

Franck, Thomas M., *Race and Nationalism: The Struggle for Power in Rhodesia-Nyasaland*, New York, 1960.

Franklin, Harry, *Unholy Wedlock: The Failure of the Central African Federation*, London, 1963.

Gann, L. H., *A History of Northern Rhodesia*, London, 1964.

Gann, L. H., *The Birth of a Plural Society: The Development of Northern Rhodesia Under the British South African Company*, Manchester, 1958.

Gelfand, Michael, *Northern Rhodesia in the Days of the Charter*, Oxford, 1961.

Gluckman, Max, and Colson, Elizabeth, *Seven Tribes of British Central Africa*, Manchester, 1959.

Gray, Richard, *The Two Nations: Aspects of the Development of Race Relations in the Rhodesias and Nyasaland*, London, 1960.

Hailey, William Malcolm, Lord., *An African Survey*, London and New York, 1957.

Hall, R. S., *Kaunda: Founder of Zambia*, Lusaka, 1964.

Hall, R. S., *Zambia*, London, 1965.

Hancock, W. Keith, *Survey of British Commonwealth Affairs II: Problems of Economic Policy, 1918–1939*, London, 1942.

Hanna, A. J., *The Beginnings of Nyasaland and North-Eastern Rhodesia 1859–1895*, Oxford, 1956.

Hanna, A. J., *The Story of the Rhodesias and Nyasaland*, London, 1960.

Kaunda, Kenneth, *Zambia Shall Be Free*, London, 1962.

Kaunda, Kenneth and Colin Morris, *Black Government?*. Lusaka, 1960.

Keatley, Patrick, *The Politics of Partnership: The Federation of Rhodesia and Nyasaland*, London, 1963.

Legum, Colin, *Pan-Africanism*, rev. ed., London, 1965.

Leys, Colin, and Pratt, Cranford, *A New Deal in Central Africa*, London, 1960.

Mair, Lucy P., *The Nyasaland Election of 1961*, London, 1962.

Mason, Philip, *The Birth of a Dilemma: The Conquest and Settlement of Rhodesia*, London, 1958.

Mason, Philip, *Year of Decision*, London, 1960.

Morris, Colin M., *The Hour After Midnight*, London, 1961.

Mulford, D. C., *The Northern Rhodesia General Election*, Nairobi, 1964.

Padmore, George, *History of the Pan-African Congress*, London, 1963.

Post, K. W. J., *The Nigerian Election of 1959*, Oxford, 1963.

Richards, Audrey I., *Land, Labour and Diet in Northern Rhodesia*, London, 1939.

Rotberg, Robert I., *Christian Missionaries and the Creation of Northern Rhodesia 1880–1924*, Princeton, 1965.

Rotberg, Robert I., *The Rise of Nationalism in Central Africa: The Making of Malawi and Zambia. 1873–1964*, Cambridge, 1965.

Sanger, Clyde, *Central African Emergency*, London, 1960.

Sklar, Richard L., *Nigerian Political Parties*, Princeton, 1965.

Welensky, Sir Roy, *Welensky's 4,000 Days*, London, 1964.

Wills, A. J., *An Introduction to the History of Central Africa*, London, 1964.

B. *Newspapers and Periodicals*

Mutende, Lusaka ,1936–52.

Northern Rhodesia News Survey, Los Angeles, 1959–60.

Nshila, Lusaka, 1957–63.

The African Mail, Lusaka, 1960–62.

The Central African Examiner, Salisbury, 1957.

The Central African Mail, Lusaka, 1960–2.

The Central African Post, Lusaka, 1948–62.

The Northern News, Ndola, 1943–.
The Northern Rhodesia Advertiser, Ndola, 1935–55.
The Rhodesia Herald, Salisbury, 1892–.
The Zambia News, Ndola, 1963–4.

C. *Articles and Pamphlets*

Banda, H. K., and Nkumbula, Harry, *Federation in Central Africa*, London, 1951.
Baxter, G. H., and Jodgens, P. W.,'The Constitutional Status of the Federation of Rhodesia and Nyasaland', *International Affairs*, October 1957.
Clay, Gervas, 'African Urban Advisory Councils in the Northern Rhodesia Copperbelt', *Journal of African Administration*, Vol. I, 1949.
Heath, F. M. N., 'The Growth of African Councils on the Copperbelt of Northern Rhodesia', *Journal of African Administration*, Vol. V, 1953.
Kaunda, Kenneth, 'Rider and Horse in Northern Rhodesia', *Africa South*, Vol. III, July–September 1959.
Kaunda, K. D., 'Some Personal Reflections', *Africa's Freedom*, London, 1964.
Kirkwood, Kenneth, 'British Central Africa: Politics Under Federation', *Annals of the American Academy of Political Science*, March 1955.
Mulford, D. C., 'Northern Rhodesia: Some Observations on the 1964 General Election', *Africa Report*, February 1964.
Rotberg, R. I., 'The Lenshina Movement of Northern Rhodesia', *The Rhodes-Livingstone Journal*, Vol. XXIX, 1961.
Rotberg, R. I., 'The Federation Movement in British East and Central Africa, 1889–1953', *Journal of Commonwealth Political Studies*, Vol. II, 1964.
Temple, Merfyn, and Sokoni, John, *Kaunda of Zambia*, Lusaka, 1964.
UNIP Election Worker's Handbook, Lusaka, 1962.
UNIP Policy, Lusaka, 1962.
Voice of UNIP, Lusaka, 1960–4.
Week by Week, Lusaka, 1958–62.
Zambia Spark, Ndola, 1961–2.

D. *Published Government Documents and Reports* (arranged chronologically)

Debates of the Northern Rhodesia Legislative Council, 1924–63.
Report of the East Africa Commission, Cmd. 2387, 1925.
Report of the Commission on Closer Union, Cmd. 3234, 1929.

Memorandum on Native Policy in East Africa, Cmd. 3573, 1930.

Statement of the Conclusions of His Majesty's Government in the United Kingdom as Regards Closer Union in East Africa, Cmd. 3574, 1930.

Correspondence with Regard to Native Policy in Northern Rhodesia, Cmd. 3731, 1930.

Report of the Commission Appointed to Enquire into the Financial and Economic Position of Northern Rhodesia, col. no. 145, 1938.

Rhodesia-Nyasaland Royal Commission Report, Cmd. 5949, 1939.

Reports of the Two Commissions Appointed to Enquire into the Disturbances in the Copperbelt, Northern Rhodesia, Lusaka, 1935 and 1940.

Statement by the Government of Northern Rhodesia on the Recommendations of the Report of the Copperbelt Commission, 1940, Lusaka, 1941.

Conference on the Closer Association of the Central African Territories: Proceedings of a Conference Held at the Victoria Falls Hotel, Southern Rhodesia on September 18 to 21, 1951.

Central African Territories: Comparative Survey of Native Policy, Cmd. 8235, 1951.

Closer Association in Central Africa: Statement by His Majesty's Government in the United Kingdom, Cmd. 8411, 1951.

Southern Rhodesia, Northern Rhodesia, and Nyasaland: Draft Federal Scheme, Cmd. 8573; *Report of the Judicial Commission*, Cmd. 8671; *Report of the Fiscal Commission*, Cmd. 8672; *Report of the Civil Service Preparatory Commission*, Cmd. 8673, 162.

Southern Rhodesia, Northern Rhodesia and Nyasaland: Report by the Conference on Federation Held in London in January, 1953, Cmd. 8753, 1953.

The Federal Scheme for Southern Rhodesia, Northern Rhodesia and Nyasaland Prepared by a Conference Held in London, January 1953, Cmd. 8753, 1953.

Report of the Committee Appointed to Investigate the Extent to which Racial Discrimination is Practised in Shops and in Other Business Premises, Lusaka, 1956.

Northern Rhodesia Government Gazette, 1957–54.

Proposals for Constitutional Change in Northern Rhodesia, Lusaka, 1958.

Notes of the Proposals for Constitutional Change in Northern Rhodesia, Lusaka, 1958.

Northern Rhodesia: Proposals for Constitutional Change, Cmnd. 530, 1958.

Report of the Commission Appointed to Inquire into the Circumstances Leading up to and Surrounding the Recent Deaths and Injuries Caused by the Use of Firearms in the Gwembe District and Matters Relating Thereto, Lusaka. 1958.

Report of an inquiry into all the Circumstances Which Gave Rise to the Making of the Safeguard of Elections and Public Safety Regulations, 1959. Lusaka, 1959.

General List of Chiefs, Lusaka, 1960.

Report of the Commission of Inquiry into Disturbances in Certain African Schools, Lusaka, 1960.

Report of the Advisory Commission on the Review of the Constitution of the Federation of Rhodesia and Nyasaland, Cmnd. 1148–50, 1960.

Northern Rhodesia: Proposals for Constitutional Change, Cmnd. 1295, 1961.

Northern Rhodesia: Statement by the Secretary of State for the Colonies on Proposals for Constitutional Change, Cmnd. 1301, 1961.

Northern Rhodesia: Proposals for Constitutional Change, Cmnd. 1423, 1961.

An Account of the Disturbances in Northern Rhodesia, July to October 1961, Lusaka, 1961.

Report of the Delimitation Commission, Lusaka, 1962.

The Northern Rhodesia (Constitution) Order in Council, 1962.

Report of the Central Africa Conference, 1963, Cmnd. 2093, 1963.

Report of the Commission of Inquiry into Unrest on the Copperbelt, July–August, 1963, Lusaka, 1963.

The Federation of Rhodesia and Nyasaland: Commentary on Statements Relating to the Establishment of the Federation and their Bearing on the Withdrawal of Nyasaland, Cmnd. 1948, 1963.

Report of the Delimitation Commission, Lusaka, 1963.

Report of the Northern Rhodesia Independence Conference Held in London in May, 1964, Lusaka, 1964.

E. Orders in Council

The Northern Rhodesia Order in Council, 1924.
The Northern Rhodesia (Amendment) Order in Council, 1928.
The Northern Rhodesia (Amendment) Order in Council, 1931.
The Northern Rhodesia (Amendment) Order in Council, 1939.
The Northern Rhodesia (Amendment) Order in Council, 1941.
The Northern Rhodesia (Amendment) Order in Council, 1947.
The Northern Rhodesia Order in Council, 1949.
The Northern Rhodesia Order in Council, 1951.
The Northern Rhodesia Order in Council, 1954.
The Northern Rhodesia (No. 2) Order in Council, 1954.
The Northern Rhodesia Order in Council, 1957.
The Northern Rhodesia (Legislative Council) Order in Council, 1959.
The Northern Rhodesia Order in Council, 1960.
The Northern Rhodesia Order in Council, 1961.
The Northern Rhodesia (Electoral Provisions) Order in Council, 1962.

The Northern Rhodesia (Delimitation Commission) Order in Council, 1962.

Unpublished Materials

F. Public Archives

I. National Archives of Zambia

African Administration: General (Franchise), MN 0001/1/1, Box 1672.
African Mineworkers Union, N/2709/4, Box 225.
African National Congress (1956 Boycotts), MN/2154/2 conf., Box 189.
African Participation in Local Government in Urban Areas, N/2156/1, Box 2999.
African Provincial Councils—General, N/2190 conf., Box 3513.
African Representative Council—General, Sec./Nat. 113.
African Representative Council, N/0052 conf., Vols. II and III, Box 1682.
Biographical Notes on Africans, N/0118, Box 205
Chiefs and Politics, MN/129/10, Vol. I., Box 4348.
Closer Association, C/1016 conf., Vol. I, Box 4349.
Congress of African Societies, Sec./Nat,/353 conf.
Constitution of African Councils, N/0088, Vols. I, II and III, Box 204.
Disturbances in Chinsali District, 1955, N/0001/2/15/4 conf., Box 188.
Disturbances in Mporokoso District, 1955–56, N/0003/2/15/3 conf., Box 188.
General Election, 1959: Registration of Voters, General Correspondence, 329/1, Box 3309.
General Election, 1959: African Administration, Territorial Election Procedure (Franchise), MN 1/4, Vol. I, Box 1672.
General Election, 1962: Election Procedure Policy, MS/2615/37/3 conf., Vol. I, Box 4353.
General Election, 1964: Election Procedure Policy, MS/2615/37/3 conf., Vols. II and III.
Meetings Held by Members of Legislative Council Nominated to Represent African Interests, N/0073, Box 203.
Moffat Resolutions, N/0047/8, Box 201.
Northern Rhodesia Constitution Changes: Registration of Voters and Publicity, General Election, 1959, MS/2615/16 conf., Box 4352.

Northern Rhodesia Constitution: General Policy, C/2615, Box 861.
Northern Rhodesia Constitution—General, MS/2615, Vol. II, Box 3678.
Official Visitor, Lord Home, Secretary of State for Commonwealth Relations, 1957, MS/2602/124, Vol. II.
Proposals for Constitution in Northern Rhodesia, MS/2615/9/1, Vol. I, Box 3767.
Race Relations, C/2616, Vol. I, Box 1894.
Rules for Electing African Members to the Federal Assembly, MN/1/3, Vol. I, Box 1672.
Tours by Members of Legislative Council Nominated to Represent African Interests, N/0073, Box 203.
Visit of Secretary of State Macleod, MS/2603/300, Box 4069.
Visit of Secretary of State Maudling, Record of Meetings, MS/2603/382/2 conf., Box 4069.

II. Africa Studies Centre, Leiden, Holland

The Africa Studies Centre holds a small but valuable collection of A.N.C. documents, early A.N.C. newsletters, records of A.N.C. party conferences, correspondence between A.N.C. leaders and sympathetic persons and groups in London, 1950–8. The collection also includes some materials on Z.A.N.C. and U.N.I.P., including statements of U.N.I.P.'s ideas on constitutional change in 1960. Particularly interesting are the newsletters and other correspondence produced by Kaunda while still General Secretary of A.N.C.

G. *Collection of Official Government Documents and Party Materials not held in Public Archives.*

A.N.C. General File, TS/S 123/01.
A.N.C. Financial Aims, GHTS/S 123/02.
A.N.C.-P.D.C. Split, DG 123/01.
A.N.C. Activities by Province:
  S/S 123/2/01 Central Province.
  S/S 123/3/01 Eastern Province.
  S/S 123/4/01 Luapula Province.
  S/S 123/5/01 Northern Province.
  S/S 123/6/01 Northwestern Province.
  S/S 123/7/01 Southern Province.
  S/S 123/8/01 Western Province.
African Trade Unions, S/S 128/64/01, Vols. I, III and V.
Barotseland Anti-Secession Movement, S/S 119/05.
Capricorn Africa Society, GHS/C 277.

Correspondence with and about Welensky, GHS/S 201/012.
European Mineworkers Trade Union, S/S 128/130/01.
European Politics, S/S 119/130/01.
Grim Peep into the North, S/S 208/012.
Peoples Democratic Party, GHS/S 119/016.
Political Leaders Series:
    Changufu, Lewis, S/S 201/014.
    Chona, Mainza, S/S 201/07.
    Dunlop, W. G., S/S 201/013.
    Kamanga, Reuben, S/S 201/022.
    Kapwepwe, Simon, S/S 201/023.
    Liso, Edward, TS/S 201/028.
    Mwanakatwe, John, S/S 201/029.
    Nkoloma, Matthew, S/S 201/026.
    Nkumbula, Harry, S/S 201/05.
    Roberts, John, GHS/S 201/09.
    Stubbs, Francis, S/S 201/024.
    Wina, Sikota, S/S 201/105.
Political Situation Files by Province:
    DG 58/1/01 Barotseland.
    DG 58/2/01 Central Province.
    DG 58/3/01 Eastern Province.
    DG 58/4/01 Luapula Province.
    DG 58/5/01 Northern Province.
    DG 58/6/01 Northwestern Province.
    DG 58/7/01 Southern Province.
    DG 58/8/01 Western Province.
Preservation of Public Security Regulations, S/S 98/81/02.
Record of Discussions between Kaunda and the Chief Secretary, S/S 108/014.
Societies Ordinance, S/S 82/81/01, Vols. I–V.
The 1961 Disturbances, S/S 57/011.
U.F.P.-A.N.C. Pact, 1962 Election, GH/S/S 119/010.
U.F.P., Constitutional Development and Activities of, S/S 107/012.
United National Freedom Party, S/S 119/01.
U.N.I.P. Activities in Luapula Province, S/S 108/4/01.
U.N.I.P. Activities in Eastern Province, S/S 108/3/01.
U.N.I.P. Activities in Northwestern Province, S/S 108/6/01.
U.N.I.P. Activities in Southern Province, S/S 108/7/01.
U.N.I.P. 'African Life', S/S 108/010.
U.N.I.P. Finance and Accounts, S/S 108/02.
U.N.I.P. Representation and Activity in America, S/S 108/07.
U.N.I.P. Youth Brigade, GH/S/S 108/015.

H. *Private Collections*

Arthur N. L. Wina papers, Lusaka, Zambia.
Phillip Emanuel collection, Leiden, Holland.

I. *Manuscripts*

Wina, A. N. L., 'A study of Nationalism in Northern Rhodesia',
    1960.
Michello, J. E., 'The Northern Rhodesia African National Congress,
    1951–1960', 1960.

J. *Author's Collection*

Listed below are the types of documents which comprise the author's
collection:
Administrative circulars for the registration of voters and electoral
    arrangements, 1962 general election.
Biographical material on European and African political leaders.
Miscellaneous documents on constitutional negotiations.
Miscellaneous party newsletters and publications.
Notes on political meetings, August–December 1962, and December
    1963–January 1964.
Official voting analyses of the 1959, 1962 and 1964 general elections.
Party campaign literature and manifestoes.
Records of racial breakdowns in constituencies, 1962 general
    election.
Reports of Provincial Administration Officers on the conduct of the
    1962 general election.

INDEX

National Progress Party (N.P.P.), 306, 325–6, 328, 331

National Republican Party (N.R.P.), 243

Native Authorities, 13, 17, 31, 33, 39, 40, 61, 65, 68, 71–2, 82, 84, 108, 117, 137, 138, 140–2, 148, 151, 156, 157, 159, 160, 165–70, 175, 184, 203, 205, 207, 212, 241, 275, 320, 339–41

Ndilila Sykes, 15n., 119, 134, 269, 295, 296

Ndola, 67, 69, 78, 85, 92, 94, 101, 116, 121, 153, 199, 319, 326, 328

Ndola East (upper roll) constituency, 259, 260

'New men', see U.N.I.P., 264–5

New York, 239

Ngalande, Matiya, 135

Ngambela, 213, 216, 218, 219, 220, 279, 314

Ngandu, J. C., 70

Ngoni, 3, 330

Ninda, 280

Nkolomo, Mathew, 42, 43, 44, 46

Nkomo, Joshua, 176, 179, 182

Nkula, Chief, 41

Nkrumah, Dr. K., 5, 80–1, 86, 335

Nkumbula, Harry (A.N.C.), 20–1, 36–7, 39, 43, 45, 46, 55, 61–7, 69–76, 77, 79–81, 86–91, 96, 98, 100, 109, 110–1, 113–9, 121–3, 125, 127, 128–30, 133, 135, 143–4, 158, 170, 175–6, 182, 189, 190, 209, 237–8, 241, 243, 252, 267–9, 271, 274–5, 277, 282, 288, 290–300, 304–11, 315–7, 319, 321–2, 324–5, 334–6, 342–3

Nomination of candidates, 88–90, 274, 313, 322–3

Non-racial politics, 56–61, 98, 185, 230, 244–5, 302

Northern (lower roll) constituency, 250, 253, 259, 260, 275, 276

Northern electoral area, 250, 253

Northern News, 64, 65, 75, 104, 194

Northern Province, 13, 23, 39, 63, 73, 74, 78, 93, 96, 112, 122, 139, 146, 148, 152, 153, 156, 159, 161, 162, 167, 169, 192, 200–7, 233–4, 237, 250, 253, 324, 327, 334, 337, 340

Northern Rhodesia Coalition, see Coalition

Northern Rhodesia Constitutional Conference, 178–84

Northern Rhodesia constitutional development
1890–1924, 6–7
1924–1958, 6–13, 33

1959 Constitution, 6, 54–5, 56–61, 73–4, 78, 181, 335–6, 338

1962 Constitution, 150, 175, 178, 184–8, 194–7, 208, 223, 229–31, 244, 247, 254, 301–4, 318, 332, 337–9

1964 Constitution, 312–5

Northern Rhodesia High Court, 175

Northern Rhodesia Police (Amendment) Bill, 66

Northern Rhodesia Reformed Trade Union Congress, 173

Northern Rural (upper roll) constituency, 258, 259, 260, 271, 272

North-Western constituency
1959, 92
1962, 250, 259, 260

Northwestern Province, 23, 79, 82, 112, 117, 122, 131, 135, 140, 149, 163, 258, 320, 324, 330, 337

Ntambo, Johnathan, 135

Nyanje, 330

Nyasaland, 3, 5, 6, 13, 19, 93, 95, 96, 103, 126, 130, 132, 137, 149, 151, 179, 336

Nyerere, Dr. Julius, 295, 328, 342

Nyirenda, Wesley, 70, 279, 305

'Ordinary' constituencies, 57–61, 97–9

'Ordinary' voters, 57–61, 97–9, 335

Pacts, see Alliances

P.A.F.M.E.S.C.A. (Pan-American Freedom Movement for East, Central and Southern Africa), 291–5, 339, 342

Pan-Africanism, 80, 144, 243, 291–5, 339, 342

Paramountcy, 7–9

Paris, 309

Parliamentary secretaries, 300, 306

Partnership, 28–36, 38, 53, 242

Party co-operation, see Alliances

Party organization, see also specific parties, 25–6, 143

Passfield, Lord, 7

Passfield memorandum, 7–9

Patel, C. C., 164

Patel, G. H., 273

Pemba, 273

Penal Code, 66–7

Peoples Democratic Party (P.D.C.), 311, 316–7, 319–20, 322

Percentage requirements, minimum, 195–7, 208, 230–1

Petauke, 61, 148, 156

Polling, 297

Ponde, Jonas, 173

Population quota, 254, 255